Annelise.

CADOGAN
CITY GUIDES

PRAGUE

Cadogan Books Ltd
Mercury House, 195 Knightsbridge,
London SW7 1RE

The Globe Pequot Press
6 Business Park Drive, PO Box 833,
Old Saybrook, Connecticut 06475–0833

Copyright © Sadakat Kadri 1991, 1993
Illustrations by Oldřich Dufek 1991, 1993,
Pavel Bezděk (Introduction) 1991

Book Design by Animage
Cover design by Ralph King
Cover illustration by Faranak
Maps © Cadogan Guides, drawn by Thames Cartographic Ltd
Macintosh: Alexander Manolatos, Typography 5

Editing: Vicki Ingle
Indexing: Dorothy Frame
Proofing: Eric Smith

Series Editor: Rachel Fielding
Managing Editor: Vicki Ingle

A catalogue record for this book
is available from the British Library

ISBN 0–947754–47–4

Library of Congress Cataloging–in–Publication Data
Kadri, Sadakat
Prague/Sadakat -- 2nd ed.
p. cm. -- (Cadogan city guides)
Includes index.
ISBN 1–58440–175–8
1. Prague (Czechoslovakia) -- Guidebooks.
I. Title. II. Series. Cadogan Guides.
DB2607 K33 1993
914.37' 120443 -- dc20
92–28240
CIP

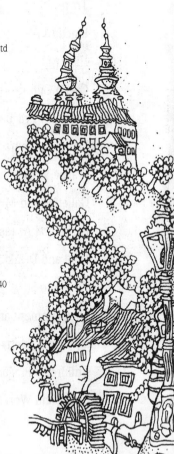

The authors and publishers have made every effort to ensure
the accuracy of the information in this book at the time of
going to press. However they cannot accept any responsibility
for any loss, injury or inconvenience resulting from the use
of information contained in this guide.

Typeset in Weidemann and produced on Apple Macintosh with
Quark Express, Photoshop, Freehand and Word software.

Printed and bound in Great Britain
by Redwood Books,
Trowbridge, Wiltshire on
Selkirk Opaque supplied by
McNaughton Publishing Papers Ltd.

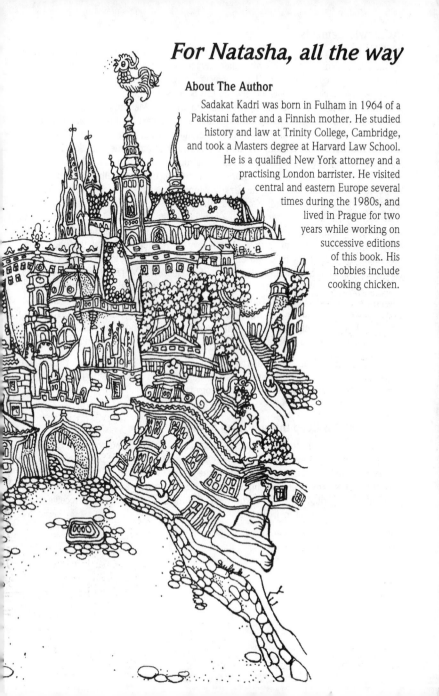

For Natasha, all the way

About The Author

Sadakat Kadri was born in Fulham in 1964 of a Pakistani father and a Finnish mother. He studied history and law at Trinity College, Cambridge, and took a Masters degree at Harvard Law School. He is a qualified New York attorney and a practising London barrister. He visited central and eastern Europe several times during the 1980s, and lived in Prague for two years while working on successive editions of this book. His hobbies include cooking chicken.

Acknowledgements

My first thanks go to my parents for their support throughout my Prague adventure. Salutations to Paul Lewis for his wit, generosity and determination to meet new people, no matter what the cost. Thanks to Hana Syslová for a volatile friendship and invaluable help, and to everyone else who was there when this book was just a contractual obligation: Jiří Kučera, Vojtěch Sysel, and the spirits of David Chirico, Marianne Decleire and Mark Kuzmack. Much love to my Charles Bridgers for a year of fun—Klára and Katka Hrubešová, Petr, Šarka, Tom Whitehouse, Simona, Helena, Alicie, Richard, Sael, David and Pavel Bezděk—and greetings to innumerable others, from Annie to Zack, whose paths I crossed while weaving through the magical metropolis. Many thanks to all the custodians of Prague who opened up a little more of the city for me, especially Dr Peter Biely at London Čedok, Petr Horák at the Žižkov Monument, Jaroslav Hrbek at the Military Research Institute, Dr Frank Kadlec at the castle, Helena Koenigsmarková at the Decorative Arts Museum, Mr Šidlovský and Jan Pařez at the Strahov Monastery and Literature Museum, and special thanks to Mr Ženaty at the Rudolfinum for letting me onto his roof to look for Wagner's nose. Much love to Harriet Fennell at the Olga Havel Foundation for constant help and encouragement. For multifarious reasons thanks to Karolinka Vočadlo, Mary-Margaret and Anne-Caroline, Julia Money, Michaela Valenová, Oldřich Dufek, Mr Bradley at the British Embassy, Georgia Schaller, Catherine Paugam, and a raised carafe to all at The Thirsty Dog. At Cadogan, continuing gratitude to my editor Rachel Fielding, thanks to the ever-helpful Vicki Ingle, and appreciations to Eric Smith and Dorothy Frame for their proof-reading and indexing skills respectively. Finally, many thanks to anyone who said nice things about the first edition of this book.

The publishers would particularly like to thank Alex Manolatos for his high standards and hard work; Horatio Monteverde and Kicca Tommasi for their style; and Emma Johnson for stepping in when technology failed.

Please help us keep this guide up to date

We have done our best to ensure that the information in this guide is correct at the time of going to press. But city life is constantly changing: standards and prices in hotels and restaurants fluctuate; bars and nightclubs come and go. We would be delighted to receive any comments concerning existing entries or omissions, as well as suggestions for new features. All contributors will be acknowledged in the next edition and will receive a copy of the Cadogan Guide of their choice.

Contents

Introduction

The flim-flam of hundreds of tourist brochures now makes Breton's homage sound almost clichéd, but there is something mighty surreal about Prague. Floating in the architectural flotsam of a thousand years, its domes, dungeons, rickety rooftops and spires are about as close as life gets to fairyland. Its central bridge is bent, one of its clocks turns backwards, an entire 13th-century town is buried three metres under its alleys, and surveying its domain from the hill above the river is a castle in the air. The city lies at the crossroads of Europe, and its spirit has been formed and deformed by the cataclysmic pressures of a millennium of continental madness. Dogs of war have dumped on it from every direction, its streets are filled with the petrified dreams of dissembling monks and cuckoo monarchs, the Communists practised their jiggery-pokery behind an iron curtain for four decades—and yet it survived the hullaballoo to emerge as one of the most enchanted cities in Europe. The spell that it evokes isn't some two-bit trick with a slipper and a pumpkin, but the almost tangible energy of images, ideologies and myths with which every European has grown up. Give it an inch of imagination, and it will unleash a mile.

Years of smears and smokescreens have added to the mystery that now surrounds Prague. It is the capital of Bohemia, which has been a byword for outlandishness for centuries. The kingdom began its ascent into the clouds in the mid-1400s: the pope spread the word that Bohemians made love on the streets, while in France a group of expelled gipsies waved their safe-conducts as they passed through, and the French duly noted that *un bohémien* was a gipsy—as he still is today. By the early 1600s, Shakespeare could get away with describing the landlocked and forested kingdom as 'a desert country near the sea' (*The Winter's Tale*); and in 1938, disingenuous ignorance was elevated to foreign policy by Neville Chamberlain. Ten years later, Prague—further west than Vienna, and considerably closer to Dublin than to Moscow—became lost in 'Eastern Europe'. The city of dreams turned into a 41–year nightmare, but in the west, Bohemia did little more than to hover across from Bloomsbury to somewhere between Hampstead and Haight-Ashbury. And then in 1989, a few million people pinched themselves, the tin-pot emperors of Communism shivered, and the city returned to where it belongs—the heart of Europe.

Prague is now the capital of the Czech Republic—made up of Bohemia, Moravia and a slice of Silesia—and comprises some 1,190,576 inhabitants (with an inexplicably decreasing proportion of men); 503 spires, towers and sundry aerial protrusions; 495 sq km; ten districts; eight islands; seven hills (like most legendary cities); and an agglomeration of what were historically five separate towns. Since 1989 it has shrugged off the torpor of its long night, and to the rhythm of pile-drivers and the glare of oxyacetylene torches, the magical metropolis is beginning another transformation—into one of the most vital cities on the Continent. It's still scarred by the barbed-wire wounds of the Cold War, but as it busks, dances, works and kisses its way back into the light, the old divisions are being healed on its streets. Prague doesn't *always* feel so dreamy—particularly as you chew through its accursed dumplings or cross swords with a hobgoblin of the bureaucracy— but if you pack your senses of humour, adventure and romance, a visit is an unforgettable jaunt into a city where history is in the making, and where a thousand years has already been made.

Travel

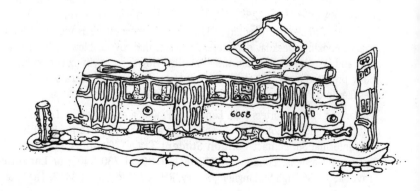

The best source of information on holidaying in Prague is still Čedok, the former national tourist agency. You pay a hefty and sometimes extortionate premium for its services, but its erstwhile monopoly means that it knows the tangled ropes of the Czech service industry better than anyone. Although sloth and inefficiency have characterized it for too long, it can arrange flights, accommodation and a series of entertainments ranging from nights at the opera to dire evenings of 'traditional' beer and sausages in five-star hostelries. For further information, contact your local office (17-18 Old Bond St, London W1X 3DA, ✆ (071) 629 6058, 10 East 40th St, New York, NY 10016, ✆ (212) 689 9720). Since 1989, scores of smaller agencies have also begun to organize holidays to the Czech Republic. Bridgewater Travel at 37 King Street West, Manchester M3 2PW, ✆ (061) 834 7444, provides a flexible service including charter and scheduled flights and accommodation in hotels and private homes throughout the country. Intra Travel at 44 Maple St, London W1P 5GD, ✆ (071) 323 3305, offers hotel and flight packages, and tours that also extend to other capital cities of central and eastern Europe.

Cultural tour organizers are listed under Specialist Holidays (*see* p. 5).

By Air

British Airways flies daily from London, and has services from many major North American cities. Czech Airlines (ČSA) has a daily service out of London and at least two flights a week from Manchester. It also flies directly to Prague from New York, Chicago, Toronto and Montreal.

BA: ✆ (081) 897 4000 (London); ✆ 800 247 9297 (New York).

ČSA: ✆ (071) 255 1898 (London); ✆ (212) 682 5833 (New York).

Both airlines charge exactly the same range of return fares,—£224–502—from London. BA offers $718–2590 (Club Class) return from New York City while ČSA offers $672–2720 (Booking Class C). The cheapest deals require 14-day advance booking, weekday departure, and a stay that covers at least one Saturday night and lasts no longer than three months. However, anything is possible, if you're prepared to pay. There are cheaper fares for anyone under 25. Delta Airlines flies into Prague daily from its Frankfurt hub.

Regular and cheap charters from London to Prague are run by Usit/London Student Travel and Lanzotic Travel. The flights are *not* restricted to students: for more information, contact **London Student Travel/Campus Travel** at 52 Grosvenor Gardens, London SW1W 0AG, ✆ (071) 730 3402; or **Lanzotic Travel** at 33–35 High St, Lingfield, Surrey, RH7 6AA, ✆ 0342 83412. The latter company also offers accommodation and mini-package tours to the city. A good place for bargain-hunting in the US is **Council Travel**, 205 East 42nd St, New York, NY 10001, ✆ (212) 661 1450. There are regular Prague-orientated offers among the classified ads in the UK's Sunday papers and London's *Time Out*; in New York, you could try the *Village Voice*.

Prague's small international airport is **Ruzyně**, situated some 20 km to the west of the city centre. The terminal isn't on a metro line, but it's linked to Dejvická station (line A) by buses 119 and 254. Pick up a ticket *(jízdenka)* at the souvenir stand in the airport lobby. Czech Airlines runs a shuttle service to and from the main railway station (Hlavní nádraží), via its office at Revoluční 25 and Dejvická station. It operates at least once every thirty minutes from the early morning until around 6.30 pm. Plenty of taxi-drivers loiter outside the airport building. Their metres are occasionally rigged, and you might want to fix a fare in advance: don't pay much more than £10 ($15) for the ride into the Old Town.

Airline Offices: All are open on weekdays only and most close by 4 pm. Airport information can be obtained on 334 11 11.

Aeroflot (CIS): Pařížská 5, ✆ 232 33 33.

Air France (France): Václavské nám. 10, ✆ 26 01 55.

Austrian Airlines (Austria): Pařížská 1, ✆ 232 27 95.

Balkan (Bulgaria): Pařížská 3, ✆ 232 45 00.

British Airways (United Kingdom): Staroměstské nám. 10, ✆ 232 90 20/40.

ČSA (Czech Republic): Revoluční 1, ✆ 231 25 95, 235 27 85.

Delta Airlines (United States): Pařížská 11, ✆ 232 47 06.

KLM (Netherlands): Václavské nám. 37, ✆ 26 43 69.

Lot (Poland): Pařížská 18, ✆ 231 75 24.

Lufthansa (Germany): Pařížská 28, ✆ 231 74 40.

Malév (Hungary): Pařížská 5, ✆ 232 82 45.

By Train

There are three time-honoured routes from London to Prague. The quickest is via Paris on the Paris–Praha night express, which you pick up at the Gare de l'Est. Another possibility is to travel through Ostend and Köln, setting off from London Victoria in the morning and early afternoon and arriving in Prague in the morning or late afternoon of the next day. Finally, you could stop off in Berlin, and then catch one of the many Prague-bound trains from Berlin (Lichtenberg), a journey of about 7 hours. A return journey from London via

Paris costs about £280 ($420) at the time of writing, and you can check that, along with other information on all the routes, at any major British Rail station or on (071) 834 2345. All international rail tickets are valid for up to two months' worth of stopovers. Non-European residents should note that at the time of writing, the Czech Republic is not covered by the Eurail Pass; however, that may change and you can get the latest information by calling Council Travel in New York, or French Railways at 179 Piccadilly, London W1V 0BA, ✆ (071) 409 1224.

Anyone under the cursed age of 26 is eligible for the set of deals that transform Europe's trains into mobile youth hostels during the summer. Campus Travel sells direct tickets via Köln for about £100 one way, as well as rovers covering a clutch of European capitals including Prague for around £220. The Inter-Rail pass covers the Czech Republic, but it is no longer the bargain that it once was, the network having been deserted by France, Italy and Iberia and the price having skyrocketed. The pass is available to anyone who has been resident in Europe for six months or more; and it's also worth noting that there are now Inter-Rail tickets for those aged 26 and above. There are no reductions for either young or studious foreigners within the Czech Republic, but anyone connected to the British or US educational systems (including over-25s, academics and accompanying spouses and children) can buy a Czech Explorer Pass *before leaving the UK*, which lets you travel the length of the country in a week for about £25 (2nd class) or £40 (1st class). You can buy the pass in many UK travel agencies including Campus Travel. You would have to spend your entire holiday on a train for it to save you money, but it's a useful way of queue-barging if you intend to use the rail system a fair amount.

Trains to Prague arrive either at **nádraží Praha-Holešovice** or, most likely, **Hlavní nádraží** ('Main Station'). Both are on line C of the metro network. Hlavní nádraží is by far the grander, four floors' worth of station, three of which somehow emerge onto the street. Train information is provided in an office on the first floor (6 am–10 pm) and on the maps and roller timetables on the same floor. The Prague Information Service (PIS) will sell you maps, and dispense more or less wise advice from its booth in the main hall below (8 am–7 pm). On the top floor—the core of the original Art Nouveau station—is a shabby dining hall, decorated with stained-glass windows and tiled mosaics (6 am–10 pm). En route, be sure to see the magnificent half-dome, some 25 metres high, that greeted arrivals to Prague until the confused postwar reconstruction of the station. The taxi rank is to your left as you enter the station interior from the platforms. The left-luggage counter is in the basement, and is open 24 hours a day (minus short but potentially disastrous breaks—make sure that you aren't caught short as your train pulls out). The nearby lockers are a cheap and quick alternative, but they are rifled on an almost daily basis. Grimy travellers can clean up in showers under the station's main hall.

Since 1989, Hlavní nádraží has sunk to the level of most European railway stations—a popular spot for gratuitous violence, public urination and erratic screaming—and you won't want to spend too much time there. All-night strip shows and slot machines attract low-life hedonists, and at the men's public toilets the attendant has been known to rent out single pages from pornographic magazines. Between June and September, AVE operates a 24-hour exchange and accommodation service (*see* p. 321), and during the rest of the year it's closed only from 12 midnight–6 am. Try to time your arrival accordingly. Otherwise if you find yourself up the creek as you stagger off your Berlin milk train, you're best advised to check your baggage into the left-luggage counter and set off for the 24-hour exchange office at the foot of Wenceslas Square. It's a five-minute walk from Hlavní nadraží and a 45-minute trek from Holešovice. You could also investigate the late-night possibilities listed in the Entertainment and Nightlife section of this book (*see* pp. 323–36). Staying in the station is a bad idea but if you are determined to do so, at least avoid nodding off. All that you will lose will be a few snatched anxiety dreams, and Prague will begin to reawaken at around 5 am.

By Coach

Thrice-weekly coach services from London are run by both Kingscourt Travel and Adco Travel. The journey is precisely as cheap as it is hellish (around £100 and two days' recovery time for the round trip). The former has offices at 35 Kingscourt Rd, London SW16 1JA (*©* (081) 769 9229 and (081) 677 6403), and Antala Staška 60 in Prague 4 (*©* 49 94 56); the latter is at 142 West End Lane, London NW6 1SD (*©* (071) 372 0323).

Specialist Holidays

Several British companies now organize trips to Prague for culture buffs. The following all offer flights, comfortable hotel accommodation and up to 10 days of excursions and like-minded conversation partners, at prices ranging from £800–1000. Explorations of the musical traditions of the city are run three or four times a year by **Travel for the Arts** at 117 Regent's Park Rd, London NW1 8UR, *©* (071) 483 4466. The trips romp from Mozart to Janáček through all the most melodious halls, stages and churches in the capital. Friends of Covent Garden are eligible for a discount. If you're the solitary type, the company can even arrange an itinerary just for you. **Prospect Tours** at 454–458 Chiswick High Rd, London

W4 5TT, © (081) 995 2151, organizes another set of musical holidays, and also offers meanders through the city's galleries and churches led by an art historian. Finally **Martin Randall Travel** runs a number of extremely high-quality artistic and architectural tours to Prague, led by very wise lecturers. The company is based at 10 Barley Mow Passage, London W4 4HP, © (081) 742 3355.

Within Prague itself there is one company that may be of interest: **Wittman Tours**, which specializes in trips exploring the Jewish history of Prague and Bohemia. It organizes regular tours of the Jewish Quarter and the former ghetto at Terezín, often led by Jews who lived through the Nazi occupation, and can arrange individual itineraries on request. The company has an office at Uruguayská 7 in Prague 2, tel/fax 25 12 35.

Customs Formalities

A full passport will get you into the Czech Republic, although if it has less than a year to run you could have problems. A British Visitor's Card won't be accepted. West Europeans and US citizens no longer need a visa, but if you plan to stay for longer than three months, the bureaucracy still wants to know (*see* p. 357).

Since 1989, Czech customs officers have undergone an almost miraculous transformation. Entry and departure used to involve running a gauntlet of psychological warfare techniques, complete with Mutt-and-Jeff teams, rivet stares, and very sweaty moments while passports were examined and occasionally taken away for questioning. You're unlikely to face more than the most perfunctory examination these days. On arrival, you're allowed to import unlimited amounts of personal effects and up to 250 cigarettes, two litres of wine, a litre of spirits, and half a litre of perfume. Any extra should be declared and duty paid, although the happy-go-lucky customs information service claims that long-term visitors can bring in any amount that's proportional to their stay—a suggestion that sounds ludicrous, but could possibly be offered in mitigation if you're nabbed. Gifts worth up to 1000 kcs can also be imported duty-free. There is a 500-kč limit on exports from the Czech Republic. As inflation rots the currency, that will either change or become even more meaningless than it already is. The standard prohibitions apply to both arrival and departure—no hard porn, no heroin, no Semtex, etc.—and Czech currency is still not meant to be imported or exported. X-ray machines can cumulatively damage films, and a single stroke by a metal detector can conceivably wipe out computer data. If you have either, it's a good idea to pack it separately and have it inspected by hand. For more information, contact the laid-back customs bureau at Havlíčkova 11, © 232 22 70.

The curves and cobbles of central Prague have a mobile life of their own. Most of the streets are no more than the patches of ground that no one has ever wanted to build on, and in their medieval madness, they often lead you on a merry dance and occasionally pull off the startling trick of coaxing you back to your starting-point after a 30-minute meander. Things aren't made easier by the name-change mania that has gripped the nation since the 1989 revolution. Countless streets, metro stations, parks and buildings were renamed in the first wave of anti-Communism, a fair proportion then had their names restored on the basis that not all the Communists' heroes deserved oblivion, and the process doesn't seem to be over yet. Slovak names will probably be the next to go. The messy result is that many people in Prague aren't quite sure where they live, a problem exacerbated by the cantankerous old Communists and mischievous youths who insist on using the wrong name. At the time of writing, you need at least three maps to master the permutations involved. The most recent should be adequate for a short visit, but you should be alert to the fact that all is not what it seems.

The only specific source of **transport information** is the enquiry centre at 29 46 82, but you'll be lucky to speak to an Anglophone. Daytime routes of buses and trams are marked on most city maps. There's a standard ticket ('*jízdenka*') for the buses, trams and metros, costing 4 kčs, which you can buy from the yellow machines in metro stations and on street corners (make sure that the green light on the top is on). You can also get them in tobacconists, newsagents and several cafés, but you *can't* buy them on trams or buses, so it's worth getting a bunch at a time. Validate them by punching them in the machines that you'll find on board the tram or bus, and in the vestibule of metro stations. The system relies on your honesty, backed up by plain-clothed inspectors (usually recognizable by their anoraks, shoulder bags and forlorn demeanour) who levy on-the-spot fines. Each ticket is valid for one ride, up to 60 minutes long. **Day passes** covering all three services can be bought from the red machines in most stations; and you can get passes up to a week from almost any *tabák*. Don't try to validate them. If you are under 10 or over 70, you have a free ride—and if you're not, you should be particularly careful not to cross one of Prague's most distinctive sub-cultures, female pensioners with time on their hands. Although the *babičky* congregate wherever there's a moral priority to be claimed—in supermarket queues, for example—you're most likely to encounter them joyriding on the transport system. Trams are their favourite. By law they are entitled to your seat, and may raise hell if you don't offer it spontaneously. During rush hours, the best policy is to stand throughout, unless you can somehow trump them. Physical disability obviously works; schizophrenia is another possibility.

By Metro

This is the easiest way to get around town. The chrome-plated Soviet-built network still has the legendary efficiency of totalitarianism, and the three lines and three intersections present few difficulties to even the worst sense of direction. Trains run from around 5 am–midnight, every few minutes at peak hours, and stops are scattered all over the centre of town. The junctions are at Muzeum (lines A and C), Můstek (lines A and B) and Florenc (lines B and C). The authorities do their best to make sure that things run smoothly: as on the trams, a recorded message announces the name of each stop (which has led to mass confusion on the rare occasions that it's slipped out of synch), and an unseen eye even watches the platforms to snap at you if you look as though you might leap off.

By Tram

These quaint beasts shudder across Prague in droves, rattling and raining down showers of sparks as they go. Their cream-and-crimson livery has been a feature of city life for decades, but in recent years several have begun to sport exuberant advertising logos. The departure from tradition has only made them more surreal than ever, with motorized cans of M & Ms and electrified Benetton jumpers now slithering colourfully across the city. An added pleasure on winter nights is that most seats are heated. Tram timetables are so simple that they look mystifying. Each of the city's hundreds of stops has its own, regularly updated, and the times given apply only to that stop. You can usually rely on them almost to the minute. The regular service runs from 5 am–midnight. A system of **night trams** then takes over all the major routes; there are nine (routes 51–59), and all pass through Lazarská street in the New Town. Night tram routes aren't marked on street maps, but there is a simple plan on most stops. To find one near you, look out for a white number on a blue background on your local stop.

By Bus

These avoid some parts of the centre, but otherwise most of the same rules apply as for trams. The timetables are less reliable (tram jams are rarer); and if you're working from a map, take into account that the stops are much further apart. Night buses are marked on the bus-stop plans, but are only really useful if you are living in one of the hellhole housing estates in the suburbs.

By Taxi

These are the source of much tourist unhappiness. Most cabbies will add several hundred per cent to your fare if you let them. As a general rule, you should ask

PRAGUE METRO

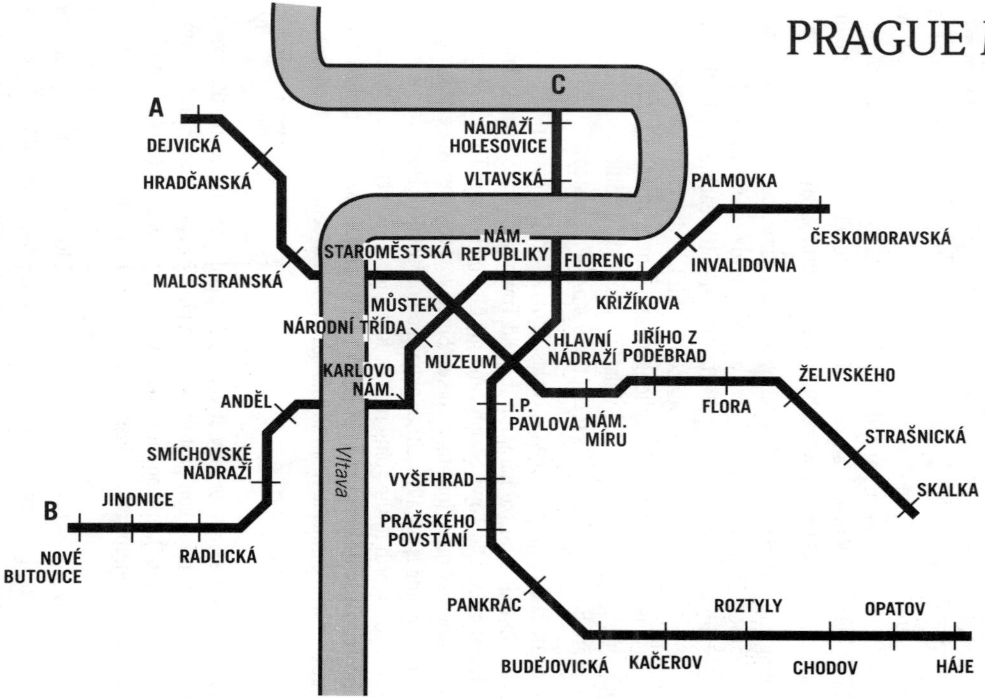

the price before setting off. An equally general rule holds that the cabby will demand from you between three and six times what he would from a Czech. A fair fare, allowing for a moderate level of extortion, is about £3 ($4.50) for 3 miles. Drivers are legally obliged to use their meters, but usually snort if you remind them. It may be no better if a driver eagerly waves you in. That could well mean that the cab has a zapper, a piece of electronic wizardry that sends the meter into overdrive; there's no real way of telling, and all you can do is shrug your shoulders and gesticulate wildly as the display blurs into triple figures. You should also check that he doesn't flick a switch from 1 to 2—the latter is the more expensive tariff that only applies outside Prague city limits. In cases where you feel that you've been zapped, or taken from A to B via Z, you could try just handing over, in silence, a fair sum. The technique relies on shaming the driver, and as such it should never work, but it can be surprisingly effective.

Haggling and settling is usually a fairly amicable game, but if you have real problems, you could take out a pen and ask for the driver's number. Licences are priceless, and an understanding is often reached if a cabbie thinks that there's even a chance of losing it. However be careful: taxi drivers have been known to turn very nasty indeed when challenged, and lone women in particular should avoid serious confrontations. For what it's worth, you could also note that taxi-drivers are bound to give you a receipt *(paragon)* if requested.

The main taxi-ranks are in Wenceslas Square, on the corner of Národní and Spálená, in Malostranské nám., on the Old Town side of the Charles Bridge, outside Bonal in the Old Town Square, and next to the Powder Tower. Most taxis are Škodas; you pay more for other makes. Since you will almost certainly pay over the odds, tipping is usually neither expected nor justified. However, if you meet a driver who's worth it, the going rate for foreigners is 10 per cent. There's a useful **24-hour minicab service** at 20 29 51–9, with 500 radio-controlled cars, and controllers who can usually speak enough English to send one in your direction.

By Car

Cars drive on the right, usually at very high speed. For the record, the speed limit in built-up areas is 60 kph (just under 40 mph). On open roads that goes up to 90 kph (about 55 mph), and on motorways you can travel at up to 110 kph (70 mph). Seatbelts are compulsory, unless you are less than 1½ metres tall, in which case you should sit in the back seat. Driving with *any* alcohol in your bloodstream is punishable by an on-the-spot fine of just under £400 ($600). Finally, don't mess with the trams. They have full right of way, even—nay, especially—if that involves careering across your lane at full speed. At stops without a pedestrian island you should never pass on the right while passengers are being disgorged. Disembarking tramsters comprise a fair proportion of Prague's dead pedestrians each year.

Until the 1970s, motor traffic trundled uninterrupted through the winding alleys and broad boulevards of Prague. However, large tracts of the capital have since been closed or restricted to those with special permits. You can buy a good driving map that shows which roads are navigable *(Praha pro motoristy*, available from all good map shops) but the best rule of thumb is to park on the periphery and continue your journey by public transport. Wenceslas Square and the surrounding streets are off-limits to almost all passenger traffic. If you try to drive along them you'll be waved down by a policeman holding a big red lollipop, who will either fine you or, if no one is looking, let you off with a bribe.

The influx of polished Mercedes with rusty engines, which followed the collapse of the Berlin wall, destroyed much of the mystique that once surrounded western cars. Nowadays BMWs and Audis are commonplace, and as Prague's first generation of yuppies emerges, Czech-registered Porsches and Mitsubishi jeeps are making an appearance. As a result, tourists' cars are no longer significantly more at risk than any other, but auto-theft generally is on the rise. Always conceal or remove valuables, and consider keeping your car in a guarded garage; you'll find them next to the National Theatre, near the main station, and under the Hotel Intercontinental, Hotel Atrium, nám. Jana Palacha and the Kotva department store. Outdoor guarded carparks are also common, are often safer and are always cheaper; they can be found, for example, in Karlovo nám., Malostranské nám., Národní street, and at both ends of Revoluční street. Otherwise, about 97 per cent of parking in the centre is for residents only. If you park illegally, you're likely to be clamped or towed away within a couple of hours of stopping. In the latter case, you'll find your baby being guarded by a man with a pistol and a porn mag in a barbed-wire suburban pound. The police will provide the address if you call 158.

Petrol pumps remain few and far between in Prague. When you get to one, fill up. The following stations, marked on most maps, are open 24 hours a day:

> Karlínské nám. (Prague 3).
>
> Olšanská (Prague 3).
>
> Plzeňská (Prague 5).
>
> Strakonická (Prague 5).
>
> Evropská (Prague 6).
>
> Argentinská (Prague 7).
>
> Českobrodská (Prague 9).

Czech roads leave a lot to be desired. Check your suspension carefully before leaving home—in Prague your car will face an obstacle course of potholes, runway-size ramps, tramlines, and most teeth-rattling of all, several stretches of cobbled dual carriageway. If your engine explodes or you otherwise sputter to a halt, call 154 and a car full of so-called Yellow Angels will charge to the rescue. The Angels will tow your hulk to the **24-hour repair service** at Limuzská 12 (✆ 77 34 55); and if you haven't entirely run out of steam, you can drive there directly. There is a certain etiquette about **road accidents** in the Czech Republic. After the usual exchange of details, apologies, blows, etc., you're expected to report the news to the police on 236 64 64. If you've moved your car an inch or if you test positive for alcohol, it's curtains for your insurance claim. *See* pp. 362–3 for information if you are bringing a car over for some time.

Car Hire

The following firms all offer a range of western cars, and permit drop-offs at offices outside the Czech Republic. All take major credit cards.

Budget	Hotel Intercontinental, ✆ 280 09 95. Daily 8–8.
Europcar	Pařížská 26, ✆ 231 02 78. Daily 8–6.
Hertz	Karlovo nám. 28, ✆ 29 78 36. Daily 8–8.
Avis	Elišky Krásnohorské 9, ✆ 231 78 65. Mon–Fri 7.30–6, Sat 8–5, Sun 8–12 noon (weekend times provisional).

If you don't need drop-off facilities, the state-owned Pragocar company at Opletalova 33, ✆ 22 23 24, hires out cheaper Škodas and Opels. It's open 365 days a year from 7 am–7 pm. A small private firm, Esucar, at Husitská 58 (✆ 691 22 44) offers rates that are among the lowest in Prague. On the other hand, if money is no object you might consider cruising Prague in a white stretch limo: chauffeur-driven Lincolns can be hired at Namarně 4, ✆ 34 27 91.

Motorbikes

The maximum speed limit is 60 kph (40 mph) in built-up areas, and 90 kph (55 mph) elsewhere. Driver and passenger have to wear helmets and may not smoke while riding, under any circumstances. Dipped headlights must be used. If your dream machine is damaged, basic repairs are carried out at Jeseniova 56, ✆ 27 90 21.

Inefficient Travel

Messing about on the Vltava is a useless way of getting from A to B, since you have to go back to A eventually, but it's fun. *See* pp. 348–9 for **boating** details. A **horse-and-carriage** is only marginally more functional, and you can mount one at the Old Town Square. You can also catch a **choo-choo train** in the square during the summer, and go on a hooting and jangling trip through town. No Czech rides a **bicycle** across the asthmatic hills of smoky Prague, but odd foreigners can get away with it: hire one at Cyclocentrum, through the courtyard at Karlovo nám. 29 (open Mon–Fri 9–6, Sat 8–1). A final opportunity to expend vast amounts of energy is provided by the Czech Aeronautical Research and Testing Institute (VZLU) at Beranových 130 in Prague 9, tel/fax 850 18 90. As well as charters of executive jets and light aircraft, it can put you into an L39 Albatros **turbojet trainer** alongside a watchful man with dual controls. For about $1000 an hour, you can speed over the Czech Republic at 500 kph in the same plane used to teach an entire generation of Warsaw Pact pilots how to evade NATO and wipe out the west, as and when it might become necessary.

Long-Distance Travel

Prague's main bus station is at Florenc (on lines B and C of the metro), and there are smaller termini at Želivského (line A), Smíchovské nádraží (line B) and nádraží Holešovice (line C). Arrive with time in hand; long queues often build up well before the bus leaves.

Trains going vaguely northwards usually leave Hlavní nádraží or nádraží Holešovice, and those to the south run from Smíchovské nádraží. Trains also shoot off in all directions from Masarykovo nádraží (on Havlíčkova, in the New Town). Tickets should be bought in advance, but if you're in a hurry just jump on board and pay the small supplement to the conductor. There are timetables on rollers in all the stations; look up your route on the map, and then refer to the corresponding table. The word for 'arrival' is *příjezd*; 'departure' is *odjezd*.

Fares within the Czech Republic are still extremely cheap. Sample 2nd-class fares are £1 ($1.50) for 50 km, £1.50 ($2.25) for 100 km and £2.50 ($3.75) for a 200-km journey. There's a small supplement on fast trains, which you can identify on timetables by the abbreviated number of stops. The difference between 1st- and 2nd-class carriages is negligible on short journeys, but on longer trips the extra legroom is sometimes worth the 50 per cent premium. Couchettes and sleepers are a bargain—even a night of bliss in a 1st-class bed will only set you back an extra £5 ($7.50). There are no special fares for foreign students or young people travelling within the Czech Republic, but see p. 4 for details of the Explorer Pass.

Prague may be only one stop on your grand tour. Wasteels, on the first floor of the main station, can book onward BIGE tickets to most European destinations. There are other exciting offers available at the ČSD agency, near the taxi-rank at Hlavní nádraží (Mon–Fri 9–1, 2–5, Sat 8.30–12 noon). Prague's once-legendary travel bargains (Moscow for £2 or $3, for example) have followed the Communist bloc into the dustbin of history, but travelling east remains cheap. ČSD sells tickets to Warsaw for £12 ($18) and to Budapest for £8 ($12). There are further reductions to ISIC-card holders—25 per cent on the Warsaw fare, and a full half for the Budapest run. A ticket to Moscow costs £40 ($60), and for about £120 ($180) the agency can aim you towards Beijing on the Trans-Siberian Express (subject to the average waiting-list of five weeks). The best of British luck to anyone who intends to get through the Commonwealth of Independent States; embassy addresses are on p. 27.

Praguers themselves tend to avoid Russia and China. They go west and south on coaches, on surreal sightseeing expeditions that do their best to make up for 40 years' lost travelling time. It's not unusual to spend longer on the coach than at the destination. Further information on day-trips to Paris and Istanbul, as well as more standard coach journeys, is available at ČSAD (in the passage at Na příkopě 31) or at Bohemiatour on Zlatnická 7 (Mon–Thurs 8–5, Fri 8–4).

Travellers with Disabilities

Even the most powerful electric wheelchair is likely to whine to a halt when confronted with some of Prague's hills, and its crowded public-transport system can be inaccessible to even the most able-bodied, but at last the city is beginning to address the problems of people with limited mobility. The first post-revolutionary mayor, former dissident Jaroslav Kořán, set the ball rolling by smoothing 3000 kerbs during his time in office. Although Kořán has moved on and now edits the Czech edition of *Playboy*, having been ousted by a gang of dull monetarists, he still regards that as his most worthwhile achievement and he did much to raise awareness of the needs of disabled people in Prague. Olga Havel, the wife of Václav, has also worked hard for disabled people, and the foundation that she created is the capital's most useful source of information for all those with visual, dietary and auditory problems, as well as wheelchair users. It's known as the Výbor dobré vůle (Committee of Good Will), and you'll find it at nám. Maxima Gorkého 2 (a.k.a. Senovážné nám. 2), © 235 24 94. Extremely helpful English-speaking workers are always around. They can also put you in touch with the Red Cross, which lends wheelchairs out to anyone who needs one. The capital is slowly providing for the special needs of blind people. Metro entrances have been bleeping for about a decade; on the trains a voice announces when the doors are about to close and what the next stop will be (the latter also on trams); and traffic lights click or squeak when it's safe to cross. Prague's first tactile exhibitions were organized in late 1992, and one, at the National Sculpture Gallery, is intended to be permanent (*see* pp. 258–9). You could also wander along to Palata, a 6-acre retreat of flowers, herbs and wind chimes at Na Hřebenkach 5 designed by the City Architect.

Those sites and businesses in Prague that provide most assistance to disabled visitors are the following:

Hotels

Atlantic—four rooms, with adapted bathrooms on each floor.

Atrium—fifteen rooms adapted for wheelchair users.

Axa—two rooms, but a small set of rampless stairs in the lobby.

Belvedere—four rooms (access through only one of the main entrances).

Diplomat—six rooms and one non-smoking floor.

Forum—four rooms.

Harmony—five rooms and one suite.

Hoffmeister—one room.

Karl-Inn—ramp and no barriers. No special rooms.

Meteor—four rooms. Underground car park includes special provision for disabled drivers.

Olympik II—two rooms.

Palace—two rooms.

Panorama—one bathroom on fifth floor.

Pension City—no special features, but this is the pension most suitable for wheelchair users (as well as the most pleasant for everyone). Lift, no barriers on the floors, and helpful pleasant staff.

Penta—three rooms. Special non-smoking rooms.

President—adapted WC on ground floor; ramps and wheelchair access to all floors.

Union—one room.

Vaníček—ten rooms with adapted bathrooms.

All the above hotels can are listed in the Where To Stay section, where mention is also made if a place is particularly *unsuitable* for wheelchairs. You could also contact **Metatour** at Štefánikova 48, © 55 10 64, fax 55 10 49, a travel agency for Czech disabled people, which hopes to open its own hotel in a Renaissance palace. The stumbling block is that the building is being reclaimed by its pre-Communist owner, and a spirited court battle is in progress to decide who owns what. Should Metatour win, and construction go ahead, the hotel will have extensive facilities for disabled people.

All the city's department stores (*see* p. 343) are accessible to wheelchair users. However, only Kotva has an adapted toilet and attendant-controlled lifts. It's also the best.

Concert Halls and Theatres

The following three venues all have unusually good facilities for wheelchair users.

Estates Theatre (Stavovské divadlo)—full wheelchair access, adapted and exclusive bathroom. All seats have headsets for those with hearing difficulties.

Vinohrady Theatre (Divadlo na Vinohradech)—full wheelchair access, 50 per cent discount.

Rudolfinum—full wheelchair access, adapted and exclusive bathroom; 50 per cent discount.

Galleries and museums

Wheelchair users can visit most of the city's collections if they telephone with enough warning, but don't expect an easy ride. Only the National Museum of Technology has an adapted loo. The main (ground) floor of the excellent Galerie Pallas is fully accessible, albeit by two separate entrances. The Jednorožec s harfou (Unicorn with a Harp) contains both a gallery and café, and has been specifically designed to be navigable by wheelchair. (*See* pp. 344–5 for addresses.)

The Czech Republic's spas are said to help scores of medical conditions, from cerebral palsy to psoriasis. Each watering hole has its particular specialities. For further information, contact **Balnea** in Prague at Pařížská 11, ✆ 232 37 67, fax 232 19 38.

The best source of general information in the UK about travel across Europe is **RADAR** at 25 Mortimer St, London W1N 8AB, ✆ (071) 637 5400, which publishes *Holidays and Travel Abroad—A Guide for Disabled People*. In the US, get hold of *Access to the World—A Travel Guide for the Handicapped* by Louise Weiss (H. Holt & Co.).

Practical A–Z

Like street names, the significance of dates in Prague has become very obscure as of late. Many anniversaries that were once charged with anti-Communist significance are now all but ignored and the only new public holiday created since 1989—Czechoslovakian Independence Day—was observed twice before the country that it commemorated disappeared from the map. The replacement for the holiday has still not been decided. That, along with the fact that a clutch of Communist feast days were abolished, means that the Czech Republic has a dearth of long weekends. On the other hand, it has an excess of so-called State Holidays (marked with a ★) and Memorial Days (marked with a +) which no one quite knows how to celebrate. Public holidays, during which most of the capital closes down, are listed in bold.

January

1—**New Year's Day**.

19—Anniversary of Jan Palach's Death. Inexplicably, this lasted as a Memorial Day for only a couple of years after 1989. Scores of people will still light a candle at his grave (*see* p. 276).

February

28—Victorious February. Anniversary of Communist takeover in 1948. Used to involve 'vast popular manifestations' in the Old Town Square.

March

7—Tomáš Masaryk's Birthday. The first president of Czechoslovakia, stooped, bearded, intellectual and much loved. This short-lived Memorial Day was celebrated with about as much enthusiasm as Victorious February.

April

The year's excitement begins. In the fortnight before Easter, street vendors sell willow switches (*pomlázky*) bedecked with ribbons, and grandmothers to granddaughters across the country suck eggs. The preparations reach fruition on:

Easter Monday (Pondělí velikonoční). A fun-packed day. Until noon, Prague's men thrash their women with the willow sticks to keep them fresh for the coming year. The newly-fertilized women then give their menfolk a painted egg, and pour buckets of water over them. The bizarre ritual is universally observed.

1—**Labour Day**. Slowly reverting to another day of feasting and fecundity. However, mass unemployment may spoil the fun.

5—Anniversary of Prague Uprising+ (*see* p. 58).

8—Day of Liberation from Fascism★. In 1991, the Czech Republic joined western Europe in celebrating VE Day on the 8th, despite the fact that on that day in 1945 ferocious fighting was still continuing in Prague.

9—The day that the Red Army reached Prague in 1945, at the cost of several thousand lives. Cancelled as a holiday in 1991.

12—Anniversary of Smetana's Death. Musicians walk from his grave in Vyšehrad to Obecní dům and play his masterpiece, *Má Vlast.* Prague Spring music festival begins.

June

18—Anniversary of the killing of the assassins of Reinhard Heydrich. Memorial mass held in the Church of SS Cyril and Methodius (*see* pp. 269–70).

21—Summer solstice. Prague has an active contingent of hippies and starchildren and you can expect strange goings-on on hillocks and mounds around town. Also, 27 spectres spend the night pottering about in the Old Town Square (*see* p. 158).

July

Karlovy Vary International Film Festival (every even year).

5—SS Cyril & Methodius Day★.

6—Anniversary of Jan Hus's death (and birth)★.

August

In 1992, a German corporation instituted what is intended to become a traditional annual Prague beer festival. Popular though it was among very small groups of German corporate executives, it failed to ignite the popular imagination and its future remains unclear. If you're desperate, you could ask around.

21—Anniversary of Soviet-led invasion in 1968.

29—Anniversary of the 1944 Slovakian National Uprising+.

September

Annual Mozart festival held throughout the city. The Wolfgang-fest ends with a multimedia party on the Charles Bridge. Far-out patterns are beamed onto the swirling Vltava below.

28—Independence Day★. This was established as a public holiday in 1990 to mark the birth of Czechoslovakia in 1918, and celebrated with acrimony and fist fights for the last time in 1992. It's now been demoted to a 'state holiday' and will probably be forgotten before long.

31—All Saints' Eve. Appropriated by accountants and attorneys with pumpkins. Retreat to your favourite cemetery and wait until …

2—All Souls' Day. The day on which the medieval Church decreed that prayers be said for 'all the dead who have existed from the beginning of the world to the end of time'. Praguers still observe the custom, and turn their graveyards into galaxies of candles.

17—Anniversary of the first demonstration of 1989 revolution+. More candles lit in Národní street and under the St Wenceslas monument. General retreat to cafés to discuss what went wrong.

Last Thursday in November—Thanksgiving Day. Prague's resident Americans invite each other to dinner. Prague's resident American newspapers, the *Prague Post* and *Prognosis*, both run stories on the phenomenon.

5—St Nicholas's Eve. An event-filled day. Public-spirited folk dress up as devils or angels and, accompanied by a crozier-toting St Nick, stalk the streets of Prague handing out coal to evildoing tots and sweets to the good ones. More troublesome kids toss firecrackers around. Drunken trios can be found propping up bars across the capital after the day's good work is done.

8—Anarchists and youth protest John Lennon's death at the John Lennon Wall (*see* p. 196).

20—Tubs containing carp appear on Prague street corners around this time, and the roads foam with rivulets of blood and water. The creatures are the Czech equivalent of the British turkey, and normally placid Praguers spend several minutes each day watching gizzards being removed. Don't stand too close—the *coup de grâce* generally sprays fishy brains across a wide radius.

24—**Christmas Eve**. Children spend the day trying to fast, in the hope of seeing golden pigs. Carp are taken out of the bath and fried. Baby Jesus or Grandfather Frost bring the presents. St Nicholas makes the occasional surprise appearance.

25—**Christmas Day**. Nothing happens. More carp is eaten.

26—**St Stephen's Day**. More carp is eaten.

31—**New Year's Eve**, a.k.a. St Sylvester's Day. Half of Europe comes to Prague; the other half is in Berlin.

Climate and Best Time to Go

There's nothing extraordinary about Prague's climate. The average temperature hovers around freezing point between December and February (and is often considerably below), climbing into T-shirt weather from May. July and August are the hottest months, reaching the high 20s regularly; and the chill of autumn usually sets in towards the end of September. The driest month is February and the wettest July, when warm showers of Bohemian acid rain drop lazily in the late evening.

Average Temperatures in °C (°F)

January	*February*	*March*	*April*
−4/1 (25/34)	−2/3 (28/38)	1/7 (33/45)	9/13 (48/56)
May	*June*	*July*	*August*
9/18 (48/64)	13/22 (56/72)	14/25 (58/78)	14/25 (58/78)
September	*October*	*November*	*December*
11/20 (52/68)	6/12 (43/54)	2/5 (34/40)	−1/1 (30/34)

About 80 million foreigners visited Prague in 1992. Surveys, admittedly non-scientific, suggest that about half of them came in August. In that month tourism reaches critical mass, and the city temporarily becomes a combination of Torremolinos and Euro Disney. Praguers take fright and evacuate to their country cottages every weekend, leaving the city almost devoid of Czechs. The August explosion can exert a horrible fascination on high-energy types, but those of a calmer disposition should consider arriving in late June or early July. Even better is early September, when the almost-statutory holiday periods of much of Europe are over, but twilight lingers and cobbles remain warm. Prague's buskers are still out in force, its gardens and islands are in late bloom, and the city heaves a sigh of relief at having survived the deluge. As autumn turns to winter, pensive types can watch leaves yellow and die, or head for the city's cafés and restaurants, which develop a jolly intimacy that lasts throughout the big chill. In November Praguers turn on the central heating, and to the sound of organ recitals and the smell of lignite they rush towards Christmas. Prague becomes a peasoup of pollution between about November and February, and if you have respiratory problems stay away. The capital closes down between Christmas Eve and Boxing Day

(St Stephen's Day). New Year's Eve became a street fiesta in 1989, but since those heady revolutionary days it has degenerated into the same confused night searching for a purpose that it is everwhere else in Europe. February is the cruellest month, but also the time when you're most likely to see Prague swathed in snow, not the mushy rubbish of the west, but the creaking stuff of Good King Wenceslas. Buds pop, sap rises, and public displays of affection reach new heights at the beginning of April. The end of the month is another of the best times to come to the city and when the Prague Spring music festival begins in early May, the tourist season has turned full circle.

Communications

Prague's **Main Post Office** is in the New Town at Jindřišská 14, © 26 41 93. Fax, telegram, post and telephone services are available at all hours of the day and night. Counter 28 of the cavernous main hall will keep correspondence for you if you don't know where you'll be staying—letters should be addressed to you at 'Poste Restante/Jindřišská 14/110 00 Praha 1'. Have your passport when you collect your mail (Mon–Fri 6.30 am–8 pm, Sat 6.30 am–1 pm). (An alternative mailing address, often more efficient, is Prague's American Express office—*see* Money below.)

There are several other post offices in the city centre, including one in the Old Town at Kaprova 12, another in Malá Strana at Josefská 4, and one opposite St Vitus's Cathedral in the Third Courtyard of the castle.

Post

Stamps can be bought from tobacconists, souvenir shops and the like, as well as from post-office counters. Correspondence can take anything from five days to two weeks to reach home; there's an express service that doesn't cost much and can halve that time. As a general rule, you should never expect post offices to sell anything as obvious as envelopes or wrapping paper, for which you should look for a shop marked *papír* or *papírnictví*.

Telephones

Cardphones have hit Prague, and if you anticipate making anything over a handful of calls, your best bet is to invest in a card. There is less likely to be a queue at a cardphone booth—thanks to Praguers' continuing distrust of plastic— and the phone is more likely to work. Otherwise, there's a certain knack to using Prague payphones. With the small orange or black ones, place a 1 kč coin in the groove, and it will drop automatically when the phone is picked up at the other end. The grey phones also take larger value coins—flick the coin in immediately *after* you're connected. The phones with digital displays take your money in advance, and should regurgitate unused coins. Public telephones generally gurgle for a while before connecting you, so don't assume that the first noise you hear is an engaged tone.

Local calls cost 1 kč for an unlimited time. Prague telephone numbers can be from four to eight digits long. The word for extension is *linka*.

Long-distance calls can be made from all but the 1-kč phone boxes. You can chat to an international operator by dialling 0135—and to reverse the charges, call 0132 and say '*na účet volaného (London/New York* etc.)'. If you find that impossible, the operators all speak English, although 'collect call' is more widely understood than 'reverse charge call'. You can also make long-distance calls from a post office. Calls cost the same at all times of the day or night. International directory enquiries are answered at 0149. The dialling code to the UK is 0044, and to the USA it's 001; the code *for* Prague is 01042(2) from the UK and 01142(2) from the USA. There are more useful phone numbers on pp. 367–8.

Faxes

Slimy sheets of paper can be sent at all hours from the central post office at Jindřišská 14. It also acts as a reception service at 232 08 78, 232 09 78 and 26 04 60 (all prefixed by the relevant code).

Telegrams

These can be sent from all the post offices listed above.

International Courier Service

DHL Couriers can be booked at Na poříčí 4, ✆ 26 75 25 (Mon–Fri 8–6).

Crime

As in the rest of one-time Communist Europe, a massive increase in (usually) petty crime has been an unwelcome aspect of the Czech Republic's transition to democracy. One reason was the fresh start that Václav Havel (an ex-con himself) magnanimously offered the hoodlum community in the heady first days of his presidency, when in early 1990 he signed an amnesty releasing thousands of petty criminals. More generally, popular respect for all forms of authority took a battering after the Velvet Revolution, and with the Czech–Slovak split, the legitimacy of national institutions is being tested to the limit. The boom that accompanied economic liberalization in Prague has also done much to turn the capital into a Dodge City for the 1990s, awash with cash and cowboys on the make. Although serious crime remains extremely low, the city hums with anarchistic potential. Scores of shiny cars without number plates drive around with impunity, and at least one branch of the State Bank politely requests that handguns be left at the door. Apocryphal stories abound of the Italian Mafia's interests in swish nightclubs, the dying Russian arrested with a plutonium-filled cigarette packet, or the Serbs who are channelling heroin and arms through the city, and—although you'll actually *see* nothing—there's a kernel of truth to most of the tales. Armed guards patrol any business with delusions of grandeur: McDonald's has a man in a shiny black uniform, and less salubrious enterprises make do with thugs in camouflage gear, sporting Alsatians and truncheons. A final straw in the wind is the culture of self-defence that has taken hold. The wide boys selling duty-free cigarettes and Red Army hats have their switchblades, taxi-drivers hide stun guns under their seats, and even the gentlest Prague love-child might well have a can of tear gas tucked away in the folds of her flares.

The deteriorating law-and-order situation is mirrored by the messy state of the Czech Republic's police. They have had a rough few years. The former state force, the VB, was held in almost universal contempt for its zealous support of the old regime, obsessive enforcement of jay-walking legislation, and legendary depths of stupidity. Officers patrol in threes, and Praguers used to claim that one was there to write the arrest warrant, another to read it, and the last to keep an eye on the two intellectuals. After the revolution, they virtually went into hiding for several months, and only after being purged and reorganized during 1991 did they re-emerge as a force to be reckoned with. Unfortunately, low pay and status mean that the new recruits are often little better than the old. Swaggering bravado, racism and corruption are ubiquitous. As a result, most Praguers still harbour a healthy suspicion of the boys in green, even if, as crime rises, they are slowly having to come to terms with the time-honoured quandary of who else to call when the flat gets burgled.

All in all, you should probably avoid the lawmen almost as carefully as you do the outlaws. Always carry your passport with you; leaving it at home is a very minor offence, and can lead to hopeful officers spending long minutes angling for a bribe. In a real crisis, look for a patrol car marked 'Policie'. Prague's central police station is at Konviktská 14 in the Old Town. The **emergency telephone number is 158**. The city also has its own police force (the *Městské policie)*, in black uniforms, who have less jurisdiction than the greenies but are often more helpful.

Despite everything, Prague is not yet New York—no matter what some bemused citizens might say. In fact Prague remains one of the safer capitals in the world, and elementary precautions should keep your property and person intact. Physical assaults are still rare. However, you would do well to avoid early morning strolls through Wenceslas Square and the main station: not only are they the most seedy and alcohol-drenched parts of town at night, but during the summer they are also the scene of regular sweeps by squads of Prague police. The most common form of thievery is the gentle art of pick-pocketing. Crooks usually operate in pairs, and are particularly active wherever tourists gather—be especially careful on the Charles Bridge in the summer. Distraction and commotion are the nastiest weapons that you're likely to face. If someone thrusts a map in your face, or asks an improbable question (e.g. 'Didn't I meet you last year in Marienbad?'), reach for your wallet immediately. Plan for the worst by making notes of your passport details (number, date, place of issue), and traveller's cheque and credit card numbers. Travel insurance policies usually require you to file a report within 24 hours of a theft; go to the main police station at Konviktská 14. You could also contact your embassy for help; the British Embassy is particularly sympathetic and can help you have money transferred out. Optimists could also try the lost property office at Bolzanova 5, © 236 88 87. If you're waylaid—or forgetful—on a train, each station also has its own lost-property office.

Lone women will probably find Wenceslas Square doubly uncomfortable at night, since it's a well-known promenade for prostitutes, pimps and sad men. The same applies to the area around Uhelný trh, which has become Prague's kerb-crawling precinct and the haunt of a thousand fishnets. According to an international survey in 1992, Czechoslovakia had the worst incidence of sexual assault in the world: it's not a statistic that many foreign women residents would agree with, but it may be worth knowing. The streets are far safer for women than those of London or most large US cities, although keys, knees and umbrellas are useful weapons to keep in reserve. Czech hairspray is a traditional and effective blinding agent, but as mentioned above, it's slowly being superseded by canisters of CS gas, available from all good tobacconists.

Finally, anyone black or even marginally off-white should expect to come across a certain degree of racism. It's often of a fairly innocent kind (much of the former Warsaw Pact seems unaware that the word 'nigger' is impolite), but it can create the occasional uncomfortable situation for foreigners. The concept of a black American is widely understood (although it's best if he or she knows a lot about rapping) but anyone who is British and not white remains something of a riddle to many in Prague. However, it's the local non-whites who bear the brunt. One of the most unpleasant of the many genies to slip out of the velvet bottle in 1989 was a contempt for the 30,000-strong Vietnamese population, and most notably of all, the open hatred now expressed towards the country's several hundred thousand gipsies (*cikány*), or Roms. As well as the skinhead gangs who occasionally lob gas grenades into their pubs, there is a less obvious racism at work in the capital, where many restaurants and clubs operate a colour bar. Although gipsies can be raucous and certainly commit a disproportionate share of the country's crime, it's near impossible to find a Praguer who could even preface his stereotypes with the assurance that one of his best friends is a gipsy.

Customs and Traditions

Praguers tend to be polite and shake hands a lot, but there are only a few peculiar habits that you really need to know. They can be mastered in a day, and often ease social intercourse considerably.

- When entering a Czech house, make as if to remove your shoes. Your host may well waive the requirement, but the reflex will be seen as a sign of good breeding.

- If you are staying in a private flat and find yourself receiving strange looks as you walk around your tenement, say *dobrý den* (good day) and smile. The greeting is ubiquitous even among perfect strangers, and elderly folk can get particularly cross if they're ignored.

- If you are sharing a café table with Czechs and they are served food, say *dobrou chut'* (bon appétit). Smile graciously in the reverse situation. On leaving, it's traditional, if untrue, to say *na shledanou* (see you later).

- When in a pub, *never* pour beer from one glass into another. If you do, an awestruck hush is almost certain to descend over the table, and in extreme cases, you may be asked to leave.

- Still on the theme of drink, you must always stare into your companions' eyes when drinking a toast. Failure to do so implies a certain untrustworthiness, and an unwillingness to abide by drunken oaths.

- Men should always precede women into an unknown Prague bar or café. The theory is that, should a brawl be taking place, the man is thus poised to fend off the barstools. It's unclear how the rule applies in the case of groups: one school of thought favours sexual alternation, but another holds that all the men should enter together, presumably to minimise the risk of being picked off one by one.

- Perhaps related to the above, women can expect to be treated as sex objects or sweetly incompetent morons by almost all male Praguers. You'll come across a huge amount of naked flesh and tissue paper pornography during your stay.

Electricity

Prague's voltage is usually 220 ac, but you'll need a plug with two round prongs before anything will fire up. Buy adaptors before leaving home. The best is the universal kind, because it can deal with the earthing prong that sticks out of some sockets. If you're staying in private accommodation in an older part of town, the voltage may be 110 ac. That's fine for US equipment, but UK hairdryers will work at half-speed, while your laptop and fax won't work at all. Pack a transformer, if in doubt.

Embassies

Most diplomatic missions are to be found in Malá Strana, or around the Dejvice area in Prague 6.

Austria: Viktora Huga 10, ✆ 54 65 57.

Bulgaria: Krakovská 6, ✆ 26 43 10.

Canada: Mickiewiczova 6, ✆ 312 02 51.

Commonwealth of Independent States: Pod kaštany 1, ✆ 38 19 40 (embassy); Korunovační 34, ✆ 37 37 23 (consulate).

France: Velkopřevorské nám. 2, ✆ 53 30 42.

Germany: Vlašská 19, ✆ 53 23 51.

Hungary: Badeniho 1, ✆ 32 24 81.

India: Valdštejnská 6, ✆ 53 26 42.

Israel: Badeniho 2, ✆ 32 24 81.

Italy: Nerudova 20, ✆ 53 06 66.

Mongolian People's Republic: Namarně 5, ✆ 312 15 04.

Pakistan: Dejvická 30, ✆ 32 87 89.

People's Republic of China: Pelléova 22, ✆ 312 32 45.

Poland: Valdštejnská 8, ✆ 53 69 51.

Romania: Nerudova 5, ✆ 53 30 59.

United Kingdom: Thunovská 14, ✆ 53 33 47.

USA: Tržiště 15, ✆ 53 66 41.

Yugoslavia/Serbia: Mostecká 15, ✆ 53 14 43.

The British Embassy acts on behalf of citizens from the Republic of Ireland and New Zealand. The Australians closed down their embassy in 1992 because no one used it, and nationals of that country should trek on to Warsaw or Vienna.

Insurance

Medical cover is less important for holidays in Prague than in some other cities, since British citizens receive free treatment and prices are low for everyone else. However when it comes to insurance it's worth looking on the dark side, and Prague is not a place where you want to have an operation. If you anticipate major surgery, you could consider a policy that will repatriate you in such circumstances. When it comes to theft and loss, check whether stolen cash is reimbursed, and go through the even smaller print detailing exclusions and limitations. The latter may result in your recovering only half a camera, and an even smaller fraction of a lost suitcase. US students with an ISIC card have free (albeit limited) cover from the moment they venture out of the home of the brave.

Medical Emergencies

Ambulance/Doctor—© 155

Fire—© 150

British citizens receive accident and emergency treatment free of charge in the Czech Republic, thanks to a reciprocal agreement between the two countries. Everyone else has to pay. In an emergency, calling 155 will get you an ambulance with life-saving equipment. If it's practical, you could go directly to the Nemocnice Na Homolce on Roentgenova 2, off V úvalu, © 52 92, which is the hospital that's both best appointed and most accustomed to handling foreigners. Less urgent matters can be dealt with at the Fakultní Poliklinika, on the second floor at Karlovo nám. 32 (Mon 7.15–5, Tues–Thurs 7.15–3.45, Fri 7.15–2.30). You can redeem your prescriptions at any pharmacist *(lékárna)*. One of the most convenient—open 24 hours daily—is at Na příkopě 7.

Starved of resources and foreign contacts for too long, Czech medicine falls short of several western standards. Although doctors are usually well trained and conscientious, you are well advised to avoid letting anyone tamper with you too much. But if you need treatment, don't be carried away by your nightmares; needles are clean, surroundings are sterile and as a foreigner, for better or for worse, you'll get better treatment than would most Czechs.

Dental treatment is available at the Poliklinika. If your agony doesn't coincide with its opening hours, Prague's **emergency dentist** at Vladislavova 22 will temporarily cap or permanently extract the offending tooth, from Mon–Fri 7 pm–7 am and all through the weekend, © 26 13 74. The waiting room alone can be a harrowing vision of purgatory, and the services provided are again surrounded by so many Prague folk legends that you should probably grin and bear it until you get home—or at least until the Poliklinika reopens.

Opticians can be found where you see a sign saying *oční optika*. If you can't find one, feel your way to Fokus Optika at Mostecká 3 (*open Mon–Fri 9–7, Sat 12 noon–7*).

AIDS is on its way, and most observers agree that in Prague HIV will spread through its young heterosexuals just as quickly as it will through the male homosexual population. Remarkably few Czechs use condoms; however, there are vending machines in the vestibules of most metro stations, all open 24 hours. Look for the boxes with the sign 'Men's Shop'. On a related theme, women spending some time in Prague might note that while the Czech contraceptive pill is less fearsome than it once was, it's still more hormone-unfriendly than western varieties. Information on sources of help in times of crisis can be found on p. 363.

Money

The Czech currency is the crown (*korun českých*, abbreviated to *kč*), which is made up of 100 heller *(haléř)*. As of early 1993, the country's banks were offering about 42 kčs to the UK£ and 28 to the US$. However, unless the Czech Republic experiences a monetarist miracle, you can expect those figures to become laughable as inflation erodes the crown. The exchange rate is likely to adapt itself to price increases, and **almost all prices in this book are given in pounds and dollars. An exchange rate of £1:$1.50 is assumed.** However, it's still only possible to give very rough estimates of how much your stay will cost. Assume prices about 30 per cent lower than those at home, and if hyperinflation hits, you will be in for a pleasant time, even if no one else is.

When changing your money, don't bother with the black market. The street rate used to be twice the official one, but with the crown on the verge of full convertibility there is no longer any real difference. More importantly, you will be conned: 99 of every hundred street transactions end in a confused scuffle, mutterings of 'police!' and the tourist left holding a wad of waste paper or near worthless Polish zloties.

Exchange Offices

These exist in every hotel and accommodation agency, and gleam out of the medieval centre of the town. There are several 24-hour Chequepoints, including one at the foot of Wenceslas Square, on 28. října 13. However, the commission they extract—often 10 per cent—is painful, and you should always change your money at a bank, which usually takes two per cent. Most banks close at 6 pm and throughout the weekend. There's a 24-hour banknote-changing machine at the Bank Austria on Havelská 19. You can reconvert crowns if you have your original receipts.

Cash

The plastic revolution is on its way, but cash is still ubiquitous. Some western currency *(valuta)* is useful for emergencies, since it's usually easy, if illegal, to spend it directly. Putting aside a high-denomination note, Czech or foreign, can be useful for bribery, but although the practice remains common you should be very careful before attempting it. Slipping someone a sweetener can lead to extremely embarrassing situations unless you know exactly what you are doing.

Credit Cards

Major cards can now be used in all the swankier restaurants, shops and hotels. Cash advances can be obtained from all banks and exchange offices. Holders of Mastercard/Access and Visa (and Cirrus cards) can also use the Automated Teller Machines scattered around the centre of town. There's one outside the Komerční banka on Na příkopě 5. American Express has an office at Václavské nám. 56. It's open from Mon–Fri 9–6, Sat 9–4, and the ATM outside is open 24 hours. Lost Amex cards can be reported on 235 24 68 during office hours; at other times call UK (0044) 273 526 840. In the case of other cards, the Živnostenská banka (© 236 66 88) will help you have them cancelled before too much damage is done.

Traveller's Cheques

Few shops are yet prepared to accept these in payment, but cheques are the only safe way to carry around small fortunes in Prague. If your cheques are pilfered, you can obtain a more-or-less instant refund at the following addresses.

American Express—Václavské nám. 56, © 235 24 68 during office hours, or at other times call the UK, © (0044) 273 571600.

Thomas Cook—Václavské nám. 47, © 26 31 06, 26 66 11, 26 43 25. (Mon–Fri 9–7, Sat 9–4.)

Visa and Eurocheque—Živnostenská banka, Na příkopě 20, © 22 35 51 (Mon–Fri 8–5.)

Telegraphic Transfers

Komerční banka has connections with Barclays, Midlands and NatWest in London, and with BankAmerica International, the Bank of New York and Citibank in New York City. The Živnostenská banka also has a branch in London. Thomas Cook and American Express can also arrange cash transfers to their Prague offices.

Packing

There is very little left that you can't buy in Prague. As a result, the time-hallowed Eastern European packing list—Marlboros, Levis, anti-State propaganda and the like—is no longer applicable. It might be worth bringing your optical prescription (if you have one), a torch for exploring dark spots, and an alarm clock. Czech wine bottles can't be opened with corkscrews, and if you picnic bring a sharp knife. A set of passport photographs is useful for onward visas and student cards.

Prague is in a state of flux when it comes to fashion. The Warsaw Pact's traditional outfits of stonewashed denims, acrylic blouses and brown suits live on in many wardrobes, augmented by the Praguers' peculiar penchant for lycra micro-skirts, white socks, furry boots and tassled shoes. Only in the city's stiffest restaurants will throats be cleared and threatening eyebrows raised at scruffs and even at the opera, jeans are common. On the other hand, snazzy dressers are no longer regarded with awe. Thousands of foreign businessmen and an increasing number of Czechs now wear charcoal suits to the office every day, while anything goes elsewhere: from the velvet flares and amulets of the Czippies to the camouflage and Davy Crockett uniform of the youthful survivalists who gather on the Charles Bridge on Sunday afternoons.

Religious Affairs

Religion has been through strange times in Prague. A population that was 90 per cent Protestant by the early 1600s reverted to Catholicism *en masse* over the next century, faced with a daunting combination of late Baroque churches and cruel and unusual punishments. Schizophrenia is thus lodged in the psyche of Czech Catholicism, which has also always had to face the uncomfortable fact that the national hero, Jan Hus, was burned with the connivance of a pope. As a result, Catholicism never acquired the stridency or nationalistic leanings that the creed did, for example, in Poland (although Prague's Cardinal Tomášek latterly became a much-admired figure of the opposition to Communism). For corresponding reasons, nonconformism has recovered considerable ground since the

Counter-Reformation. The Czech national church is the neo-Hussite Unity of Czech Brethren, established in 1918 as a gentler version of the almost-Calvinist Union of Bohemian Brethren (see pp. 47–8).

A more recent chapter of Bohemian history has had a crucial impact—still reverberating—on religious practice in Prague. Shortly after seizing power, the Communists pronounced an anathema on God. On 14 April 1950, the secret police launched "Akce 'K'"—"Operation 'K'", for Klášter or Cloister—and during the course of one night, every monastery and convent in the country was closed down. Several thousand clerics were taken away, to what even official documents referred to as 'concentration camps' until an alert aparátník noticed that the phrase could have unfortunate connotations. The name was changed to 'centralization camps'. During the rest of the decade, the Communists maintained a ferocious onslaught on religion: churches were looted and closed, anti-Zionism was often used as a cloak for anti-Semitism, and a subject called Scientific Atheism became part of the national curriculum.

Policies became less repressive from the mid-1960s, but only in 1989 were the many practical obstacles to religious observance dismantled. Early 1990 saw a massive upsurge in churchgoing, but interest has steadily receded as the Church has lost its image as a symbol of anti-Communism. Catholic surveys report that 65 per cent of the population are Catholic, and about 5 per cent Protestant, but others suggest that only some 30 per cent of Czechs are religious at all, and that the proportion in dark satanic Prague is even lower. Prague's Jews have dwindled to a minority of little over a thousand, as a result of assimilation, emigration and extermination. In 1700, they formed 25 per cent of the city's population, and before the war one in twenty Praguers still defined themselves as Jewish. The Czech Republic has so far remained little touched by the anti-Semitic tide flooding back into the rest of Central and Eastern Europe, although a closely-typed hate-sheet that appeared on newsstands in 1992 caused a few spines to shiver.

With established religion losing its grip and the country in the throes of convulsive change, sects and cults have been trying to move in. However, although Scientologists have made the thoughts of L. Ron Hubbard available to the city, and a jolly woman called Shri Sumtingwara regularly comes to Prague from Poona to teach yogic flying, true raptures remain rare. The grandest success of the cults has been culinary: between them, the Seventh Day Adventists and the Hare Krishnas operate the best vegetarian eateries in town (see p. 292 and p. 306).

For a city that has seen so much religious division, Prague is displaying an almost miraculous ability to heal its wounds. Properties have been returned to their former owners, and smiling monks and nuns now drift through the supermarkets and subways of the capital as though they had never been away. British and American clerics have also hit town, and several English-speaking services are held. Sunday Mass is at St Joseph's Church, and you can confess your holiday sins at 10 am, 30 minutes before the service begins. An Anglican Sunday service is held at 11 am in St Clement's on Klimentská, the Church of Scotland holds one at Korunní 60 at 11 am, and ecumenical prayers are said at 11.15 am at Cirkev Bratrská on Vrázova 4. An international Baptist congregation meets at Vinohradská 68 at 11 am on Sundays. Details of Czech-language services are pinned up outside the churches concerned, and the times of non-Christian services are as follows:

Buddhist

Prague's Hare Krishnas hold services at 2 pm on Sundays at Na Blanseku 24. During the summer, chant-ins also take place at strategic locations in the city centre, often in front of politely clapping crowds. All are welcome. If you have forgotten the mantra or never knew it in the first place, it runs as follows: 'Hare Krishna, Hare Krishna, Krishna Krishna, Hare Hare/Hare Rama, Hare Rama, Rama Rama, Hare Hare' (repeat as necessary).

Jewish

Orthodox: Staronová Synagoga, Červená ul. Sabbath services are held on Friday evenings, Saturday mornings and Saturday evenings. Morning services are also held during the rest of the week. Times are pinned up in the vestibule.

Conservative: Jubilejní Synagoga, Jeruzalémská 5. Times are pinned up in the vestibule of the Old-New Synagogue.

Muslim

There is not yet a mosque in Prague, but *insh'allah*, one shall arise. Contact the Pakistani embassy for further details.

Services

Beautification

Shaggy travellers and those with dirty fingernails should head for U zlaté koruny (The Golden Crown) at Železná 3, © 235 40 27. Give them a few days notice and they will paint, manicure and clip whatever you require. *The salon is open from Mon–Fri 7 am–8 pm.*

Dirty clothes

Laundries are common. Look out for the sign *prádelna* or *prádlo*. Prague finally has a launderette, **Laundry Kings**, founded by a friendly man from Mobile, Alabama, and used by about half the foreigners living in Prague. It's become an ex-pat institution, with active noticeboard and a range of while-U-wait entertainments including coffee, beer and a reading rack. *You'll find it at Dejvická 16, and it is open from Mon–Fri 6 am–10 pm, Sat–Sun 8 am–10 pm. Last loads must be in by 8 pm.*

Photographs

Express processing labs are ubiquitous; the Fotoexpress Minilab, on Lázeňská 15 offers a 1-hour service (*Mon–Thurs 9–7, Fri 9–6, Sat–Sun 10–6*). There's a passport photo booth on the ground floor of Kotva, and you can get a less grimacing likeness from one of the many Polaroid Studio Express shops. There's one in the subway half-way down Wenceslas Square open from Mon–Fri 8–7. Traditionalists might prefer the black-and-white studio at Bartolomějská 1 (*Mon–Fri 8–6*).

Express Shoe Repairs

Hobble up to the fourth floor of the Bat'a shoe store on Václavské nám. 6 (*Mon–Fri 8.30–7, Sat 9–4*).

Smoking

Prague lives under a sooty coat. Its winter smog can be as bad as that of 1950s London—no mean feat in city where only one in five adults owns a car. Deep breathing will provide plenty of carbon monoxide, but if you need nicotine as well, the city remains a congenial retreat from the passive smoking lobbies of the UK and US. The foreign influx since 1989 has included a well-intentioned group of radically-non-smoking people, many from California, who have done their best to clean up the city, but most Praguers still think of them as unhealthy obsessives. The government has also jumped on the bandwagon by banning tobacco ads, but the spunky fighters of the tobacco cartels will doubtless see off that threat. Slow-motion suicide looks safe for the foreseeable future.

The first thing to do is to divest yourself of your duty-frees and go native. Czech cigarettes are far cheaper than those of the west, and often only slightly more destructive to your health. The mildest are probably the Bulgarian *Select*, but *Femina* also provides a smooth drag (blue packs; the reds are slightly stronger, and green are menthol). *Milde Sorte* are Austrian, and have a certain cachet among the upwardly mobile, but Prague's favourite has to be *Petra*, as endorsed by 40-a-day Václav Havel. *Sparta* are the Marlboros or Camels of the country, rugged, manly and frightfully strong. The Constructivist lettering of *Mars-M20* makes them useful as souvenirs; but the closest thing to the late, lamented tubes of Soviet cardboard has to be the filterless *Start*, the humble favourite of penniless conscripts and addicts past the point of no return. It's fair to assume that *Start* smokers die at a rate ten times greater than puffers of other brands, and in a desperate bid to maintain its market share the company introduced *Start Filter* in 1992. The concept makes about as much sense as alcohol-free Stolichnaya, and the done thing is to bite off the filter immediately prior to lighting up.

There are only a few other things that smokers need to know. You should be very careful about asking a Czech for a light (*'máte oheň'*). If you're preferred a lit cigarette, never remove it from the other person's hand unless you know exactly what you're doing. To take it is usually regarded as very bad manners, but can also be construed as an erotic suggestion. Similarly, never scrounge someone's last cigarette, and don't press yours onto someone else, as Czechs have a colourful phrase for such situations. Finally, almost all Czech beer joints ban the weed in their dining rooms for a couple of hours at lunchtime. Waiters hurl ashtrays onto the table the minute that it's over, and almost enough nicotine emanates from the furnishings to keep addicts going throughout, but it's the closest thing to a smoke-free zone that you're likely to find in Prague.

Students

Despite the insistent claims of many UK youth-orientated travel agencies, there are no travelling discounts available to students already within the Czech Republic, unless you're travelling on to Poland or Hungary. However, there are several deals available before you leave (*see* pp. 2–5), and holders of an ISIC card are also eligible for reductions in Prague's museums and galleries. You can buy the card at student union offices and a number of travel agents, including London's STA Travel and Campus Travel and New York's Council Travel (*see* pp. 2–3). In Prague, a scrap of paper that vaguely implies that you're enrolled somewhere should persuade the staff of the International Students' Union to issue you with the card. *See* p. 367.

Toilets

There are toilets in every subway station, and in strategic locations across town. If you are desperate, it's acceptable to rush into the nearest café or wine bar and ask for the *záchod*, a.k.a. WC (pronounced *ve tse)*. On the other hand, if the urge is more theoretical, you could stroll towards Malé nám., where you'll find what many argue is the finest Gothic lavatory in central Europe. 'Men' is *muži*; 'women' is *ženy*. One of the stranger of the many jobs created to keep Prague's *babičky* off the streets is that of Toilet Paper Custodian, and in several public conveniences you'll find one sitting at a table near the entrance, snarling and mumbling as she folds and neatly lays out small scraps of tissue paper. The procedure varies, but generally you have to pay a crown for admission and/or a piece of paper. It can all be terribly embarrassing, and it's generally advisable to carry spare supplies. Otherwise, there are few differences between Prague's loos and those of NATO countries.

Tourist Information

The official **Prague Information Service** (PIS) has its main offices on Na příkopě 20 and Staroměstské nám. 22. The latter has the longer opening hours: *Mon–Fri 8–7 (6 in low season), Sat–Sun 9–5.* PIS has a telephone helpline on 54 44 44. It also runs sightseeing tours, as does almost everybody else in Prague during the summer.

The best weekly listings magazine is *Program*, which you can buy from most newsagents and street vendors. It has English summaries of all its sections. There ia even more accessible information in *Prognosis* and the *Prague Post*.

When booking tickets, you're best advised to go directly to the venue concerned. However, if you're pressed for time or want advice in drawing up an itinerary, there are a couple of particularly useful booking agencies. Bohemia Tickets International at Na příkopě 16 (*©* 22 87 38) can book seats for the Národní divadlo, Nova Scena, Státní opera and the Stavovské divadlo, as well as most of Prague's less grand venues (*open from Mon–Fri 9–12, 1–6, Sat 9–4*). Smaller theatres, pop concerts, and the cheap and cheerful balls that are often held in the city, are dealt with by two agencies hidden in shopping arcades: SLUNA on Václavské nám. 28 (*Mon–Fri 10–12.30, 1.30–6*) and Melantrich at Václavské nám. 38 (*Mon–Fri 9–7*). Tickets for all the cinemas in the centre of town can be bought at the SLUNA office in Panská 4. The only place to buy tickets for the Prague Spring music festival is at Hellichova 18. It's only open for a month from mid-April onwards, but advance information and tickets can be ordered from Bohemia Tickets International/ P.O.B. 534/ Praha 1—111 21.

History

Those who lie on the rails of history must expect to have their legs chopped off.

Rudé právo (Communist Party newspaper), 1979

The thousand-year history of Prague is one of the most inspiring and tragic of any European city. Glory, betrayal and martyrdom litter its pages, while its magnificent skyline has grown to maturity, bloodied but unbowed, through centuries of invasion and war. Prague's citizens—who conceived nationalism before it even twinkled in the eyes of the rest of Europe—have seen their country both liberated and dismembered in the last few years. What the future holds for the Czech Republic is anyone's guess—but if history is any guide, it's not going to be dull.

The First Přemysl is Found

The story begins with the establishment of Bohemia's first ruling dynasty, the Přemysls, at some time around the end of the 8th century. Myth and history are intertwined, but according to the former, the Čech tribe had established itself at Vyšehrad ('higher castle'), a rocky outcrop on the Vltava river that still bears the same name. Čech himself was a mass-murderer on the run; but it was his son, Krok or Crocus, who went down in legend as the putative founding father. However, he had one fundamental weakness—try as he might (and he tried at least three times) he was unable to produce a male heir. Of his three daughters, Libuše, Kázi and Teta, Libuše was the most impressive and the one who succeeded him. According to Bohemia's venerable chronicler, Cosmas of Prague (c. 1045–1125), she was:

> ... a wonderful woman among women, chaste in body, righteous in her morals, second to none as judge over the people, affable to all and even amiable, the pride and glory of the female sex, doing wise and manly deeds; but, as nobody is perfect, this so praiseworthy woman was, alas, a soothsayer.

Cosmas spins a good yarn, but he rather wanders around a very simple point. Sex was the crucial issue for the Čechs. Following Libuše's decision in a boundary dispute, the losing party complained that only a husband could knock some sense into hysterical Libuše, and the cry was taken up by the men of the tribe. Libuše's response was to go into a trance. Pointing towards the distant hills, she told them to follow her horse, which would take them to a ploughman whose descendants would rule over them for ever. The horse trotted off, the people dutifully followed and a sturdy farmer named Přemysl was brought back to wed Libuše. A dynasty had begun.

The city of Prague (as distinct from the settlement at Vyšehrad) also owes its legendary origins to one of Libuše's prophecies. According to Cosmas, she was overcome by a vision involving two golden olive trees and 'a town, the glory of which will reach the stars'. Again the loyal subjects trooped off to a spot described by Libuše, where they found a man building a door-sill (in Czech, *práh*—hence the name Praha or Prague) for his cottage. Legend has it that this spot was on what is now Hradčany, or the Castle District. Building started in earnest and the rest, as they say, is history.

Archaeological finds and other scanty evidence suggest that the first people in the area were a Celtic tribe known as the Boii, who lived here at the turn of the Christian era and stayed long enough to leave behind the name 'Bohemia'. In the 2nd century AD, Marcus Aurelius briefly considered incorporating the region into the Roman empire but thought better of the idea—the place was just too wild. In about the 5th century, the Čechs, a Slavonic tribe from Croatia, are thought to have established a powerful presence in the area, but there's no record of Crocus, and it's only in the later 9th century that the first historically-attested Přemysl, **Bořivoj**, appears on the scene as ruler of Bohemia. The little princedom was still an insignificant cog in the Greater Moravian empire, which included most of the Slavs of central Europe, and which was engaged in endless bloody tussles with the German Frankish state—known as the Holy Roman Empire—to the west.

The Great Schism between the Roman and Byzantine Churches had already begun to open up, and German monks were scurrying across the Moravian empire with their version of the Good Book. As far as the Slavonic kings were concerned, that represented enemy propaganda—but Christianity was clearly the coming thing, and in about 863, the empire's ruler, Rostislav, turned to the eastern Church for help. Emperor Michael sent along **Brothers Methodius and Cyril**, two Greek Holy Rollers who arrived with a Bible and a liturgy written in a new Greek-based alphabet (Glagolitic, or Cyrillic script) that could deal with the grunts peculiar to the Slavs. Jealous Germans levelled the usual charges of heresy, but the two men remained on fairly good terms with Rome until their death. In Bohemia, Bořivoj was dunked into the new religion by Methodius in about 874. Mass abandonment of storm and fertility gods followed.

Bohemia Takes Off

Although the Slavs had little sympathy for the Holy Roman Empire, its power couldn't be ignored. As the Přemysls struggled to control Bohemia, they began to turn away from the east—and the influence of Germans in Bohemian affairs, which was to become a tragic motif over the next millennium, began to grow. In 885, Pope Stephen V declared the Slavonic liturgy to be heretical. The Přemysls took his word for it and began the switch away from Cyrillic, for which western tourists can be eternally grateful. Bohemia remained subservient to the Moravian empire until the beginning of the 10th century, when that empire suddenly disappeared from the map, seized by rampant Magyars who had recently marauded across from central Asia. The invaders' conquests included the land of Slovakia, which was to stay under Hungarian control for almost all of the next thousand years, but little Bohemia was left untouched. No one knows why it was spared, but it is from this point that its history hots up.

In about 921, **Prince Wenceslas** (Václav) became Bohemia's sovereign. A gentle Christian who seems to have spent his life attending church foundation ceremonies, he may have been a suitable subject for imaginative 19th-century carols but he just wasn't up to the rough-and-tumble of Dark Age intrigue. In 935, he was murdered on the way to Mass by his brother, **Boleslav the Cruel**. What Boleslav lacked in kindness, he made up for with political skill: by selective extermination, he removed the remaining rivals to the Přemysls in Bohemia; he extended his dominions massively, punching a large hole into Magyar territory and marrying his daughter into the Polish ruling family; and he successfully resisted political pressures from Rome. In 973, under the rule of his less cruel son, Boleslav the Pious, Bohemia's strength was acknowledged by the pope, who finally consented to the founding of a bishopric in Prague. Two more Boleslavs followed—Boleslav the Third, who reverted to type and murdered several unruly nobles at a banquet, and his brother, Boleslav the Brave. The last was called in from Poland by the Bohemian nobility to sort out his sibling, which he did, by blinding him.

Over the next two centuries, Bohemia was pulled ever deeper into the tangled web of the Holy Roman Empire, and its interminable struggles between power-hungry popes, German princes and whoever had mustered the support to be elected emperor. In the early 13th century, both pope and emperor allowed Bohemia's princes to call themselves kings and wear a crown—which was as unimpressive as it sounds, and laid the ground for future emperors to claim the right to appoint Bohemia's king. An explosive brew was also building up at lower levels of society. Under the reign of King Wenceslas I (1230–53) German merchants were invited to Prague and other parts of Bohemia, where they were allowed to govern themselves according to their own laws. Native nobles eyed the influx with growing suspicion. They had accumulated a great deal of power, thanks to the murderous tiffs of the Přemysls, and had no intention of letting it pass by default to the Germans.

Wenceslas' successor, **Přemysl Otakar II**, gave further ground to the colonists, quite literally, by founding Malá Strana on the left bank of the Vltava for their benefit in 1257. During his reign (1253–78), the city developed into three autonomous units—the Old Town, the Castle District itself on Hradčany, and Malá Strana. A Jewish community in the area around Malá Strana was expelled to make way for the Germans—if Jews wanted to stay in town, they joined another Jewish community in the north of the Old Town which had been walled into a ghetto some years before. Gipsies are thought to have first come to Bohemia at about this time in the wake of the short but savage incursions of the Tartars in 1241–42—although, somewhat inexplicably, Romany lore claims that they arrived from Egypt, far from the Tartars' route of conquest across Russia. Trade and finds of silver deposits around nearby Kutná Hora helped to fund Prague's first building boom, and its Romanesque basilicas and houses gave way to Gothic grandeur.

However, the city's expansion was soon stopped in its tracks—a victim of Přemysl Otakar's own success. By the early 1270s, his skills at marriage, politicking and war had created a Bohemian kingdom that stretched from the Baltic to the Adriatic; which did nothing to satisfy the country's nobles that they could control their all-devouring king, but was more than enough to shake Germany's princes out of their internecine struggles. Otakar made a last-minute lunge for the emperor's throne in 1273. He missed—and Rudolf, count of Habsburg, stepped into the imperial driving seat. Three centuries later, Rudolf's descendants would burn their name into Bohemian history, and he made a memorable initial impact in 1276, when he led 100,000 soldiers into Bohemia. He was greeted by an emissary offering Přemysl Otakar's unconditional surrender. According to Thomas Carlyle, the Bohemian king tried to retain a shred of dignity by begging to be allowed to genuflect in the privacy of a tent. Rudolf agreed, only to have its walls whisked away at the crucial moment. Otakar was allowed to stay on his throne, but the powerful empire that he had built lay in ruins.

Anarchy and Chivalry

In 1306, the Přemysl dynasty sputtered to a halt with the murder by persons unknown of the 17-year old Wenceslas III. Libuše's foresight had turned out to be finite, and finding a successor was no easy matter—the German townspeople had their own axes to grind, and the nobility was split in several directions. The issue was temporarily solved when the Emperor Albert stepped in and suggested that his son, another Rudolf of Habsburg, would found a new hereditary dynasty for Bohemia. It was an offer that, in the light of recent events, was hard to refuse; but young Rudolf failed to live up to his father's expectations and died a year later. By now, tensions were high. Albert invaded to protect the good name of the Habsburgs, and was promptly assassinated; while one stormy Diet in Prague ended in mass murder after an Austrian suggested that if the Bohemians wanted a native king, they should get on their horses and find a peasant relative of Přemysl the Ploughman.

Anarchic Bohemia badly needed a monarch, and by 1310, everyone was longing for a strong hand. Their favour settled on 14-year old **John of Luxemburg**, the son of the new German emperor, Henry VII, who seemed well suited to provide the stability required.

The young king confounded everyone's expectations. Henry died on his way home from the coronation, and some blame John's oddball character on lack of parental control during his formative years. He spent most of his reign on a warring spree across Europe: for a time, he conquered northern Italy; he occasionally helped out with the pope's crusades against the tenaciously pagan Lithuanians; and he skilfully bagged Silesia a few days after it had foolishly thought his absence in the Baltic made it safe to declare war. He cared little what Prague got up to so long as it kept the royal coffers full, and burghers and nobles all made the most of the new opportunities: during John's reign, the Old Town got a town hall, a legal code and formal supremacy over every other town in the kingdom. John's interest in Bohemia waxed briefly around 1319: he invited Europe's most celebrated knights to Prague in order to re-establish Arthur's Round Table (no one turned up); and he had his baby son imprisoned, because a friend suggested that his wife would put the child on the throne while he was away making war. Although John's errantry took him far across Europe, he was an obsessive Francophile, and any gains that Bohemia made were a by-product of his desire to serve French interests. He happily paid the price in the end, dying a surreal death in 1346 at the Battle of Crécy, fighting for the French against the Black Prince's English army. Old and blind, John tied himself to two Czech noblemen and charged into the heart of the enemy ranks, leading 500 horsemen to annihilation under the arrows of Welsh archers. A Bohemian historian reports the dubious news that on hearing of John's death, King Edward III burst into tears and cried: 'The crown of chivalry has fallen today; never was anyone equal to this King of Bohemia'.

The Golden Age

John's son also fought at Crécy and narrowly escaped with his life. He could hardly have been less like his father. The German princes certainly agreed: scatter-brained John had been repeatedly blackballed for the imperial throne, but they had just elected his son **Emperor Charles IV**. On his return from Crécy, he was also offered the Bohemian crown. He doesn't seem to have borne his father a grudge for having imprisoned him, and loyally joined most of his mad dad's crusades. But Charles's reign was to be the mirror-image of that of his father.

John had been sure to give his son a good French education, but Charles systematically used the skills that he picked up at the Parisian court in a way which would have been entirely alien to the bluff Francophile. In 1356, he finally regularized the imperial electoral system, putting power squarely in the hands of the princes, thereby undercutting those who had voted against him, and dealing a body-blow to the temporal ambitions of the papacy, which had had an effective veto for centuries. (Future popes would find plenty of other ways to stick their oars into the empire's affairs.) He repaid the French debt by taking advantage of the battering that the country was receiving at the hands of the English (the Hundred Years War had only just begun) to reduce it almost to vassal status. The feeble state of both France and the papacy was symbolized by Charles's ability to persuade Pope Urban V to return to Rome from his Avignon 'prison' in 1367. The French cardinals looked on aghast as their man left (supposedly shrieking in unison, 'Oh wicked Pope! Oh Godless brother! Whither is he dragging his sons?'); Charles met his boat, and accompanied him to Rome where Urban crowned the emperor's fourth wife Elizabeth of Pomerania.

For Prague, having a calculating and ambitious monarch on the throne after a series of gamblers and crazies was a godsend. Charles may or may not have been a good patriot—but like any monarch with a family to consider, he acted like one. Charles hoped that by making a power base out of Bohemia he would enable his successors to continue his good work. He spoke fluent Czech (along with several other languages); he encouraged the development of the country's language and traditions; and he wrapped his reign in a series of legends, going back to Libuše and St Wenceslas (his mother was the daughter of King Wenceslas II, and he milked the Přemysl connection for all it was worth). Charles's dreams for Prague were spectacular. He had adopted his name at the age of 30 in honour of Charlemagne, the first Holy Roman Emperor and the last to rule over an undivided empire, and he had hopes of recovering all the ground that had been lost over the years. With the help of his friend and former tutor, Pope Clement VI, Prague had already been elevated to an archbishopric in 1344, and Charles got permission to invite monastic orders from the furthest-flung reaches of the eastern Church. While the Black Death devastated the rest of Europe during 1348, Bohemia lay protected by a screen of mountains and began to emerge as the most vital centre of Gothic art and architecture on the Continent. As befitted a medieval town with pretensions of grandeur, it got a new bridge, cathedral and the first university in Central Europe. For decades this was an academic vortex, sucking in scholars from as far away as Oxford. In the same year Charles founded the New Town, incorporating the straggling settlements outside the city walls into a system of broad streets and marketplaces that must count as the most successful and lasting piece of urban planning in Europe since the efforts of the Romans.

Nationalism and Hussitism

The peace and prosperity enjoyed by Bohemia during Charles's reign were not to last. For two centuries tensions had been building between the country's German and Czech populations. The native nobility, although far from homogenous, resented the political influence wielded by the Germans; traders and workers were jealous of their economic influence in Prague and other cities. Popular anger soon found potent expression in a movement for religious reform—one which began a century before the birth of Martin Luther, and which was one of the first signs of the conflict that was to tear Europe apart.

Charles probably could have done little to prevent the forthcoming explosion— unfortunately, he actually did his bit to shorten the fuse. While distancing himself from the political influence of the papacy, he relied heavily on the support of Bohemia's clergy, which grew particularly fat under his reign. His policy of inviting scores of religious orders to Prague also aroused hostility. Monasteries and convents were set up across the city, and Praguers realized with angry fascination not only that medieval monks and nuns were as prone to screw around as anyone else, but that here they were being subsidized to do it. The Church was brought further into disrepute by one of Charles's personal obsessions, a mania for collecting religious relics. He spent a small fortune on saintly organs, pieces of the True Cross and the like, and even persuaded the pope to create a Day of Relics, on which his collections would be exhibited to huge crowds in Prague's cattle market. The fetishistic fairs were extremely popular. Apart from the fact that indulgences were sold at knock-down prices by special agreement with the pope, hundreds of miracles were regularly recorded—but the gatherings usually degenerated into drunken orgies, and in the cool light of day, many began to wonder if the Church's time hadn't come.

In reaction to a corrupt Church, anticlericals, reformists and chiliastic lunatics of all sorts began to flood into Prague. The **Flagellants** were characteristic of the age. Said to have been founded by a mysterious group of 'gigantic women from Hungary', they sought to combat the plague and pave the way for the Messiah's expected return by not washing, and whipping themselves in public, for periods of 33 days at a time. In populist terms, you couldn't go far wrong with an idea like that in medieval Europe, and the movement made dramatic advances during the Continent's *annus horribilis* of 1348. The flailing trains of Flagellants that wound across the dying landscape were usually greeted with hopeful hysteria when they arrived at a town's gates, often followed by the annihilation of the local Jewish community, but they had less success in healthy wealthy Prague. They hit town in March 1349, by which time the movement's star was on the wane: Pope Clement, who had led some group whipping himself a year earlier when it seemed politic to do so, was seeking advice and help from the scholars of the Sorbonne and was soon to anathematize the movement. Although Flagellants put on a number of respectably attended lash-ins in Prague, Charles IV ruthlessly suppressed them within months (which, say some wags, is just what they wanted all along). There were plenty more fanatics where they came from. One of the most influential was **Jan Milíč of Kroměříž**. His ominous contribution to the debate was the announcement—made to a startled imperial court in 1366—that Charles was the Antichrist. He was wrong (the emperor died peacefully in 1378) but although the seven seals remained closed, the next decades saw the fissures in western Christianity grow ever wider.

Charles IV's eldest son, **Wenceslas IV**, took over as both emperor and king of Bohemia. The new ruler wasn't the man demanded by the difficult times. Both anticlerical and Church chroniclers disliked him, and the picture of the monarch that emerges is a bleak one. They record that from the moment that he urinated into his christening font, his reign only got worse. He apparently went on to soil the altar at his coronation, and spent the rest of his reign in an alcoholic stupor, punctuated only by acts of random violence such as the roasting of his cook and the incarceration of his first wife in a brothel. Although said to be popular among the hoi polloi (he had a flair for populist gestures, including the old favourite of dressing up in paupers' clothes and then executing anyone who sold him short measures), his relations with the high and mighty were fraught with difficulties. He tended to give jobs to his lowly chums, so the Old Town nobles imprisoned him in 1394; he got out eventually, but watched haplessly as he was stripped of his imperial title by the German electors in 1400 and constantly outsmarted by his replacement as emperor, wily half-brother **Sigismund**.

In 1402 a young priest, **Jan Hus** (John Huss), much influenced by the teachings of the Oxfordshire parish priest, John Wycliffe, was appointed rector of the Charles University. Although Hus would never have regarded himself as anything but a Catholic, his fiery sermons moved further and further from the party line. His assertion that clerical and even papal decrees had to be tested against scripture amounted to a direct political attack on the power of the church—there were hundreds in Prague alone who lived off the notion that contact with the Almighty was cheapened if it wasn't made through duly-appointed intermediaries. Like the Protestants who were to follow, the Hussites preached in the vernacular, and in about 1414 began the practice that was to characterize the movement, allowing the congregation not only the bread, but also the wine of the Eucharist. They became known as the Utraquists (from the Latin for 'in both kinds'), and adopted the chalice as their emblem. The Church was not pleased. A sentence of excommunication against Hus was published in 1411, and in 1414 he agreed to appear before a General Council of the Church at Constance to defend his views. He should have set them out in a letter. A safe conduct provided by the fiercely orthodox Emperor Sigismund proved to be worth considerably less than the paper it was printed on. Hus was locked up on arrival. The emperor issued a mild public protest, while secretly urging the assembled bishops to barbecue Hus without delay. The inquisitors actually gave Hus several chances to recant everything that he'd ever said, but he refused—and on 6 July 1415, he was burned at the stake. His ashes were scattered into the Rhine to discourage souvenir hunters.

News of his death enraged his supporters back home. Wenceslas made clear his sympathies for the nationalists, but many pro-Roman officials remained, and he was under constant pressure from his brother to keep the heretics under control. In 1419 things went from bad to worse when councillors at the New Town Hall were **defenestrated** and killed by a Hussite mob—a novel form of political violence that was to become a regular feature in Bohemia's history. The pressure finally became too much for Wenceslas, who bowed out of history by succumbing to repeated apoplectic fits.

In 1420, sneaky Sigismund tried to succeed his brother as king of Bohemia. No one quite knew what had happened at Constance, and the delegation of Prague citizens and noblemen who received him weren't initially averse to his claim. It became clear, however, that he intended to restore Church privileges and suppress the Utraquists, and the last straw came in 1420 when Pope Martin V declared a crusade against Bohemia. During the next decade he would announce four more, while the Turks merrily hammered into Christendom. Bohemia found itself at war with most of Europe; even Joan of Arc took an interest in 1429, warning the Hussites in doggerel Latin that once she had finished with the English, she'd come to sort them out. However, she herself was sizzled two years later by ungrateful Catholics; and the brilliant one-eyed general, **Jan Žižka** (c.1360–1424) developed an almost invincible army that successfully repulsed each crusade, and made 'Hussite' a word that Catholic mothers across Europe would frighten the kids with. At the same time, papal propaganda successfully tarred the Hussite movement with the brush of the Adamites, a breakaway movement (brutally suppressed by the Hussites themselves) which practised a medieval form of free love involving arcane nudist rituals, and the word 'Bohemian' entered the vocabulary of several European languages as a synonym for weirdo. As early as 1421, a more important division developed among the Utraquists, between moderates who sought a compromise with Rome and a more radical group which was beginning to think in terms of a total break with the Church. Many Bohemian nobles, and a large part of the Old Town, allied themselves to the more moderate cause; while the others were based in the poorer New Town and outside Prague at a camp and commune known as Tábor (*see* pp. 384–6), giving rise to their nickname, the Táborites. The conflict between the two groups came to a head in 1434. The new pope, Eugenius IV, reluctantly granted the right to administer and receive communion in both kinds (an agreement known as the Compacts of Basle). The extremist Táborites rejected the proposals as insufficient, so the moderate aristocrats wiped them out at the Battle of Lipany in 1434.

Sigismund, finally recognized as sovereign of Bohemia, died a few months later. His successor, Albert of Habsburg, followed suit in 1439, time enough for him to impregnate his wife, Elisabeth, who produced Ladislav the Posthumous in 1440. Ladislav reigned briefly from 1453–1457 when he died of the flu; but the real ruler of Bohemia from 1440–1471 was an Utraquist nobleman, **George of Poděbrady** (Jiří z Poděbrad), who ruled as king from 1458. George staunchly defended the new religion against a backsliding Holy See, which tried to steal the Compacts of Basle at one point (1448) and excommunicated George at another (1466). Although he had high hopes of establishing a native dynasty and expanding an independent Bohemian empire, he was living in messy times and found himself concluding a treaty with the pro-Catholic **Vladislav II of Jagellon** of Poland, in order to fight off the equally pro-Catholic Matthias Corvinus of Hungary.

Vladislav was elected king in 1471, and it was under his reign that the last flickers of popular Hussitism went out. Anti-Catholic feelings still ran high among the population—a riot against Vladislav's officials in 1483 produced Prague's second defenestration, this time from the Old Town Hall (along with the lynching of several Germans and Jews for good measure)—but the nobility began increasingly to look after their own interests. Taking advantage of the king's long absences (he preferred Hungary's Buda castle), nobles introduced serfdom in 1487, and began to brew beer (a long-standing privilege of the towns) on their feudal estates. Many nobles kept to the Utraquist faith, but in their hands it came to signify little more than a tipple at communion. The Hussite mantle was largely taken over by the Union of Bohemian Brethren, an ascetic bunch who subscribed to a mixture of predestinarianism and resistance to the Antichrist (i.e. Catholic kings). The movement grew in strength among ordinary Czechs, but it was rarely in favour with authority, and Protestant nobles tended to sniff at it with suspicion. But even if the first flowering of Czech nationalism was over, Prague and Bohemia had nevertheless established themselves as a centre of anti-Catholicism—and were to pay heavily over the next centuries.

The Habsburgs Arrive

Although vacillating Vladislav managed to produce an heir, Ludvík, the latter managed to drown in a marsh while running away from the Turks at the Battle of Mohács in 1526. Another would-be dynasty had bitten the dust, and princelings and archdukes from across Europe headed for Prague to vie for the vacant throne. The fateful choice of the divided electors was **Ferdinand I of Habsburg**. He seemed tolerant enough for a Catholic—he had been educated by liberal Erasmus—and after years of fratricide, some had the forlorn hope that a strong monarch might turn his attentions to the Turks, who had strolled ever deeper into eastern Europe during the Hussite wars. The nobles made it clear that he was being *elected* to the throne, and didn't take very seriously his occasional mutterings that the Habsburgs had had the right to rule Bohemia for over 300 years. They had forgotten their predecessors' promises to Albert—and the Habsburg chicken was coming home to roost.

In the 1520s, many of Bohemia's Germans fell under the Lutheran spell, while the Bohemian Brethren found affinities with Calvinism—and although estimates vary, the population was probably 90 per cent Protestant by the middle of the century. The religious issue came to the fore gradually. Ferdinand began his reign tolerantly enough, while he battled away with the Turks, and his first concern was to consolidate Habsburg rule. He had a minor triumph in 1541, when a fire raged through Prague and destroyed all the state documents. In the absence of the papers that would have proved otherwise, he somehow persuaded the Estates that whatever they might have said 15 years earlier, he had ascended the throne by hereditary right. Peace with the Turks in 1545 allowed him to turn his mind to matters spiritual. Ferdinand was religious and Catholic, but his opposition to Protestantism was strengthened by more mundane concerns: in the empire as a whole, Catholicism was a usefully universal ideology under which to establish centralized rule; and in Bohemia, Protestantism still had a dangerously nationalistic tinge, even though many of the country's Germans now shared the religion of the Czechs. He had long been trying to forge an alliance between Catholicism and old-style Utraquism—but although Prague's Protestants had been suspicious since his trick with the documents in 1541, it was only in 1547 that he laid his cards on the table.

In that year he sweet-talked them into financing an anti-Turkish army, which then marched westward to attack Protestants in Saxony. Representatives from across the country met in Prague and decided that enough was enough—the king would respect the Estates' privileges and their right to elect the monarch, or else. They could have chosen a better time to make a stand. Ferdinand's troops massacred the Saxons in weeks, and were back in Prague before the Estates had got their own army off the drawing board. They made the best of a very, very bad job, and surrendered unconditionally. Ferdinand held a meeting with them at Prague Castle, and after chopping off the heads of three of the most troublesome leaders, convinced them of what he'd long believed—that his family was to rule Bohemia for ever, and that the powers and privileges of Prague and other Bohemian towns were to be cut down drastically.

It was dramatic stuff, but in 16th-century Bohemia, agreements were made to be broken, and Ferdinand made sure to have his eldest son **Maximilian** crowned king while he was still alive. The Habsburg family had recently had a squabble, and its Spanish section had hived off, so Ferdinand was Old Town Hall particularly anxious to consolidate his western empire. That meant coming to terms with Germany's Lutheran princes, and at the Peace of Augsburg (1555), it was established that a territory's religion would depend on the preferences of its ruler. The unsteady compromise did little to help Bohemia, ruled by the Habsburgs themselves. Ferdinand introduced the fiercely proselytizing Jesuit order into Prague in 1556 to counteract the spread of Lutheranism, and in 1563 Pope Pius IV launched the militant programme of the Counter-Reformation at the Council of Trent. It was to be another half century, however, before the interests of the Habsburgs and those of the papacy were fully to coincide, in an explosive fashion.

Ferdinand died in 1564, to be succeeded as emperor by Maximilian (who was already king of Bohemia). In return for continued funding for his anti-Turkish forays, Maximilian granted Bohemia's Lutherans the right to organize independently of the old Utraquist church. The concessions enabled him to have his son elected king of Bohemia with little difficulty in 1576, and when Maximilian died later that year, the same son succeeded him as **Emperor Rudolf II**.

Rudolfine Prague

The Turks were now within 100 miles of Vienna, the traditional seat of the Habsburgs. The Czech Estates offered to pay off a fair chunk of the empire's debts, and rebuild the castle, if Rudolf moved to Prague. By 1583—despite frantic lobbying by Viennese nobles—the emperor had decamped to his new capital. Prague became the centre of an empire for the first time in two centuries.

Rudolf was the most singular monarch that Prague had seen since Charles IV. In a very different way from his predecessor, he too presided over a cultural rebirth in the city (*see* pp. 69–71). The papacy had high hopes for the young emperor— educated in the powerfully anti-Protestant atmosphere of the Spanish Habsburg court, he seemed just the man to give Bohemia its comeuppance. Unfortunately for the Catholic Church, Rudolf turned out to be a very strange fish indeed, imbued with an almost mystical spirituality that was far from the new orthodoxy the Church was trying to promote. Fanaticism was almost entirely alien to him— the Lutheran astronomer Johannes Kepler was just one of those who found a haven at his court—but his education left him torn between the ideal of a universal truth and the reality of a Christianity that was being reduced into two armed camps. High in the castle, his artists and scientists tried to transcend a world that was falling apart, but the deeper his court delved into the esoteric mysteries of the symbolic and the occult, the heavier grew the burden of the religion into which Rudolf had been born. The sensitive emperor was never able to resolve the dilemma, and teetered between profound pessimism and mild insanity for most of his reign. He sought absolution regularly, but his public pronouncements were rarely confessions of faith—in 1605, an increasingly perplexed papal nuncio reported back to his boss that Rudolf had just declared, 'I know that I am dead and damned; I am a man possessed by the devil'.

Legend and history came to remember Rudolfine Prague as a fantastic city of alchemy and astrology, suspended in time, but its surreal atmosphere was very much the product of the moment. The Counter-Reformation was gathering force in neighbouring Austria and Styria; a part-time lunatic and full-time melancholic was on the throne; and mystics and zealots of every hue were massing in the city. Prague had become the nerve-centre of Europe's schizophrenia. Although Rudolf's reign was remarkably peaceful for two decades, waves of panic regularly spread across the capital. As the silver-tongued Jesuits made slow but steady advances, rumours grew that they were planning an armed insurrection; alarmed fury greeted the pope's theft of 11 days in 1583, when the Gregorian calendar was introduced into Bohemia; and in 1588, the sun entered the fiery trigon for only the second time since the birth of Christ. As the century drew to a close, Prague's seers shivered like animals before a storm, and issued the time-honoured announcement that the world was coming to an end.

It would have taken a genius to steer the empire peacefully through its crisis, and Rudolf's temperament, though unique, was ill suited to the job. His Spanish education had given him a powerful belief in the Habsburg mission, but his interest in politics was combined with an utterly irrational set of policies. He was terrified of popes and monks, and although he passed several anti-Protestant laws in the later years of his reign, he rarely enforced them—a combination that made few friends and plenty of enemies. Another problem was the succession issue. While in Spain, Rudolf had spawned a brood of bastards (including Don Giulio, a clockwork-obsessed sexual deviant and psychopath), but in Prague he tenaciously refused to marry, and withdrew at the last minute from unions with two hopeful princesses. As the years passed and his nobles clucked nervously, he would fly into a rage if the subject was publicly mentioned—although as late as in 1608 he had his henchmen go on a furtive trawl through Europe's marriage market to see 'what sort of nubile princesses or even high-ranking countesses are available'.

But by then, the game was almost up. His younger brother **Matthias** had been intriguing against him since his first major bout of insanity in 1600. Matthias steadily picked up support from other princes, whose patience with madcap Rudolf had reached an end. By 1606, Matthias had launched an open mutiny, and two years later he forced his brother to hand over all his realms save Bohemia, which was to be Rudolf's posthumous gift. Prague's nobles were happy with the compromise, having stayed loyal to Rudolf with the aim of extracting concessions in his moment of weakness. They were disappointed. The would-be autocrat had become a failed has-been, and in the last years of his reign, Rudolf swung wildly from promises to threats against his Prague nobles while making frenzied plans for revenge. It all ended when he offered his cousin, Leopold, the empire, just to deny it to Matthias. Leopold mysteriously acted as though Rudolf still had something to give, and his armies marched into Prague in 1611. Matthias did the same, Leopold left as swiftly as he had come, and an exhausted Bohemian nobility recognized Matthias as king. Rudolf was forced to abdicate and died alone in his castle a year later, and his brother was elected to the imperial throne.

From Defenestration to Massacre

In 1617, Emperor Matthias, as heirless as his brother had been, proposed his cousin **Ferdinand** as his successor to the crown of Bohemia. Ferdinand had made a name for himself as a rabid anti-Protestant while archduke of Styria, and it's hard to understand why the electors agreed to recognize him as king. As the policies of both Matthias and their new monarch turned more militant, the Bohemians began to ask themselves the same question—and on 23 May 1618, they finally took their stand against Catholic rule. The two most hated of Ferdinand's councillors were William of Slavata and Jaroslav of Martinic (the latter was known to chase his serfs into Mass with dogs, and to have wafers stuffed down the throat of anyone who insisted on a spot of wine at communion), and it was decided to give them a traditional Bohemian lesson. In full armour, the Protestant Estates entered the Court Chancellery in Prague castle and, egged on by a crowd, hurled the two royal councillors and a secretary through the window. All three survived the 50-foot drop—the Catholic Church attributed it to a miracle; others claimed that their fall had been broken by a dungheap. Prague's third defenestration threw Europe into the religious fratricide of the Thirty Years War. By its end in 1648, the Continent was in ruins.

Bohemia didn't have to wait that long. Prague's nobles swiftly set about looking for a royal champion. Europe's Protestant princes had long expected the lid to blow on the Peace of Augsburg, but although Ferdinand and allies were massing their forces against Prague, no one was yet sure if this was the Big One. Only one was eager to take up the gauntlet—**Frederick of the Palatinate**, who had had his eye on the Bohemian crown for some time. He arrived in 1619, accompanied by his English wife, Elizabeth—who was, incidentally, pregnant with Prince Rupert, later to be an impetuous if unsuccessful scourge of the Roundheads. Everyone agreed that Frederick had excellent manners (although the low dresses of Elizabeth's English maids set tongues a-wagging for several years) but it's hard to see how the Bohemians could have made a worse choice. The allies he was expected to carry with him, including Elizabeth's father, King James I, flaked away as he spent the winter in Prague. By the following November (1620), Ferdinand's Bavarian allies were within reach of the city, and Bohemia's nobles had resorted to frantic negotiations with the Turks. It soon became apparent that the 'Winter King' had never fought before in his life—and the morale of his Bohemian army gently collapsed as he nervously shuttled from battlefield to castle and made repeated attempts to persuade his wife to leave town (she was made of sterner stuff, and refused). The two armies finally met at the **White Mountain** *(bílá hora)* just outside Prague, on 8 November. It was the mother of all Bohemian battles, and a sorry end to over two centuries of anti-Catholicism in the country. The Czech and Hungarian allied armies scattered into headlong retreat. They can't altogether be blamed—their enemies included Polish Cossacks, who charged into Protestant ranks with a sabre in each hand as they held their reins between their teeth; and the Virgin Mary apparently made an appearance—but Frederick emerges with no credit whatsoever, unless love of life counts for something. He had already virtually deserted his troops; and when news of the rout reached the banquet he was holding in the castle, he decided to scarper. His wife persuaded him to stay firm, and he uncertainly agreed to rally his forces for an orderly withdrawal—but as he watched her and little Rupert ride off in a carriage, he cracked and gave the signal for mass flight.

There's one strange postscript to the battle. Among those who fought with the Catholics was **René Descartes**, who was sowing his wild oats as a mercenary before settling down to his epistemological enquiries. His presence at the battle has given rise to Prague's most absurd legend. He's said to have been wounded, and on recovering from unconsciousness, to have declared with relief, 'I think—therefore I am'—a reflection that, when honed, would transform the course of European thought.

The Bohemian Counter-Reformation

Ferdinand, who had become emperor after Matthias's death in 1619, proceeded to exact a terrible revenge from the upstart Bohemians. A few days after the battle, he was given some advice by one of his court favourites, a Capuchin friar called Brother Sabinus. Quoting Psalm 2:9, the holy man ventured to suggest that, 'Thou shalt break them with a rod of iron; thou shalt dash them in pieces like a potter's vessel.' In March 1621, judges were sent to Hradčany Castle from Vienna to consider cases against 27 Protestant leaders. Two months later, on the anniversary of the defenestration, all were sentenced to death. Twenty-four were beheaded, the longstanding privilege of the nobility (although two suffered the discomfort of having their tongue and a hand chopped off before getting it in the neck), while three commoners went to the gallows, all in Prague's Old Town Square.

The Thirty Years War ravaged Europe until 1648. It began as a struggle to assert Habsburg power, but by the 1630s almost the entire Continent was sorting out its political differences by fire and sword. Germany's princely armies made mincemeat of each other; Sweden's Gustavus Adolfus made a spectacular entry on the Protestant side in 1630; and pragmatic Cardinal Richelieu of France busily encouraged the anti-Habsburg cause and threw his country into a pussyfooting war with Spain in 1635. As Richelieu's policies testify, the battle-lines were far from cleanly religious—but in Prague that made little difference. Bohemian Protestantism and nationalism were inseparable; while Ferdinand soon hitched the imperial cause firmly to that of the Church. Even before the war's end, he and his monkish allies extinguished the city's ancient powers. In 1624, he removed the court to Vienna and sent in German-speaking bureaucrats to carry out the metropolis's edicts; while in 1627, a new constitutional settlement finally established hereditary Habsburg rule over Bohemia. Protestantism was made a capital offence, and the independence of the Czech Estates was destroyed. Thousands of families emigrated for ever, while turncoats and parvenus decended like locusts on vast tracts of confiscated land. The **Peace of Westphalia** (1648) was a compromise not far removed from the Peace of Augsburg a century before—but no one disputed Habsburg control over Bohemia any more, and its Protestants were denied even the very limited religious freedoms guaranteed elsewhere. The last battle of the war was fought on Prague's bridge, between the Swedes and a motley crew of soldiers, newly-Catholicized students and Prague Jews. When the dust settled, Bohemia was left with its population reduced by over a third, and the country plunged into a decline that lasted two centuries.

Nothing Happens

Frederick the Great invaded Prague twice in the mid-18th century; but otherwise the city became a backwater where you went when the bright lights of Vienna became too much. The spiritual shock troops of the Counter-Reformation, the Jesuits, led the consolidation of the new faith with a Baroque building programme that transformed the face of the city, but even they had to leave town when the work was done. They were placed under a worldwide ban by a jealous pope in 1773; and in 1781, the despotically enlightened **Emperor Joseph II** abolished most of the empire's other monasteries and convents. The corollary was the restoration of individual religious freedom for all save the weirdest sects. Prague's Jewish population was finally allowed out of its ghetto, but just in case they got any uppity ideas, an imperial decree of 1789 prohibited all males save the eldest son from receiving a marriage licence.

The Nationalist Revival

During the early 19th century, Bohemia began to breathe again. Europe's tide of nationalisms swept across the country, and after centuries of German meddling and oppression, Czechs began to hanker for a purely Slavic alternative. The

Czech language, which had all but died out since the Battle of the White Mountain, was resuscitated by a handful of writers and researchers—František Palacký and Josef Jungmann being among the most notable—whose painstaking efforts can almost be compared to those of Eliezer Ben-Yehudah in creating modern Hebrew. In 1848 the citizens of Prague were up in arms again, this time joined by the rest of the empire in a revolt against Metternich's iron rule from Vienna. Prague's Czechs split with the German revolutionaries by refusing to take part in the German National Assembly at Frankfurt, and a Slavic conference was held in the city in June. Imperial forces soon shot their way through the barricades, but although it was not apparent at the time, the Habsburg empire was slowly dying. Composed of a score of different peoples, it was to prove incapable of accommodating the new power of nationalist sentiment. As it sickened, the Czech nation quickened. On the cultural front, composers such as Smetana and Dvořák dug deep into the national consciousness to emerge with a music fit for a new country. On the political front, nationalists wrested a series of concessions from Vienna towards the end of the 19th century, including language ordinances and the creation of an autonomous Czech division of the Charles University. Within the neighbouring province of Slovakia, nationalism also emerged in reaction to Hungarian rule; but despite common pan-Slavist sympathies, few in either state had yet developed a clear programme of autonomy, let alone joint independence.

From Independence to Dependency

As the pattern of European alliances emerged in the years before 1914, many Czechs and Slovaks felt with apprehension that in any future war, their interests lay firmly in the enemy camp. Lingering pan-Slavism encouraged sympathy even for the corrupt Russia of Nicholas II, while democratic ideals and anti-German sentiment made others look towards France and Britain. When war broke out, two men—**Tomáš Garrigue Masaryk** and **Edvard Beneš**—set out on a four-year tour to persuade the world that Czechoslovakia was an idea whose time had come. In 1918, Masaryk was in the United States. President Woodrow Wilson had made clear his support for the principle of self-determination, but neither he nor anyone in the White House was quite certain which European tribes existed, let alone which should get independence. Masaryk signed a deal with Slovak émigrés in Pittsburgh, and although he very quickly reneged on his promises, that was enough to persuade Wilson to give 'Czecho-Slovakia' the green light.

Masaryk and Beneš wasted no time. On 28 October 1918—while artillery fire still thundered in the west of the Continent—independence was declared. Within two weeks, Masaryk had been elected president of the new Czechoslovakian Republic. As the western allies pondered how to neutralize the losing powers and contain the Bolshevik incubus, Masaryk and Beneš, now Foreign Minister, unilaterally staked out the borders of the new state. These encompassed the largely German-populated Sudetenland to the west, as well as areas claimed by the Hungarians and the Poles, but at the peace conferences the victors ratified the *fait accompli* with little discussion and no plebiscite.

The youthful democracy flourished economically and culturally, and its capital embraced the new age with vigour; but the 1920s weren't the best of times to consolidate democracy. Although the country's political structures rode the Depression with a stability astonishing in a country so young, the latent and ancient problem of the German minority was soon to explode with unparalleled ferocity. An ongoing separatist movement in the Sudetenland found a champion in Hitler, and Czechoslovakia became the eye of the building European storm. Under the notorious 1938 **Munich Agreement** Britain, France and Italy gave Hitler *carte blanche* to seize the Sudetenland. The disingenuousness of the British Prime Minister, Neville Chamberlain, has made a contemptuous reference to appeasement obligatory for visiting western politicians ever since—although Hitler was sweet about him, saying that, 'He seemed such a nice old gentleman that I thought I would give him my autograph as a souvenir'. In Czechoslovakia, many gave up hope on the west and in a strange echo of pan-Slavism came to regard the Soviet Union as Czechoslovakia's last best hope—an attitude that was fatefully to influence Beneš's policy during and immediately after the war. Within six months, the 'quarrel in a faraway country between people of whom we know nothing' (as Chamberlain described it in a BBC radio broadcast) had led to the invasion of Czechoslovakia by the German army. Britain and France remained silent as the **Reich Protectorate of Bohemia and Moravia** was declared in March 1939 (Slovakia was made a puppet republic), and only after the invasion of Poland six months later did they declare war on Germany.

The war left Prague's buildings almost unscathed. Its population was less fortunate. Tens of thousands of intellectuals, politicians and gipsies were imprisoned or killed, while of the 90,000 Jews who remained in the Protectorate in late 1939 (about 26,000 had emigrated in the six months after March), only some 10,000 survived the war. The town of Terezín (Theresienstadt) in northern Bohemia was turned into a 'model' ghetto to show the Red Cross—while 140,000 other visitors passed through on the way to Auschwitz, Ravensbrück and Treblinka. Hitler chose Prague's old Jewish Quarter to be the site of an 'exotic museum of an extinct race', to which artefacts from exterminated Jewish populations throughout Europe were sent. The macabre decision has meant that, thanks to the Nazis, Prague now has the saddest and finest memorial to prewar European Jewry on the Continent.

Beneš had taken over as President in 1935, and fled three years later, having received indications that Hitler personally wanted his head. He was making the twilight rounds of the North American lecture circuit when war broke out, and swiftly crossed back to London to establish a government-in-exile. Czech pilots, evacuated at Dunkirk after the fall of France, were integrated into the RAF and over 500 died in its service. Czechoslovakian troops (including Jan Lodvik Hoch, who would end the war as Captain Robert Maxwell) fought with the British army; some made their way through the USSR and the Balkans to Palestine, where 800 fought in the battle for Tobruk. Within the Protectorate itself, somewhat to the surprise of the Nazis whose armies had invaded without even token resistance, armed underground movements began to operate, directed largely by the London government. Some Czech Communists were also active, but had to play a doubly surreptitious role, as the Party was stymied by the tortuous logic of the Nazi–Soviet pact. The Resistance annoyed Hitler sufficiently for him to appoint **Reinhard Heydrich** as *Protektor* in place of the namby-pamby Von Neurath in late September 1941. Heydrich proceeded to liquidate the Resistance by wholesale public executions and the banning of all public gatherings on pain of death. He lived for nine more months, time enough for him to chair the Wannsee Conference in Berlin in January, at which he ironed out the administrative aspects of what he called 'the coming Final Solution of the Jewish problem'. In June 1942 he died from infected wounds after an assassination attempt by London-trained Czech parachutists. Hitler ordered savage reprisals. 1331 Czechs were summarily executed, and seven Resistance fighters, including the two assassins, were holed up in a Prague church where they died to a man (*see* pp. 269–70). Seven villages around the capital were chosen at random to be wiped off the map. The small mining town of **Lidice** became the best-remembered. For much of the outside world, the destruction of Lidice (filmed and publicized by the Nazis themselves) threw a baleful light for the first time on the night and fog that had descended over Central Europe. After burning down the houses, Gestapo and SS troops shot dead its 172 male inhabitants. The 195 women were sent to Ravensbrück; seven babies out of 90 children were judged sufficiently Aryan to be sent to German adoption homes. None was ever found. Not only did the Nazis kill the village's current inhabitants, they also traced all those who had been born there in order to execute them. A story told by the Czech writer, Josef Škvorecký (and fictionalized by another, Bohumil Hrabal) is that they missed one man, who was serving a jail sentence at the time. On his release, he returned to his village only to find it a desert of asphalt, and went insane. The local Gestapo refused to shoot him as he demanded, and he died of drink a few years after the war.

On 5 May 1945, the capital's Resistance groups broadcast a call to arms and thousands rose up against the remnants of the occupying Nazi forces in the city. The **Prague Uprising** lasted only four days, but street fighting and last-minute executions left up to 5000 Czechs dead. Plaques and graves throughout the city mark where they fell. On 9 May 1945 the Soviet Red Army entered Prague to a rapturous reception. A provisional national assembly, under Beneš as president, was set up in October, and set about solving Czechoslovakia's German problem once and for all. While mobs lynched collaborators, the country's three million Sudeten Germans were expelled, resulting in the deaths of thousands. The policy was official, indiscriminate, and approved by the Allies at the Potsdam Conference.

Communist Consolidation

The Czechoslovakian Communist Party led by **Klement Gottwald** swept the board in the 1946 elections, with 38 per cent of the votes. (Even before the war, it had been one of the strongest in Europe, winning 10 per cent of the votes in 1935.) Beneš appointed Gottwald prime minister of a coalition government, but Uncle Joe Stalin had no intention of letting his protégé go to bed with a bourgeois. Gottwald's rabble-rousing skills and Beneš's weakness led to the former's assumption of the presidency in February 1948. Within a month the popular foreign minister, **Jan Masaryk**—son of Tomáš—who was less accommodating to the Communists, had died in a mysterious fall from his office window late one night. A fourth defenestration began 40 years of Communist rule, and the Party was pleased to report 89 per cent support in new elections in May.

Within a year the Terror had begun. Gottwald, prodded on by Stalin, imprisoned thousands of political opponents, and executed over 200 after show trials that were as fraudulent as the best of Moscow's in the 1930s. The most notorious was the **'Slánský Trial'** of 1952, in which 11 high-ranking Party members (almost all of whom were Jewish) were condemned as 'Trotskyite Titoists, bourgeois nationalist traitors and enemies of the Czechoslovak Republic and of socialism', and sent to the gallows. (The trial has been dramatized in a moving French film, *L'Aveu*.) Slánský (who was actually guilty of far worse than the ludicrous charges on which he was tried) wasn't rehabilitated until 1990. Rudolf Slánský Jnr. became a respected figure of the opposition to Communism, and in a fitting gesture, was appointed democratic Czechoslovakia's first ambassador to the Soviet Union in 1990.

From Socialism with a Human Face to Normalization

Gottwald caught pneumonia at Stalin's funeral, and followed his mentor into oblivion nine days later. His death of 'Moscow flu' still brings a smile to the face of many Czechs when they talk of their 'first working-class president', as he was invariably referred to in official publications until 1989. During the mid-1960s reformers at the lower levels of the Party began to work on revitalizing its links with the rest of society. In 1963, the Kolder Commission published a terrifying report on the 'violations of socialist justice' of the 1950s. Large numbers of victims were rehabilitated, posthumously in all too many cases. In January 1968, **Alexander Dubček** was elected to the post of First Secretary. Dubček was no closet liberal—his politics were formed in the crucible of the 1930s Soviet Union, and he would never lose his sentimental attachment to the country in which he spent his youth—but in the heady days of 1968, he finally began to listen, and learn. During the so-called **Prague Spring**, he proposed ever-more radical reform of the country's political and economic institutions, partly out of his changing convictions but largely at the urging of more committed forces and individuals both within and outside the Party. The Soviet Union—which had actually backed pliant Dubček for the leadership the year before—began to stir. General-Secretary Brezhnev was soon considering how to help the Czechoslovak proletariat stave off 'a return to the bourgeois-capitalist system'. He took soundings of all the other leaders of the Warsaw Pact, and on 21 August, Czechoslovakia was invaded by five armies. Maverick Nicolae Ceaușescu was the only Warsaw Pact leader to stick to the principle of non-interference. Molotov cocktails greeted the tanks, while road signs were reversed and street names removed in a quixotic attempt to disorientate the invaders, who killed scores of civilians on Prague's streets. On the day of the invasion, the reformers were bundled onto an Aeroflot jet and taken to Moscow for urgent discussions, and the Prague Spring suddenly turned very cold.

The cultural and political renaissance of the mid-1960s had been strangled in its cradle. The times were desperate. Fourteen philosophy students at the Charles University drew lots, and agreed to burn themselves alive one by one until press freedom was restored. 'Torch No. 1' was **Jan Palach**. On 16 January 1969, the 20-year old emptied a can of petrol over himself in Wenceslas Square, and flicked a lighter. Before he died, three days later, Palach begged his doctors for news of the reaction to his act. They told him that flowers and phone calls ran into the thousands—and that the government had said nothing. Palach died asking that none of his friends follow him. Two weeks later, Jan Zajíc, not connected to the group, immolated himself in northern Bohemia. Over the next month, so too did many others.

Dubček had lingered on, racked by a sense of responsibility for the invasion and half-heartedly dismantling his reforms, but he had become yesterday's man. The Soviets began looking for a stooge. Several Central Committee members applied fairly directly for the job, but even Brezhnev could see that they were too widely loathed. In April 1969, Dubček was replaced by **Gustáv Husák**—Resistance hero, victim of the Terror and supporter of the Prague Spring. Few understood how he got the job. Brezhnev was among them. He's said to have murmured, 'If we can't use the puppets, we'll tie the strings to the leaders'; and within a year, Husák began to dance. Some 500,000 people were deprived of their Communist Party membership, either for what they had done pre-1968 or, in the case of those who wouldn't publicly support the invasion, for what they now refused to do. The process was called 'normalization' (*normalisace*); and when it was finished, the government declared that Czechoslovakia had achieved a state of *realní socialismus*, an eerie phrase that's usually translated as 'real existing socialism'.

A new generation grew up without even the memory of hope. The signatories of the 1977 human rights manifesto, **Charter 77**, were ruthlessly persecuted, and apathy led tens of thousands of non-Party members to sign a government-backed petition condemning the organization. The possibilities for change seemed less than zero.

The Velvet Revolution

Even as late as mid-1989—with Hungary and Poland well on the path to reform—few observers saw Czechoslovakia as likely to follow in the near future. But as the East German regime tottered, refugees from the country began to flood into the West German embassy in Prague. The revolutions of 1989 had begun. On 10 November the west woke to the news that bulldozers were demolishing the Berlin Wall, and on 17 November Prague's students confronted a baton-wielding police force on the streets of the New Town. The filmed scenes of police brutality, against students armed with candles and flowers, aroused the population from two decades of torpor. Media reports that a student had been killed set off popular fury, and within a week a million people had taken to the capital's streets to demand that the government resign. For the next six weeks, Prague was enfolded by a 'Velvet Revolution', an anarchic hubbub of strikes, pickets and celebrations which culminated in the election of playwright and recently-released political prisoner, **Václav Havel**, to the presidency on 29 December 1989.

Truth Will Out

The postscript to the Velvet Revolution was written some months later. During early 1990, it emerged that the 'dead' student was alive and well, and had been living on the payroll of the secret police (StB). The November clash had been organised by the StB and the KGB, with the intention of replacing the hardline regime led by Miloš Jakeš with one more in tune with Gorbachev's Soviet Union. Fortunately, matters soon slipped out of the conspirators' hands and Communist rule died. The bloody fate of the Romanian uprising, also nudged forward by the Kremlin, shows the forces that could have been unleashed had Czech Communism fought back.

Other messy truths have been tumbling out ever since. Praguers are teaching themselves democracy with impressive alacrity, but the crucial tests lie ahead. Their country spent decades blindly tying itself up, and disentangling the confusion is going to hurt. The most spectacular casualty so far has been the country itself. In under three years, Slovakian nationalism grew from a vague regionalist sentiment to a fully-blown independence movement, fomented by **Vladimír Mečiar**—an old Communist with a new cause. Czechoslovakia gave up the ghost on New Year's Eve 1992, seen off in Prague by shrugged shoulders and fireworks, and in Bratislava by brief jubilation. Many older people felt a twinge of sadness, but the dominant attitude in Prague was relief; the shadow of Yugoslavia had been hanging over the country as a horrifying reminder of what can happen when dialogue runs out.

The Czech Republic's racial problems don't have a solution as simple as the 'Velvet Divorce'. The country's gipsies, or Romanies as most prefer to be called, have suffered from official neglect and public ignorance for decades. In health, education and employment statistics they lose out to whites, and in crime they beat them—a combination that has turned them into pariahs. A wave of immigration from Slovakia and the Balkans is exacerbating racial tensions, but few in the majority population are interested in understanding the complex problems, let alone solving them. Ordinary folk often favour relocation (sometimes sterilization) of 'problem gipsies'; politicians promise to 'get tough' or spout neo-fogey banalities about cultural cohesion; and at the end of the line, skinheads batter gipsies, or Vietnamese, or Arabs, or Bosnians, when they sit on the wrong tram seat or dance with the wrong girl.

The psychological legacy of Communism also fractures the country. As late as May 1988, the Party had over 1.7 million members—over one in ten of Czechoslovakia's *total* population—and humdrum compromises with the regime were struck by millions more. Only the most arrogant or the most saintly would condemn them for that; but paradoxically, it's only the most courageous (and often the least implicated) Czechs who will now admit to having reached any *modus vivendi* with totalitarianism at all. The desire for a scapegoat is everywhere: on one level, accusations of closet Communism may fly immediately prior to the fists in Prague's rowdier pubs; on another level, hardly more elevated, it was seen at newsstands in mid-1992, when long queues formed to buy directories containing the names of 300,000 'collaborators' taken from secret police files. The material was riddled with inaccuracies, and included many people the police had only thought *might* collaborate—one day. Among those named were dedicated former dissidents such as Jan Kavan and Zdena Salivarová, the wife of author Josef Škvorecký (both of whom are still making the impossible attempt to prove their innocence); on an earlier file had appeared one 'Havel, Václav'. Meanwhile, the real villains of the time suddenly found that their guilt had been submerged in a huge sea that had unexpectedly risen up around them.

Supporters of anti-Communist measures often draw an analogy with denazification in postwar West Germany, and although the comparison is an emotive and arguable one, the moral arguments for countering the influence and privileges of old Party members are strong. That said, the Party is a shrunken shadow of its former self, and a blanket assault on all those competent professionals and middle managers who dully did well out of Communism would deny the Czech Republic many badly-needed skills for no compelling reason. Furthermore, a phenomenon that has caused much anger over the last few years—the Communist who successfully turns into capitalist entrepreneur—may actually be a figment of the popular imagination. Many of the old dogs are proving amusingly incompetent at learning the free market's new tricks, capable only of declaiming some memorized yuppy jargon before being wiped off the floor by the liquidators. But even if the possibility of a Communist resurgence isn't real, the fear is, and a *lustrace* law ('lustration', or ritual purging) promises to bar Communists from the civil service for several years. It's anti-democratic, but perhaps the minimum catharsis that the Czech nation needs.

On the brighter side, the country's political institutions are standing firm. Although Communists regularly poll over 10 per cent (far less in Prague), and the besuited thugs of the ultra-right Republican Party have had a parliamentary toehold since 1989, their anti-democratic pincer movement is still extremely weak. A coalition of centre-right forces, led by the Civic Democratic Party (*Občanské demokratické strana* or *ODS*) of **Prime Minister Václav Klaus**, has dominated government since 1991 and is set to do so for the foreseeable future. The party was born out of the ruins of the movement that swept into power after the 1989 revolution, the Civic Forum (*Občanské fórum* or *OF*). Klaus et al. are a hard-nosed crew compared to that rainbow wave of dreamers and dissenters, but for many Czechs the idealism of the anti-Communist opposition no longer has any political relevance. It remains to be seen how that harsh judgement will affect the fortunes of Prague's own philosopher-king, Václav Havel, who was re-elected president (by parliament) in January 1993. His once-stratospheric levels of support have shrunk dramatically, and he himself senses the new delicacy of his position. As well as brushing his hair, taking his hand out of his pocket and hiring a spin-doctor, he has promised to play a more ceremonial role. Few believe him, given his evident sense of presidential mission, and many fear that if social divisions widen, his liberalism will put him on a collision course with his own government.

But it's the economy that represents the fundamental test for the new democracy. The country's institutions and social fabric will hold or break according to the ease with which the transition to capitalism is made. At the time of writing, the situation certainly *looks* optimistic, particularly in Prague. Foreign investment is pouring in, led by the United States, France and Germany (in that mildly surprising order); state enterprises are being privatized and either sold off, or auctioned to ordinary Czechs, each of whom has been given a wad of vouchers to invest; and streets are filling with shimmering shops and proud owners. But there's a dreamy unreality about the boom, and the strange sense that everyone is just playing lifesize Monopoly for a while. Innumerable businesses deal in luxuries such as holidays and hi-fis, while Praguers spend while they can, cushioned by years of savings and unaffordable state benefits. The latter include most people's jobs: in early 1993, some 80 per cent of businesses were running on empty, technically bankrupt. The deluge can't be held off forever. The first wave of closures has already begun, and even state forecasters say that up to 15 per cent of the workforce will be on their bikes by early 1995.

A crucial issue is how Czechs adapt to capitalism's inequalities. The first beggars have appeared, slumped against the cobbles and restaurants of the Old Town, and Praguers sometimes gaze at them with a shocked incomprehension that's striking to a westerner. The country has an egalitarian tradition that dates back to Hussitism and Habsburg repression and was a cause, rather than effect, of the Communist rise to power—and discontent will grow with every new person thrown onto the scrap-heap. Another question mark hangs over the city's relationship with the tens of thousands of foreign residents who have invaded since 1989. Most Praguers are still enthralled by the newcomers—whose clubs, new-fangled ideas and above all, money, are helping to turn their city into one of the most dynamic on the Continent—but tensions exist. Czech magazines report on the foreign men who urinate in Baroque fountains and sleep with three Czech women a night, and even the most tolerant Praguer is beginning to resent that he or she sometimes has to speak English to order a drink nowadays. The city can contain divisions like that, but if they ever explode into the age-old charge that the country is being sold out to foreigners, its stability will face a far more threatening challenge.

But no matter how distressing some of the creatures that have squirmed into the light since 1989, a great deal of hope remains alive in Prague. For two years the capital hummed with surreal tension, as it awaited a big bang that never sounded. Now that the explosion has come, no one is standing still. The city has its problems, but in its scores of journals and hundreds of cafés they are at last being argued out. For every down-and-out, there are scores of other people who can travel to see the Pyramids or study Romany or own a café for the first time in their lives. Prague has become a living town again. The penultimate thought belongs to President Havel, whose gravelly words are as fitting now as they were back in December 1990. 'The happiness is gone. The second act is called crisis. The crisis will be chronic and then the catastrophe will happen. Finally the catharsis will come, and after that everything will start to go well.' Prague has been through it all before.

Czech Culture

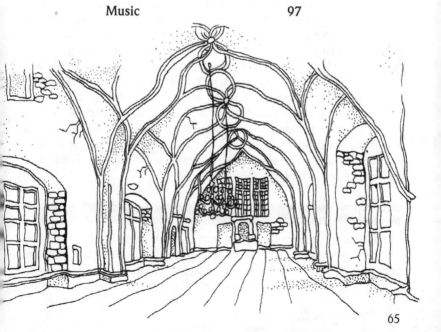

Art and Architecture

The golden ages of Prague have been short and few, and yet the city has emerged with one of the richest architectural legacies in Europe. Purists may object that it's a visual cacophony; anyone with an ounce of romance will be dumbstruck. Czech painters have perpetrated some atrocities over the years, but Bohemia's Gothic art and the riot of modernism of the first half of this century were superb. Catholic oppression helped, by providing the city with an unforgettable Baroque skyline; the Nazis spared it their artistic efforts, but did their bit by holding off the tanks until the last week of the war; and the city is now one of Europe's most complete if haphazard selections of a millennium of cultural endeavour.

Romanesque

A century was a tender age for a town in 10th-century Europe—but in 965, at a time when most urban centres in the north of the continent comprised a few wooden hovels, Prague was already a thriving town of stone and mortar. The Jewish merchant Ibrahim Ibn-Jacob said as much in his travelogue, noting also that it was very rich and that man and beast would easily find enough to live on. The earliest architecture was Romanesque, deriving from what Europe could remember of the old empire's building skills, and the first churches follow a standard basilican ground plan, with nave and aisles separated by a colonnade. Stone was heavy, but no one yet understood how the clever Romans had supported the weight of their roofs. As a result, Romanesque buildings were either covered with wood or supported with massive pillars; narrow church naves might be given simple tunnel vaults; tiny rotundas, whose tops were supported by a circular wall, were built. Prague's best surviving example of a Romanesque church is St George's Basilica; and three of the mushrooms survive, one of them on Konviktská street. The structural deficiencies of these building methods were slowly solved across Europe after about 1100, but Prague stuck with crude Romanesque architecture for two centuries after that.

Gothic

The style of architecture that spread from French cathedral design of the later 12th century was named 'Gothic' centuries later by Renaissance-minded Italians who felt that it could only have been produced by vandals. Weight problems were solved by the realization that pointed arches could redistribute stresses throughout a building, that ribs could be used to hold up a vault and then filled in with light material, and that external walls could be bolstered with exposed flying buttresses. These engineering feats were only the means by which a new spirit was brought into architecture: pointed arches and tremendous steeples drove heavenwards; walls, which no longer had to support the weight of the building, became a field for rich sculptural decoration; and sheets of glass, framed only by decorative tracery, flooded the interiors with light.

The first glimmers of the new architecture arrived in the mid-13th century with the building of St Agnes's Convent, and Gothic features also crept into Prague's Old-New Synagogue. Its effect on the city had been delayed, but it was to be complete. Prague owed its existence to its river, but this had its disadavantages. In the late 1200s, the Vltava submerged the town once too often, and the burghers retaliated with the drastic step of burying their town under several metres of earth. Romanesque Prague became subterranean Prague (much of it still in existence under the Old Town), and a new one was built in Gothic style, using decoration and glass to a greater extent than ever before.

It was under the reign of Emperor Charles IV (1346–78), that Prague entered the European stage. Charles was well-travelled (he studied at the French court and invaded northern Italy while a youth); had a deep reverence for relics, gemstones and painting; and was driven by a proud determination that before he was through, his capital would outshine Paris. Under the influence of his harebrained Francophile father, he imported a French architect, **Matthew of Arras**, to begin his new cathedral; but by the mid-14th century, it was Germany that was leading the Continental field in church design, and in 1353 Matthew's timely death brought 23-year-old **Peter Parler** to Prague. The Swabian's father, Heinrich, had just completed the first of Germany's great hall churches at Schwäbisch Gmünd; but Peter outdid him with St Vitus's Cathedral, one of the grandest late Gothic churches of Continental Europe. It would take five centuries before the finishing touches were put to the work; but Parler, who was also an accomplished sculptor, assembled a team that left an indelible imprint on the capital.

Bohemian artists also began to produce the first work that was recognizably unique to the country. Its earliest art had come from Constantinople, along with Christianity, and Byzantine art continued to be the model even after Bohemia threw in its lot with the pope (see p. 40). The oldest paintings to survive, however, date from the first half of the 13th century, and show how artists were beginning to break free of the rigid rules of Byzantium. The lead followed was that of Siena, where the grace of the older tradition was maintained but its strict iconography gave way to personal interpretations of the tales and characters concerned. The individualist trend in Bohemia manifested itself in ever-heavier modelling, which reached a peak in the work of Charles's court artist, **Master Theodoric**—whose outstanding portraits of saints in Karlštejn Castle (*see* p. 395) ranks as some of the most distinctive work of any royal artist in 14th-century Europe. The emperor's mystical taste for glass and precious stones spills out of Theodoric's work; and the expensive fashions set by Charles were reflected in the creation of Prague's first artistic guild in 1348, which united painters with goldsmiths and glass-blowers.

Charles died in 1378, and although Peter Parler and sons continued to hammer Gothic Prague into existence for another two decades, the assertive spirituality of Charles's art was replaced by a mood of self-indulgence among the court and clergy of his son, Wenceslas IV. Painting and sculpture moved towards a sophisticated and idealized style; while sculptural decoration grew ever more personalized, erupting occasionally into fantastic beasts or obscene tableaux. They added richness and colour to the city, but were out of tune with the popular mood. In 1420, the outbreak of the Hussite Wars called an abrupt halt to cultural development. Although the Hussite movement called for spiritual regeneration, art and architecture weren't high on its agenda—paintings represented idolatry, Church property was theft, and the clergy was the enemy. St Vitus's Cathedral, which had got as far as its central tower, was ransacked; most of the city's other churches were looted or burnt; and only two of its religious orders were left *in situ* after they took the cowardly, albeit revolutionary, decision to side with the masses.

When the dust settled in the 1470s, under the reign of Vladislav II, Prague's Gothic architecture ended in a series of splendid explosions. The king gave his name to the last phase of late Gothic architecture in Bohemia—and the magnificence of the structure that best exemplifies it, the Vladislav Hall, shows that by the end of the 15th century Prague Gothic had gone just about as far as it was possible to go. The ribs of the vault, flowing with gay abandon, have less in common with the structural supports of early Gothic architecture than with the spatial invention of Prague's late Baroque (*see below*); and the hall is filled with features from the Italian Renaissance, working their way up from Italy via the court of Matthias Corvinus in Hungary, decades before its influence was to be felt in western Europe.

The Renaissance

The Italian Renaissance had a haphazard effect on Prague's architecture. The coronation of Bohemia's first Habsburg monarch, Ferdinand I, in 1526 encouraged the flow of Italian ideas to Prague, but they made limited headway through the narrow lanes of Gothic Prague. Ferdinand built his sublime Royal Summer Palace (1538–63), and when land prices on the left bank plummeted after a huge fire in 1541, a series of imposing Renaissance palaces were built by nobles anxious not to appear unfashionable; but the town's burghers were a more conservative bunch. Windows might be enlarged and straightened, *sgraffito* was often plastered over façades, the more adventurous might even build a miniature courtyard at the back; but the sturdy Gothic structures themselves stayed firm until the tidal wave of the Baroque. North Italian craftsmen poured into Prague towards the end of the 16th century, but they were second-rate peddlers of an architectural style that was already old hat at home.

Mannerism

During the reign of **Emperor Rudolf II** (1576–1611), Prague became one of the leading centres of Mannerist culture in Europe. The term, like so many others in the vicious world of art appreciation, was originally one of abuse; when the new style emerged in northern Italy at the beginning of the century, its apparently distorted and unnatural proportions were often seen as no more than an affected (or untalented) departure from the classical beauty of the High Renaissance. Mannerism was a clear retreat from the notion that art could best capture the essence of the world by trying to reproduce it in its most noble form. In a troubled century of religious uncertainty, the attempt to penetrate beyond the appearance of things was part of a widespread and urgent search to find a more solid basis for a universal truth. Rudolf's court crossed national boundaries and modern-day disciplines. The old order was collapsing, and no one really knew what its replacement might look like. Alchemists and astrologers were just as likely to have useful ideas as painters and sculptors, and the fine arts of Rudolfine Prague are packed with the symbolism of the esoteric and the occult.

Rudolf II's art collection was one of the largest of its time, and as well as buying works, he summoned artists to Prague from across Europe. The Milanese painter, **Giuseppe Arcimboldo** (1527–93) followed the emperor to Prague, having loyally served the Habsburg court since the days of Ferdinand I. He is best known for his allegorical portraits, surreal compositions that drew on an arcane system of correspondences between man and nature. They began when Ferdinand, with Habsburg humour, had asked him to draw the syphilis-ravaged face of the court doctor. Arcimboldo produced a likeness made up of animals and cooked fish, which impressed everyone, not least the Surrealists, who rediscovered the artist some four centuries later. He created many more of the heads while in Prague, and organized Rudolf II's pageants in the castle. Many of the emperor's other favoured painters came from the Low Countries. Among them was **Bartholomeus Spranger** (1546–1611), who proved central to the development of the court's art. He settled in Prague in 1581 after travelling across France and Italy. Spranger's style—shimmering with colour and movement, and highly sophisticated in form and composition—expressed itself not just in classical and religious themes but also in a series of allegorical paintings that pulled together motifs from alchemy and astrology to glorify the emperor and the imperial mission. The apotheosis of Rudolf—Christian hero against the Turks and patron of the arts against dark ignorance—was a theme to which most of his artists turned their hand at some point. **Hans von Aachen** (from Köln—1552–1615) was appointed to the imperial service in 1597. Aachen had spent a decade in northern Italy, during which he had kept Rudolf up to date with developments in the art market (the emperor sent him across Europe to snap up Dürers and the collections of the recently deceased); and one of his occasional jobs was to travel to foreign courts to paint pubescent princesses during Rudolf II's doomed search for a suitable match. His work comprised elegant portraits and religious scenes; but like Spranger, he also painted nudes, tinged with an eroticism that sometimes went beyond a respectable Renaissance fascination with the human form. The trend permeated the art of the court—largely due to sad Rudolf himself, who often stipulated his preferred views. An almost morbid voyeuristic spirit lurks behind many of the classical love scenes that he commissioned, usually drawn from myths telling of deception and weakness, and generally capturing highly advanced stages of courtship. The emperor's sculptors came from Italy on the recommendation of Giovanni Bologna, who stuck with the Medicis despite repeated Habsburg attempts to buy him out. **Hans Mont** gave up the art after being blinded while watching a game in Rudolf II's tennis court; but **Adriaen de Vries** (1545–1626), a talented student of Bologna, stayed in Prague until his death.

Rudolf II's curiosity stretched to the natural world, and among his still-life artists was the Flemish **Roelandt Savery**, who arrived in 1604. He stayed for a decade, pottering around the emperor's fabled menagerie and gardens, and produced Europe's first paintings of exotic animals (and in the case of the dodo that he found in Prague, probably its last). The emperor's court was also the centre of one of the grandest collections ever assembled, rivalled only by that of Uncle Ferdinand in Ambras Castle. As well as a panoply of 15th- and 16th-century art, Rudolf II's thirst for knowledge led him to amass clocks, perpetual motion machines, gemstones and endless lists of curiosities—including a homunculus pickled in alcohol, remnants of the clay used by God to create Adam, Brutus' dagger, and four stones that fell from a clear sky onto a Hungarian battlefield.

Rudolf II's court was an ephemeral Camelot that began to evaporate from the moment of the emperor's sorry downfall in 1611. His successor, Matthias (with whom Rudolf had fought a long battle over a unicorn horn), spirited parts of the collection over to Vienna a year later; and almost all the rest was systematically removed in 1648, when Swedish troops invaded Prague specifically to steal the collection for their own unbalanced Queen Christina. Although engravings of Spranger's paintings were an important influence on the earliest work of the Haarlem Academy, Rudolfine Mannerism was a vortex of talent, rather than an explosion; and its mood was far removed from that of the city below. Prague's visual arts were going through another crisis in an atmosphere of quasi-Calvinism, and the Estates sold off an unknown amount of Rudolf II's collection in 1619. Local engravers gave some of the emperor's art a wider audience, but the reasons for their popularity were sometimes dubious—as was widely noted after 1612, when a local artist died and was found to have painted a varied collection of pornographic works for unidentified patrons. The court's introverted intellectualism led it to an interest in the Jewish cabala, and its contacts with ghetto scholars reinforced the otherworldly image of Rudolfine Prague that has been fixed in the city's popular imagination. It began with *Satyricon*, a trashy but influential 17th-century satire, which reached its high point when the narrator was led to a thinly-veiled Rudolf, engrossed in conversation with a sinister type clutching formulae and retort—and was told by a courtier, 'That, my lord, is the most favoured person in the whole palace—a Jew'.

Rudolf II's architecture has also been lost. Much of what was built still clung on to Gothic motifs (the church of St Roch is a good example that's still around); and the few grand schemes of the emperor, such as his rebuilt castle, have been all but destroyed by later remodelling. There are remnants of his summer palace at Stromovka (*see* p. 282), and its artificial pond is fed by a mile-long tunnel, one of Rudolf's pet projects.

The Baroque

Mannerism asked imponderable questions; the style that followed declared violently that it had the answer. The Baroque emerged in Rome in the late 16th century, at almost exactly the same time as the Council of Trent laid down its demand that art was to glorify the Church. It took some time to get to Prague and by the time it did so, its Counter-Reformatory zeal had been all but spent in its home town. But here it was part and parcel of the Catholic reconquest of Bohemia, and within a century it had utterly transformed the face of the city.

There was no return to the balanced harmony of the Renaissance, but the Baroque used ideas such as movement, disproportion and unnatural light with a consistency that overwhelmed rather than intrigued. The new architecture elbowed its way into the vast **Waldstein Palace**, which represents a transition between the two styles; but while the Thirty Years War progressed, most Catholic orders and newly-rich nobles bided their time. When it ended in 1648, building began in earnest, helped along by another burst of land-clearance in 1689 when a fire destroyed most of what remained of the Gothic Old Town.

The first Baroque architects in Prague were imports, usually shadowy figures about whom little is known. **Carlo Lurago** (1615/18–84) was born in Tessin, but seems to have worked only in Prague; some trained in Rome itself, such as the classicizing Frenchman **Jean-Baptiste Mathey** (c. 1630–95); but the majority came through Vienna, which had become a centre of the new architecture since Ferdinand II had stormed back to his ancestral home in a post-White Mountain huff. Of the latter group, the most prolific were **Francesco Caratti** (?–1677/9) and **Giovanni Alliprandi** (1665–1720). All brought some of the most distinctive features of Roman Baroque to Prague. Ovoid halls and domes stretched through their palaces and churches, replacing the serene circles of yesteryear; and the huge dramas of their palatial façades loudly announced that Prague had lost the war, and the victors had come to stay.

By the beginning of the 18th century, northern Europe had firmly snatched the baton of the Baroque from its homeland; and Prague and Vienna were setting a scorching pace, each encouraged by the inventiveness of the other. Two of the city's greatest architects were **Kristof Dienzenhofer** (1655–1722), born in Cuckoo Hill, Bavaria, who settled in Prague around 1685; and his native-born son **Kilian Ignaz Dienzenhofer** (1689–1751). Kristof's contemporary, the Viennese court architect **Johann Fischer von Erlach**, also designed several works in Prague. All three men were heavily influenced by the undulating rhythms of Borromini's work in Rome and the quivering geometry of Guarino Guarini, who had visited Prague and drawn up unrealized plans for a church in Malá Strana in 1679. The influence of the two Italians appears most strikingly in the Dienzenhofers' joint masterpiece, the Jesuit Church of St Nicholas in Malá Strana, one of 18th-century Europe's finest.

Prague Baroque has been called 'the fruit of oppression' and 'the flowers of evil' by the modern Czech author Milan Kundera, and it has an ideological element that took it to a realm of deception and power that it rarely reached elsewhere in Europe. It's apparent in the vast palaces built on confiscated lands, but most especially in the city's churches. A population that was 90 per cent Protestant and had started the Thirty Years War had to be taught a lesson—and the city's religious orders knew that if you yanked the heartstrings violently enough, the mind would follow. The Jesuits were the most notorious masters of the Baroque propaganda exercise, and produced St Nicholas's Church as the evidence, but all the religious architecture of the period is permeated with missionary zeal. The mysterious abstraction of Gothic vaults was replaced by vast illusionistic paintings and frescoes; the Marian cult and miracle-working icons found their way into almost every church; and splendid but fake marble, gold and silver appeared throughout. The trick worked: Praguers headed like moths towards the Catholic flames, and by the 18th century, a majority of the city had reverted. It's sometimes difficult now to appreciate the hypnotic power of the churches—to the modern mind they often appear little more than tacky works of triumphalist propaganda—but the greatest can still reduce you to a moment of stunned silence.

The architecture wasn't entirely alien to the city's traditions. Even in St Nicholas's, the flowing vault harks back to the Gothic style; and the work of the third great architect of Bohemian late Baroque, the Prague-born **Giovanni Santini** (1667–1723), is even more explicitly Gothicizing. His churches—especially outside Prague (*see* Day Trips—Kutná Hora, pp. 397–400)—are replete with tall towers and pointed arches, and the ribbed vaults of many look like nothing so much as the floral extravagance of the Vladislav style.

Throughout Europe, the Baroque saw a reintegration of architecture and sculpture, after the Renaissance insistence that both were independent elements of a building. Baroque statuary became one of the most distinctive features of Prague's architecture. Coming so soon after the tail-end of a long late Gothic phase, a tradition was thus established that influenced design into the 20th century, and has given Prague's streets one of the highest concentrations of sculptured façades in Europe. Baroque sculpture began with the relative restraint of **Jan Bendl** (1620–80) and **Matthias Jäckel** (1655–1738), but at the end of the 17th century, a combination of lessons learnt from Rome and the accelerating pace of the Counter-Reformation gave rise to the epic works of **Matthias Braun** (1684–1738), born in the Tyrol, and **Ferdinand Maximilian Brokof** (1688–1731), born in Prague of Slovakian origin. Neither ever attained the virtuosity of Rome's Bernini, but their work—Madonnas brimming with sexuality and atlantes straining with their spheres—shows the superhuman sensuality with which the Catholic conquerors titillated and ultimately subdued the natives.

Baroque painting in Bohemia isn't up to the sculpture. **Karel Škréta** (1610–74) was the first of its early Baroque artists. Škréta studied in Rome, and developed a style that made use of most Italian art of the previous century, rounded off with the classicist restraint of Nicolas Poussin whom he's thought to have bumped into briefly. He had left Prague a Protestant exile, and returned a fervent Catholic; and apart from portraits, he produced vast amounts of work for the busy monks of the day. **Michael Willmann** (1630–1706) was another convert, who produced messy (albeit deeply felt) moments of religious anguish and passion, which were sorry homages to the exuberance of Rubens. The most accomplished works of Prague Baroque were the experiments with light and colour of **Petr Brandl** (1668–1735); but even in the 18th century, the most important development in the painting of Germanic countries, their ever-more-glorious frescoes, found few worthy practitioners in Prague. The only notable exception is the work of **Franz Anton Maulpertsch** at the Strahov Monastery (*see* p. 205).

In the second half of the 18th century, the enervating force of the Baroque had almost eaten itself up. Prague's architecture was briefly affected by the **Rococo**, which transformed the mobility and dramatic light-effects of the earlier style into playful elegance. Its most characteristic features were the use of pale colours and asymmetrical motifs, most notably in the dangling stucco decoration of the Goltz-Kinsky Palace and the Sylva-Taroucca Palace on Na příkopě. The fey creature only lasted a few decades in Prague, before both it and the Baroque were finally extinguished in the late 18th century.

From Neo-Classicism to Neo-Gothic

Under the reign of Emperor Joseph II, the city's culture suffered a series of rapid blows. Fripperies had no place in the monarch's coolly rational world. What remained of Rudolf II's collection was auctioned at giveaway prices in 1782, and most men of the cloth were turfed out of their monasteries, which were then turned into barracks. The Jesuits had already been disestablished in 1773, and the disappearance of religious orders from Prague had particularly serious consequences. As the wealth of the aristocracy had flowed towards Vienna, the Church had emerged as the most important patron of art and architecture in the capital. Although the new clergy had arrived as conquerors, it had made a huge contribution to its cultural life. In the last years of the century, this all but ended.

There was little originality in the few buildings that appeared in Prague in the years between 1780 and the middle of the next century. Architecture was typified by a dry classicism inspired by France. Buildings continued to use many of the motifs rediscovered during the Renaissance: triangular pediments and Grecian pillars or, more often, pilasters. But they were no longer piled together with the bombast of the Baroque and sculptural decoration was no longer used on façades. The change was particularly noticeable in Prague, which had taken to the earlier style so completely, but neither classicism nor the Empire style, which followed, had much impact on the centre of the city. The cool façade of the Philosophical Hall of the Strahov Monastery, housing the last flourish of the Baroque in the form of Maulpertsch's ceiling fresco, represents the transition; the genteel Estates Theatre shows the new style at its best. The late 1700s also saw the greening of Prague. The palaces of Malá Strana were given the gentle lawns and terraced slopes that characterize the area today; avenues were planted; and the city's first parks were tamed for the great Prague public over the next decades.

Nation-Building

In the middle of the 19th century, Prague's architecture became engulfed in the national revival movement (*see* pp. 54–5), which demanded monuments to reflect Bohemia's glorious past. Like the rest of Europe, the city was swept by a vogue for rehashing older architectural styles, and the favoured choice for buildings of national significance was the Renaissance. It didn't matter that Prague had been little touched by the real thing and non-existent in the age of antiquity, nor that what little had appeared was imported by the Habsburgs. Huge pediments were triumphant, and stacks of disordered columns were thought to be noble. The result appears most clearly in Prague's National Museum. The later 19th century also saw a wave of restoration of Bohemia's Gothic architecture, which (with more reason) was also seen as an expression of the national spirit. However, the zealous bunch concerned, led by **Josef Mocker**, often destroyed more than they created, since they frowned on anything that had appeared in the intervening centuries—which, given Prague's messy architectural history, was often most of the building concerned. One exception was St Vitus's Cathedral, to which the same architects began to add a western half some 550 years after construction had commenced. Artists also played a heroic role in the national revival, adorning the new buildings with mythological and allegorical works to express the aspirations of the patriotic movement. The work was a useful visual aid for a public whose literacy in the recently revived Czech language was often shaky, and you can consider it in the National Theatre and the museum at St Agnes's Convent (*see* pp. 172–3).

Opening the Doors to Europe

By the turn of the century, Habsburg rule had begun to crumble, and directly political concerns gave way to introspection over what the future held in store for little Bohemia/Czechoslovakia. Although Vienna remained an important channel for new ideas, artists and architects went searching for inspiration across the Continent, and France in particular was to have a important influence on the country's cultural development until the Nazi invasion in 1938.

Art Nouveau and Symbolism

Prague's architecture at the turn of the century was dominated by Art Nouveau—or rather, the Europe-wide attempt to escape the slavish historicism of the dying century's art and architecture that came to be known by at least seven names across the continent. This book uses the term 'Art Nouveau' throughout, but the Bohemian *secese* was actually a confluence of two distinct currents.

The first came from France, and aimed to create a unified new style from diverse natural forms. A distinguishing feature of French Art Nouveau—which Prague tradition had no problem in accommodating—was the use of extensive sculptural decoration in the new buildings. Most motifs with fecund or sensual connotations had their place—rampant vine leaves, exploding lilies, drowsy nudes—but it was the disciplining energy of the whiplash curve that gave this form of Art Nouveau its coherence and driving force. The city's most glorious examples are the Hotel Evropa (*see* pp. 231–2) and Municipal House (*see* pp. 148–9), but the top floor of the Wilson Railway Station (Wilsonovo nádraží, or Hlavní nádraží) and the embankment at Masarykovo nábř. are also impressive excursions into the new style. Enthusiasts could also investigate the sunburst lamps and wrought-iron angels of the Svatopluk Čech Bridge, and the bourgeois mansions of nearby Josefov (in the northern Old Town), erected after slum clearance in the early 1900s. Outside the centre, vegetation-covered tenements can also be found peppering the suburbs of Vinohrady and Vršovice, interspersed among the more modern buildings built after a wave of bourgeois-mansion clearance by Allied bombers at the end of the Second World War.

The second form of Art Nouveau—having little in common with the first variety other than a shared concern to leave the past behind—looked instead to rectilinear structures, abstract, self-contained and stripped of ornamentation. It was born in Glasgow but reached Prague from Vienna, and was to have a powerful influence that would run through four decades. The leading light was **Jan Kotěra** (1871–1923), whose turn-of-the-century work has more in common with postwar Constructivism (*see below*) than the popular flowery idea of Art Nouveau. His own house, an angular assembly of brick boxes on Hradešínská, is a typically stark example.

Art Nouveau found decorative expression in the work of sculptors such as **Ladislav Šaloun** (1870–1946) and **Stanislav Sucharda** (1866–1916), and most notably, in the many talents of **Alfons Mucha** (1860–1939). During the 1890s Mucha lived in Paris, where he became one of the most distinctive poster artists of the age as well as an acolyte cum lover of Sarah Bernhardt, for whom he designed graphics, jewellery and stage sets. He returned to Prague in 1922, but the exuberance of his early work gave way to sombre tributes to the Slavic race and the occasional stamp or banknote design. Two of the most original artists to emerge during the 1890s, however, were mystical types less concerned with the new forms that had been developed by Art Nouveau than with the spiritual values that could be expressed with the new freedom and greater level of abstraction. The first was the sculptor **František Bílek** (1872–1941), who studied in Paris in the early 1890s. Using a huge variety of techniques and materials, Bílek linked ideas spanning music, literature and religion to produce a complex and fascinating body of work. His house has now been turned into a museum (*see* p. 259). **František Kupka** (1871–1957) settled in Paris after 1896, but much of his most important work has found its way back to Prague. Kupka's earliest paintings concentrated on ideas of rebirth and renewal; but after several years as a medium, he moved on to produce some of Europe's first intentional abstract art, such as his *Amorpha, Fugue in Two Colours* (1912). His better-known contemporary, Vassily Kandinsky, shared similar beliefs in visual music, but is thought to have painted his first non-figurative composition one year after Kupka.

Cubism

In 1902, a belated exhibition of the French Impressionists and a Rodin retrospective caused a storm among the city's artistic community. Three years later, however, all eyes were on an exhibition of the anguished work of the Norwegian Edvard Munch. As a result, Prague took a crash course in the clash of philosophies that had been building in Europe over the previous decade, between the view that art could and still should show what the world *looked* like, and the idea that it should express the emotions of the artist and the subject. Drawing inspiration from the two very different starting points, the capital's painters, sculptors and architects were soon immersed in the artistic ferment of prewar Europe.

Prague's first modernist painting came out of *Osma* ('The Eight'), a group of artists founded in 1907. Its initial inspiration was the raw force of Munch, but as early as 1910, Czech artists such as **Emil Filla** (1882–1953), **Bohumil Kubišta** (1884–1918) and **Antonín Procházka** (1882–1945) had picked up on Parisian Cubism. For the next decade, Prague was to be perhaps the most important centre of the new art outside its birthplace. For a time, Czech artists developed a form of Cubo-Expressionism, using Cubist techniques but packing their work with a powerful psychological punch. The most interesting paintings of Czech Cubism were produced in these first years, but Filla and Procházka left to set up the more formally Cubist *Skupina* ('Group') in 1911, and began to move away from capturing moments of existential crisis to more orthodox examinations of structure (and, later, movement). Kubišta wouldn't join the Skupina, and his fascinating work, riddled by dark questioning, was cut short only by his death in the 1918 flu epidemic. Two other artists to emerge during this period—**Josef Čapek** (1897–1945) and **Jan Zrzavý** (1890–1977)—also dabbled with Cubism, but were more concerned with the primitivism that had inspired it. Each produced a set of simple and beautiful paintings, with a lyricism that in the case of Zrzavý in particular, signposted the way to developments in the 1920s.

Kubišta notwithstanding, Prague's painters largely followed the lead set by Picasso and Braque, but the sculptors and architects in the Skupina produced maverick works that are unparalleled in the world. The leading sculptor was **Otto Gutfreund** (1889–1927), who studied under Bourdelle in Paris, but returned in 1911 to create a series of works that are uncategorizable. Most of his early work exemplifies the ideas of Cubo-Expressionism. The formal method of Cubism, its disciplined and coherent use of angular spaces, was used to explore emotional states (*Angst* and *Hamlet* were two of his earliest efforts); but he also explored Czech Baroque's use of imbalance to express energy, and the Futurist fascination with movement, to develop ways of capturing tension in sculpture. The most extraordinary three-dimensional experiments of Czech Cubism were made in architecture. Three members of the Skupina—**Pavel Janák** (1882–1956), **Joseph Gočár** (1880–1945) and **Josef Chochol** (1880–1956)—openly rejected the harshness of their teacher Kotěra's work, and tried to restore depth and flexibility to their buildings by using three-dimensional geometrical forms on the façades. The idea was to translate one of Prague's oldest architectural traditions into the idiom of Cubism; how far they succeeded is open to question, but in Prague you can see examples of the only systematically theorized and practised Cubist architecture in the world. (You can find examples of the strange results at Celetná 34 and Neklanova 2 and 34.)

The interwar years were among the most exciting in the history of Prague's cultural life, spiced with a political content with which the postwar Communist government had serious problems. Some of the best work of the period lay under wraps for decades and has only begun to re-emerge since 1989.

Clean breaks are rare creatures in history, but in 1918 much of Prague's artistic community thought that it had just lived through one. The old world didn't look too good after the carnage of war; Czechoslovakian independence had finally been won; and over in the east, a rosy Bolshevik dawn was rising. In 1920, a group of young artists, led by the breathtakingly energetic **Karel Teige** (1900–51) founded *Devětsil* ('Nine Forces'), which was to throw itself into the van of the European avant-garde during the next decade.

There was probably never a time when the old cliché of Prague laying at the heart of Europe was as directly relevant to developments in the city. With a population that was almost 10 per cent German-speaking, influences from the north and the south were unavoidable (though Germany became more important than Vienna); French contacts continued unabated; and the spectacular explosion of creativity in the east was to have cultural effects in Prague long after it had been snuffed out at home. One of the most significant arrivals was **Roman Jakobson** (1896–1982), who came as Soviet press attaché in 1923; the ideas he developed in the Prague Linguistic Circle were seminal to Structuralism, and he was a signal member of Devětsil during the interwar years.

The firmly-stated political philosophy of the group was Soviet-style Marxism, but after a very brief tinker with the idea of 'proletarian art', Devětsil spent the rest of the 1920s bobbing and weaving through a maze of artistic experimentation that led one exasperated Party critic to describe the group as 'the fruit of late capitalism'. The roller-coaster began in 1924. Teige hurled the group into the mêlée of European -isms with his *First Manifesto of Poetism*. Like the Soviet Constructivists, he embraced the abstract beauty of the machine age—transatlantic liners, light bulbs and the like—but he also began to lay down his own theory of 'Poetism', 'the art of pleasure', which was to condition the art produced. The balancing act was precarious—technology had just happily slaughtered millions—and Devětsil never consistently united the two elements of its philosophy. The general feeling was that art should be accessible to everyone, and not just an élite. Machine-made goods were favoured because 'their midwife is not art', and there were plenty of them, to boot. But, on the other hand, Devětsil came up with some work that would have been incomprehensible to anyone who hadn't read every manifesto published.

Despite the fact that Teige spent most of the early 1920s calling for 'the liquidation of art' (and the Artist), Poetism was characterized in its first years by a joyful celebration of creative imagination. A strong influence was the French theorist and writer Guillaume Apollinaire, who had visited Prague in 1902. To the dismay of many Poetists, he had passed through unrecognized, although he apparently met Ahasuerus, the Wandering Jew, when asking for directions. There were few constraints more rigid than free association, and the ideal was to cross sensory boundaries. The lyrical poets **Jaroslav Seifert** (1901–86) and **Vítězslav Nezval** (1900–58) worked on 'film poems' (i.e. scripts); the sculptor **Zdeněk Pešánek** (1896–1965) created visual pianos and perhaps the world's first neon fountain; and Teige turned his hand to almost every field save painting. One of the most common forms of art in the group was the collage, or 'pictorial poem' in Teige-talk. It was a democratic game that anyone with scissors could play, and appealed to the Poetists' fascination with modern images and the feelings that could be inspired by combining pictures on a certain theme. Holiday pictorial poems were a favourite—apart from allowing plenty of opportunities to use pictures of transatlantic liners, they also stressed the new international mood of the country. Not surprisingly, photography was favoured by the movement, which took the view in the early 1920s that it should and would replace the dying bourgeois art of painting. Most of the group walked around with cameras for a while, although its photography section contained only one full-timer, **Jaroslav Rössler** (b. 1902). Two other photographers emerged during the 1920s—**Jaromír Funke** (1896–1945) and **Josef Sudek** (1896–1976), and although they were never confined by the ideological posturings of the group, their prewar interests included beautiful machines and suggestive patterns of objects. One-armed Sudek also began a lifelong expedition through the light and shadow of Prague, with a beautiful series of shots of dusty St Vitus's Cathedral, taken in 1924, as the builders were putting the finishing touches on Peter Parler's masterpiece.

Devětsil's love of cameras was matched by its early celebratory attitude to movies. The group approved of cinema's popular appeal and its non-élitism (Charlie Chaplin and Douglas Fairbanks Jnr. were both drafted into Devětsil, although neither seems ever to have found out); ideas and images could be linked on film in true Poetist fashion; and to the politicos of the movement, the big screen was an ideal moving blackboard with which to instruct the masses. Members turned out endless film poems, and the first Structuralist film analysis took place in Prague, but it came to virtually nothing. The conservative studios would have nothing to do with the avant-garde urchins and Teige was moved to warn that the industry would 'probably perish on its unforgivable sins' if it didn't start producing some of the works 'alas, only on paper, in the desks of modern authors'. Although it didn't perish, it certainly wasn't very vital until after the war (*see* pp. 86–9), but it enjoyed one international success with Gustav Machatý's *Extase* ('Ecstasy'—1933), one of the world's first artistically valid erotic films (honest, guv). Devětsil had more success with the stage, and in 1926 it set up the Liberated Theatre, which was taken over three years later by the comedy and cabaret duo of Jiří Voskovec (1905–81) and Jan Werich (1905–80) (**V & W**), whose work remains popular today.

Outwardly Devětsil had many interests in common with French Surrealism, but the two groups kept at arm's length during the 1920s. Teige had issued his manifesto a month before André Breton, and he was probably jealous of the wider attention the French movement was getting, but towards the end of the decade, the darker questions raised by Surrealism began to make heavy inroads into the happy-go-lucky early Poetism of Devětsil. This was exemplified in the work of two of the group's painters, **Toyen** (Marie Čermínová) (1902–80) and **Jindřich Štyrský** (1899–1942). During the 1920s, both moved from painting geometrical abstractions to a far more personal and introspective style that relied on half-remembered images and semi-conscious associations. In 1926, during a three-year stay in Paris, they tiresomely christened their new work 'Artificialism', but their increasing concern with buried levels of consciousness was only a short step to Surrealism. Another Devětsil member, **Josef Šíma** (1891–1971), settled in Paris in 1921 and hovered on the fringes of the movement for a decade. He was regarded as heretical by the French group for his concern with the collective rather than individual unconsciousness (the result of an epiphany after a close encounter with a bolt of lightning); but although he painted too many cosmic eggs and crystals for the Surrealists' liking at first, he became an important contact between the two movements.

The supposed obstacle between the groups was political, and after the French made a doubtful pledge of allegiance to the Communist International in 1930 the way was free for increased contacts. In 1932, one of the first international exhibitions of Surrealist art was held in Prague, and in 1934 the Prague Surrealist Group was established. Teige hopped on board and took over in the same year; and giving free rein to his unconsciousness, he produced some of his most amazing and alarming collages, a series of women's bodies penetrated by machinery or otherwise dismembered. Breton and Paul Eluard boosted the troops by visiting in 1935; and Poetism had established an imaginativeness and cooperation between the branches of the arts that made Prague's Surrealist movement the second most active in Europe outside Paris through the 1930s.

Surrealist architecture would have been a fine thing. There was none of that, but Prague saw huge activity in the field of design. In the immediate postwar years, the prewar Cubist architects developed a short-lived 'Rondocubism' which it was hoped could become a distinctively national style for the new republic. The theory was impressively realized in the bizarre Banka legií on Na poříčí, designed by Josef Gočár. It was still the façade that was emphasized but, in a manner harking back to the Baroque, its elements were amassed and pushed outwards in repetitive curves. Another traditional feature of Prague architecture that the style maintained was to integrate figurative sculpture onto the building. The friezes on the Banka legií, by **Jan Štursa** (1880–1925) and Otto Gutfreund, are far removed in their simplicity from Gutfreund's earlier Cubist-inspired work. Although he died in 1927—the Vltava got him as he took a dip on a hot day in June—they were an important move towards a form of social realism that influenced many other sculptors in the later 1920s.

Rondocubism was the last effort to create a Czech national architecture for the 20th century. Between the wars, internationalism and ideology led most of Prague's architects (again, often involved in Devětsil) towards Constructivism and Functionalism. The basic difference between the two was that the first claimed that mass production and modern materials were beautiful; the second theoretically didn't give a hoot, so long as a building served its purpose. Both theories found willing adherents in Prague, and by the 1930s, the aesthetic differences, although still loudly argued over, were little more than nuances. Already primed by the Art Nouveau of Jan Kotěra, Prague (and to an even greater extent the town of Brno) hurled itself into the brave new world of glass and concrete. In 1924, Teige organized Czech participation in the first international Bauhaus exhibition; Le Corbusier came to Bohemia three times, skirting around Prague after Teige attacked him for betraying Functionalism by worrying too much about the looks of his buildings; and the Brno-born Adolf Loos built his Müller Villa on the outskirts of the capital, on Nad hradním vodojemem in Střešovice. The ideal of many of the city's architects was to use the new ideas to house the poor. Teige went the whole hog and suggested abolishing the family and socializing education in collective blocks. The most significant modernist housing built in Prague, though, was the Baba Housing Estate, a private project for well-heeled professional types. In the jaded light of the 1990s, it's less exciting than it must have appeared at the time, but if you want to see how portholes and passenger decks influenced the city's designers, the houses are around Na Babě in Prague 6.

Standing outside any movement was a radical Slovenian architect—**Jože Plečnik** (1872–1957)—whose contributions to the architecture of Prague were limited but dramatic. As a result of the efforts of Jan Kotěra, who had studied Art

Nouveau with Plečnik in Vienna, he was appointed Prague Castle Architect in 1920, and spent the next decade modernizing the castle, and designing the Church of the Sacred Heart (*see* pp. 275–6), one of the most extraordinary religious buildings of the 20th century. Plečnik's fluent architectural vocabulary—which could draw on sources ranging from ancient Egypt to Constructivism—was incomprehensible to Prague's aesthetic conservatives, whose outrage eventually bored him back to Ljubljana where he transformed the face of the city. The confidence, flair and visual appeal of Plečnik's work in Prague has made him the darling of visiting post-modernist architects in recent years. He deserves the attention, but it's worth remembering that, unlike many of the eclectic western designs of the 1970s and 1980s, riddled with irony and in-jokes, Plečnik's *œuvre* is founded on a deep reverence for tradition and history.

From Nazism to Normalization

The Nazis rolled into town in March 1939, and Prague's cultural life was crushed. Functionalist architecture wasn't glorious enough; most contemporary Czech art fell squarely within the category of degenerate art. Exile and extermination decimated the city's intelligentsia, and three years after liberation another tyranny moved in.

With the accession of a Communist-led government in 1948, creativity in painting and the plastic arts was sacrificed on the altar of Socialist Realism. The doctrine, invented by Moscow in the 1930s, was a monolithic officially-controlled programme of extolling the class struggle and the onward march to socialism. Sometimes defined by Czechs as 'art so simple even the Central Committee can understand it', it produced monumental buildings and Stakhanovite murals and sculptures that still disfigure parts of the capital. The best architectural example is the tremendous Hotel International, Prague's homage to the even more mammoth University of Moscow (which Muscovites used to claim wasn't all bad, since it was the only place in the city from which you couldn't see the University of Moscow). The prewar avant-garde was an abomination in Communist eyes; not only was its work too unReal, but the Surrealists had spent the later 1930s flirting with Leon Trotsky. Turncoats were granted dishonourable rehabilitation; those who resisted were tempted back into the fold by a variety of means, notably spells of hard labour in Czechoslovakia's uranium mines. Karel Teige lived long enough to see his dreams turn to dust. He's said to have committed suicide in 1951, with a warrant out for his arrest.

After the death of Stalin, the cultural constraints were slowly eased. The Surrealist movement, suppressed and banned in the years after Teige's death, raised its head above the parapets in the late 1950s—and when it realized that the shooting had stopped, it whooped into life again. Two important artists of the period were **Mikuláš Medek** (1926–74) and **Václav Tikal**, and, perhaps most impressive of all, **Jiří Kolář**. Kolář began as a banned poet in the early 1950s, but in the early 1960s started to experiment with collage, just as Teige had before him. His assemblages of image and word, as playful as they can be political, have won him an international reputation over the past two decades. As the thaw became a rushing stream, the artistic energy of flower power engulfed a city that seemed headed towards a benign revolution. In 1965, Prague's cheering students elected Beat poet Allen Ginsberg as their king and carried him shoulder-high up the length of Wenceslas Square; and by 1968, the mildly insane **Milan Knižák** had introduced the capital to the Happening and was slaughtering chickens to loud rock music in the city's leading art galleries.

The party ended on the night of 21 August 1968. 200,000 Warsaw Pact troops turned the Prague Spring into winter. Within two months, Louis Aragon (who had been one of the first French Surrealists to make the leap to Stalinism) had coined a phrase that was to haunt the next two decades, when he warned that Czechoslovakia was on the path to becoming a 'Biafra of the spirit'. Within two years, the government had launched a programme of 'normalization', which was more of a threat to independent thought than anything since the Counter-Reformation. Potential centres of ideological resistance—such as theatre companies and the Writers' Union—were dissolved and reconstituted; individual artists who had supported the Prague Spring were anathematized; and most importantly, the government all but gave up the idea of promoting the Party line through art. The form of cultural control was more insidious than Socialist Realism, or even Baroque churches. So long as artists were prepared publicly to recant earlier errors, they were often grimly snatched back into the bosom of the Establishment; and what they *said* subsequently in their art was often less significant to the government than the persona that they presented to the public. In the case of those artists whose work was only tangentially political, official acceptance (and a livelihood) might depend only on their being prepared to utter a few words; and the characteristic feature of the country's officially sanctioned art over the next two decades, most especially the 1980s, isn't a slavish portrayal of the Party line, but a coy evasion of thorny issues. The government had learnt to smile at gentle experimentation; and those who kept quiet could now even include the occasional in-joke at the regime's expense.

Those who wouldn't play the game weren't sent to uranium mines—just prevented from ever using their talents again. Ph.D.s and artists found work as stokers and taxi-drivers, and were harassed for 'parasitism' if they couldn't find anyone brave enough to employ them. Scores found fame abroad. The most courageous signed the **Charter 77** manifesto (*see* p. 60).

Resurrection

Since 1989, some of the artists who left after 1968 have returned. The cultural return has had a number of significant effects: not only is it helping to bring new (and old) ideas to the capital for the first time, but the bridge between west and east is helping to untie the past's ideological knots—without which Czech culture will be stymied. An interesting example is the naïve painting of **Milan Kuns**, whose canvases of bright Coca-Cola-sucking smiles and lonely parking lots of shiny automobiles stand next to equally livid icons of Communism and piles of rusty building equipment. Few Praguers can stomach it when westerners glibly compare capitalist alienation to Communist despair, but the lonely vision of the exile can at least warn that materialism is going to exact a price. Other artists based overseas have held up a mirror to their former compatriots: a pastime that's as useful as it it may be arrogant, and typified by the stark photographic record that **Josef Koudelka** has made of the neglect and poverty of the country's gipsies.

Apart from exiles, hundreds of Prague-based artists are now exhibiting in the city's galleries. The collective attempt to piece back the nation's shattered cultural life draws inspiration from innumerable sources. Young artists have rediscovered the work of the interwar avant-garde with enthusiasm—despite its leftward political leanings—and Surrealism in every sense has made its regular return onto the Czech cultural stage. Milan Knižak—the *enfant terrible* of the Prague Spring—is now the head of the Academy of Arts. Foreign influences are also pouring in, and the city is suddenly being engulfed by aesthetic debates that began in the west years ago. For example, many are considering (or dismissing) the difference between erotica and pornography for the first time; Czech art often has an unself-conscious lasciviousness about it that can be odd and occasionally unpleasant to western eyes. The work of photographer **Jan Saudek** is illuminating in this respect: known in the west for his portraiture and a much-reproduced image of a male torso with baby, his subject-matter also ranges from tender kissing scenes to spanking scenarios with uniformed girls. Finally you should at least be aware of **David Černy**, whose art has included painting a tank pink, spraying a Trabant gold, and putting up anonymous posters in London to advertise a day of random killing (a joke). Like many over-eager performance artists, Černy claims inspiration from both Andy Warhol and the Situationist anarchists of 1968 Paris, but even if the desire for 15-minute fame is there, Černy's spectacles more conform to prevailing expectations than challenge them. However, his work reflects a fascinating question for the future of Czech art: how much it will profit from the recent past and recast the innumerable issues raised by Communism—the meaning of individual integrity, kitsch versus irony, idealism versus realism—and how far it will sink into the vacuous pastiche, commercialization and sensationalism that freedom now allows.

As for the architecture of Prague, it endures. The redevelopers are moving in and the city of *Amadeus* has begun to echo to a faster beat, but the ancient stone jigsaw of the centre will survive. Even the Communists didn't dare tamper with that.

Film

Early Czech cinema produced *Extase* (1933), a classic of cinematic erotica starring Hedy Lamarr; but it was only after 1945 that the medium took off. It has had a chequered history, but its high points have given Czech film and animation an international reputation for excellence.

Prague's Barrandov studios emerged from the war as Europe's largest functioning film complex outside Italy and France—all thanks to the Nazis, who had confiscated it and expanded the facilities considerably, with an eye on what was expected to be a postwar audience in serious need of relentless propaganda. Their cinematic dreams fell through, but it soon became clear that others had similar ideas. In 1945 Barrandov was nationalized. The decision was taken for honourable reasons, and supported by many film-makers, but it meant that when the Communists took over in 1948 they could, and did, swallow it whole. The studios began to churn out classics of Socialist Realism, a gooey mess of sanitized folk traditions and heroic furtherance of Five Year Plans, often with a romance thrown in (e.g. handsome Party official meets naïve but zealous peasant-ess, CIA plot to destroy tractor factory, sabotage thwarted, hands held at sunset). The films were never popular—but there may be a kitsch revival, in which case you could keep your eyes open for *Tomorrow There Will be Dancing Everywhere*.

The 1950s were lean years, but even then talented film-makers began to break free of the censors' stifling attentions. Czechoslovakia's huge international reputation in the field of animation began to develop with the work of three directors, **Hermína Týrlová**, **Jiří Trnka** and **Karel Zeman**, which combined animation, live-action and puppetry to an extent that was then all but unique. The films won kudos at a time when little else in Czechoslovakia's cultural life was celebrated abroad, and were sometimes even lauded by the government. The jittery camera and savage cuts of the Surrealist **Jan Švankmajer** added a new punch to the genre when he produced his first short feature in 1964. By then, the liberalization that was to culminate in the Prague Spring was in full swing, and for some five years an extraordinary generation of Prague film-makers created and rode the crest of what became known as the **Czech New Wave**.

Most of the new directors emerged from the Prague Film School (FAMU), where, in the words of one of the best known, **Miloš Forman**, the students 'first learnt to read between the lines, and then to write between the lines'. Working in close collaboration with talented new authors such as Bohumil Hrabal, they produced work that broke entirely from the conventions of the recent past. The casting of amateurs presented a world that remains spontaneous even today, while a playful eroticism replaced the heroic and chaste embraces of the previous decade.

Simply by representing a real world, the new directors found themselves making political statements from the outset. Forman's first two films, *Lásky jedné plavovlásky* ('Loves of a Blonde'—1965) and *Hoří, má panenko* ('Firemen's Ball'—1967), were both examinations of society in microcosm, where entire villages were drafted in, and bumbling officialdom presented in all its gentle mediocrity. **Věra Chytilová** had her film, *Kopretiny* ('Daisies'—1966), banned for misrepresenting Czech youth, who, the authorities seemed to believe, were immune to the summer of love. It was in 1967 that the outside world first realized that something special was happening in Prague, when another FAMU graduate, **Jiří Menzel**, won an Oscar for Best Foreign Film with his *Ostře sledované vlaky* ('Closely Observed Trains'—1966), the celluloid version of a novel by Bohumil Hrabal. This superb film takes the favourite Communist theme of anti-Nazi struggle and subordinates it to the significantly less heroic concerns of a prematurely ejaculating railway apprentice. In one celebrated scene, a station-master advances up the thigh of pretty Jitka Zelenohorská with a selection of official rubber stamps. Menzel was strongly advised to remove the shot, but arranged for a private screening at the village where the film had been made. The inhabitants insisted that it should stay, and the Bottom Stamping Scene is now a legend. It's also one of the most touching scenes of Czech cinema.

In the years leading up to the Prague Spring, several films stepped beyond gentle mockery into powerful allegory. **Jan Němec**'s *O slavnosti a hostech* ('The Party and the Guests'—1966) was set at a grim outdoor feast, where straying guests are brought back by worried diners; eventually, dogs are used to make sure that no one misses out on the fun. Few Czechs were in much doubt as to whose Party it was, least of all beleaguered President Novotný, who considered a libel suit. **Jaromír Jireš**'s adaptation of Milan Kundera's ascerbic novel, *Žert* ('The Joke') was filmed while tanks rumbled through the streets in August 1968. One of the last, and most daring, films was *Nezvaný host* ('The Uninvited Guest'). This 1969 graduation film by FAMU student **Vlastimil Ventzlik** revolved around two sets of neighbours, each of which finds that a lumbering and unknown visitor has decided to stay indefinitely. Each is uncouth—but one eventually wins over his hosts by buying them a better present than the next. It was an accurate assessment of the social divisions that were to arise over the next 20 years, and Prague's real guests took offence. The film was seized, much of the rest of the work of the previous five years was banned, and FAMU's teachers were dismissed.

The New Wave sank into the quagmire of the 1970s. Many directors took their chances and fled to the west. Among them was Miloš Forman, whose 1975 *One Flew Over the Cuckoo's Nest* gave him the security of an international reputation. That reputation, and perhaps more importantly the US passport that he acquired, enabled him to return to Prague in the early 1980s to film *Amadeus*. Menzel decided to stay, and after signing a statement in support of the 1968 invasion, was permitted to make anodyne films during the 1970s. In the 1980s, Chytilová and Menzel both produced work that had a better popular reception, but although Czech cinema of the past decade had a wryly critical humour that could easily be understood by the Czech audience, it was far from the exuberant spontaneity of the New Wave.

After the 1989 revolution, several films that had been locked away since 1969 were shown for the first time. Apart from most of the works listed above, they include **Karel Kachyňa**'s chilling *Ucho* ('The Ear'); Menzel's adaptation of another Hrabal novel, *Skřivánci na niti* ('Larks on a String'—1969); and Evald Schorm's *Konec faráře* ('The End of the Priest'—1968), based on a story by Josef Škvorecký. But the way forward is unclear. Barrandov is now being run as a private company, and because of its size and cheapness it has become a favourite facilities house among foreign film-makers: recent productions have included *The Young Indiana Jones* and Stephen Soderbergh's *Kafka*. The business could have gone to Poland or Hungary, and it means that a Czech cinematic industry will survive, but whether the investment and skills will find their way into Czech film is less certain. To make things worse, the Czech–Slovak split has cut the maximum domestic audience for any new release by a third; it was never large anyway, and now every successful new film will need mass appeal just to break even.

Those post-revolutionary productions that have emerged so far do little to stake out a bold new direction for Czech cinema. Jiří Menzel, Věra Chytilová and Jan Němec have all made gentle comedies and historical romps that were loyally applauded by audiences and universally panned by critics. There's also little sign of a renaissance at FAMU. Early hopes that a new generation of students would pick up the baton of the New Wave from Menzel, the school's new director, came to nothing: he took little interest in his job and was forced to resign by a strike of the student body (which accused him of the rather impressive charge of absentee draconianism).

But the outlook isn't entirely bleak. There are glimmers that Czech film is beginning to tackle contemporary issues. One director worth watching is **Juraj Jakubisko**, a Slovak who now lives in Prague and whose *Lepšie byt' bohatý a zdravy ako chudobný a chorý* ('It's Better to be Rich and Healthy than Poor and Ill') received much critical acclaim when released in 1992. Most impressive of all has been the work of a grizzled survivor of the 1960s, Jan Švankmajer. Over the past two decades, his uncompromising work was variously banned, sabotaged and sponsored by the confused authorities, while it slowly established him as one of the leading animation artists in the world. Since 1989 his reputation has drawn the all-important foreign investment to allow him to resume production in force. In an age of teenage mutant turtles, Švankmajer still swears allegiance to the dark interests of Surrealism and the Mannerist Prague of Rudolf II and Arcimboldo; and his eerie, sometimes brutal, and unerringly witty use of cartoon and puppetry shows the deep influence of both. Since 1989 he has trained his machine-gun lens onto the politics of his country: having disposed of Stalinism in a 1990 short, he is now taking Surrealistic aim at the all-consuming free market. Look out for *Faust*, for his unforgettable feature-length *Alice* (1987) and for anything else with his name on it. Along with the classics of the Sixties, his work remains the best Czech film now showing in the city.

Literature

A common complaint of modern Czech writers is that their country's literature has never been given the international audience that it deserves. It's a fair comment—albeit one that applies to most other small nations—but modern Czech writing has actually done remarkably well on the crowded world stage, particularly when you consider its late start.

Until 150 years ago Czech literature was all but non-existent. After the suppression of Cyrillic script in the late 11th century, Latin remained the usual written language until the mid-1300s. There are very few earlier examples of Czech literature, and one of them consists of obscene doodles on a prayer book scrawled by a bored nun at St Agnes's Convent. Charles IV (1346–78) encouraged the use of the language; and the Hussites produced a series of Bibles in the vernacular, later given definitive form in the Kralice Bible (1579–94). In 1623, the exiled Protestant and pedagogue **Jan Ámos Komenský** (Comenius) published his *Labyrinth of the World and the Paradise of the Heart*, a questing allegory that plodded through most of the mortal coil—and then what little there was of a Czech literary tradition fizzled out. The cause was the Thirty Years War, which left Bohemia devastated and saw German replace Czech as the language of the educated classes. It was only with the linguistic revival of the early 1800s that modern Czech literature began.

Romanticism and Nationalism

The founding father, acknowledged as such by almost every writer who followed, was the dashing **Karel Hynek Mácha** (1810–36). He cut a Byronic figure even unto death: the Englishman had been cut down by a malarial mosquito in the fight for Greek freedom; Mácha lay lingering with pneumonia after hurling himself at a blazing building. In true Romantic style, he left a fiancée, pregnant with his illegitimate son, and an epic poem, *Máj*. Although it was prefaced with a message to the Czech nation, Mácha's passions lay far from the progressive nationalism of his day. The lyrical poem is a macabre examination of a doomed love; and the May of the title isn't so much springtime as one of the months that comes before winter. That didn't stop patriots seizing on it as an expression of the national genius—but Prague's Surrealists of a century later were almost closer to the mark when they declared him a kindred spirit.

In fact, although the nationalist current of the 19th century flowed through every other area of the arts, it inspired very little literature of note. **František Palacký** (1798–1876) published a seminal Czech history, but the only major novel to draw on the rural themes so dear to the hearts of the patriots was *Babička* (Grandmother—1855) by **Božena Němcová** (1820–62). The journalist and writer **Jan Neruda** (1834–91) snatched realistic vignettes from Prague life, particularly Malá Strana, which aimed to be accessible to the new reading public but were closer in spirit to Charles Dickens than to the blood and soil of Czech nationalism.

Armed with the neologisms and background reading that had been provided by 19th-century linguists and translators, Czech literature was finally ready to tackle the world. French Symbolism was the first modern movement to affect Prague. The poets concerned centred around the journal *Moderní Revue*. This morbid crowd was typified by **Karel Hlaváček** (1874–98), whose last years were spent dying of tuberculosis and capturing the experience in verse. Over the next 40 years, Prague's avant-garde went on an exhausting trek from Cubism to Surrealism, and had little time for the outworn conception of the novel. However, the work of Guillaume Apollinaire remained a powerful influence on the Devětsil group (*see* p. 79 *et seq.*), which produced the poets **Jaroslav Seifert** (1901–86) and **Vítězslav Nezval** (1900–58). Nezval, whose career was to end rather ignobly after the war, turned the language into liquid with lyrical poetry that—along with the work of **Vladimír Holan (1905–80)**—is still often regarded as the best Czech poetry after Mácha. Seifert's work tends to attract loyal affection rather than acclaim nowadays, despite the fact that he picked up a Nobel Prize in 1984.

The first major Czech writer of the 20th century was **Karel Čapek** (1890–1938), whose work was infused with the democratic spirit of the interwar republic that died in the same year as he did. A recurrent theme was a suspicion of technology, and he harboured a (mutually felt) contempt of the angry young men and women who were then busy celebrating the machine ethic. Another preoccupation was a fascination with presenting all sides of a story—a technique that he developed with a triple-faceted set of novels *(Hordubal, Meteor* and *An Ordinary Life)*, each independent but each contributing to a whole truth. Čapek attributed the typically liberal idea to the Cubist paintings of his almost-as-famous brother, Josef Čapek. The writer's best-known work is his 1920 science-fiction play, *R.U.R*, standing for the English phrase 'Rossum's Universal Robots'. A smash on Broadway and in most of Europe's capitals, it gave the world the word 'robot', from the Czech *robota*, meaning 'hard labour'.

A very different character was **Jaroslav Hašek** (1883–1923). A fair portion of his classic *The Good Soldier Švejk*, chronicling the archetypal anti-hero's perceptive bumblings through Europe's 1914–18 war, is assumed to have been written while drunk. The novel broke new ground in Czech, simply by ignoring most of the established differences between the spoken and written language. Hašek was no cerebral moderate like Čapek, but he was even more isolated from his literary milieu, uninterested in the pretensions of the avant-garde and unable to focus his radical temperament on anything for long. He lasted 30 months as a commissar in the Red Army—but far more typical was his swift dismissal from his editorship of *Animal World*. It came after he wrote a detailed report on the fossil, remarkably well-preserved, of an antediluvian flea, and inserted a classified advertisement offering two thoroughbred werewolves for sale. (*See* also Visionary Prague, pp. 107–8).

Čapek and Hašek notwithstanding, it was Prague's Germans who made the literary running in the first decades of the century. So many of this 35,000-strong, 8 per cent minority were authors that, according to the popular journalist **Egon Erwin Kisch** (1885–1948), 'If people hear you're from Prague, it's simply taken for granted'. An even more distinct subset existed: 85 per cent of the city's Germans were Jews and Prague, along with Vienna, was a centre of the last flowering of Jewish culture in Europe. (Among the many who passed through was Albert Einstein, Professor of Theoretical Physics at the Charles University from 1911–1912.) Only one non-Jewish German writer is much remembered today— **Gustav Meyrinck**—and even his major work is a best-selling retelling of the story of the golem, the Prague ghetto legend *par excellence*. In German countries, **Franz Werfel** (1890–1945) is still read; **Max Brod** (1884–1968) was a highly successful novelist in his day; and one of Kisch's schoolmates, less well known than any of his contemporaries while alive, was **Franz Kafka** (1883–1924), who has probably done as much to influence modern thought as any other author this century.

Kafka's universe—so distinctive that it gave birth to an adjective—was created in Prague, where he lived for all but a few months of his life. The effect of the city on his work is often overstated, most audaciously by the foreign tour guides who tell visitors that museum-like Hradčany inspired the mental labyrinth of his novel *The Castle*—but it had a powerful psychological impact. Prague was known familiarly to Czechs as *matička* ('mama'), and in 1907 Kafka wrote to a friend, 'This mama has claws. We ought to set fire to it at both ends ... and maybe then it would be possible to escape.' Like the hapless insects and litigants of his fiction, he spent a lifetime trying to make sense of the background into which he had been born. In his brutal *Letter to His Father* he analyzed his childhood with a detail that matched his novels' most nightmarish logic. He handed it to mother; she never passed it on.

Towards the end of his life, he finally began to tackle one of the biggest riddles, his Jewish background. He bolted to Berlin in 1923, and having begun lessons in Hebrew, began to make plans to emigrate to Palestine. Six months later he was dying, and back in Prague, he wrote his last story, an allegory of the Diaspora told by one of the mice of the threatened tribe. Mama reclaimed him, and he now lies buried in the New Jewish Cemetery.

Max Brod, Kafka's closest friend, was an extraordinarily appealing character, selfless in his support of the city's artists, some now world-famous, some forgotten. He had Hašek's *Švejk* translated into German, and it found its way to Bertolt Brecht in Berlin; he personally translated the libretto of Leoš Janáček's *Jenůfa* and gave the composer an international audience; and the supreme irony for a man who was a literary star while Kafka was an insurance official is that he lived to see his independent claim to fame evaporate. Kafka's last will asked his friend to burn most of his unpublished manuscripts. As Brod remarked, the author knew that Brod was perhaps the least likely person in the world to follow the instruction, and as a result he has gone down in history as the man who saved Kafka's work from the incinerator.

Occupation and Holocaust

Countless other books died with Prague's Jews in the ghettos and gas chambers of the Second World War. Wartime experiences inform many postwar Czech works, but two deliberate chroniclers of the Holocaust were **Jiří Weil** (1900–59) and **Arnošt Lustig**. Lustig's works, sparse and often almost cinematically direct, record his voyage from Terezín to Buchenwald to Auschwitz. If such a thing can meaningfully be said, Weil's perspective is even more unique. When the documents arrived ordering him to attend for transportation to Terezín, he successfully faked his suicide. He waited out the war, in hiding and officially dead, in the capital—a time of despair and hope that he captured, to exceptional effect, in his novel *Life With a Star*.

The only notable literature to have actually appeared during the war was *Reportage from the Gallows* (1943), an avowal of Communist faith smuggled from the condemned cell of journalist **Julius Fučík** (1903–43). It was translated into 70 languages after the war, and Fučík became one of the postwar regime's favourite heroes—and as a result, one of the more unfortunate victims of the 1989 revolution. It's common nowadays to hear Praguers claim—on the basis of a Radio Free Europe programme broadcast at the height of the Cold War—that the *Reportage* was a forgery, and that Fučík was a collaborator who died peacefully among his ageing Nazi chums somewhere in South America. But although he took foolish risks and may well have broken under torture, graphologists have now established that he wrote the testament and there's every reason to believe that he was hanged for his anti-Nazi activities.

> *'When an ordinary person stays silent, it may be a tactical manoeuvre. When a writer stays silent, he is lying.'*

Jaroslav Seifert

The Communist takeover of 1948 had a more threatening effect on literature than perhaps any other area of Czechoslovakia's cultural life. The doctrine of Socialist Realism (*see* p. 83) regarded writers as the 'engineers of souls', a phrase usually attributed to Uncle Joe himself. There was no shortage of time-servers prepared to take on the task. The poet Nezval hurriedly excised God and death (favoured themes) from his collected work, and until one or both caught up with him in 1951, he was an eager mechanic for the regime. Few honest authors could accept the job with integrity, however, and after the first revelations of Stalinist misdemeanours in 1956, it became all but impossible. According to the novelist **Josef Škvorecký**, whose first work appeared during the late 1950s, frowned-on writers began to devise ever more ingenious ways of slipping past the censors, such as placing fiction into obscure scientific journals, or handing their work to sympathetic but tolerated fellow-writers who would print it under their own name.

During the liberalization of the early 1960s, the literary thaw was symptomized by an absurd but important conference in May 1963, where literary critics successfully argued that Franz Kafka's work was relevant to the socialist aspirations of modern-day Czechoslovakia. Kafka—a socialist sympathizer himself, in the days when it meant something rather different in Prague—would probably have appreciated the irony. It was rather too subtle for the post-1968 government, which pronounced the conference to have been one of the first assaults of the Czech counter-revolution.

Through the 1960s liberalization advanced on all fronts. Absurdist drama was developed by a number of playwrights, of whom the best-known was **Václav Havel**. His first play (The Garden Party—*Zahradní slavnost*) was published in 1963 and The Memorandum *(Vyrozumění)* appeared in 1965. Many of the country's best authors, such as Arnošt Lustig, Josef Škvorecký, **Bohumil Hrabal**, and **Milan Kundera**, worked in close conjunction with the Czech New Wave film-makers (*see* pp. 86–7), and Kundera taught at the film school. Much of the newer writing was tinged with an eroticism that had been long suppressed by officialdom, and which has become one of the more distinctive features of modern Czech literature. Hrabal's fascination with sex is tender, if sometimes bizarre; while in the case of **Ivan Klíma**, the popular Beatle-fringed president of the Writers' Union during 1968, a more melancholic and less exuberant view of human relationships has tended to come to the fore. Kundera's approach is the best known in the west, as a result of his filmed novel *The Unbearable Lightness of Being*, and is most remarkable for the cerebral world of betrayal and often cruelty in which his lovers are steeped. Although often accused of being misogynic, his early works, like the writings of Klíma, can be seen as studies of an atomized society in microcosm, and are branded with the searing history of the Prague Spring.

Through the 1960s, the influence and confidence of the writers grew. They were among those leading the external pressure on the Communist Party to introduce structural reforms, which reached a head in July 1968 with the publication of the polemical '2000 Words Manifesto', written by the journalist **Ludvík Vaculík**. Leonid Brezhnev got on the phone to ask Alexander Dubček how it could have found its way into the newspapers. Dubček's response was too vague, and within a month the Prague Spring had been crushed by the fraternal tanks of the Warsaw Pact.

The illusion of reform was over, and the next 20 years saw it replaced by the bread and circuses of 'real existing socialism'. The lies of the post-1968 government were clearer than those of any of its predecessors, but a dispirited population all but gave up caring; and Czech literature now fought the most crucial battle of its short history. Authors engaged the government in a struggle for the country's language, unparalleled in its scale outside postwar Communist Europe. Havel's plays parodied the obscurity and deceptions of bureaucratic speech, while his articles developed one simple theme—that the regime would win if it could change the meaning of words, and would be subverted if people refused to play its semantic game. The idea that truth alone would threaten the government might seem idealistic, but the only common feature of the hundreds of works suppressed was that they made no allowances for the censors' tastes. From the early 1970s, individually typed 'Padlock Publications' (*Edice Petlice*) of banned literature began to circulate. Some, such as Vaculík's *feuilletons* (translated into English as *A Cup of Coffee with My Interrogator*), were direct attacks on the day-to-day injustices of the regime. Others, such as the works of Ivan Klíma were often little more than honest stories set in an unadorned Prague. Some of the country's leading writers, such as Havel, Vaculík and **Pavel Kohout** were instrumental in forming Charter 77. Others chose to leave: among them were Kundera, Lustig and Josef Škvorecký. The last-named set up Sixty-Eight Publishers with his wife in Toronto, which was responsible for publishing hundreds of Czech works and smuggling them back into the country. It was a huge contribution to keeping the nation's literary culture alive, which has won him honours and respect in post-1989 Prague; an absurd paradox is that his no less committed wife has had to wipe off the smear of collaboration (*see* p. 62).

Literature Unlocked

At the time of writing, the Czech Republic is the only country in the world to have as its president a man who has been both a brewery worker and a published playwright. Václav Havel is potent evidence of the political power of Czech literature since 1968, but as he has said in a different context, that's a shaky criterion by which to judge any work of art. The new struggle is to find a literary voice appropriate to the post-Communist era, and the task will be a tremendous one. Innumerable 20th-century writers—from Hemingway to Nabokov—remain all but unknown in the Czech Republic. Publishers are sticking with sure sellers, and catering to the massive trend towards escapist literature that has occurred since the revolution. *Lord of the Rings* and *Dallas* have both been best sellers, and science-fiction has reached new heights of popularity. Czechs had their noses rubbed into a particularly tawdry form of the real world for a long time, and the desire for fantasy is eminently understandable—but one important feature of some of the best modern Czech literature has been its refusal to tease its targets with half-hearted analogy and allegory. If its analytical power is subverted by the retreat into unreality, it will be the worse for it.

However, a far more optimistic view is possible. Ever since the Romantic poetry of Mácha, the mystical and the surreal have flowed through the country's writing, and, *Dallas* notwithstanding, the new escapism just may be the first signs of a return to the lyrical heritage of Czech literature. One link is the long-banned **Ladislav Klíma** (1878–1928), a tortured chap with ping-pong eyes, crinkled brow and walrus moustache, who wrote in early 20th-century isolation. Since 1989 his cerebral, solipsistic and visionary writing has been rediscovered, and he is now one of the favourite authors of the young Prague literati. No English translations of his work are yet available, but if you get to see a photo of Klíma, ponder the fact that many Czechs believe his work to be even more fantastic and disturbing than his appearance. Another writer to watch is **Egon Bondy**, a.k.a. Zbyněk Fišer, a fascinating character of the pre-1989 underground. During the 1970s and 1980s, his *samizdat* works popularized esoteric knowledge from eastern mysticisms to Jewish fairy tales, which—in conjunction with his unfolding philosophy of Communist Buddhism, fiercely asserted cowardice, and regular collaboration with the secret police—have carved him out a unique and uncategorizable place in contemporary Czech literature. Since 1989 Bondy has gone to ground, emerging only occasionally to warn that capitalism will be as bad as the other one, but he remains a cult hero to some. Finally, his long-standing friend Bohumil Hrabal personifies the creative potential of apolitical fantasy: he compromised with the pre-1989 regime to the extent that he signed a petition attacking Havel and his other Charter friends, and yet his swirling fiction, swimming in a joyful humanity and a sense of the absurd that makes politics almost irrelevant, is widely regarded as the pinnacle of contemporary Czech writing.

As well as their unconventional lives and styles, one feature common to Hrabal, Bondy and Klíma is that each represents a different model for young writers wanting to forget the literary agenda of totalitarianism. For those authors who tackled Communism head-on, the transition will be harder and the writers who will fall are those who were so locked into the anti-Communist struggle that they were defined by it. Some argue that the most eminent example is Václav Havel himself, but as yet there is no way of telling. Other than his superbly crafted speeches, he has published nothing since 1989 and has even said that he can't write anything while president. Given the potential subject matter, it's a creative impasse that many hope he will conquer soon.

Music

Prague music rode the storms that regularly shattered every other area of the capital's cultural life. While the Hussites were stringing up choirmasters, they composed some of the first recorded martial hymns; and as the Counter-Reformation burned Bohemia's language and literature out of existence, Prague Jesuits performed mysteries that gave birth to Czech opera. One of the leading Baroque musicians of the period was the organist **František Brixi** (1732–71).

Prague's 18th-century status as a glorified suburb of Vienna had certain musical advantages. In January 1787, **Wolfgang Amadeus Mozart** (1756–91) made the first of four visits, and swiftly wrote his *Symphony in D.K504 ('Prague')*. While Vienna never quite understood Mozart, Prague fell in love with him: *Figaro* was a roaring success; he conducted the premiere of *Don Giovanni* in the city; and he composed *La Clemenza di Tito* for the Bohemian coronation of Leopold II in 1791. 3000 Praguers attended a requiem (by a Czech) nine days after Mozart's death, as he lay little-mourned in a third-class section of Vienna's St Mark's cemetery. The city has revelled in its recognition of Wolfgang's genius, helped by Miloš Forman's cinematic tribute to his home town, *Amadeus*.

However, it was another half a century before Bohemia found a musical language appropriate to Romanticism—in the **polka**. Peasants had been raucously skipping to a 2/4 rhythm for centuries, and in the mid-1800s patriotic composers decided that the dances expressed the essential genius of the country. Simultaneously, the reinvention of Czech now made home-grown librettos possible. In 1866, rustic traditions brought to life the first great national opera, *The Bartered Bride* by **Bedřich Smetana** (1824–84) in which the composer showed a deftness for comedy and characterization that was compared to Mozart at his best. Two years later, his operatic fusion of rural Bohemia and its legendary landscape reached almost Wagnerian heights in *Dalibor* (1868). His symphonic masterpiece, the six-poem cycle of *My Country* (Má Vlast; 1874–9), transformed national myth into a sweeping and universal lyricism. The composer went deaf in 1874 and never heard it performed. He incorporated the last screeching E note that he ever heard into his autobiographical *String Quartet in E Minor* (1876). Even in his lifetime Smetana was regarded as the father of Czech music (though he never quite got his tongue round the language), and in 1881, he conducted his opera *Libuše* at the opening of Prague's National Theatre. It burned down two weeks later (the firemen were at their boss's funeral), and Smetana died insane and syphilitic in 1884, but his reputation endures.

The second great figure of 19th-century Czech music was pigeon-fancier, model-railway enthusiast, and protégé of Brahms, **Antonín Dvořák** (1841–1904). Dvořák spent 1891–5 in the United States (to which the optimism of his *9th Symphony (From the New World)* was a homage), but he too was strongly influenced by folk music (*Slavonic Dances*). It also permeates his symphonic works, which have the rich melodiousness of Smetana but a more disciplined feel. His chamber music is highly regarded, and his *Cello Concerto* represents the composer at his best.

Prague's critics fiercely debated the merits of Smetana and Dvořák, but showed almost unmixed hostility to Moravian-born **Leoš Janáček** (1858–1928)—in part because he had reviewed a work by the influential National Theatre director as 'so-called music, filled with menacing obscurity, desperate screams and dagger stabs'. Janáček was a close friend of Dvořák, and shared his interests in folk music (*Lachian Dances*). He became convinced that it was born from the cadences of speech, and from the late 1880s he scribbled down sounds in a notebook wherever he went—from the monkey shrieks at London Zoo to the death rattle of his daughter. He never used the notes directly, but his concern for authenticity gave birth to work that, combining spare but extraordinarily powerful melodies with a deeply humane philosophy, is some of the most inspiring classical music of the 20th century. Look out in particular for his operas *Jenůfa* and *House of the Dead*; his orchestral works, *Taras Bulba* and *Sinfonietta*; and his two rarely performed but excellent string quartets. His *Glagolitic Mass* is also exceptional.

Even more prolific was **Bohuslav Martinů** (1890–1959), who produced over 400 uncategorizable works, with names such as *Thunderbolt P.47*. Czechs admire him; foreigners are often at a loss.

The most notable postwar music in Prague has been that suppressed by the government. To two generations, **Marta Kubišová** is the personification of the 1968 Prague Spring: an outlawed Sandie Shaw whose *Modlitba pro Martu* reduced thousands to tears when she sang it for the first time in 21 years during the demonstrations of 1989. The **Plastic People of the Universe** became the Sex Pistols of Prague—*very* roughly speaking—when in 1976 they were put on trial for singing 'shit' once too often. As a direct result, the capital's intelligentsia founded Charter 77; and as an indirect result of that, Václav Havel became president.

Since 1989 Czech music has thankfully been able to avoid politics. Prague's favourite crooner, wolf-grinning heart-throb **Karel Gott** always did the same, but no one minds that he kept his nose clean and he's been a perennial favourite of the capital's lusty housewives for over 30 years. At the other end of the scale, the slightly alternative tendency among the city's youth favours a cacophonous thrashing noise that has become a distinctive feature of modern music in Prague. Leading exponents of the genre are **Garáž** (Garage), while **Psí vojáci** (Dogs of War) are ever so slightly jazzy. **Půlnoc** (Midnight), a reconstituted version of the Plastic People, add the touch of a droning viola. Many other new groups are experimenting with world music, resulting in as many kettledrum-and-castanet atrocities as you'd expect. One noteworthy exception is **Shalom**, whose dreamy tunes, Jewish symbolism and rabbinical attire are making Judaism almost fashionable among a section of Prague's flower-children—all the more surprising given that the group were all born Gentiles. Finally, you could listen out for a legendary stalwart of the pre-1989 opposition, the accordionist **Jim Čert**. He's a pot-bellied loon with a very long beard, whose trademark is to turn venerable Czech folk melodies into furious squeeze-box punk rock. The Communists could never quite believe that he existed, and used to broadcast his performances on TV simply to warn children what anti-Communism might turn them into. (Not surprisingly, he became a folk hero.) Čert remains a favourite of Václav Havel's cultural entourage, and he's now known as the President's Accordionist. But if none of that is your bag, you could settle back with a recording of Beethoven's 9th Symphony with its concluding *Ode to Joy* by Schiller. It was played at the first classical concert of post-Communist Czechoslovakia and is still very hopefully called the anthem of the United States of Europe.

Visionary Prague

A cockeyed outlook on the world permeates the history of Prague. For centuries, the capital has stalked wild geese and built monuments to chimeras. What follows is a ramble through a jungle of delusions, from alchemy to Communism, in which only glimmers of sanity have ever appeared.

The ear of Rudolfine Prague was attuned to speculations on all the highest planes, and soothsayers, croakers, necromancers and prophets of every description found the emperor's court a congenial staging-post. In Rome, the shadow of the stake was a powerful disincentive to weirdness; in Prague, the character of an emperor whose horoscope had been cast by Nostradamus demanded it. His vast curiosity cabinet included mandrake root fetishes (thought to scream when pricked); he apparently carried moss from the bones of a hanged man in his back pocket; and his courtiers were at the sharp end of contemporary scientific thought. Wherever there was a mystery to be pondered, Prague thinkers could be guaranteed to deepen it. The emperor's private secretary published an acclaimed thesis on squaring the circle; others wrote influential works on a Silesian boy reported to have been born with a gold tooth in 1593; and when a bone was unearthed in the capital, the city was consumed by a debate on whether it was an elephant's tusk or the shin of an antediluvian giant.

Two of the earliest visitors to the capital were the extraordinary Jekyll and Hyde duo of John Dee (1527–1608) and Edward Kelley (1555–95?), who pulled into the capital on a coach from Cracow in 1584. Dee, a Fellow of Trinity College, Cambridge, and astrologer to Queen Elizabeth I, was a scholar in search of a question; but quite what drove Kelley, whose experiments in England had included the disinterment and quizzing of a corpse, has never been satisfactorily established. It does a disservice to his warped genius to call him a mere fraud, but Rudolf would still have done well to ask him why he had no ears (they had been shorn for counterfeiting). Instead, the emperor put both men on the imperial payroll.

The partnership revolved around crystal balls. With Kelley gazing, and the doctor asking the questions, they had already clocked up hundreds of hours of crystalline conversations with maverick quasi-Christian angels, all conducted and recorded in Enochian, an entirely new 117,649-character language. Rudolf seems, remarkably enough, to have been uninterested in Dee's outline of the hallucinations, and soon dispensed with their services. However, there were plenty of other takers, and the duo were to spend five eventful years in and around Prague.

Their unholy alliance came to an end before they left Bohemia, however. In April 1587, while peering into the crystal, an astounded Kelley (32) informed Dee (60) that Madimi, one of the regular cast of angels, was taking off all her clothes. Under protest, Kelley also revealed that she was also ordering the two men to 'share all things in common, including our wives'. Kelley assured Jane Dee (also 32) that 'my heart pales at the arrangement'. Jane was considerably more upset than the earless grave-robber; the thoughts of frumpy Mrs Kelley are nowhere recorded; but a pained John Dee decided that, imponderably mysterious though they were, the angels' commands had to be obeyed. A covenant of sex and silence was signed between the group in May 1587. Kelley then seems to have had problems getting his act together, and tetchily locked himself into his laboratory for several days, but it's interesting to note that Theodore (Gift of God) Dee was born 9 months and 2 weeks later. The angels never spoke again, and Kelley soon fled the lugubrious love-nest. In 1589, the Dees were on their way back to England; at which point Kelley reappeared in Prague and entered another department of Rudolfine science—alchemy.

Rudolf II's court was the Los Alamos of the alchemical age. Europe's wild golden-goose chase peaked in the late 1500s, and to questing types everywhere the emperor was the latest incarnation of Hermes Trismegistus, the mysterious quasi-divinity who had been the first to crack the transmutation secret. Unfortunately, Hermes' gnomic utterances—notably, 'that which is above is like to that which is below; but that which is below is like to that which is above'—kept a tight lid on the Hermetic wisdom. The concept of the philosopher's stone ('the stone which is not a stone, a precious thing which has no value, a thing of many shapes, this unknown which is most known of all') did little to advance matters, but its discovery was one of Rudolf II's obsessions. Anyone who could show proven alchemical ability was given board and lodging, and all the technology that money could buy. As they slaved over their stills, alembics, crucibles and hot-ash baths, Rudolf II's alchemists produced interesting results—hair-restoring potions, hair-removing potions, laxatives, philtres and new recipes for mulling wine—but the nature of the experiments (among other factors) ensured that the stone remained elusive. Congelation, calcination, cibation and mortification were among the standard processes; when those failed, they could be combined with ceration, the addition of wax, or inhumation, which generally involved burying the substance concerned in dung.

The stakes were high in the alchemical quest: possibly eternal life, certainly ultimate wisdom, and depending on the Hermetic tract that you read, anything from a million-fold increase in gold to a thousand billion. The scope for quackery was immense. On one celebrated occasion, a mysterious Arab drew into the capital and invited hundreds to a banquet at which he swore to multiply contributions by a thousand; to general consternation, he and the money exploded into a puff of smoke instead. The dangers were no less dramatic. Dungeons and mercury inhalation were occupational hazards, and in Prague unmasked charlatans faced the added possibility of being paraded in tinsel and hanged from a yellow rope on a gilded scaffold. Alchemical theory had accommodated the risks, by suggesting that the philosopher's stone could take up to 12 years to ripen. By that time a nimble failure could be long gone, leaving behind only a steaming heap of wax and dung; but for those who talked big and failed to deliver, time could run out far sooner.

Kelley was one of those who learnt the hard way. The Englishman had stumbled upon the stone while pottering around the ley lines of Glastonbury during happier times with John Dee. Although his claims were relatively modest (an increase in gold by a factor of 72,330), he was taken on by Rudolf in 1589. He began impressively, transmuting a pound of lead into gold with a drop of blood-red oil (leaving a ruby at the bottom of the pot), and he was promptly knighted by the emperor. By 1591, however, he was under pressure. England's Lord Treasurer had written to ask for 'a token, say enough to defray the expenses of the Navy for the summer', and Rudolf was finding that the gold he was receiving was significantly less than the amount he was paying his knight. Kelley was incarcerated on suspicion of heresy and sorcery. He enjoyed an Indian summer in 1593, when he was reported to be at liberty and making gold 'as fast as a hen will cracke nuttes', but his incredible career was drawing to a close. Suitably enough, no one knows where or when (or, say some, if) he died. Legend claims that he lost a leg or two jumping from a tower, and then poisoned himself; a neat variation on the tale is that the fatal draught was an elixir of life that he had prepared for the emperor.

Kelley notwithstanding, alchemists would soon become chemists, and the stargazers of Rudolfine Prague also stood at a turning point in the history of science. In the space of a few decades, the universe had been shaken to its core. For some 1500 years, the moon, planets, sun and stars had orbited the earth attached to Ptolemy's harmonious crystal spheres, but in 1543 the Pole Nicolaus Copernicus had revived the ancient heresy of heliocentricity. No one knew how to look at the universe any more. When a Paduan arrived with a set of concave mirrors, they were snapped up by the thinkers of the court; Giordano Bruno stopped by in 1588 with his theories of infinite worlds; and as comets, a supernova and fateful conjunctions hurtled through the firmament during the last decades of the century, the capital battened down the hatches and prepared for darkness at noon and the end of empires.

Successive imperial mathematicians at Rudolf II's court personified the critical juncture to which the heavens had come. The work of the first, the little-remembered Nicholas Ursus, was inextricably linked to that of the second, the Danish Tycho Brahe, who served between 1599 and 1601. While still in Denmark, Brahe accused Ursus of plagiarism, setting off an arcane intra-Continental row that became vitriolic even for an age when scientists didn't mince their words. Ursus published a defence from Prague in 1597. It interspersed an erudite survey of astronomy's history with constant references to one of Brahe's supporters as 'Snotface', taunts about Brahe's own disfigured nose, and the observation that the

Dane's daughter was 'not yet nubile and so not of much use to me for the usual purpose'. Brahe never quite matched his opponent's invective, but he was no more stable. Some said that his departure from Denmark had been inspired by another dispute, this time over the ownership of a dog; and although his stellar observations did their bit for rationalism by putting the boot into Ptolemy's crystal spheres, in Prague he subjected poor Rudolf to endless astrological prophecies of doom. The emperor was told variously that he would die before 50, that he would be killed by a monk, and that he would follow his pet raven to Hell.

Brahe's successor as imperial mathematician (1601–12), Johannes Kepler, went further than any of his contemporaries in developing a rational philosophy of science, but the wisdom of the ancients continued to permeate his work. His laid down the laws of planetary motion, but linked them to the idea that each of the five planets corresponded to one of the musical ranges from bass to treble. His suspicion of superstition (reinforced when his mother was tried for witchcraft) meant that when it came to astrology, he was cautious. He suggested that the aspects affected the world only in the limited sense that a peasant could affect the shape of a pumpkin, and he sensibly warned that 'one must keep astrology entirely from the emperor's mind' (although he actually cast several horoscopes for Rudolf). His contributions to scientific debate were incomparably more elegant than those of his predecessors, often written in Latin verse or Ciceronian orations. However, neither the mode of expression nor the caution demanded by the dangerous times fully account for their elliptical sound to the modern ear. His comments on those who now questioned Copernicus' views are a suitably oblique memorial to an absurd Prague that has never quite disappeared.

> 'They castrated the poet
> Lest he copulate;
> He lived without testicles.'

Rabbi Loew

Every community mythologizes its history, but with the legendary Rabbi Loew, Prague's Jews personified it. Loew (as in 'I just *lurve* sushi') was a celebrated scholar in the relatively tolerant Prague of the late 1500s, but the stories that came to envelop his life encapsulated the centuries-old experience of the ghetto— where pogroms and the evil eye were omnipresent dangers, and only the rabbi could really explain why life was so abysmal.

The legends begin on a touching note. When young Loew arrived in the capital, he was smitten by Pearl, daughter of one Reb Schmelke. Schmelke then went bankrupt, but Loew was so in love that he agreed to wait until the dowry could be raised. Impetuous it may have been, but it was only 10 years before Reb Schmelke was back on his feet, thanks to a bag of gold that a contemptuous cavalier tossed at Pearl as he stole a loaf of bread. Loew, by now steeped in the Talmud, declared that that had been no ordinary horseman, but Elijah. The stage was set for an exceptional life.

Certain themes run through all the tales. The ghetto is under constant threat from Christians, the wickedest of whom is Brother Thaddeus, whose very mention brings a hiss to the throat. There is also the occasional good *goy*, most notably the weak but fundamentally sympathetic Emperor Rudolf. Pulling the strings together is mild-mannered Rabbi Loew, who checks Brother Thaddeus at every turn, dares to reveal to the emperor that his real mother was Jewish, and exchanges tips with other super-rabbis across Europe in his dreams. After 300 clerics ask Loew to answer questions such as 'Are the Jews guilty of killing Christ?', his eloquence wins them over to a man. On the innumerable occasions that Rudolf begs him for help, the rabbi rescues him from jail, dethrones an impostor and overturns expulsion edicts. When a jealous flunky persuades the vacillating emperor to order Loew to hold a banquet, the scholar transports a shimmering palace from a distant land into his humble ghetto abode; and to the now-jovial Rudolf II's uproarious laughter, the luckless lackey pockets a goblet and is rooted to his seat. The picture of Rudolf that emerges is about as far from reality as it's possible to get. The emperor summoned the rabbi to his castle once, to discuss a matter that was never revealed, which was clearly more than enough material for generations of Jewish myth-makers.

The legend now inextricably linked to Loew is that of the golem, or artificial man. The word, meaning 'unformed substance' (or 'unmarried woman') in Hebrew, is first found in Psalms 139:16; and the idea that humanity could create life comes from the mystical cabalistic tradition that each mortal contains a spark of the divine. Jewish history is littered with pre-Loewian golems, and they have stalked Europe's ghettos for centuries. Jakob Grimm found one in Poland in 1808, but Rabbi Loew's has become the most famous, turned into a German silent film (1920), a French talkie (1937) and a tale to alarm good Jewish boys and girls everywhere. It all began while Loew was communing with the cosmos one night. He was warned that a great danger loomed, and told to make a golem, pronto. With his two youthful rabbi sidekicks, he hurried to the banks of the Vltava. Chanting melancholy psalms and working by torchlight, the trio built a man out of mud, walked around it several times, and Loew then placed the unknown name of God (the *shem*) in its mouth. 'Joseph Golem' was born. His adventures are laced with slapstick ghetto humour—such as the moment when he follows orders too literally and floods long-suffering Pearl's kitchen—but most are of a grimly heroic nature. Joseph once rescues a girl from being forcibly baptized; and when the community is on trial for ritual murder, he arrives with the exonerating evidence as the verdict is to be announced. The allegation that Jews kneaded Christian blood for their Passover *matzoth* (unleavened bread) echoes throughout, and as well as thwarting the remorseless Brother Thaddeus, Joseph constantly intercepts shadowy Christians wheeling dead babies into the ghetto in order to lay the ground for a pogrom.

Joseph was eventually laid to rest in the roof of Prague's Old-New Synagogue. The annihilation of the capital's Jews gave rise to the last golem legend. It had been said that he would return if needed, but as the Nazi cattle trains filled and emptied, those Jews who remained declared that he had died forever. It sounds likely, but Praguers still claim that on stormy nights, Joseph's footsteps can be heard on those streets of the ancient ghetto that survive.

Švejkism

20th-century literature in Prague has produced two -isms that go far to illuminate the absurdity of Czechoslovakia's modern political experience. The first was Kafkaism, which a literary lackey of the Communist Party dismissed in 1963 as 'a knife severing the veins of progressive traditions'. The comment contained its own unintended admission of moral harakiri; but it's with Švejkism that authority generally, and the Communists in particular, faced irony in its purest form.

The Good Soldier Švejk, written by the Czech Jaroslav Hašek in the years around the First World War, became the first great anti-hero of the modern age; and via the theatres of Berlin took the Continent by storm (Bertolt Brecht died with the book by his bed, admittedly along with 60 others). Švejk was Sancho Panza and Don Quixote rolled into one and set loose on the battlefields of Europe. Armed with an eagerness to ape formalities and observe rules to the letter, and the ability to shine the occasional shaft of common sense on the hecatomb around him, Švejk survived—which is what the doctrine is all about.

Hašek himself was the first Švejkist. The alcoholic anarchist began with fairly minor journalistic hoaxes: he conducted pseudonymous polemics against himself in the two major party newspapers of the day; and during his time at *Animal World*, Prague's animal-lovers were buffeted with illustrated accounts of a musk-rat invasion of the capital and blood-curdling reports of rampaging packs of collies in distant Patagonia. The -ism really began to emerge in 1911, when he wrote the earliest Švejk stories. Hašek announced that his newly-formed Party of Moderate Progress Within the Bounds of the Law would contest the Imperial elections in

June. It lost, despite a rousing song (chorus: 'To arms, to arms, to arms!/ Moderate progress is our aim!') and the offer of a pocket aquarium to anyone who voted for the party. Hašek then wrote the party's social and political history. In 1915, he checked into a hotel in feverishly anti-Russian Prague as 'Ivan Fyodorovich Kuznetsov, born in Kiev and coming from Moscow', giving as his reason for visiting 'to check up on the General Staff'. Habsburg secret police cordoned off the block; a relieved Hašek told them that he had been worried about the lax security in the capital, and got away with five days in jail.

Most Czechs now claim that there's a heavy dose of Švejkism in the national character, but as usual with stereotypes, that's only half the story. The characteristic emerged with full force during the 1968 invasion. The commander of the Warsaw Pact armies, Marshal Grechko (nicknamed El Grechko after his troops strafed a particularly interesting design onto the National Museum), warned Czechoslovakia's president that 'We have all read Švejk and that's all that's happening here'. Alexander Dubček remained in power, promising everything and doing nothing; Praguers would politely translate road signs for tank crews, not mentioning that they had just reversed them; and according to Milan Kundera, an address to a students' meeting by the new First Secretary, Gustáv Husák, had to be cancelled when the audience wouldn't stop shouting 'Long live the Party! Long live Husák!'.

However, demoralization is the kiss of death to Švejkism, and it was often a far darker, Kafkaesque, streak that came to the fore under Communism, particularly after 1968. Too many came to believe in the powers-that-were. Although mockery continued behind closed doors, Praguers absorbed the lies and methods of the government rather than hurl them back. It was the Poles who were the true heirs of Švejk during the 1970s and '80s, and as even many Praguers admit, it's no coincidence that Czechs were so late joining the 1989 revolutions. The symbol of Kafkaism—the man who destroys himself in the search to make sense of another's world—is also the symbol of Prague's modern history. For all his incredible bravery, Jan Palach was Josef K., not Josef Švejk, when he burned himself to death in 1969.

Communist Kitsch

When the Czechoslovak Communist Party moved into the driving seat in 1948, official culture embarked on a headlong descent that was to last four decades. The fetish of the Five Year Plan, gigantomania, and the celebration of vulcanization processes were to leave no one entirely untouched.

The Party's first plunge into truly execrable taste was the transformation of President Klement Gottwald into a mummified icon after his death in 1953. The procedure was in its infancy in the Communist world, and Gottwald proved too rotten for formaldehyde—in part because alcoholism had already pickled him. An alarmed government turned to the prop and make-up wizards of the Barrandov film studios, who effectively rebuilt Gottwald in plastic, limb by putrefying limb. Only in 1962, by which time the original president had been reduced to a head, did the Central Committee call it a day. The lecherous drunkard then became 'Czechoslovakia's First Working-Class President', immortalized until 1989 in a metro station, a town, countless roads, museums, a bridge and a banknote.

Stalin himself was the subject of Prague's most mind-boggling piece of cultural junk, when in 1953 the government constructed a 30-metre-high statue in his honour, glowering from a hillside over Prague's Old Town. 600 workers spent 500 days building the colossus, which showed Stalin leading a Soviet worker, woman heroine, soldier and botanist into the future. The designer, Otakar Švec, did the decent thing and shot himself before its completion, but the Czechoslovak Communist Party apparently had every reason to be satisfied with its magnificent display of unctuousness. Triumphant speeches were held as it was unveiled in 1955, and workers from across the country danced polkas at the base. But within a year, things had gone badly wrong. Stalin's successor, Nikita Krushchev, let slip that Uncle Joe had, objectively speaking, deformed socialism—and what's more, that a personality cult had apparently grown up around him. The Party took a quick look at its 14,000-ton masterpiece, and shrouded it in scaffolding. In January 1962, a commission was set up. A panicky Mr Štursa, who had seen the project through, wrote to suggest that Stalin could be sliced off the botanist et al., and replaced by 'an allegory—perhaps a woman holding a bouquet?'. The commission never replied, and in October 1962 the dynamite boys went in. The heroes were destroyed by a series of night-time detonations; a single explosion would have ripped away most of the hillside and the bridge below.

Mass activism was essential to many of the bizarre rituals of Communism. Most Praguers now draw a discreet veil over their participation, but as the Party would have said, the statistics speak for themselves (although it confused matters by also saying things such as, 'We do not bow to facts'). The Spartakiáda, a quinquennial gymnastic exhibition inaugurated in 1950, continued until 1985, but the 1960 week was typical. 800,000 athletic types filled Prague's Strahov stadium, and displayed synchronized contortions on themes such as 'Towards New Tomorrows' and 'Life Wins Over Death'. Vast crowds waved red flags at Prague's May Day rallies, where Party luminaries saluted missiles and spoke on peace; work teams would compete, albeit very half-heartedly indeed, for the 'Brigade of Socialist Labour' award, a piece of cardboard that could still be found in Prague factories in early 1990; and the shibboleths of a hollow regime emerged from the mouths of thousands of otherwise-honest folk.

It's hard to tell whether long-term damage has been done to the Prague psyche by the cultural atrocities perpetrated by their side of the Cold War. During the 1950s, many actually believed in the slush and the cant, but it was in the 1970s and '80s that kitsch very nearly triumphed, by implicating hundreds of thousands in a world of schmaltz. The aspirations were noble, but they were enshrined in hyperbole which threatened to destroy critical functions entirely. The dangers have become clear since 1989: one example is that years of seeing banners celebrating racial harmony have led many to conclude that anti-racism is somehow equatable with Communism.

Visible vestiges of the Communist interregnum are hard to find these days. The crimson placards that lined Wenceslas Square until early 1990 (saying things like 'We shall overfulfil the plan by 143%!') have been replaced by advertisements for photocopiers and computers; statues have been toppled and history is being re-rewritten. But ghosts survive. Hundreds of megaphones, which once blared martial tunes and speeches on festival days, sit silently on lampposts across the capital. Epic friezes and mosaics cling on (notably at the Anděl metro station), spared destruction by their size and yet mutely pleading for it by their ugliness. And most formidable of all is the Hotel International, a masterpiece of Socialist Realism. Since 1989, its pride has turned into insouciance, but it remains as arrogant now as it must have been on that hazy day back in 1954 when the Defence Minister stepped out to unveil his granite tower to a jubilant crowd.

There has been endless talk since the revolution of the need to exorcise the spirit of Communism, and an essential stage will be the opening of a gallery of revolutionary culture. The perfect site exists: the former Communist Party mausoleum, a marble temple to totalitarian necrophilia (*see* pp. 274–5). The vast sepulchre would take some filling, but there is no shortage of exhibits. The hundreds of statues that now lie in storage across the capital could line the long approach road in welcome—nymphs caressing olive branches would mingle with scrums of bearded thinkers, while droves of bald men with goatees could point visitors onward, ever onward. Several items from the now defunct Museum of the National Security Corps and Army of the Interior Ministry could also find a new home there. They celebrated the valour and vigilance of the border patrol: among the threats to the nation that the brave boys had seen off were packs of strange cigarettes (accompanied by photographs of their bewildered hippy owners) and the home-made helicopter and pretend tank of very hopeful would-be escapees. Most stirring of all was Brek, an almost legendary guard dog who pounced on 60 fleeing miscreants, sustained two shotgun wounds, and was eventually stuffed for his pains.

It is hard to draw up a Prague top ten, but if you're only in town for a couple of days—or if you prefer roaming free to following walks—you may want to do so. The following list represents a few of the most impressive sights and experiences that the capital has to offer. No explanation for the choices is given, but you can double-check their interest value by looking them up in the main body of this book.

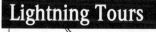

Lightning Tours

Art Nouveau	Municipal House; Evropa Café.
Baroque churches	St Nicholas's Church; St James's Church.
Bridges	The Charles Bridge. No others.
Cemeteries	Malá Strana Cemetery; Old Jewish Cemetery.
Evening drinking	Evropa café in winter; Michalská street in summer; cup of *burčák* on the Charles Bridge in September.
Galleries	Šternberk Palace (European Art); St George's Convent (Czech Gothic and Baroque art).
Gothic architecture	Cathedral of St Vitus; Vladislav Hall; Old-New Synagogue; St Agnes's Convent; Stone Bell House.
Islands	Kampa; Žofín (Slovanský ostrov); Střelecký ostrov.
Modernist architecture	Baba Housing Estate; Church of the Sacred Heart; Žižkov Tower.

Museums	Museum of Decorative Arts; National Technical Museum; Military Museum in the Lobkowicz Palace; Anti-Nazi Resistance Memorial.
Preposterous Baroque shrines	Loretto; *Bambino di Praga*; St John Nepomuk's tomb.
Quirky miscellanies	National Memorial (Communist mausoleum); John Lennon Wall.
Rides	Funicular up Petřín Hill; tram 22; rowing on Vltava.
Romantic strolls	Winding path down Petřín into Malá Strana; Kampa Island; Nový Svět; streets around St Agnes's Convent.
Subterranean spots	House of the Lords of Kunštát and Poděbrady; U zlaté konvice (wine bar).
Views	From a table at Nebozízek restaurant; the orange tiles of Malá Strana from the top of Nerudova street; from a room in the Hotel Praha.
Walled gardens	Waldstein Gardens; courtyard in Clementinum; cloister of St Giles's monastery; Vojan Park.

Hit-and-run Itineraries

The following lists assume a hunger for sensation, efficient planning and taxis throughout. If you have all three, you can conquer Prague, and have the photos to prove it, within 72 hours.

One Day

St Vitus's Cathedral, Vladislav Hall and Golden Lane; Old Jewish Cemetery and Old-New Synagogue; Charles Bridge; St Nicholas's Church (Malá Strana); a walk down Wenceslas Square and a drink in the Old Town Square. Skip lunch and snatch a sausage for supper.

Two Days

Add the Church of St James; Museum of Decorative Arts; Waldstein Gardens; the gallery of St George's Convent. Have lunch in the Evropa café and dine at U mecenáše.

Three Days

Add Strahov's libraries, Loretto and Nový Svět; the John Lennon Wall; St Agnes's Convent. Have a glass of wine in U zelené žáby and make a reservation for Nebozízek up on Petřín Hill.

A walk through old Prague is a stroll through a labyrinth of the senses. Wherever you turn, you're confronted by come-hither tunnels, lanes disappearing into mysterious curls, or the distant sound of music. Secluded gardens peep through tiny doorways, unseen organists practise in empty churches, and the city's bells are chiming for the first time in decades. Crawling through its hidden staircases and cloisters will take you through a treasure chest of ages, and—on occasion—a *déjà vu* of a childhood dream.

The walks are structured around the ancient divisions of the capital. Prague castle—in fact an entire city of regal follies—is covered in Walk I; and Walk IV is a stroll through the hush of the surrounding district. The higgledy-piggledy Old Town is divided between Walks II (northern half and Jewish Quarter) and V (southern half); and Walk III criss-crosses Malá Strana, the cream of Prague Baroque. Apart from Wenceslas Square (Walk V),

Prague Walks

*Malá Strana
from Charles Bridge*

the dusty chaos of the New Town isn't covered in the walks. However, despite its name it is 600 years old, and if you're in town for more than a week you could explore its hidden surprises (*see* pp. 268–72). On the other hand, if you only have a couple of days, the order of the walks corresponds very roughly to their level of interest—although Walk III heads the list for smoochability, Walk IV wins for its becalmed quirkiness (and it contains Prague's best art gallery), and the Astronomical Clock and Charles Bridge in Walk V are the quintessence of the magical city.

Each walk is headed with a list of the main sights on the route, followed closely by possible lunch stops, and details of where it starts and ends. The best time for the walk is also mentioned: in a nutshell, *avoid Walks I and IV on a Monday, Walk II on a Saturday, and Walks III and V if it's raining.* All the walks should be begun by midday if you want to see everything, but Walk III is a good choice for an evening meander. Where an admission fee is charged, '*adm*' appears after the opening times. How long each trip will take is suggested: a fairly brisk approach is assumed, and if you're a dawdler at heart, you can easily add 50 per cent.

There are two minor considerations to bear in mind before setting off. One of the most absurd juxtapositions of past and present in Prague is that two systems of house numbering, on red and blue signs, exist. Only the modern blue numbers are used in this book. Also, you may notice that pedestrians at traffic lights are reluctant to move until they see a little green man. The obsession isn't as developed as in the anally-retentive nations of the north, but expect to face the basilisk glares of a line of grimacing, growling *babičky* if you dare to cross against the lights.

Start: Ⓜ *Malostranská (Line A); or trams 12, 18 and 22.*
Finish: *about 20 metres from where it begins.*
Walking time: *3 hours, longer for gallery addicts.*

I: Prague Castle

Tomb of St John Nepomuk

From its beginnings as a pagan mound to the day when Václav Havel was sworn in as president, Prague's history has unrolled in Hradčany Castle. Its neo-classical veneer now stretches half a lazy mile over the capital, but it's the onion domes and demented prongs of the cathedral, rising from its core, that hint at what really lies within. This walk uncovers the city's medieval heart and arcane mind. It explores St Vitus's Cathedral, the monument to a monomaniacal emperor and one of the grandest churches of the 14th century; and it takes you through the Vladislav Hall, a late Gothic masterpiece with early Renaissance windows through which three men and the Thirty Years War were launched. By the end, you'll have begun to sense the forces, large and small, that have made Prague tick so strangely for so many centuries. Every building has its secrets, from the laboratory of Emperor Rudolf II's alchemists, to the minuscule pastel cottages of the 400-year-old Golden Lane.

This walk is one of the best for a rainy day—unless that day is Monday, in which case everything is closed. Get moving in the morning—the doors start to shut as early as 3.45 pm. If you have the energy at the end of the walk, you can happily start Walk III through Malá Strana, which is at its best in the evening. Another possibility is to take tram 22 four stops up the hill, which deposits you neatly at the beginning of Walk IV.

---

lunch/cafés

Eating opportunities are limited within the castle walls. However, during the summer a number of seasonal cafés spring up to service the stomachs of the thousands who pass through daily, and you'll have little difficulty finding a passable pizza or a minute steak. The following are the best spots; for added variety, those places listed in Walks III and IV are all within easy reach.

Valdštejnská hospoda (Waldstein Inn), in Valdštejnské nám., just before you begin the climb up to the castle. *11.30–4 pm (lunch)*. Duck, venison, veal and steak in elegant surroundings. Pricier and more satisfying than the other options listed here.

U krále Brabantského, at the foot of the New Castle Steps. *11–10*. The charming façade and location are rather let down by the interior, and this is best described as a Renaissance diner. Nevertheless, it has an ancient history (Wenceslas IV used to stop by) and it's a pleasant place to stop if you fancy soups, sauerkraut, goulash or strudel.

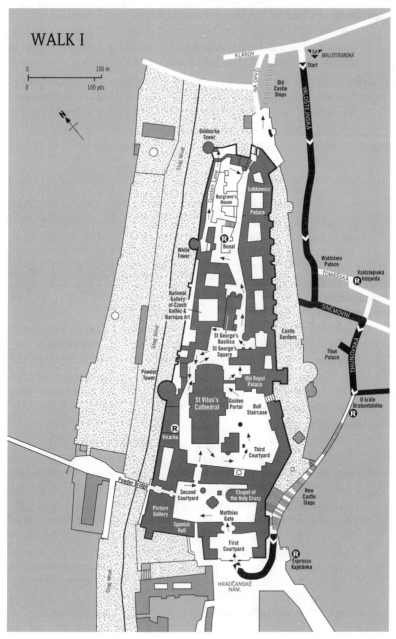

WALK I

0 ———— 100 m
0 ———— 100 yds

N

KLÁROV

MALOSTRANSKÁ

M

Start

NA OPYŠI

Old Castle Steps

VALDŠTEJNSKÁ

Daliborka Tower

Golden Lane

Burgrave's House

Lobkowicz Palace

White Tower

R Bonal

Waldstein Palace

Valdštejnská hospoda R

TOMÁŠSKÁ

National Gallery of Czech Gothic & Baroque Art

ŠNĚMOVNÍ

St George's Basilica
St George's Square

Castle Gardens

Thun Palace

THUNOVSKÁ

Old Royal Palace

Powder Tower

St Vitus's Cathedral

Golden Portal

Bull Staircase

U krále Brabantského R

R Vikárka

Third Courtyard

Powder Bridge

Second Courtyard

Chapel of the Holy Cross

New Castle Steps

Picture Gallery

Matthias Gate

Spanish Hall

Stag Moat

First Courtyard

Espresso Kajetánka R

HRADČANSKÉ NÁM.

Espreso Kajetánka, at the top of the New Castle Steps. *Tues–Sat 11–10, Sun–Mon 11–8.* Suspended on a terrace just above Malá Strana's canopy of quaint orange tiles and smoky chimneys. Come for the view; the food is limited to a handful of snacks and fresh fruit tarts.

Vikárka, in the lane next to the cathedral. *11–10.* Both a busy lunchtime restaurant and a cavernous beer hall, serving all the classics of Czech cuisine. The latter is the jollier alternative and you'll find it below stairs, near the Mihulka tower.

Bonal, just before the Golden Lane. *10–5.* Stand-up café with excellent coffees and fresh sandwiches to go.

Hills were much in demand in the dangerous Dark Ages. Prague's venerable chronicler, Cosmas, was particularly complimentary about the Hradčany hill, comparing its shape to 'the back of a dolphin or a sea-pig'; and he was writing in the 12th century, when the topography would have been clearer than today. Despite the legend that Prague's history began with the soothsaying of Libuše at Vyšehrad (*see* pp. 38–9), the castle is almost certainly the oldest continually-settled part of the city. The Přemysls, Bohemia's first dynasty, fortified the area towards the end of the 9th century. They coexisted happily with their neighbours, a community of cockerel-worshipping pagans, until Prince Bořivoj got Christianity and founded a church. Relations became strained, the infidels revolted, and Bořivoj left town for a while. By the beginning of the 10th century, however, the family was firmly in control. Until the end of Bohemian independence in the 17th century, the castle was home to most of the oddballs to rule the country—and behind the monotonous palatial grandeur of its façade, it's a vast monument to centuries of regal madness.

> *To get up to the castle from Malá Strana station, walk along Valdštejnská. To your right are the glorious gardens of the Polish Embassy (Fürstenberg Palace). They are meant to be closed to the public, but you could always lose your way looking for a visa. Gloomy palaces hem you in for the rest of the street, which leads into Valdštejnské nám. The palace of General Waldstein, whose glorious gardens and life story you'll find in Walk III, runs along one side. The palace is now the Czech Ministry of Culture, and houses a very dusty museum devoted to philosopher and pedagogue, Jan Ámos Komenský (Comenius). Walk up the cobbled street opposite. Turn left at the quiet leafy triangle, and then right up Thunovská. You'll approach a grotesque bust of Winston Churchill, more bullfrog than bulldog, which was a dubious Czech gift to*

*the British Embassy (Thun Palace) lurking at the end of the cul-de-sac to your right. That building's devious location is somehow appropriate—the Baroque façade expands into an unseen Renaissance palace that was the eventual bounty of Major Walter Leslie, one of the assassins of the no-less-treacherous General Waldstein. At the end of the narrow lane in front of you, buttresses straining to keep the sides apart, you begin the climb up the **New Castle Steps** (Nové zámecké schody). Never trust the word 'new' in Prague—there have been steps here since the early 15th century, and the climb follows a 13th-century route from Malá Strana to the castle. At the top of the steps, you'll find the gates to your right. Recover your breath and take in the view of the city.*

The pomp of the castle's façade dates from 1753–1775, when, after centuries of sieges, fires and royal building projects, it had become a crazed accretion that sorely displeased pernickety Queen Maria Theresa. Although the Habsburgs had moved to Vienna over a century before, she still regarded the palace (and Bohemia) as a pleasant little possession, and hired her Viennese court architect, Nicolo Pacassi, to clean it up. He filled in moats and added neo-classical façades with dull abandon although, behind it all, huge chunks of the medieval castle survive. At least Maria Theresa tried in her tasteless way to make the castle pretty; her son, Joseph II, attempted to turn it into a barracks, and succeeded in part. In the century before Czechoslovakia was born in 1918, the castle was all but deserted by the distant Habsburgs. The last emperor to spend any time here was Ferdinand the Gracious after his forced abdication in 1848. A. J. P. Taylor once claimed that Ferdinand's most significant statement was 'I am the Emperor and I want dumplings'. He brought little glory to the castle as he ended his days here. In 1918 it became the seat of the president—a tradition maintained by the Communists, and one that continues today with Václav Havel's occupation of the castle.

*Enter the castle through the main gateway under the Art Nouveau Battling Giants, and take a look at the **castle guards**, resplendent in their bright blue uniforms.*

They wore dull khaki until 1989, but when Václav Havel moved in as president, he got a friend, Theodor Pištěk, to design something more jolly. Pištěk's previous major job had been as costume designer for *Amadeus*, and the gulping guards look dimly aware that they are the victims of a presidential prank. At the changing of the guard ceremony every hour, sweaty rookies often look on the verge of tears and sometimes crack up into blushing laughter when confronted with one video camera too many. Another of Havel's wheezes during the humorous honeymoon that followed the Velvet Revolution was to dress the brass band in red and have them play a tune every Sunday morning. If you're here at midday, keep your eyes left, and on the first floor you'll see them emerge onto the window ledges to blast out a lilting classical piece composed by Michal Kocáb, rock musician and erstwhile MP for central Prague.

> Walk through the first courtyard. Between the pine flagpoles is the **Matthias Gate** (1614), thought to have been designed by Vincenzo Scamozzi. The Vicenza-born architect worked in the service of Emperor Matthias and visited Prague in 1599–1600. He was a close follower of Andrea Palladio, but the elegant serenity of the master's influence gave way in Scamozzi's later work to some of the earliest hints of the Baroque—and this grand gateway is one of the first signs of the new architecture to have appeared in the capital. The Roman triumphal arch is now unhappily immured in a building dividing the first two courtyards, but it originally stood proud and alone between two bridges crossing the outer moats of the castle. As you walk through the gateway, glass doors on either side open up onto broad staircases. On the left is the **Hall of Columns** (Sloupová síň), built between 1924 and 1926.

Three rows of Ionic columns line the walls around the stone staircase, which marches up to doubled iron doors under a copper-panelled roof. The hall is the work of Jože Plečnik (*see* pp. 82–3) who did more to transform the appearance of the castle than anyone since Pacassi. He was appointed Castle Architect in 1920, with an unenviable brief: to modernize the castle in a way unimposing enough to suit the democratic ideals of the new Czechoslovakian state, dignified enough to honour that democracy's president, and tactful enough to complement the existing architectural scheme of the castle. In the context of the monumentalism that surrounded him, it's a balancing act that he carried off with aplomb.

> The staircase leads up to the **Spanish Hall** (Španělský sál).

The hall is used for concerts but otherwise accessible to the public only occasionally. When it is opened, the queues of Praguers that snake through are immense. Their curiosity isn't inspired by the garish neo-Baroque interior, a stucco cavern of mirrors and chandeliers, but by the fact that it used to host the regular meetings of the Communist Party Central Committee.

> Opposite the Hall of Columns another glass doorway leads into the presidential rooms. Once the isolated enclave of Communist greymen, they are now occupied by the team of Václav Havel.

Havel has calmed down considerably since the days when he would ride a scooter through the corridors of power, and his gang now wear more suits than ever before. However, you still may see a relic from his freewheeling past: look out for lank-haired chaps clutching dog-eared reports, or one of the female bodyguards of whom he was notoriously fond.

> *Walk into the second courtyard. Directly in front of you is the **Chapel of the Holy Cross**, designed by Nicolo Pacassi. Turn left and walk across to the northern end of the courtyard, past the Baroque fountain (1686) and the disused well. Through the gateway the **Powder Bridge** crosses what was the northern moat of the castle (see Walk IV). Make as if to walk through the arch, and then suddenly turn left into the **Picture Gallery of Prague Castle** (Obrazárna Pražského hradu), containing works of art kept in the castle since the reign of Emperor Rudolf II (1576–1611). (Open Tues–Sun, April–Sept 9–5, Oct–Mar 9–4; adm.)*

Rudolf summoned artists from across the Continent to Prague, and the court that he assembled became one of the centres of European Mannerism. His collecto-mania became legendary, even in an age when curiosity cabinets cum art galleries were a dime a dozen among Europe's nobles. No inventory survives, but as well as rhinoceros horns, nails from the Ark and the like, Rudolf is thought to have installed some 3000 pictures and 2500 sculptures. This is a sad tribute. The gallery was pillaged by occupying Protestant forces during the Thirty Years War: a moderate pruning by the Saxons in 1631–32 was followed by a systematic ran-sack by Swedes in 1648. (Their naughty Queen Christina later sold most of the loot, reverted to Catholicism and lived off the proceeds in Rome.) Lots of what remained was sold off by Joseph II in 1782. However, the gallery is worth a brief visit to get a feel of the eclectic taste of Rudolf—more of whose collection pops up later on this walk—and the decline of his Habsburg successors.

> *At the time of writing, the collection is temporarily closed, pending a full-scale security review. Two visitors walked off with a Cranach during opening hours and replaced it with a cheap Rembrandt reproduction. The normally Argus-eyed babičky who guard each room didn't notice that anything was amiss for several hours. However, it should have reopened by the time you're reading this.*

The small first room contains the art most closely related to the emperor himself. The portrait skills of one of his court artists, Hans von Aachen, are displayed in two rather atypical works, showing none of the stylized proportions or mild eroticism for which he's best known. It probably had something to do with the subject-matter: his *Head of a Girl* is touched with the affection that a father might be expected to show his daughter, while his full-length *Portrait of Emperor Matthias* flatters the peacock-grandeur of the hated brother who usurped Rudolf's throne. (Aachen waited for Rudolf to die, and then jumped onto

Matthias's payroll.) There's a bust of Rudolf himself by his sculptor, Adriaen de Vries; and the strange work of Joris Hoefnagel, who painted innumerable studies of creatures of the deep and crawlers of the earth, showing a fascination with the order (and decay) of things that was typical of Rudolfine Mannerism (*see* pp. 69–71). The audacious art-swappers took one work by Lucas Cranach the Elder but left behind his *Mocking of Christ*. That can only hint at the cruelty of which the artist was capable, and which made him one of Rudolf's favourite painters.

The Swedes and Saxons were discerning hordes, judging from what they left behind. The rest of the gallery contains works that lay around in the castle for three centuries and were identified only by scientists with X-ray machines in the late 1960s. However, the next room contains an intriguing *Amnon and Tamar* by Lucio Massari. The saga of incest and rape is mysteriously treated as a story of unrequited love: topless Tamar gazes wistfully at her hunk of a half-brother, while the men at the door look as though they're about to break up a tryst rather than leave the scene of the imminent crime. An Oedipal sphinx sitting cryptic under the bed is about the clearest reminder of the incestuous theme.

The next rooms contain a motley collection of 16th- and 17th-century Italian works, but highlights include Guido Reni's *Centaur Nessus abducting Deianeira*, Gentileschi's *Triumphant Amor*, and a *Flagellation of Christ* by Tintoretto (who is also credited with two mediocrities). There's a pretty work by Titian (*Toilet of a Young Lady*) and four paintings by Veronese; the *Portrait of a Jeweller, Jacob König*, shows his shrewd friend who landed the job of Venetian buyer for Rudolf II. The end of the largest room is dominated by the vast *Gathering on Mount Olympus* by Rubens—an exuberant feast of divine nudity where the gaze of ashen-faced Cassandra, peeking out from the wall of flesh, seems to have been the only concession to a moral message that fun-loving Rubens was able to make.

The stone portal at the other end of the room is a remnant from the days when the gallery used to be Rudolf's stables (housing 300 thoroughbred horses), and leads to some dignified portraits by Jan Kupecký, and an excellent *Still Life with Cards and Letter* by Samuel van Hoogstraten (1627–78). Hoogstraten spent his life exploring the effects of perspective, and this work, an almost abstract composition, is imbued with a sense of experimentation that's immediately apparent to the 20th-century mind.

The last room contains some astonishingly bad portraits of assorted Austrians and Spaniards. Rudolf II may have not been the healthiest of Habsburgs, but if you take the portraits of Marie Eleonoro and Marie Leopoldina at face value, it was with these two that the inbreeding finally took hold. The museum has taken the unusual step of advertising the paucity of its own collection by showing photographs of paintings that are now elsewhere in Europe. Take a look at the surreal composite heads by the Milanese Mannerist Giuseppe Arcimboldo, court painter for three generations of Habsburgs between 1562–1587. His portrait of Rudolf as a bunch of fruit (*Vertumnus*, Roman god of the garden) was eagerly awaited in Prague, and the emperor loved it. Ageing Arcimboldo, who had served the Habsburgs for decades, was allowed to return home in 1587, but he continued to receive a salary until his death, and he was awarded the highest imperial title, that of Count Palatine.

> *From the gallery, retrace your steps and turn left through the arch into the Third Courtyard—and stop dead before* **St Vitus's Cathedral** *(Katedrála svatého Víta), looming up before you as you emerge from the tunnel.*

Prince Wenceslas (a.k.a. Good King) founded the first church, a rotunda, on the site in 929 after receiving St Vitus's arm as a token of friendship from the Saxon King Henry I. He dedicated it to the saint in honour of the limb, but also because he hoped to convert the local pagans, who worshipped a four-headed war and fertility god called Svantovít (St Vitus in Czech is *svatý Vít*). The trick was made even easier by the fact that Svantovít liked cocks, a symbol shared by Vitus. Between 1060 and 1096 the church was enlarged into a basilica, but it was under Charles IV that the present construction, one of the finest 14th-century churches in Europe, began to take shape. Building commenced in 1344, months after the future emperor had persuaded his ex-tutor, Pope Clement VI, to promote Bohemia to an archbishopric. Charles hoped to make Prague into a great imperial metropolis, and the cathedral was to be its centrepiece. Having been brought up in Paris, he turned first to a French architect, summoning Matthew of Arras from the papal court at Avignon. Matthew built the east end of the chancel on standard French lines, but luckily for Prague's Gothic architecture, he died in 1352. His replacement, called to the court from Swabia, was **Peter Parler**, the scion of a distinguished family of German masons. His new plan for the nave inaugurated a half-century during which Prague became the most significant centre of Gothic architecture in Europe. Although the church was unfinished at his death in 1399, most of its most notable features are his work. The Hussite wars brought construction to a halt, and the building was closed with a temporary wall which stayed for centuries.

The entire western part of the church, including the grand façade you're looking at, was only completed between 1871 and 1929. Prague's neo-Gothic mania at the end of the last century did its fair share of damage to the town, but the architects' efforts here can hardly be faulted. Their work completed a symbol of Bohemian history, and gave Prague's skyline a focus it had lacked for 500 years.

Although there's an almost too perfect industrial precision to some of the pinnacles and sculptures on the façade, you would be hard-pressed to find the joins in most of the building.

As you launch your gaze through the mammoth pillars lining the noble arch of the nave, you're in the monument to the greatest king ever to rule Bohemia. Charles, on his way to becoming one of the most powerful men in Europe, almost certainly hoped to be canonized after his death à la Louis IX. But he was taking no chances. The Black Death was marching across Europe, and Prague's clerics were warning that the Apocalypse would take place sometime between 1365 and 1375. To add insult to prospective injury, one of the city's leading preachers had recently accused Charles of being the Antichrist. As well as putting his capital firmly on the medieval map, Charles's magnificent offering to God was private insurance that, when weighed in the balance, he would not be found wanting.

The first three chapels on each side date from the early 20th century. Although topped up with older decoration, they are filled with neo-Gothic sculpture that's as lifeless as St Ludmilla, throttled and serene in the first chapel to your right. The stained glass is another modern addition dating from the 1930s. The original Gothic church is thought to have had only one coloured window, and its bold use of clear light was one way in which architect Parler broke from the church's French origins. The windows have a certain garish splendour, but here at least it's hard not to wonder how different a completed 14th-century church might have been. The window in the third chapel was paid for by an insurance company, and celebrates prudent risk-assessment with the psalm 'Those who Sow in Tears Shall Reap in Joy'.

> Walk past the Renaissance tombstones, and the tower of the old cathedral. Its view is the highest in Prague, and as breathtaking as you would expect from a climb of 287 steps (open April–Sept; adm). You're now in the original part of the building. To your left is the **choir** (1557–61), designed by Ferdinand I's court architect, Bonifaz Wohlmut, and surmounted by a tremendous organ dating from the later 18th century. Originally, it closed the western end of the church, but the whole shebang was moved in the 1920s. Just to your right is the shining goldmine of the **Chapel of St Wenceslas**, built between 1362 and 1367 by Peter Parler.

Gentle Wenceslas died at the hands of his brother Boleslav in 935, and has wielded more influence from his grave than he ever did during his life. After killing him, Boleslav cheekily decided that to be the brother of a martyr was no bad thing, and he had the remains transferred to the original rotunda in 939.

Charles exploited his ancestor in a far more systematic fashion. From the example of St Louis, he had learnt how useful national cults were in cementing together a kingdom, and even before his arrival in Prague, he began to turn his ancestor's grave into a shrine. He had the old tomb decorated with silver statues of the Apostles (which his father, John of Luxemburg, immediately pawned to finance his latest foreign adventure); and when the cathedral was begun, he had Parler change his plans for the nave to build this chapel on the site of the original grave.

There are two doorways. The northern portal in the nave contains the ring to which the saint allegedly clung as he was hacked to death, although the church where the deed occurred, outside Prague, has always indignantly claimed to have the knocker concerned. The arch is flanked by sculptural warnings—on the left, a crumbling figure of Peter denying Christ, and on the right a vicious demon yanking Judas' tongue from his mouth—but the interior is an inviting mosaic of gilt plaster and semi-precious stones, unevenly framing and crowding over the painted Passion scenes below. The chapel is a Gothic painting in three glittering dimensions, suffused with the shot of mysticism that ran through the otherwise eminent worldliness of Charles. The number of stones (about 1370) corresponds to the date of its construction (and, if Prague's clerics were to be believed, the rough date of the Second Coming); and if you can lay your hands on a Bible, take a look at ch. 21 of the Book of Revelations. The chapel is a literally-conceived model of the Heavenly Jerusalem, whose arrival would herald the end of history.

The full ramifications of the original decoration, which Charles illuminated with 144 perpetually-burning candles, would have been hard for the modern mind to appreciate; but impressive as the chapel is, there have been some changes over the years. The emperor and his wife are still kneeling near the crucified Christ over the chapel altar, but the (heavily restored) paintings on the upper part of the wall date from 1509. They show scenes from the *Legend of St Wenceslas*, as well as portraits of Vladislav II of Jagellon and his rather unappealing wife Anne, who flank the arched window. The **tomb** in the centre was once as gold-plated and jewel-encrusted as the rest of the chapel (and contained small reliquaries for 18 more saintly scraps) but Charles's sons proved as impious as their grandfather, John of Luxemburg, had been. Wenceslas IV melted down bits and pieces to make gold coins, while Sigismund turfed the saint out and carted away the whole coffin during his occupation of the castle in 1420. Wenceslas's semi-precious home dates from the early 20th century, and represents one of the rare occasions when Prague's pedantic neo-Gothic restorers didn't even try to match the original work.

The chapel also contains a Gothic statue of the saint by Peter Parler's nephew, Henry; some more odd stained glass (a translucent vision from the late 1960s);

and in the south-east corner is a sanctuarium, built here by Charles so that Wenceslas could guard the cathedral's wine and wafers. The emperor also gave the chapel tremendous secular significance by establishing a new coronation ceremony linked closely to the cult of the saint. Much of it took place here, and the forged door in the south-west corner leads to a small room containing the old **crown jewels** of Bohemia. You'll have a job getting to see them, though; the door is closed with seven different locks and to track down the scattered keys, you'd have to sweet-talk some fairly imposing figures, ranging from the President of the Republic to the Archbishop of Prague. In any case, any pleb who puts them on signs his own death warrant. The legend was last fulfilled (or just possibly created) in 1942, when *Reichsprotektor* Reinhard Heydrich is said to have sneered with Teutonic arrogance when the grizzled guardian of the jewels warned him of the curse; shortly after trying on the crown, he was cut down by assassins. An extension of the story, which begins to damage its own case, is that Heydrich's two sons also had a go. One died a fairly predictable death on the eastern front, and Nemesis apparently caught up with the other at the end of a mad stallion's hoof.

> *Good King Wenceslas was one of the first buried here, but like any cathedral worth its salt, St Vitus's in its heyday served as a necropolis for the corpses of the high and mighty. In the central aisle is the white marble **Habsburg mausoleum** (1566–89), containing the remains of the first two generations to rule Bohemia.*

Ferdinand I died in Vienna, but the family decided to honour St Vitus's with his posthumous presence to shore up their shaky claim to be the hereditary rulers of Bohemia. His wife joined him, and in 1577 Maximilian II arrived here at the head of a funeral procession that chroniclers noted was the grandest that Prague had ever seen. All three characters were sculpted sleeping on top of the tomb, next to each other and in full regalia. Maximilian's peculiar son, Rudolf II, made his own arrangements (as you'll soon see), as well as those of his mother when she died in 1603. The funeral procession that he organized for her was a suitably lavish affair, marred only by the fact that Rudolf himself failed to turn up, despite plans to attend in disguise.

> *The Habsburg contingent only topped up a church that was already brimming with human tissue, thanks to Charles IV's mania for collecting relics. Cultured and cosmopolitan he may have been, but he was truly medieval when it came to saintly souvenirs. On his jaunts abroad, he begged, borrowed and, according to legend, stole (once, from the pope) about 200 sacred objects. When his nephew, Charles V of France, asked the emperor in 1356 for help in recovering his father (John the Bountiful,*

> who had been confiscated by the Black Prince at the Battle of Poitiers),
> Charles agreed to mediate with the victorious English only after being
> given two thorns from Christ's crown and splinters of the True Cross. In
> 1354 he proudly wrote to Bohemia's first archbishop, 'I do not think that
> you will find another place in the whole of Europe, except Rome, where
> pilgrims can seek out so many holy relics as in the cathedral of St Vitus'.
> If you go to the **St Andrew's Chapel**, next to that of Wenceslas, you'll
> see that Prague did not yield second place to Rome for want of trying.

The chapel contains a picture known as the **vera icon** (true image). The Vatican also has one—a messy state of affairs, given that the *vera icon* is the miraculously-imprinted hanky used by the (strangely anagrammatical) St Veronica to wipe the sweat off Jesus on the road to Calvary. The story goes that Charles set his heart on the thing and asked if he could have it; the pope said no way, so the cunning emperor asked if he could copy it instead. The weak point of the story is that the pope trusted Charles enough to agree—otherwise, it's not hard to believe the punch line, that the emperor returned the copy and you're looking at the original. The castle catalogue casts some doubt on the matter by listing the work as a 'Gothic panel painting from about the year 1400'.

> In the next chapel is the entrance to the **crypt of the cathedral** (open
> 9–4.45; adm). The tour is a confusing journey through the convoluted
> architectural history of the cathedral. Columns and tombstones
> unearthed over the years litter your path as you wend through the 11th-
> century crypt of the basilica, the cathedral's foundations and those of its
> original choir, 20th-century masonry, and the northern apse of
> Wenceslas's rotunda. A plan of the two older churches in the penulti-
> mate room may help you piece together the puzzle, although it's hardly
> any less complicated. The wooden steps take you back out into the nave,
> but first take a look at the **royal crypt** in the room to the right, next to
> more of the basilica's foundations.

The spotlit sepulchre is the bizarre resting place of Bohemia's greatest kings, silently awaiting Gabriel's trumpet in an avant-garde collection of stainless steel and granite sarcophagi—all were given a postmortem and reinterred here during the final stages of the church's completion in 1928–1935. You'll find Charles IV here, next to his four wives who have all been tossed into the same stone box. Rudolf is in his original pewter coffin, but he's a lost and lonely character even in death. He is separated from his forebears (in the mausoleum upstairs), his internal organs (in the Saxon chapel), and his successors (who deserted Prague altogether after the Battle of the White Mountain—*see* p. 53—and now lie in the Capuchines in Vienna).

From the crypt, you emerge back into the centre of the nave, a good point from which to compare the medieval part of the cathedral with its 20th-century extension.

From here you can see one of Parler's most significant contributions to the design of the church, the net-vault of the choir, which breaks free of the purely practical concern of cross-ribbed vaulting, the need to stop the roof from falling down, and shows the move towards abstraction that came to characterize late Gothic architecture across Europe. Parler is thought to have borrowed his ideas from England, possibly after Charles IV's daughter married King Richard II. The work is actually a model of restraint compared to the exuberance of English vault design over the previous century; nevertheless, it was the first time that the ideas had been used in a major Continental church. Up in the triforium are a series of busts by Parler and his workshop. They're among the earliest portraits in Gothic art, but you'll need binoculars to see them properly. As well as Charles and family, Parler and Matthew of Arras are represented—an unusual honour for the time, which shows the respect that Charles had for his architects.

The line of chapels on the right continues with the **Royal Oratory**, designed for Vladislav II by his court architect, Benedict Ried, and built in 1493. The vault and the entrance are decorated with fantastic branch-like ribs, gnarled stone bows bent across the vault. Ried, like Parler, had radical ideas when it came to vaulting, as he showed to magnificent effect in his design for the Vladislav Hall, which you'll see soon.

*Walk past the **Waldstein Chapel**, containing the Gothic tombstones of the cathedral's two architects. Opposite the chapel is a relief showing what looks to be a very orderly iconoclastic rampage through the cathedral, which occurred in 1619. You're now entering the oldest part of the church, but to go any further you have to get round the incandescent Baroque **tomb of St John Nepomuk**, fashioned from 3700 pounds of solid silver after a design by Fischer von Erlach the Younger.*

What John would have made of it all can only be guessed. Larger-than-life angels support the coffin; the swooning saint clutches a crucifix above the lid; and four heavenly bodies float over it all, dangling from wall-brackets. The cleric had been venerated in an unassuming way from the moment he was lobbed off the Charles Bridge in 1383 (*see* p. 253), but three centuries later he suddenly found himself at the heart of the Jesuit drive to re-Catholicize Bohemia. The monks needed a native saint, and John fitted the bill—he was untainted (to both sides) by any involvement in Europe's religious schism, he was Czech, and he was dead. In 1715, a canonization committee gathered in Prague to investigate the old legend that John had been martyred for refusing to tell King Wenceslas IV what the queen had said in the confession box. When his rotting coffin was exhumed from his chapel (opposite the tomb), the confessor's skull was found to contain a lump of organic matter. The committee's three doctors examined it, solemnly swore that it was John's incorrupt tongue—a useful organ, given the basis of his proposed canonization—and the 100 or so commissioners hurried to Rome with the news. The pope promptly beatified John—and sensing that they had backed a winner, the Jesuits pulled out all the stops. Six years later their doctors declared that not only was his tongue still throbbing with life, but growing steadily. That clinched it, and in 1729 John was canonized. To make his cult even more palatable to Praguers, the Jesuits filled the castle fountains with beer and wine on his annual feast day. They couldn't quite get the cathedral renamed, but after John was reburied in this awe-inspiring piece of kitsch in 1736, it effectively became the high altar. Curious scientists examined the tongue in the early 1980s and declared that it was actually a desiccated brain. Sadly, it's no longer available for public worship, having been removed to an inaccessible part of St Vitus's treasury. It apparently resembled the condom-like object being pointed out by the priggish cherub on top of the coffin.

> *The next chapel along contains yet more bodily remains—the two Přemysl Otakars in tombs sculpted by Parler, and under the slab marked with the Habsburg double-headed eagle, a vault containing Rudolf II's exiled viscera. There are also fragments of a mural painting* (The Adoration of the Magi) *which may have been painted by Master Theodoric, court artist to Charles IV—you'll see some of his most exceptional work later on this walk (see p. 137). As you pass the centre of the cathedral, pay your respects to the **altar to St Vitus** on your left, especially if you're afflicted with an annoying twitch or you've been bitten by a mad dog. Vitus hasn't done well over the years, outshone first by Wenceslas and then by John Nepomuk, and his tomb is an insignificant 19th-century affair. At least Charles IV did him the courtesy of cobbling together a full body.*

On the left as you pass the next two chapels are two more **oak reliefs**, dating from 1631, which show the flight from Prague of Frederick of the Palatinate (motto: I Know Not How to Turn) after the defeat of his Protestant armies at the Battle of the White Mountain. Malicious they may be—they were commissioned by the victorious Ferdinand II—but the second is a lovely snapshot of 17th-century Prague, all the king's horses and men galloping in hasty retreat from the medieval castle across the bridge and through the Old Town Square.

On the right just past the choir is an amazing **wooden altar** (1896–99) by the Czech sculptor František Bílek. Its simplicity, and the pain that it exudes, owes much to the humanistic traditions of late Gothic art in Bohemia, but Bílek's Symbolism developed a spiritual language independent of any single religion or country. His **Crucifixion** is a masterpiece: Christ rising slowly from the ropes and nails of his cross, locked into meditation while a heedless humanity despairs at his feet; and on the altar, the return of hope, portrayed by a single arm stretching up with its offering.

> *Bílek's sculpture is a modern addition that works; the Art Nouveau stained glass by Alfons Mucha (a 1931 comic-strip celebrating SS Cyril and Methodius) is one that doesn't. You're back in the 20th-century half of the cathedral. The chapel now contains the grave of Cardinal Tomášek, Archbishop of Prague until his death in 1992, and an ever-more vocal focus of opposition in the years before the 1989 revolution. In 1987, the Communists mocked him as a 'general without an army'; by the time of his death, they had lost the battle and the mourners who attended the funeral here included two underground fighters who had become presidents, Václav Havel and Lech Wałesa.*

> *From the cathedral, turn left into the expanse of the Third Courtyard, where you'll find a large granite obelisk (a memorial to the dead of the 1914–18 war), and at the far southern end, the offices of the president. On the southern façade of the church is the central **tower**, which marked the front of the cathedral until its modern completion.*

It's almost 100 metres high, although a fair chunk of that (38 metres) is made up of the multi-storey Baroque dome added by Pacassi in 1770. Four bells hang in the tower, of which the largest is **Sigismund**, an 18-ton monster on the first floor. Bells caused no end of trouble in the 16th century. They couldn't be touched by anyone impure (a category that included all women), and pubescent boys dressed in white had to be engaged to transport them from foundry to belfry. Sigismund, dating from 1549, was the successor to two earlier bells. The first was dragged on sledges from the Old Town by hundreds of pretty urchins in 1534; after several days, they got it to the gate of the castle, only for it to roll out of control and break into pieces. No chances were taken with the next one, which was cast in the castle grounds and hung in 1538—three years before smashing to the ground during the great fire of 1541. Sigismund finally made it in 1549. Like the carillon of Loretto, it survived the great Austro-Hungarian bell massacre of 1918 (*see* p. 210) and can be heard booming across Hradčany on Sunday mornings. The ornate golden grille in the arched window dates from Rudolf II's reign (hence the 'R' just above)—so too do the two clocks, the higher of which shows the hour, the lower the minute.

*To the right of the tower is the **Golden Portal**, once the main entrance to the cathedral.*

The emphasis on the southern façade is unusual in church design—Charles effectively turned the cathedral around, so that Wenceslas could have the prominence that he deserved (his chapel is just to the right of the doorway). Another of Peter Parler's notable touches appears under the bullet-shaped arches, where ribs spray into the air from the door, again inspired by England and again unique for its time on the Continent.

*Above the gate is a **mosaic of the Last Judgment** dating from 1370–71.*

The mosaic, thought to have been pieced together by Venetians after a cartoon drawn up by artists in Charles's court, is the largest on any Gothic building other than Orvieto Cathedral. Kneeling below Christ the Judge are patron saints; to the left, on Christ's right hand, the luckier resurrected corpses emerge from their coffins; while to the right, wretched sinners wail and gnash their teeth as they're herded into Hell. The not-so-humble suppliants on either side of the central arch, crowned and ermined, are Charles and his fourth wife, Elizabeth of Pomerania. The epic theme ought to shine out in glorious technicolour, but it has become an almost monochromatic smudge. Quartz, opals and chalcedonies were used in the design, but so too were 30 chemically unstable shades of enamelled glass which have finally faded to grey under the impact of the late 20th century. The Getty Institute has promised to fund restoration, and by the time you read this the mosaic should be either a veiled mystery or a radiant blaze.

*Directly opposite the mosaic is the **Bull Staircase**, another ingenious Plečnik construction, which runs down to the Garden on the Ramparts. That contains benches, pavilions and two obelisks that commemorate a miracle to be described shortly. Pop down to have a look and then enter the **Old Royal Palace** (Starý královský palác), on your right as you re-emerge up the stairs.*

Since the castle was first fortified, this has been the site of the royal residence, and inside are three layers of palace, spanning the Romanesque and the Renaissance. The older halls are now below ground level—a feature you come to expect in Prague—as a result of the original unevenness of the Third Courtyard, which sloped steeply towards the east until paved during Rudolf II's reign.

*The topmost palace, and the one you'll see first, is the **Vladislav Hall** (Vladislavský sál). (Open Tues–Sun April–Sept 9–4.45, Oct–Mar 9–3.45; adm.)*

The hall was built between 1486 and 1502 by Benedict Ried, court architect to Vladislav II of Jagellon. Over the previous century the palace here had been deserted: in 1383 rollicking Wenceslas IV had taken the toadies and flunkies of his court to the high jinks to be found in the Old Town, where he built a new Royal Court, and the castle fell into ruin. For decades the only visitors were passing Hussite mobs or the invading army of Wenceslas's brother, Sigismund. But in 1483 life returned suddenly. Vladislav was now king, and city pressures had become too much—his Catholic officials had just been defenestrated by Hussites from the Old Town Hall, and the final straw came when he opened the windows of the Royal Court one morning to be greeted by an arrow carrying the scrawled message, 'Get out of town, Polack'. He left in a hurry, crossing the Vltava by boat at night, and wasted no time in fortifying and expanding the desolate castle.

Vladislav built a new hall above the old palace partly because of his belief—all too often disproved in the castle's history—that 'high' meant 'safe'; but it was also the expression of the worldly grandeur that now permeated the court. The structure represents the culmination of the Bohemian late Gothic style named after the Polish king (*see* p. 68). In its magnificent vault, ribs shoot up like monstrous tendrils from its wall shafts, intertwining across five gently articulated bays and somehow meandering into star-like flower petals in the centre. Ried used anything that seemed to fit the opulence required: the broad rectangular windows are pure Renaissance, sneaking into Bohemia years before the Italian influence began to be felt in western Europe; spiralling pillars and classical entablatures frame the doors of the hall.

Surrounded by the almost tangible space of the hall (62 x 16 x 13 m) you understand the awe of the chronicler who breathlessly recorded, 'There was no other building like it in all of Europe, none that was longer, broader and higher and yet had no pillars'. Horses fitted in here comfortably; mounted stewards and cupbearers lined the sides during banquets, and tournaments were a regular feature. Under the reign of Rudolf II, it became a bazaar; a contemporary engraving shows it full of high-hatted and haggling merchants, and even a small scrum of bargain-hunting Persians. Since 1918, the president of the Republic has been sworn in here, and this was where Václav Havel took the oath of office that ended 40 years of Communist rule in December 1989.

> To the right of the entrance is a door leading to the **Ludvík Wing**, built in similar style by Ried between 1502 and 1509, and named after Vladislav's successor, Ludvík of Jagellon (who ruled from 1516–1526). Inside, on the same floor as the hall, are the two rooms of the **Czech Chancellery**.

Walk through the portal of the first room (marked with Ludvík's initials) into the next chamber, in which the chancellor and the governors used to deliberate under the Habsburgs.

*It was here that Prague's most significant **defenestration** took place on 23 May 1618.*

Count Thurn and other Bohemian Protestant noblemen confronted the two hated Catholic governors appointed by Ferdinand I, and after explaining their grievances, tossed both out of the window to your left (*see* p. 52). According to a contemporary account of events, 'They loudly screamed 'Ach, ach oweh!' and attempted to hold on to the narrow window ledge, but Thurn beat their knuckles until they were both obliged to let go.' Their secretary, Fabricius, protested and followed them down. All three plunged some 50 feet, but landed more or less comfortably in a dungheap. After interviewing a number of witnesses, most of whom swore that they had seen the Virgin Mary parachute the men to safety, the Church declared it a miracle; and following the defeat of Bohemian Protestantism at the Battle of the White Mountain, two obelisks were set up in what's now the Garden on the Ramparts to commemorate the glorious event. They mark where the governors came to rest. No similar honour was accorded the humble Fabricius.

From here walk back into the hall, and go through the first door on the opposite side of the hall.

The staircase spirals up to the offices of the **New Land Rolls**, a land registry institution similar to the Norman Domesday Book. The walls and ceilings are decorated with scores of colourful crests, the emblems of the clerks between 1561 and 1774. If you walk through to the next room, you'll see a mid-16th-century cabinet containing the rolls themselves, highly unofficial-looking hand-painted tomes decorated with rainbows, planets and various flora and fauna.

*Back in the hall, turn left and take the second door to the left into the **Diet**.*

Originally part of the palace below, it was rebuilt by Ried in about 1500 only to be completely destroyed by the fire of 1541. Ferdinand I's architect, Bonifaz Wohlmut, designed the present room between 1559 and 1563, copying Ried's vaulting and making his own contribution to the hall's Renaissance motifs with two mutant Doric pilasters, twisted like liquorice sticks into three dimensions around the door. The Diet was the supreme court in medieval times, and the place where the Estates met until 1848; if the emperor wanted to meet his Czech subjects (which was not often after the Battle of the White Mountain), they all assembled here. Nobles and clergy sat on either side of the central throne. In case the town representatives were in any doubt about their insignificance in Habsburg

Bohemia, they were given one collective vote and left to watch the proceedings from the gallery on your left.

> *As you leave the Diet, to your left is the entrance to the **All Saints' Chapel**. It was built by Peter Parler as part of Charles IV's palace, but after the 1541 fire, its vault was rebuilt, and Baroque additions have left it an unimpressive appendage to the rest of the hall. Opposite you is an **observation terrace**, a popular spot from which to look for any lingering remains of the defenestratees' dungheap (unfortunately its rough location is hidden by a covered passage). Leave the hall through the **Riders' Staircase** on your right, built by Ried in around 1500. Knights summoned to amuse the diners with a spot of horseplay would storm up these shallow steps on their steeds. The pointed cutaway section on the portal was to make sure that nothing embarrassing happened to their plumes.*

> *At the foot of the staircase, more steps on your left lead down to the predecessors of the Vladislav Hall. At the very lowest level is the Romanesque gloom of the 12th-century **Soběslav Palace**.*

Impressive though it must have been back in the 12th century, to the modern mind its gloomy arches are reminiscent of nothing so much as a short stretch of railway tunnel. Its most interesting structural feature is a Romanesque fireplace.

> *On the intermediate level are a number of chambers from various palatial extentions built between the mid-13th and the late 14th century. The largest room is the **Charles Hall**, built by Emperor Charles IV in the mid 1300s.*

Charles had little use for the sombre cavern that he found awaiting him when he moved to Prague. He used it to store the wines that he brought back from his travels, and built a new palace on top. Although only this hall survives, its high-ribbed grandeur can still hint at a building that was designed to outshine the Paris Louvre, in keeping with the emperor's peaceful megalomania.

At the time of writing, the hall contains little to see other than copies of some of the sculptures hidden in the triforium of St Vitus's cathedral. However, there are elaborate plans afoot to transform it into a fortified treasury, with display cases that would sink nightly into the Soběslav Palace, for the more spectacular baubles amassed during the castle's history. The range of exhibits will include countless monstrances and jewelled crucifixes, and possibly even the accursed crown jewels (which were stored here during the war). There is also a chance that the castle's relic collection will be put on show. Until 1989 the po-faced authorities showed a reluctance to show off their holy titbits but times are changing. Efforts have been made to release the tongue of John Nepomuk (the Church has so far put its foot down), and among the other objects that you could look out for are Moses' staff, the Virgin Mary's robe and veil, several shirts worn by Jesus on the cross, and a crystal pitcher containing the tablecloth from the Last Supper. With luck they will be labelled, but if not, read between the lines.

> *Retrace your footsteps to the Rider's Staircase and leave the palace complex. You'll emerge in St George's Square (nám. u sv. Jiří), originally much larger and the heart of the medieval castle (the buildings to the north are neo-Gothic 19th-century creations). Opposite the majestic chancel of St Vitus's is the charming early Baroque façade of the* **Basilica of St George** *(Bazilika sv. Jiří) and neighbouring* **Chapel of St John Nepomuk.** *After noting that its towers are of different widths and turning to p. 156 for the quirky reasons why, enter the church. (Open April–Sept 9–5, Oct–Mar 9–4; adm.)*

The perky orange-on-brown pilasters and dunce's cap of a dome cover an incongruously sombre Romanesque interior. The church was the second to be founded in the castle (921) and predates the Cathedral of St Vitus. Strictly speaking, its present interior dates back to 1142 when it was rebuilt after a fire, but zealous restoration at the end of the last century has robbed it of gloom and turned it into a spanking-clean model of neatly hewn pillars and masonry. To your right as you enter is the Chapel of St John Nepomuk. He and his tongue are in the cathedral, and the bones and skull grinning below the altar belong to one of the early abbesses. The church was an even more crowded cemetery than St Vitus's. Most bones were removed, but at the end of the nave are the tombs of three early Přemysl rulers. The wooden tent on the right houses Vratislav II, next to Boleslav II and then Oldřich.

Between the Baroque steps winding up to the chancel is the 12th-century **crypt**, containing the Romanesque tympanum that used to crown the southern portal of the church, with minuscule abbesses and kings attending the coronation of the Virgin. It also shelters a grim sculpture of a decomposing skeleton, shielding her groin with a gesture of modesty that seems deeply inadequate in the face of snapping sinews and an abdomen under attack by a host of creepy-crawlies. The work dates from 1726 and represents *Vanitas*, an age-old thematic reminder of the way of all flesh; although morbid Prague legend insists that it's a portrait of a murdered woman, whose killer inexplicably tried to atone for his sins by sculpting his victim's corpse.

At the top of the steps is the chancel, decorated with fading Romanesque frescoes of the Heavenly Jerusalem, and to the right is the **Chapel of St Ludmilla**. The saint was Prince Wenceslas's grandmother and spiritual adviser, strangled at prayer with her veil by his pagan mother Drahomirá, who hoped thereby to coax her son back into the cock-worshipping fold. It was an optimistic scheme, and it soon collapsed: Wenceslas took Ludmilla's side, and had her remains transferred here in 925; Drahomirá died, apparently swallowed up into Hell on what is now Loretánská street. Sadly, the chapel is inaccessible, having been firmly closed off since a 17th-century German workman temporarily absconded with some of the saint's bones.

> When you leave the church, turn right and then right again into the neighbouring **St George's Convent**. The Benedictine convent was the first in Bohemia, founded by Mlada, the sister of Boleslav II, in 973. She went to Rome to ask the pope to make Bohemia a bishopric, and he not only agreed but also gave her an abbess's staff to take home. The nuns are long gone though, having thrown off their habits when the fanatically enlightened despot, Joseph II, abolished all the empire's religious institutions in 1782. He turned the convent into a penitentiary for bewildered priests to consider the error of their ways. Despite its venerable age, successive reconstructions have left it a dull building, except that it contains the **National Gallery of Czech Gothic and Baroque Art**. (Open Tues–Sun, 10–6; adm.)

The collection is divided into two sections, Gothic art in the basement and on the ground floor, and Mannerism and Baroque on the first floor.

The earliest Gothic art in Bohemia dates from the beginning of the 14th century. The slender and elegant Madonnas in the first room of the basement, their faces half turned away, show how Bohemian art was beginning to escape the rigid formality of its Byzantine progenitors. Figures became more robust, with even heavier features, typified by the *Strahov Madonna* (c. 1350), almost struggling with her overgrown brat. The break with Orthodox art had begun to occur across western Europe; but the second feature marked the birth of Bohemia's independent artistic traditions, and during the few decades of Charles IV's rule, made its painting unique in Europe.

To your left as you leave the room is the gallant *St George*, plunging a lost standard into the mouth of a downed dragon (the flag's gone missing, but you can see it in the copy of the work that now stands in the Third Courtyard). The bronze statue, which dates from 1373, was designed as a free-standing work, one of the first in Europe to break out of the Gothic inability to conceive of sculpture (any more than painting or architecture) as an independent art form. That said, it's not easy to see what Europe's proto-sculptor had in mind; puny George is dwarfed by a remarkably life-like horse, recast with the rather different techniques and mentality of two centuries later.

In the room to your right is the *Vyšší Brod (Hohenfurth) Altarpiece*. The most notable feature of the nine paintings is their use of contrasting colours to create the illusion of depth, a century before the laws of perspective twinkled in the eyes of the clever Florentines. It's most remarkable in *The Descent of the Holy Ghost*: huddled Apostles swirl in a sea of reds and greens and indigoes, yet the space around them appears almost three-dimensional.

> *The loudmouthed creature at the bottom of the set of steps with the droopy ears is a gargoyle. It's mysteriously called* Capricorn, *though less goat-like a beast you never did see. Walk past its howling canine companion into the room containing the work of* **Master Theodoric**.

Theodoric is the first of Bohemia's painters to emerge from misty anonymity— and as you gaze at the six paintings on display here, you'll understand why. Bohemia's experiments with colour values and facial modelling reach their culmination in these panels, which have a vitality that survives six centuries. Huge saints spread onto the edges of their medallion-studded frames; their powerful human ugliness crowds forward into the small room; and with just the crow's feet of an eye or the downturn of a lip, Theodoric gives them an expressiveness deeper than anything that had come before. The panels are from the Chapel of the Holy Cross at Charles IV's castle at Karlštejn, where there are over 100 more (it's closed until about the year 2000—*see* p. 395). Theodoric was the emperor's court painter—a radical choice for a man brought up amidst the delicacy of French art, and one which almost makes his other quirks seem unimportant.

> *Up the stairs is a café, but hold your horses—a golden age draws to a close in the next room.*

With Charles's death and the coronation of his wastrel son Wenceslas IV in 1378, Bohemian art became increasingly refined. Sophistication replaced spiritual mystery, and the paintings of women take on a doll-like charm. Look, for example, at *SS Catherine, Mary Magdalene and Margaret*, languid rosy-cheeked triplets. As you walk along the next corridor, the line of Madonnas become mothers, while motherhood is heavily romanticized in the process. The *St Vitus's Madonna* shows the process in all its treacle, and it's especially apparent in the sculptures. The trend towards humanization takes a different form in most of the men of late Gothic art; the corridor is filled with hirsute and/or bald saints, while Christ suffers and is tortured with a greater intensity than ever before.

> *Up the steps and to your left is a small room containing the very big* **Tympanum of the Northern Portal of the Týn Church**, *dating from*

around 1380–90. The central scene is the work of either Peter Parler or one of his team then working on St Vitus's Cathedral.

Compare its sense of balance and perspective with the clumping neanderthals on either side, flagellating and crowning Christ, which were the work of lesser artists. The tympanum was originally gilded and painted, but the colour has disappeared, along with much of the top scene, where diabolical amphibians struggle with a rather unconcerned angel, ripping a poor soul apart in the process.

The work in the next corridor represents the final period of Gothic art in Bohemia.

By the time you get to the *Žebrák Lamentation*, the regular cast of characters mourning the dead Christ have a restraint that's still utterly Gothic, but they have begun to sprout the extra inches and shrunken pinheads that are characteristic of Mannerist art; and a strange sense of movement pervades the sculpture, from the rolling curtain of drapery to the Medusa-like locks of Christ. The floor ends with the carvings of Master I. P., a shadowy character who lived in Prague between 1520 and 1525, and who left behind a series of masterful woodcuts, showing all the devotion to north European foliage characteristic of the Danube School.

*On the second floor, the pace heats up. Despite the **Žebrák Lamentation**, the gallery's shift from Gothic to the Mannerism of Rudolf II's court painters is abrupt.*

As you walk up the stairs, you're ambushed by the rather incredible eroticism of the *Epitaph of the Goldsmith Müller*, by Bartholomeus Spranger. Sex permeated the art of the emperor's court—generally in its kinkier forms—and here Spranger has turned Christ into a coquettish pin-up, sly, pouting and wrapped in the strangest loincloth that you'll have ever seen. It was Spranger's memorial to his father-in-law, and bereaving relatives (rare portraits by the artist) line the bottom of the scene. Spranger himself thought it one of his greatest successes, and its almost reflective iridescence is one of the best examples of the feature that typified his work—but quite what the stern mourners thought about being extras in a Mannerist skin-flick can only be suspected.

The collection also contains a rippling *Hercules with the Apples of the Hesperides* by Rudolf II's sculptor, Adriaen de Vries, the only full-length work by the artist to have escaped the attentions of the Swedish art collectors of 1648 (*see* p. 121). The *Allegory of the Reign of Rudolf II* (1603) by Dirck de Quade van Ravesteyn is typical of the many apotheoses that were produced to celebrate a pipe-dream vision of Rudolf II's crisis-ridden reign. Peace, Justice and Plenty fondle each other's breasts, while an iron-clad imperial bouncer keeps a curious

Turk at the door. Finally, the landscapes by the Flemish Roelandt Savery show some of the talents of a man whom the emperor sent to the Alps when he wanted to know what they looked like.

Baroque painting begins with the restrained touch of Karel Škréta, but its dubious culmination is heralded by the Last Judgment trumpet in the ear of *St Jerome* by Michael Willmann. Removed from the sensory wonderland of Prague's Baroque churches, Willman's work, and much of that which follows, has all the unpleasant drama of a fish twitching out of water. The heroic proportions and animation of the country's Baroque sculpture make it no less peculiar under the harsh light of the gallery—but it's far more fun. The quiver that begins with Jäckel's *Mary, Mother of Sorrows* becomes an earthshaking crescendo among the statues of Matthias Braun and Maximilian Brokof, the two greatest sculptors of Baroque Prague. Braun's *St Jude* is the most spectacular example. The sculptor studied in Venice and probably Rome, and with this statue, he seems to have made an attempt to capture the ecstasy of Bernini's *St Theresa* in the frame of an octogenarian. The result is heartstopping in every sense, a whirlwind of frenzied rags and varicose veins. Brokof's armed and arrogant Moors are models of restraint by comparison.

Past the paintings by the Czech Petr Brandl, you'll find the remarkable work of Jan Kupecký (1667–1740), a melancholy Czech exile who spent most of his life shuttling between Vienna and Nuremberg. Kupecký lived off commissions from rich buyers and trod a thin line between flattery and honesty. With his superb *Portrait of the Miniaturist, Karl Brun*, he just about lets the diabolically charming subject, swathed in silk dressing-gown and furry shadow, get away with the concealment of a faraway stare, but he's less sparing of himself. He looks downright shocked by what he found when painting his *Self Portrait with the Artist's Wife*. It might just be what he met in the mirror, but it's worth bearing in mind that his wife was busily being unfaithful at the time. That's her again, clutching a Bible in the next painting, *Penitent Spouse*, and only you can judge what Kupecký thought of her oath of fidelity.

> *From the gallery, walk into the narrow lane ahead of you (Vikářská). The present buildings date from the early 18th century, but Rudolf II's **alchemists** used to live in earlier houses here. Sunk in the shadows of the cathedral's flying buttresses and vomiting gargoyles, their laboratory was in the **Powder Tower** (Prašná brána), also known as Mihulka, on your right. (Open Tues–Sun, April–Sept 9–5, Oct–Mar 9–4; adm.)*

The tower was built as an armoury in the 15th century; a foundry had been set up by the 16th century; and under the reign of Rudolf II, scientists and quacks from across Europe hopefully distilled their aqua vitae and toiled with base metals here. Despite rigid admission tests administered by Rudolf II's quality controller Tadeáš Hájek of Hájek, during which applicants had to transmute a pound of lead into gold, a motley crew of adventurers and charlatans were taken on as imperial alchemists. Among them was the incredible English duo of **Edward Kelley and John Dee**. Kelley, who lost his ears in England and his legs in Prague, was a rather magnificent fraud, but Dee was a true Renaissance scholar. He has gone down in Prague legend as the trickster who wormed his way into Rudolf II's confidence by translating bird-warbles; in fact, by the time he arrived in Prague with Kelley in 1584, his Europe-wide reputation was established, thanks in no small part to a giant mechanical dung beetle with which he had amazed the Fellows of Trinity College, Cambridge, some 40 years before. While in the capital, he had his son baptized in the nearby cathedral, but that wasn't enough to placate an alarmed papal nuncio who eventually persuaded the emperor to expel the English sorcerers from the capital. Kelley was to return, and give birth to another string of Prague legends (*see* p. 104).

Any alchemy that survived Rudolf II's abdication in 1611 ended with the outbreak of the Thirty Years War. The tower was used as an ammunition dump by occupying Swedish forces in 1648, until it blew up. It has since been rebuilt, and now houses a museum devoted to its strange history. The basement (through the gate and down a curving set of stone steps to your left) sinks to sub-zero temperatures for much of the year, and is often closed in winter. It contains a selection of objects from the foundry of Tomáš Jaroš, bell-maker *extraordinaire*. Sigismund the Bell was one of his babies, and there are two of his more minor creations here (you're still not supposed to touch). Another object that you can examine at close quarters is the copy of Rudolf II's pewter coffin, each side lined with a set of camp and repellent cherubs.

The next floor contains a paltry selection of weapons—muskets, cannon and a handful of balls—and no mention of the far more interesting lamprey *(mihule)*, which gave the tower its nickname. Folklore remembered that the vile creatures were bred here for the castle kitchens, but although the suckered and feelered pseudo-fish were indeed a staple feature of the castle diet, the lamprey tank was actually in another tower which disappeared in the late 1500s. The second level contains retorts, crucibles and stoves used by the alchemists. This was once their laboratory (and the top floor of the tower), as proved by the soot on the roof and the chimney, which survived the centuries thanks to an unthorough replastering.

The last floor contains an elegant collection of late 16th-century furniture and art, including a typically icy work by Agnolo Bronzino: *Nobleman in Red Coat.*

There's also a portrait of the young Rudolf—a rare chance to see his magnificent Habsburg chin before he was able to muster the hairs for a beard.

> *From the tower, retrace your steps and cross St George's Square. Walk along the road next to the church (Jiřská) and take the first left—follow the path round to the right and then left, and you'll emerge into the **Golden Lane** (Zlatá ulička), one of the most popular attractions in the castle.*

The huddled cottages date from the later 16th century, and look like a Matisse painting come alive—tiny blocks of colour stretching higgledy-piggledy down the street. There's barely enough room inside to fit a cat, let alone swing one. The cottages are built into the castle fortifications, and originally housed 24 of Rudolf II's marksmen. The minuscule passage used to be even tinier: woodsheds and outhouses lined the other side until the 18th century. By then, the neighbourhood was on the decline: scores of grimy artisans had moved in, starved out of the city below by the restrictive practices of the trade guilds, and had taken to tending pigs, goats and chickens. The grunting and gobbling disturbed the nuns of St George's, so the abbess closed down the local pub and wiped out the woodsheds. However, people continued to live here until 1951, when the Communists evicted the last inhabitants and turned the lane into the collection of more or less uninteresting souvenir shops that you see today.

The origins of the street's name have long caused controversy. 19th-century mythmakers transmuted Rudolf's guards into alchemists, cheating Vikářská street of its rightful claim to fame, and creating one of the most pernicious of Prague legends. In fact the lane seems to have been named after goldsmiths who lived here in the later 17th century, but in 1990, a Czech historian hurled a thought-provoking cat among the etymological pigeons. It's well known that the 24 sharpshooters shared one toilet, and even that little closet was several nerveracking minutes away on the Powder Bridge. Supported by lateral thinking (over 100 people lived here in the lane's glory days), he suggested that the 'gold' referred to was urine, dribbling down the passageway for generations.

> *Unless it's unbearably full, you may want to potter around the street for a while. There's a café in a courtyard to your left (with Renaissance painted flowers hiding on the joists), and on the right as you enter the court is the sheer wall of the **White Tower** (Bílá věž), built as part of Vladislav II's fortifications of the castle.*

For about 200 years after 1584, it was Prague's central prison. Among those held here were the 27 Protestant leaders executed after the Battle of the White Mountain. During the reign of Rudolf II, the few villains in his court unlucky enough to be rumbled were also kept here. Among them was the already mentioned Edward Kelley, who eventually fell foul of the emperor, and was imprisoned in towers across Bohemia. The nature of the dispute is unclear, but legend has it that Rudolf became convinced that Kelley was withholding the philosopher's stone from him. If he had it, it didn't do him much good—he's said to have been crippled leaping from the windows above you in an escape attempt, and then to have poisoned himself here.

Back in Golden Lane proper, take a look at the powder-blue hovel (No. 22) on the left, a tourist-trap Tardis swallowing up a coach-load of Germans at a time. Between December 1916 and March 1917, Franz Kafka lived here and wrote most of the short stories published during his lifetime. His sister Ottla, who actually rented the house, deserves to be remembered in her own right. Married to a German 'Aryan', she was exempted from the first anti-Jewish measures passed by the Nazis, but after seeing her two sisters and their husbands taken away to the Łódz ghetto, she divorced him. In August 1942, she was sent to Terezín (Theresienstadt), and died in Auschwitz after volunteering to escort a children's transport there the following year.

> *Walk on. Behind the summer sunflowers of No. 19 is a reconstruction of how one of Rudolf II's castle guards might have lived, a display that includes the telling detail of a chamber pot under the bed. A green door at the end of the street, if open, leads down to the **Daliborka** tower, built in 1496 as another part of Vladislav's fortifications. (Open April–Sept 9–5.)*

The tower was the work of Benedict Ried, but he has kept his flamboyant tendencies firmly under control here. As you walk down into the main body of the tower, bricks jut out from the crumbling masonry, and the heavy arches and immense walls fiercely announce their function. Between fending off onslaughts, the tower served as a prison for the nobility. It's named after its first inmate, a knight named Dalibor of Kozojed, who landed up here in 1498. The events leading to his incarceration are unclear. They involved a revolt of serfs on a neighbouring estate and dispossession of the landowner concerned. Dalibor may have been no more than a thieving vulture, but over the centuries he has been turned into a Robin Hood figure who returned from distant climes to find that serfdom had been introduced (1487) into once-free Bohemia, and incited a rebellion. While awaiting the chop, he's said to have taught himself to play the violin, attracting huge crowds to the tower—that's the mournful sound you hear if you're around at midnight. The story has minor flaws—the violin was only introduced to Bohemia in the late 16th century—but it was good enough for Smetana to use the motif in his epic opera named after the knight.

Most noble criminals had the privilege of having their heads chopped off when their hour was up, but those who had been especially troublesome were dealt with in less summary fashion. Through the door to the left of the main entrance is a cramped stone staircase, whose worn steps lead down into a dingy cell above the tower's oubliette. Prisoners would be bound and lowered through the narrow hole, and left to starve to death. If they got bored, they could always watch their predecessors putrefy.

If the doorway to Daliborka is closed, retrace your steps to Jiřská and turn left—otherwise, walk straight ahead past the white bricks of the **Black Tower** *(Černá věž—another debtors' prison) and turn right as you enter the street. The final stop of this walk is the* **Lobkowicz Palace**, *on the southern side of the street just before the castle gates.*

The Lobkowiczes were among the staunchest servants of the Counter-Reformation during the religious cold war of Rudolfine Prague. Zdeněk Lobkowicz was appointed chancellor by the emperor during one of his pro-Catholic moods—and his wife, Polyxena, made innumerable contributions to the cause. She gave the capital the incredible *Bambino di Praga* (*see* pp. 194–5), and it was thanks to her fortitude that the 1618 defenestratees survived their plunge from the Vladislav Hall. Fabricius et al. were far from home and dry as they emerged from their dungheap—pistol shots followed, and Count Thurn assembled a posse to complete the botched job. The stinking trio fled to the garden door of this palace, and Polyxena nobly let them in. What's more, when Thurn popped round to ask if he could kill them, she gave him such an earful that he apparently apologized and left.

The palace now contains Prague's **Historical Museum**, *a small collection containing one or two exhibits that neatly wrap up the loose ends of this walk. (Open Tues–Sun 9–5; adm.)*

The museum runs backwards, and you should start on the second floor. In the second room are copies of the elusive **coronation jewels**. The crown was designed on the instructions of Charles IV for his new coronation ceremony. The original contains the largest sapphires then known to Europe, and a hole to accommodate the Crucifixion thorns that Charles had just acquired. The emperor also established a tradition that it was to be stored on St Wenceslas's skull between ceremonies. There's also the Wenceslas Sword, one of the links to the older and more bizarre Přemysl coronation rite, in which the prospective king would be presented to a peasant on a stone throne, who would slap him about the face and then give him a sword to wave. There are more busts from the triforium of St Vitus's, including a portrait of bearded and impassive Peter Parler himself. Various oddments from the period of the Hussite Wars include a jolly relief from the Bethlehem Chapel (*see* pp. 241–2) of a disputatious bunch of Disciples, sprawled around a table and a long, pink and unidentifiable main course. They are all about to polish off the *Last Supper*, an artistic theme especially popular in the Hussite struggle to drink communion wine. The floor ends with exhibits related to the Battle of the White Mountain, including a portrait of hapless Frederick of the Palatinate, painted during his doomed sojourn in Prague; as well as the engraving of the Vladislav Hall (by Aegidius Sadeler) mentioned on p. 132. The only notable exhibit in the floor below is the sword used by Mydlář the Executioner (*see* p. 158) to slice off the various heads, arms and tongues of Protestant nobles in 1621.

Opposite the museum is the palace that used to be occupied by the burgrave (castellan) of the castle. The courtyard contains the sculpture of a bronze waif whose member merits some discreet scrutiny. It sparked off a major debate on aesthetics in the early 1960s, beginning with castration at the hands of Communist hardliners—who felt that the organ sullied the innocence of youth—and ending only when an embarrassed President Novotný stepped in to order repenification.

*At the foot of the lane is the eastern gate of the castle, guarded by two more fidgeting boys in blue—in front of which are the **Old Castle Steps** (Staré zámecké schody). As you might expect, they're newer than the New Castle Steps which began the walk, although Na Opyši, curling away on the left is one of the original paths to the castle. Both routes take you down to Malá Strana, and you'll find the metro station some 20 metres to the right. Each has its pros and cons: the road is quieter, but it's haunted by a headless driver with a flaming carriage; on the steps, you just might find a worthwhile souvenir among the junk.*

Start: Ⓜ *nám. Republiky (line B, the exit marked nám. Republiky rather than Masarykovo); or trams 5, 24, 26 .*
Finish: *you can get the same trams from Revoluční, or it's a short walk back to where you began.*
Walking time: *3–4 hours.*

II: Old Town Square, Jewish Quarter

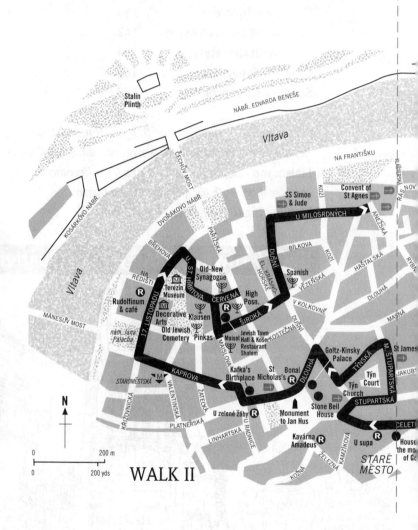

Stalin
Plinth

NÁBŘ. EDVARDA BENEŠE

Vltava

NA FRANTIŠKU

ČECHŮV MOST

SS Simon
& Jude

Convent of
St Agnes

KOZÍ

KLÁŠTERSKÁ

DVOŘÁKOVO NÁBŘ.

U MILOSRDNÝCH

RÁS NOV

ANEŽSKÁ

BŘEHOVA

PAŘÍŽSKÁ

BÍLKOVA

EL.KRÁSNO-HORSKÉ

DUŠNÍ

Spanish

KOZÍ

HAŠTALSKÁ

RYBN

U ST. HŘBITOVA

Old-New
Synagogue

VĚZEŇSKÁ

DLOUHÁ

NA
REDIŠTÍ

Rudolfinum
& café

Terezín
Museum

ČERVENÁ

High
Posn.

V KOLKOVNĚ

MAŠNÁ

Decorative
Arts

Klausen

ŠIROKÁ

DUŠNÍ

17 LISTOPADU

Old Jewish
Cemetery

Pinkas

Maisel

Jewish Town
Hall & Košer
Restaurant
Shalom

KOSTEČNÍ

nám. Jana
Palacha

MÁNESŮV MOST

Vltava

MAISLOVA

Goltz-Kinsky
Palace

St James

Kafka's
Birthplace

St
Nicholas's

Bonal

DLOUHÁ

TÝNSKÁ

Týn
Court

M. ŠTUPARTSKÁ

JAKUB

KAPROVA

Týn
Church

STAROMĚSTSKÁ

VALENTINSKÁ

ŽATECKÁ

U zelené žáby

Monument
to Jan Hus

Stone Bell
House

STUPARTSKÁ

KŘIŽOVNICKÁ

PLATNÉRSKÁ

U RADNICE

LINHARTSKÁ

Kavárna
Amadeus

ŽELEZNÁ

U supa

CELET

House
the mo
of Go

N

0   200 m

0   200 yds

KOŽNÁ

KAMZÍKOVA

STARÉ
MĚSTO

WALK II

Founded and fortified in the 13th century, the Old Town is the central European fantasy in microcosm, a topsy-turvy world of Baroque colour and Gothic gloom, public executions, legends and wonder-working rabbis. As you follow the centuries-old route to the market square, you'll shadow the life of the last Jewish storyteller of Prague, Franz Kafka, and then wander among the synagogues and ancient cemetery of the former ghetto itself. Its houses and lanes were demolished to make way for Art Nouveau mansions and avenues; elsewhere in the Old Town, history reeks from every stone, but in the Jewish Quarter, it's the transformation that speaks.

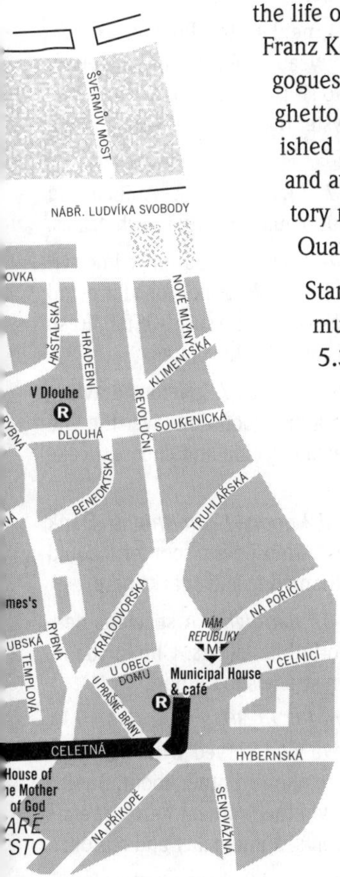

Start this walk by the early afternoon. The museums of the old Jewish ghetto close at 5.30 pm, and the latest that you can buy a ticket is 5 pm; in winter the times are 4.30 pm and 4 pm respectively. The convent and gallery at the end of the walk are closed on Monday, and on Friday afternoon and Saturday the Jewish Quarter takes a rest. Fair weather is a bonus, although there are plenty of stops where you can take shelter from a storm. The southern Old Town is covered in Walk V, and one variation on the present walk is to continue to the Charles Bridge from the Old Town Square.

Map labels: ŠVERMŮV MOST · NÁBŘ. LUDVÍKA SVOBODY · OVKA · HAŠTALSKÁ · HRADEBNÍ · NOVÉ MLÝNY · KLIMENTSKÁ · RYBNA · V Dlouhe · DLOUHÁ · REVOLUČNÍ · SOUKENICKÁ · BENEDIKTSKÁ · TRUHLÁŘSKÁ · KRÁLODVORSKÁ · NA PORÍČÍ · mes's · UBSKÁ · RYBNA · TEMPLOVÁ · NÁM. REPUBLIKY · U OBEC-DOMU · V CELNICI · U PRAŠNÉ BRÁNY · Municipal House & café · CELETNÁ · HYBERNSKÁ · House of the Mother of God · ARE STO · NA PŘÍKOPĚ · SENOVÁŽNÁ

As well as the following stops, there are innumerable eating posts scattered around the Old Town Square which will keep the wolf from the door. During summer, overlapping terraces and parasoled tables turn the square itself into one huge (and audaciously overpriced) outdoor café.

Obecní dům kavárna (Municipal House Café), next to the Powder Tower. *8 am–10 pm*. An almost elegant Art Nouveau café serving omelettes, hams, cheeses and steaks. The best place to sit is at the far end under the dribbling white marble nymph, whose mysteriously conical breasts are a traditional subject of Prague contemplation.

U supa (The Vulture), Celetná 22. *Mon–Sat 11–11, Sun 12–9*. Arched and expansive restaurant, with beer and a gamut of juicy, meaty Czech dishes.

Bonal, Staroměstské nám. 5/6. *9–9 (summer), 9–8 (winter)*. Summertime terrace café on the Old Town Square which is a perfect spot for idling and watching. As well as cappuccinos, mochas and espressos, it offers fresh cakes, crisp sandwiches and a creamily dreamy hot chocolate.

Kavárna Amadeus, Staroměstské nám. 18. *8 am–10 pm*. A gracious drawing room café, with pink lilies on the wall and a first-floor view over the Old Town Square. Snatch a window seat, sip a cappuccino and choose a cake from the photo album.

U zelené žáby (The Green Frog), U radnice 8. *12 noon–12 midnight*. Dank and gloomy chamber hung with axe-blades. Atmospheric spot for a liquid lunch, but you can't rely on getting more than wine and snacks here.

Rudolfinum Café, in the Rudolfinum. *10 am–12 midnight*. A spacious neo-Renaissance hall, structured around six Corinthian pillars. Chintz chairs, civilized service and snacks that range from strudels to salmon.

Košer Restaurant Shalom, Maislova 18. *Sun–Fri 11.30–2 pm (lunch)*. A Prague institution. The stodgy and expensive food, served with characteristically cantankerous chutzpah, is nothing to phone mother about. But it's kosher, the community needs funds, and whether you eat here depends on where you draw that elusive line between sentimentality and reason.

V Dlouhé, Dlouha 35. *Mon–Fri 11–11, Sat–Sun 11–10*. Large and unfussy, with an often delicious range of Czech dishes.

From nám. Republiky look for the ornate Art Nouveau façade of the **Municipal House** *(Obecní dům), built between 1906 and 1911 as an unusually successful contribution to the Czech national revival movement.*

The building stands on the site of the Gothic Royal Court, occupied by Bohemia's monarchs for an unhappy century, deserted for several more, and finally destroyed in the early 1900s. Its replacement, with exhibition halls and auditorium, had the standard patriots' aims of edifying the masses; but unlike all the other dire architectural monuments of the revival movement, it came late enough to express itself in the language of Art Nouveau. Scores of Prague artists and architects made contributions, and it is a cacophonous charivari rather than a tight symphony in the new style. But exploring the building is a treat if you enjoy the easy sensuality of whiplash curves and organic excrescences, and the various sculptural and artistic homages to Czechdom and civic virtues need hardly impinge on your enjoyment at all.

For years, it has been unclear how much the great unwashed is allowed to see in the so-called Municipal House. Between the wars it was the rendezvous for the nabobs of Czech-speaking society in Prague, a bourgeois heritage that made it particularly susceptible to the Communist genius for wasting space and neglecting beauty; and although the building is slowly opening up to new shops and art galleries, it remains full of locked doors and crabby caretakers. However, guided tours take place intermittently, and at other times moderate self-assertion should leave you unmolested. Stride purposefully up the stairs and peek into as many rooms as possible. The entire building is a reflecting maze of cut glass and mirrors, with wreaths, reliefs, laurels and leaves dancing up the stairs and around a central lift shaft. Highlights include the Turkish delights of the absurd **Oriental Hall** (Orientalní sál); and the **Němcová Hall** (Němcová sál), which contains an Art Nouveau aquarium encrusted with brass snails. Next door is the glittering **Sweetshop** (Cukrárna). In the circular **Mayorial Hall** (Sál primátorský) are violet windows, and paintings by Alfons Mucha: examples of the sombre late work of the man who produced some of the most distinctive posters of Parisian Art Nouveau during the 1890s. Rising through two floors at the core of the building is the **Smetana Hall**. Every year on 12 May, the Czech Symphony Orchestra arrives here hotfoot from a pilgrimage to the composer's grave in Vyšehrad (*see* p. 278); and the Prague Spring music festival bursts into life with a performance of his symphonic poem cycle *Má Vlast* ('My Country').

> Turn right from the main doors, towards the looming **Powder Tower** *(Prašná brána)*, a Gothic hulk marooned in a 20th-century sea. Tethered by a small bridge to the neighbouring Municipal House and hemmed in by grim banks and a shiny shoe shop, it's a stately but forlorn reminder of a glory that never was. (Open April and Oct 10–5, May–Sept 10–6; adm.)

As long ago as the 11th century, traders with turbans, pelts, spices and slaves would roll into Prague from the east through a gateway here; and in the later 1200s, they were joined by *nouveaux riches* from the silvery boom town of Kutná Hora, all on the way to Prague market. In 1475, King Vladislav II of Jagellon laid the foundation stone of this tower amid general festivities and merriment. He had just moved into the Royal Court next door, and the elated burghers of the Old Town had stumped up the money for the new tower as a coronation present. However, the Hussites were a mercurial crowd, and eight years later they hurled his mayor out of one window, and shot a death threat through his own. Vladislav beat a hasty retreat to the safety of Hradčany hill. The burghers stopped building. A century later, it was given a temporary roof, a use (gunpowder storage) and an unimaginative name; in 1757, it was bombarded by Frederick the Great, and emerged in an even sorrier state than before. It was finally put out of its misery by the zealous neo-Gothic touch of the Czech Josef Mocker, and the ornate decoration of the façade, and much of the interior, is his work (1875–86).

The sad tower contains two levels. Pay at the first, after negotiating the treacherous spiral staircase. From the viewing gallery, there's a broad panorama over the New Town and a sneak preview of much of this walk.

> *Walk from the Powder Tower into Celetná, named after a medieval sweetmeat—bakers used to loaf around here. The street is one of the oldest in Prague. Behind the Baroque and Rococo façades are the remnants of earlier Gothic buildings; and below them cellars that were once ground floors, buried along with the rest of the capital during the drastic flood-prevention programme of the late 13th century (see p. 67). However, the first notable building, on your left at the corner of Celetná and Ovocný trh, is a 20th-century Cubist curiosity, the **Black Mother of God** (U černé Matky boží).*

Designed by Josef Gočár, and built in 1911–12, it is recognizable by the caged Virgin suspended above the portals, a 16th-century remnant of an earlier house on the site. Black Madonnas have long been a popular sideline of the Marian cult in Catholic Europe. When this was built, Cubism was sweeping through Prague's artistic community, and Gočár was one of several Czech architects who hoped to use the principles of Braque and Picasso to restore volume and life to the façades of Prague's buildings without breaking the city's architectural traditions. The experiment sounds shocking, but tradition came out very much the winner; despite the recessed, angular window frames and two-tiered roof, the house slots almost perfectly between its Baroque neighbours.

> *Continue along Celetná. Near the end, at No. 8, is an 18th-century house called **The Black Sun** (U černého slunce).*

Prague lore would have you believe that, Madonnas apart, almost all the black creatures who have adorned the city's houses over the years were once occult talismans. This house's supposedly dark history goes back to the 15th century, but the present sign, a sorrowful but splendid Mr Sun gazing out of a Rococo cartouche, is more curious than furious.

*The Old Town Square opens up in front of you, but for now walk along Štupartská, doubling backwards away from Celetná. At the Hotel Ungelt turn left down Malá Štupartská. To your left is the entrance to the **Týn Court**, or in German, 'Ungelt'. The courtyard looks like a construction site at the time of writing, but during weekdays you can snoop among the cement mixers.*

The name 'Týn' comes from the same Germanic root as the English 'town'; this courtyard, dating from the 11th century, was the enclave of the eastern traders and formed one of the first settlements on the right bank of the Vltava. It had everything—church, inn, and even a hospice in which moribund merchants could expire in comfort. Quite why so many businessmen came to Prague to die is an imponderable question, but those who survived were a fun-loving crowd. Bohemia's kings knew that merchants meant money, and after paying their duties (*Ungelt* in old German), they were allowed to ignore Prague's laws. The consequent licentiousness apparently led to Týn becoming known as the 'jolly courtyard', and to at least one legendary murder, by a turbanned Turk who is still occasionally spotted wandering around the court with his sweetheart's head in a jewel-box. The fun lasted until the late 1500s, when the traders upped and went to the Vladislav Hall and the more abstruse pleasures of Rudolf II's castle; at which point Týn became the idyllic hideaway that it's been ever since, cement mixers and restoration notwithstanding.

The court is now a vertical accretion of centuries of building and at least four years of debris. The Baroque and Renaissance houses are piled onto Romanesque cellars that have been breached by rubbish chutes; and paradoxically, while restoration remains incomplete, Týn is one of the most tangible cross-sections of Prague's architectural history.

*Weave through the machinery to the dignified **Granovský House**, on the far right, built by the customs officer of Týn in 1560.*

The building is the grandest survival of the Renaissance in Prague other than the palace of Granovský's employer, Emperor Ferdinand I (*see* pp. 223–4), but the ravaged paintings on its first-floor loggia are still awaiting the touch of the restorers. If you see a Bacchanalian scene, *Justice*, or anything resembling the divine beauty contest of *The Judgment of Paris*, it means that work is under way.

*Leave the Týn by the same door you came in. On the other side of the street is the **Church of St James** (sv. Jakub).*

St James's, founded in 1374, escaped the overkill that turned some of Prague's churches into grotesqueries during the Counter-Reformation. Its interior is now one of the most elegant in the city, but it hasn't escaped the Old Town's stormy history. It was the target of iconoclasts in both 1420 and 1611, and was saved only by the courage and cleavers of the Butchers' Guild, whose history is intertwined with that of their church; while in 1689 it was ravaged by a huge fire, which destroyed about 800 houses in the area covered by this walk. By 1739, the interior and the façade had assumed their present appearance. The church vibrates better than any other in Prague and its organ concerts are superb; the schedule is pinned up outside.

Above the entrance, rich stucco reliefs depicting the event-filled lives of SS Francis of Assisi, James and Antony of Padua crowd out of the wall. The nave is the second longest in Prague after St Vitus's Cathedral. The illusionists in charge of the Baroque reconstruction wanted it even longer, and tapered the galleries in the narrower bays of the chancel.

Although the Gothic proportions of the hall-church keep the 21 Baroque altars

Tomb of Count Jan Václav Vratislav of Mitrovice

firmly under control, the splendid tableau of the **tomb of Count Jan Václav Vratislav of Mitrovice** (1714–16), tries its hardest to break free, at the far end of the northern aisle. Mitrovice was imperial chancellor of Bohemia at a time of strict control from Vienna, when the most important qualifications for the job were dull ambition and kneejerk reflexes. He may have slipped out of the history books, but when the daunting late Baroque duo of Vienna's J. B. Fischer von Erlach and Prague's F. M. Brokof set to work on this monument, his posthumous fate was clearly seen in more elevated terms. Earthbound Sorrow is left behind as corpulent Jan, double chins at peace and crucifix slipping from his grip, is tugged heavenwards by a delighted astronomical Muse; hoary Time states the obvious; and an angel, frozen in mid-inscription, has managed to scribble the important details—the name, office and achievements of Count Jan Václav Vratislav of Mitrovice.

None of the other decorations of the church can quite match the tomb. After a brief look at the ceiling frescoes (Life of the Virgin *and* Glorification of the Trinity) *and the* Martyrdom of St James *on the high altar, go to the left of the main doors, where you'll find a less carefully crafted monument to human folly.*

It's a scraggly **human forearm** hanging from a chain. The rag and bone is what's left of a bloodthirsty miracle that took place in 1400, when a thief tried pilfer the jewels of the Madonna on the high altar. The Virgin would have none of it and grabbed his member, refusing to let go despite the prayers and pleas of church (who must have had interesting plans for the luckless villain). The limb eventually had to be lopped off, presumably by one of the congregation's cleavers, and has hung ever since as awesome testimony to Divine Justice. The painting on the wall depicts the memorable scene.

Turn right when you leave the church. Next door is the Gothic cloister of the old Minorite friary of St James; the clerics have returned from Communist-imposed exile, and can occasionally be spotted traipsing across the flagstones and pillars of their recently-renovated home. Turn left at Týnská, which winds through to emerge under the looming chancel of the Týn Church. On the arched portal is a copy of a Gothic tympanum by members of Peter Parler's workshop; the original is in St George's Convent (see pp. 137–8). Follow the northern façade of the church, which runs into the **Old Town Square** *(Staroměstské náměstí).*

The square is the Brothers Grimm in stone. Gothic towers, a sparkling white church and a pastel wave of pink and blue Baroque rooftops provide the location; and like the Jew-baiting and sadism of central Europe's unexpurgated fairytales, its history is sunk in blood and guts. The merchants of Týn unpacked their wares here from the 12th century onwards and the hawking tradition survives to this day, but it has always been the sideshows that have proved the square's status. Romping stomping Wenceslas IV threw parties here until the Old Townies locked him up in 1394; in 1600, scholarly Dr Jessenius (an ancestor of Kafka's epistolary lover, Milena Jesenská) astonished silent crowds of thousands as he fiddled with a corpse during the world's first public dissection; and the plaza's capacity meant that it played host to all the most significant state killings of Bohemian history. Nowadays, the square—closed to traffic for well over a decade—is the strolling intersection of the Old Town, and the perfect spot to soak up rays, history and a beer on a summer's day.

The best place to get an overview is from the steps of the **Monument to Jan Hus**. Heretical Hus was burnt alive in 1415, and his death marked the beginning of decades of war in Bohemia. Two centuries later, his Protestant heirs were eradicated at the Battle of the White Mountain; but although the population reverted in droves, Hus never lost his position as the pre-eminent symbol of Czech nationalism. In 1900, as the Austro-Hungarian empire doddered towards extinction, Prague's authorities commissioned a monument to their man, in preparation for the 500th anniversary of his martyrdom. The artist chosen was Ladislav Šaloun, whose lifelong attachment to Art Nouveau techniques (until 1946) placed him outside both the mainstream and the avant-garde of Czech sculpture; and when this sculpture was unveiled in 1915, it was predictably showered with abuse. It shows Hus flowing from the bronze base, standing tall between two groups representing the crushed and the defiant. Some complained that Šaloun had created a sprawling mess, by letting his fascination with light effects run away with him; others found the very idea of allegory too disrespectful, although it's doubtful that they would have preferred Hus to be portrayed as the bald midget that he is thought to have been. However, the very fact that Šaloun was commissioned shows that the municipal arbiters of Prague taste were slowly coming to terms with the 20th century. Compare the work with the pomp of the St Wenceslas Monument (*see* pp. 230–1), unveiled only three years before.

> *A bronze line in front of the sculpture marks Prague's former meridian. A Marian column, erected in 1649 to celebrate the Bohemian Counter-Reformation, sent its midday shadow along here until it was toppled by a patriotic mob in 1918. With independence, Prague gave up the increasingly inconvenient tradition of calculating its own time. In the north-east corner of the square is the rinky-dink **Goltz-Kinsky Palace**.*

The dainty building dates from 1755–65, by which time Prague's Baroque frenzy had begun to exhaust itself. This is one of the best examples of Rococo architecture in the city, with its frilly stucco garlands and pink and white façade demanding no more than an approving coo from passers-by. Kafka studied here from 1893–1901, and the family connection was resumed some years later when his father, no-nonsense Hermann, moved his haberdashery store into the ground floor. But its moment came in February 1948. A vast crowd gathered in the square to hear Czechoslovakia's first Communist president, Klement Gottwald, roar from the balcony that the dictatorship of the proletariat had arrived. The masses cheered back and paid the price—every year workers were herded back here to celebrate their emancipation, until Victorious February was thrown into the dustbin of history in 1989. The gracious palace has now shrugged off its claim to ill fame, and spends its days hosting the National Gallery's exhibitions of graphic art, and broadcasting light arias and chamber music across the square from the music shop on its ground floor.

Go to the **Stone Bell House** *(Dům u kamenného zvonu), to the right of the palace.*

The creamy façade, stone bell set into the corner, belongs to the oldest intact Gothic house in Prague. It was built in the mid-13th century, and Emperor Charles IV is thought to have lived here as a youth—but you won't find it on any photographs older than a decade. Thorough remodellings after the late 1600s meant that only in the 1960s did restorers realize what lay within the then unremarkable neo-Baroque house. The onion-skins were peeled away, the thousands of fragments pieced together or reconstructed, and the house was opened to the public in 1986. It's now used for concerts, and some of the city's most consistently excellent exhibitions of modern art. It will be closed if there's nothing on, in which case check the notices outside for the dates of the next event.

The Gothic tower, fronting what is now a Renaissance courtyard, is the richest part of the building, but you'll find fragments of murals, pointed doorways and ribbed vaults throughout. The most complete decoration is in the chapel to your right as you walk towards the courtyard, once entirely covered with murals of the Passion (c. 1310). On the first cross-vault are symbols of medieval Christianity, including the bloody pelican, charitably dunking beak into breast to feed her squawking brood. The second chapel, on the first floor, was built some 30 years later. Flanking the former Crucifixion scene of the niche altar are two reliquaries. The first suppliant was quite likely to have been relic-obsessed Charles himself: the date fits, and the sun at the centre of the nearby vault was an especially favoured symbol in the hermetic vocabulary of the future emperor, who mused in his Latin diary (7 July 1339) that 'no body created bears so clearly the traces of the Holy Trinity as the sun'. The cheeky Dionysian orb, wrapped in vine leaves, was also a representation of Jesus in his various alcohol-related personae (true vine, wine press, blood donor, etc.).

Next door is one of the airy halls of the building, with a translucent view of the square from the graceful tracery of the reconstructed windows. After taking in the watery panorama and wandering through the other exhibition rooms, turn left as you leave the house. The next building is the Týn School, its 16th-century façade falling and rising in bulbous imitation of the church that it fronts, the **Church of Our Lady Before Týn** *(Kostel Panny Marie před Týnem)—abbreviated to the Týn Church.*

The multi-steepled towers of Týn bristle like Gothic missile batteries and dominate the square, but they emerge from behind the school, which has given rise to dark tales of Catholic conspiracies. The church was the hub of Hussitism right up to the 1620 rout; and although the Hussites were by then a minority among Bohemia's Protestants, it is said that the Jesuits decided to humiliate Prague by hiding its former parish church behind a house. In fact, the school and its even more obtrusive neighbour were originally Gothic buildings, and appeared around the same time that the church was founded (1385). Their later reconstructions were just par for the course in Prague. Týn created its own problems; it was founded on a self-effacing earlier church and just grew, adding the spires over a century later. The legend may have arisen because of the alterations that the Jesuits really did make. As well as the almost sensible decision to melt down a Hussite statue and transform it into the Madonna that now stands between the towers, the monks melted down the bells because they had been given Hussite nicknames, and then recast them into identical copies. To put the fetishism of the monks into context, it is worth remembering that this was a time when bells couldn't be touched by women or any non-cleric over the age of puberty. The lead spires with their countless golden prongs are an aerial signpost over the Old Town, but few ever notice that the tower on the right is significantly broader than its neighbour. That's the result of yet more ancient madness. Medieval rules said that a fat male tower had to protect a slim female tower from the midday sun.

> *Enter the church through the passage running from the vaulted arcade. After a fire in 1679 the central vault was rebuilt in Baroque style. The altars and decorations are also largely Baroque, but even more than in St James's, they are swamped by the cavernous Gothic structure of the triple-naved church. At the end of the northern nave, past the 1493 stone baldachin (which now canopies a 19th-century altar) and the tombstone of the dwarf to your left, is a powerful Gothic Calvary of around 1410. From here, cross the central nave. Walk across the high altar, and on the pillar to your left, you'll find the* **tomb of Tycho Brahe** *(1546–1601), Emperor Rudolf II's imperial mathematician for two eventful years.*

The red marble relief is relatively flattering. It hardly hints at the gold and silver nosepiece worn by the moustachioed Dane ever since he lost most of the original organ in a duel. Brahe was one of the most colourful men in a court that was hardly dull. He had an unnerving habit of coming up with doom-laden astrological prophecies—he once predicted that Rudolf would share the fate of France's Henry III, murdered by a monk, sending the emperor into terrified isolation for months. His own day-to-day activities were conducted according to the Delphic utterances of Jeppe, a homuncular lunatic whom he placed under the table at mealtimes (no relation to the pygmy whose tomb you've just seen). Nothing became his life so much as his manner of leaving it, the result of over-drinking at a feast when a combination of self-control and a polite reluctance to leave the table caused his bladder to implode. His death, five days later, doesn't really bear thinking about. However, when the aforementioned Dr Jessenius gave the funeral oration, he dwelt at great length on the fate of both bladder and nose—an interesting comment on the mentality of an age, and more particularly, on that of anatomically-minded Jessenius himself.

Near Brahe's tombstone, at the end of the southern nave, is the oldest font in Prague, a tin pot dating from 1414. The Gothic pulpit on the next pillar to the west dates from the 15th century, although the painting and canopy are 19th-century additions. It was from here that rabble-rousing preachers incited generations of congregations to sprees of destruction. Near the pulpit is the rich foliage and drapery of the early-16th century **carving of Christ's baptism** by Master I. P., a Dürer-influenced artist whose work is also exhibited at St George's Convent (*see* p. 138).

At No. 15, on the corner of the square and Celetná is **The White Unicorn** *(U bílého jednorožce). It now houses the lawyers of White & Case, a US law firm that likes to leave its lights blazing through the weekend. But diligent though its employees may be, the firm is a prosaic successor to its turn-of-the-century predecessor—Prague's one and only* true *salon.*

The *saloniste* was one Berta Fanta, an intellectual magpie who led the capital's thinkers on a trek that ranged from Nietzsche to the cigar-smoking and lama-trained psychic, Madame Blavatsky. Among those who attended the Tuesday meetings were Albert Einstein, who outlined his theories to the group while he taught in Prague between 1911 and 1912; Max Brod, who nodded in awe and based his novel *Tycho Brahe's Path to God* on questing Albert (although he cast the scientist as a relatively rational Johannes Kepler); and, drumming his fingers on the table, an increasingly impatient Franz Kafka. Kafka was no stranger to fads—he fretted over his bowel motions endlessly, chewed each mouthful of food a dozen times, and performed callisthenics each night by an open window—but he was a mordant and laconic observer of other people's obsessions. Berta Fanta's philosophical shopping-list would eventually become too much for him, but in 1911, he attended a series of talks by anthroposophist Rudolf Steiner, who had come to Prague to speak on 'Awareness of Higher Worlds'. Kafka's extremely limited record of the lectures ran not much further than

Mrs Fanta: 'I have such a poor memory.'
Dr Steiner: 'Don't eat eggs.'

The author spent some unhappy childhood years living at Celetná 2 and 3; for completeness' sake, stare at them and then walk across the square

*towards the tower of the Old Town Hall (which is covered on Walk V—see pp. 236–40). The houses lining the southern side of the square, like those of Celetná, are built over older subterranean houses; and at The White Pony (U bílého koníčka), through the Gothic arcade at No. 20, you can writhe in a Romanesque disco from Tues–Sat. As you approach the tower, you'll see the sharp oriel window of its chapel, dating from the later 14th century and pieced together after the Nazis reduced it to rubble in 1945. The plaque marked 'DUKLA' contains a pot of earth from a 1944 battle between the Nazis and Soviet/Slovakian forces; and to the right is a memorial to an earlier watershed in the country's history, **the executions of 21 June 1621**, which took place on the site of the 27 crosses painted on the ground.*

After the Battle of the White Mountain, Emperor Ferdinand II wasted no time. The big fish of Bohemian nationalism were put on trial; Viennese judges pondered the evidence and sentenced them to death. A scaffold was set up on this spot, and a grandstand constructed for those nobles lucky enough to find themselves on the right side. The square was shrouded in black and the drums began to roll. The appointed day began portentously—crossed rainbows were seen in the sky—but the executions went like a dream. Dr Jessenius was among those who got their comeuppance, and in a terrible echo of his most celebrated moment, he was virtually dissected himself: tongue extracted, decapitated, then quartered. Mydlář the Axeman was such a virtuoso that Praguers (who have celebrated their national humiliation with gusto ever since) took him to their hearts almost immediately. The hooded hero is still an integral character in the packed universe of Prague childhood. Mydlář plucked and amputated with legendary precision, and according to an English sightseer, the 24 decapitations were performed, 'with great dexterity, not missing one stroake, as if the winde had blowen their heads from their shoulders'. Ten of the unluckiest heads were piked and suspended over the Old Town Bridge Tower for a decade. When Protestant Saxons temporarily occupied Prague in 1631, they piously reburied the grinning ten in the Týn Church, as startled workmen found during restoration in 1766. However, all 27 martyrs apparently still come here on the night of the anniversary, on a rather futile hunt for their many other missing appendages.

Next to the town hall is the burnt-out shell of a pink neo-Gothic stump, which used to stretch across to the bright southern façade of St Nicholas's Church (sv. Mikuláš) in the north-west corner. It was a part of the town hall obliterated by Nazi tanks on 8 May 1945, a week after the suicide of Hitler, and on the same day that western Europe was celebrating V-E Day.

The last fighting on the continent took place in Prague. On 5 May 1945, the city rose up against the Nazis; four days and up to 5000 dead Czechs later, the Red Army arrived. There seems to have been none of the chicanery that surrounded the Soviet betrayal of the Warsaw Uprising; but US forces—who were within easy reach of the capital—stood idle so as not to breach the terms of the Yalta agreement.

Eight competitions have been held since 1945 to find a way of filling the hole. Endless Stalinist temples and monumental schemes were proposed, but fortunately, even the competition organizers seem to have been unnerved by them, and no one ever won. It's now hard to imagine that anyone would have the nerve to rob the square of its sunbathing green.

> *Take a look down Pařížská, the broad thoroughfare running northwards from the square. You'll probably see something odd high up on the hillside of Letná Park. At the time of writing, a giant mechanical metronome is waving from side to side, but there's talk of replacing it with a revolving glass cube filled with 100 tons of dirty water from the Vltava. The post-modernist japes are all born from the lingering need to lay the ghost of what used to stand on the Letná pedestal—a 30-metre-high* **statue of Stalin**. *As you'll notice, that is no longer there, and on its fate hangs a tale that you'll find on pp. 108–9.*

> *Walk towards the* **Church of St Nicholas**. *Since 1920 it has been used by the Hussite Church, re-established as the official creed by early 20th-century patriots.*

The church, backing into the square with its cluttered southern façade, two towers, and the rump of a chancel, is a lop-sided charmer. When built in 1735, it was respectably covered by a very large building and commanded the dim alleyways of the Jewish ghetto. To see it as it was designed to be seen, sidle along about three metres from the watchful saints and pretend that you're locked in on all sides.

> *Walk to the end and turn right. The church was stripped of its original decoration when it and its accompanying monastery (now demolished) were turned into storage space by Emperor Joseph II. The most impressive feature is the dome, hovering on a squared-off drum. Walk to the junction in front of you. The neo-Baroque mansion between the church and Maislova street stands on the site of the former clergy house of St Nicholas's. The town scribe is said once to have lived here, and suitably enough, it was also* **Franz Kafka's birthplace** *in 1883.*

Only the Baroque portal survives from the house that heard baby Franz's first scream. As astute walkers will have begun to suspect, the author spent almost all his life within this square mile. He once stood near here, tracing with his finger while telling a friend, 'This narrow circle ... encompasses my entire life'; and he wrote his final story as he lay dying in a flat over the Old Town Square, 'the most beautiful setting that has ever been seen on this earth'.

A 1966 bronze sculpture of the author's face now looks out from the corner of the house. It was produced after consultations with Kafka's life-long friend Max Brod who thought it 'admirable', but others have been less impressed by the gaunt sculpture. As well as likening it to an unfinished strudel, one 1967 critic suggested that it would be set off perfectly by installing green light bulbs in the eyes.

Except during the cultural thaw of the 1960s, no serious attempt was ever made to accommodate Kafka's bleak and incomprehensible world into the progressive literary canons of the Communists, i.e. the requirement of a happy ending. Only after 1989 did his books become freely available again. Few people bother to read them now that they're no longer banned, but Kafka as commodity has become hugely popular. The author's remarkable gaze, simultaneously as piercing as approaching headlamps and as doomed as a transfixed rabbit, stare out from T-shirts, mugs and postcards across the capital; while foreign film crews regularly troop into town to re-create his life and loves. Part of the ground floor of this building was converted into a museum in 1991. It has a few photos, accompanying quotations, and a large selection of souvenir booklets and videocassettes.

> Some 10 metres to your left on U radnice is a small restaurant called **The Green Frog** (U zelené žáby).

Frogs were once all the rage on this street; two other houses were named after the black and the golden varieties. Mydlář the Executioner used to unwind in this one after a hard day's chopping. Popular though Mydlář was, there were time-honoured taboos surrounding messy jobs, and this was the only hostelry in the Old Town where he could snatch a bite. Even here, he had to slink in through a side-door and sit in a separate room along with the town's animal skinners. If you ask politely you'll be shown the dim chamber in which he used to amuse his fellow pariahs, and the hole in the wall through which he could share anecdotes and pithy observations with the admiring, but respectable, burghers of Prague. You could even grab a bite to eat under the axe-head chandeliers.

> Take Kaprova, ahead of you veering right, the 20th-century successor of an ancient route that led from the market to the Vltava ford. It leads into **Jan Palach Square** (nám. Jana Palacha), opening up onto the river embankment and a view of distant Hradčany Castle lounging across its hillside retreat.

There is something peculiarly poignant about this square's tortured history. In mid-1945 it served as a temporary burial ground for Soviet soldiers who fell during the liberation of Prague, and was renamed Red Army Square (nám. Krásnoarmějců)—an understandable decision, but not to the thousands who gathered here in January 1969 to mourn Jan Palach. Another generation of the Red Army had invaded Prague, and Palach had just burned himself to death in protest. The crowds tore down the street signs and renamed the square after the young man, who had studied at the grim Philosophy Faculty, facing the river. The change didn't last, but in November 1989, students were again in control of the square, and their strike headquarters were in the faculty building. The street signs were repainted; a huge star-shaped tulip bed that used to squat in the centre was uprooted and (with rather unfortunate irony) turned into a symbolic grave of Communism; and after a Velvet Revolution, and a polite petition, the square was re-re-re-renamed and in a ceremony attended by the newly-elected President Havel in January 1990, Palach was officially honoured for the first time since his death. His lonely bronze face now gazes out from the northern end of the Philosophy Faculty's steps. The likeness is the work of the Czech sculptor Olbram Zoubek, and is based on a death mask that he secretly cast when Palach's three-day deathbed ordeal came to an end. Given Palach's sacrifice, it is almost understandable that the Soviet men who gave their lives here in 1945 have been forgotten; the ground that held them has become a car park.

Turn right along 17. listopadu.

This street—17 November—is one of the few roads in Prague renamed by the Communists which has survived. It commemorates a student protest in 1939 during which the Nazis shot several people dead. In November 1989, students held an officially sanctioned demonstration to mark the 50th anniversary of that event—and then used the rally to attack the government, in the belief that the authorities wouldn't risk the analogies of using force. They didn't give a damn: the police used batons, and within a month the government had been overthrown. As a result, the street now recalls both 1939 and 1989.

Cross Široká. On your left is the grand neo-Renaissance palace of the **Rudolfinum.**

The building's walnut-panelled and cut-glass rooms, ranging around a vast glass-roofed atrium, host temporary exhibitions; but the Rudolfinum is best known as the home of the Czech Philharmonic Orchestra. Its history is not purely cultural: the musicians perform under the globe-clustered chandeliers of the glorious Dvořák Hall (Dvořákovy sál), which used to host the legislative sessions of the Czechoslovak parliament until that was prorogued by the Nazis in 1938.

The building was also the scene of one of the more surreal episodes of the war. If you look up to the roof, you'll see sculptures lining the balustrades on each side. Each is of a famous musician, and according to the Czech (and Jewish) author,

Jiří Weil, *Reichsprotektor* Reinhard Heydrich erupted with fury when he noticed that the non-Aryan Felix Mendelssohn was among them. The order was barked that he be toppled, *schnell*, but the hapless workers to whom the task fell found that the statues were nameless. The solution seemed obvious—the Jew would be the one with the biggest nose—and disaster looms and Weil's novel sets off as they accordingly put a noose around the neck of Richard Wagner, the musical demiurge of fascism. No one's quite sure who is who nowadays. Mendelssohn is probably the character second from the riverside, as you face the main steps. According to Weil, Wagner is wearing a beret. However, careful inspection from the rooftop—unfortunately not yet opened to guided tours—reveals that the bewigged character on the street-side balustrade has the largest organ, by a long chalk.

> *Directly opposite the Rudolfinum is the* **Museum of Decorative Arts**
> *(Uměleckoprůmyslové muzeum). (Open Tues–Sun 10–6; adm.)*

The museum was founded in 1885, inspired by the English Arts and Crafts Movement's dream of elevating public taste in the industrial age. Many of its holdings remain in storage, but the small collection on display is a sumptuous one: four rooms of household and palace furnishings from the Renaissance through to the mid-19th century. The work includes escritoires and cabinets inlaid with gemstones, a technique imported from Milan by the Miseroni family, invited to Prague by mineral-mystic Emperor Rudolf II; and timepieces by Erasmus Habermel, who had promised Rudolf the secret of perpetual motion. The rooms also contain Baroque bureaux and chests, pumped into fat curves by the same men who were designing Prague's 18th-century churches, such as Kilian Dienzenhofer and Giovanni Santini. The porcelain—a material that fascinated the 17th-century alchemists of Prague and Europe, according to Bruce Chatwin's *Utz*—includes works from Meissen, the first European factory to unlock the thousand-year old Chinese mystery; and from Munich and Vienna, produced after treacherous Dresden workers swiftly spilled the beans. Pewter pots, cobalt jugs and fussy teacups are scattered throughout, and the tapestries include Gobelins. The collection ends with the stark furniture of 18th-century neo-classicism, rediscovered by the Functionalists of the 1920s, and ornamented neo-Rococo work of the mid-1800s.

The museum has neither the money nor the space to exhibit the rest of its huge holdings, but temporary displays are very occasionally held. The stored collections include thousands of posters and photographs, a unique collection of Cubist furniture, and one of the largest glass collections in the world. The last-mentioned begins with 14th-century Bohemian glass (which got off to a flying start under the patronage of Charles IV, another gem-fanatic) and runs through Venetian Renaissance glasswork to Art Nouveau and 20th-century pieces.

*When you leave the museum, turn right and then right again. Follow the grey wall into U starého hřbitova street. You have now entered what remains of the **Jewish ghetto** of Prague. (Open Sun–Fri April–Sept 9.30–5.30, Oct–March 9–4.30; last tickets sold 30 mins earlier; adm.)*

No one knows when the first Jews came to Prague. Even ghetto legend, which generally had an answer for everything, was unclear about precisely which lost tribe had made their way here. It often set the date at some point between the Exodus (*c.*1300 BC) and AD 33—a period that gave the community a watertight alibi to charges of Christ-killing—but folklorists sometimes settled for about AD 135, when the Jews had been expelled from Palestine. Even the last date precedes the arrival of the Czechs by about four centuries. Historical sources suggest that the 10th century is closer to the truth; and it's thought that Jews first lived in two separate communities on either side of the river. By the mid-13th century an unhappy set of events had combined to create a single community here. Přemysl Otakar II wanted the left bank for his new town of Malá Strana (*see* p. 177); the Old Town was fortified; and most importantly, the Church in 1179 had announced that Christians should avoid touching Jews, ideally by building a moat or a wall around them. Another set of walls was accordingly built within the Old Town; and three centuries before the word was coined in Venice, Prague Jews began life in the ghetto.

The daily routine was much the same as that of Jews elsewhere in central Europe—pogroms, ritual murder allegations, and occasional banishments from the land (on many occasions in the early 16th century, and in 1744–48). By day movement was free, but as the sun set, the portcullis would be lowered. The gates would be locked throughout the Easter/Passover flashpoint. Jews didn't mind, as it kept out the crowds eager to avenge Jesus on Good Friday; but the authorities' concerns were no different from those of the mob. Medieval Christendom generally assumed that the Passover lamb was a cunning codeword for Christ; and that unless the gates were locked, Christian babies and virgins would end up on a Passover plate.

During the 16th century, the ghetto became a vortex of Jewish mysticism, as interest in the cabala grew among both Jews and Christians throughout Europe. The mysterious cabalistic tradition—handed down orally from Adam—was reflected in the intellectual search of Rudolf II's court, and the exchange of cryptic data between rabbis and castle scholars became legendary. The period was to inspire a powerful image of the ghetto as a dank universe of miracles and poverty; its 7000 inhabitants living cheek-by-jowl in a shadowy labyrinth of cramped lanes, subterranean passages and hypertrophied buildings. There's more than a little truth to the picture, but although the ghetto was sealed, it wasn't all poor. The richest man in Rudolfine Prague was Jewish.

In 1784, under Emperor Joseph II, the gates were thrown open. Joseph, enlightened despot that he was, was being liberal only in an academic sense. The idea was to wipe the Jews out as an independent community: the use of Hebrew or Yiddish in business was prohibited, and separate schools were banned. That didn't stop him being honoured after 1848, when Jews were finally granted civil rights (Charles IV had made 'imperial serfs' of them in the late 14th century). The former ghetto was formally incorporated into Prague in 1850 and renamed Josefov, as it is still known. Integration proceeded apace—rich Jews moved out, poor Christians moved in. By the end of the 19th century, the district had become a set of 288 stinking slums, brothels and bars, a breeding ground for typhoid and tuberculosis. The authorities could have repaired the buildings, but they chose to destroy them, along with an irreplaceable part of Europe's history. Broad streets, crowded with turn-of-the-century mansions, now stand over winding medieval alleys. Of the old ghetto, only six synagogues, the town hall and the cemetery were spared, and still survive thanks to Hitler's macabre decision that they would house a postwar 'Exotic Museum of an Extinct Race'. Of the Jews themselves, some 80,000 of the 90,000 who remained in Bohemia and Moravia in March 1939 were killed.

After the war, the government took over the Nazi collection. It is hard to see what else could have been done, but the Communists proved unworthy custodians. A monument to a destroyed community was loaded with propaganda exalting the wartime role of the Communists, and incredibly inappropriate attacks on Zionism. Those Jews who remained in Prague continued to run the town hall and two neighbouring synagogues; but even the supposedly autonomous community organization had been compromised, as became clear after 1989—when the chief rabbi was found to have been a police informer. Since then both the community administration and the State Jewish Museum have been purged of stooges, but they remain separate bodies. A certain friction continues between the two, and the division of their responsibilities is still unsettled; in practice, that means that you will probably have to buy at least two tickets to see all the sights of the old ghetto.

Enquire about the current state of play from the museum ticket office, which you'll find in a booth at the end of the wall on U starého hřbitova.

*Next to the booth is the entrance to the **Old Jewish Cemetery** (Starý židovský hřbitov, known in Hebrew as **Beth-Chajim**, or the House of Life).*

The Jewish graveyard, the second oldest in Europe after that in Worms, is an astonishing sight—a flash of a lost world that imprints itself on your memory. For over three centuries until 1787, it was the only burial ground permitted the Jews, its elder trees the only patch of green behind the ghetto walls. As space ran out, it was covered with earth, older gravestones were raised, and a new layer of burials was begun. Subsidence has turned the graveyard into a forest of some 12,000 madly teetering tombstones. Many are half-interred themselves; many have migrated far from the person they commemorate; and as you walk through, there are thought to be some 20,000 people under your feet, buried in up to 12 subterranean storeys.

The tombs are marked with the name of the deceased and the deceased's father (for women, also that of the husband), usually with verses pointing out some especially good things about the proprietor. The many hieroglyphs include the benedictory hands of the Cohens, the anointing jugs of the Levites, and other respectable symbols born out of the rigid division of Israeli labour; but the gravestones are also peppered with figures, and even the occasional portrait. As far as the Talmud was concerned, that was the first step towards the Golden Calf. The freethinking Enlightenment is a partial explanation of the idolatrous experiments, but no one really knows what came over the ghetto Jews.

Descendants, moon-struck lovers and superstitious types leave scribbled wishes, and pebbles, on the graves. No one knows where the Jewish custom of placing stones on tombs arose. Legend provides the only suggestion: it claims that the tradition dates back to the Exodus from Egypt, when only rocks were available to mark desert graves. The cracked vaults themselves probably contain more desperate prayers; when the Nazis ripped up Jewish cemeteries elsewhere in Europe, their gruesome harvest often included treasures hidden in broken tombs by Jews whose transportation papers had arrived.

The melancholy of the graveyard has made it a favourite spot for quiet contemplation over the years, but the days when Einstein or Egon Erwin Kisch could come here to ruminate in seclusion are long gone.

Old Jewish Cemetery

> *Despite the tens of thousands of people who now visit annually, wandering between the stones was still permitted as recently as 1992. However, for many reasons—including religious sensibilities and the fact that the cemetery was being padded down by a millimetre each year—walking routes have now been marked out.*

The oldest known plot is that of poet **Avigdor Kara**, dating from 1439. In 1389, Kara lived through and lamented the most vicious pogrom in Prague's history, in which 3000 were massacred—over half of the ghetto's inhabitants. His original gravestone, now in the Maisel Synagogue, has been replaced by a copy which you'll find on the path running along the eastern wall of the cemetery.

> *On the southern edge of the cemetery is the **Pinkas Synagogue** (Pinkasova synagóga), which stands over the 11th-century foundations of what may have been the first synagogue in Prague.*

Rabbi Pinkas began the present building on this site in 1479, apparently after a dead monkey stuffed with gold coins had been hurled through his window. A man nicknamed Munka (coincidentally) enlarged the synagogue and constructed the late Gothic vault in 1535; and in about 1625, it was given its present Renaissance façade.

The first Jews of Prague may have worshipped on this spot, and after the war, the synagogue was chosen to house the Czech monument to the victims of the Holocaust: under the gilded ribs of the brick red vault were listed the names of each of the 77,297 Czech Jews who died at Nazi hands. The synagogue was reopened in 1991, after being closed for over 20 years of so-called restoration, during which the Communist authorities allowed the memorial to crumble into indecipherability. They excused themselves by blaming rising damp. As you gaze at the thousands of names, now being repainted, only their tragedy can dwarf the scale of that insult.

> *Follow the western border wall from the synagogue. Just before it turns to the left is the grave of **Rabbi David Oppenheim** (1664–1736), whose 5000-volume library eventually went on a tour across Europe, and made it to Oxford's Bodleian in 1829, where it now forms the Oppenheimer Collection. Walking routes permitting, turn right at the path and then right again. There you'll find the grand tomb of **Mordechai Maisel** (1528–1601), the mayor of the ghetto during the reign of Rudolf II.*

Maisel had to wear a yellow wheel and high hat like any Jew in Rudolfine Prague (badge and hat were an intermittent requirement throughout the ghetto's history) but he died one of the wealthiest men in Europe. His will made dispositions amounting to 17 million gulden, at a time when five would buy a fattened ox. Jewish lore claims that young Maisel was an honest urchin who found a gold coin in a ghetto alley, and tracked down the wealthy rabbinical owner. The proud rabbi wasn't pleased, as he had put it there after a trio of goblins had told him that it would be retrieved by his future son-in-law. But prophecies were prophecies, and the ragamuffin moved in; the goblins eventually returned with several treasure chests, and rabbi, daughter and Maisel lived and died happily ever after. Others claim that Maisel made his fortune thanks to the trading monopoly granted him by Rudolf II.

> *The best-known of all the cemetery's occupants, the subject of tales that are still told to awestruck New York children, is **Rabbi Loew ben Bezalel** (1512–1609). His tomb, inundated in pebbles, is along the western wall, roughly opposite the entrance gate.*

Loew, born in either Poznań or Worms, was one of the leading scholars of 16th-century Jewry. Most of his life was spent in Prague, and in 1597, he took over as chief rabbi of the ghetto; by the time of his death, he was already a legend. The stories surrounding his life—the most famous of which is his golem, a cabalistic precursor of Frankenstein's monster—are detailed on pp. 105–7; but his powers apparently extended even beyond the grave. He's surrounded by 30 faithful disciples, among whom is his grandson Samuel. Solemn Samuel set his heart on being buried next to his grandfather; Loew vowed that he wouldn't be disappointed. Bungling ghetto authorities filled the precious plot with another lucky corpse—but dead though he was, Loew had not forgotten. When Samuel expired, the rabbi and his sepulchre budged a couple of feet. Samuel's grave is the thin one on the left.

> *After leaving the cemetery, turn left into the neo-Romanesque **Ceremonial House** (1908).*

The two rooms contain an exhibition of artwork and poetry recovered from the Terezín (Theresienstadt) ghetto in 1945 (*see* pp. 379–82). The range of contributions is due to be extended, but at the time of writing all the work is by children. Much of it was produced under the direction of Friedl Dicker-Brandejsova, a dedicated Communist, until her final deportation to Auschwitz in 1944. Although the Nazis often turned a blind eye to classes in their 'model ghetto', over 80 per cent of the 140,000 people who passed through Terezín were to die. The childhood scenes, disfigured by grimacing figures and black skies, have an eloquence that defies description.

> *From the exhibition, make your way to the **Klausen Synagogue** (Klausova synagóga) on the other side of the entrance to the graveyard.*

The late 17th-century synagogue (remodelled in 1884) was built on the site of a mess of schools and prayer halls, supposedly where Emperor Maximilian I began a ghetto walkabout in 1571. Rabbi Loew taught in an older building. As well as initiating Samuel and others into the secrets of the cabala, he practised his new-fangled pedagogical theories on the ghetto children. Loew believed that the familiar was a better starting-point than the unfamiliar, and that the general would be more easily understood than the particular, which in the 16th century would probably have thrown his classes into utter confusion. The synagogue now houses a small museum devoted to Jewish customs and traditions, including a tearful cycle of early 19th-century paintings devoted to the dolorous deathbed-to-grave duties of the Jewish Burial Societies *(Hevrah kadisha)*.

> *Continue along U starého hřbitova until you come to Maislova, and the nose-diving roof of the Old-New Synagogue across the road. Opposite is the wooden clocktower of the **Jewish Town Hall** (Židovská radnice), the entrance of which is a few metres further up Maislova.*

It was donated to the ghetto by rich Mayor Maisel in 1586. Originally Renaissance in style, it was given a Rococo revamp in 1765, when the tower and the clock below it were also added. The lower clock has Hebrew figures, and just as the Jewish alphabet is read from right to left, its hands turn backwards.

The town hall is still the administrative centre of Prague's Jewish community. For years it was a symbol of the moribund state of Jewish culture in the capital, but like so much else in the city it has fizzed back into unexpected life since 1989. There are still only about 1200 registered Jews, but the number is growing and their average age (which used to be about 65) has begun to sink, in the nick of time. Since the revolution, parents have felt freer to discuss all sorts of topics which were once taboo, and many adolescents have recently found out for the first time that they have a Jewish heritage. Interest has also been revitalized by the influx of foreigners to Prague—which has included Jews from as far afield as Croatia, New York and North London—and by the young chief rabbi elected in 1992, Karel Sidon, whose dissident credentials and literary leanings make for easy comparisons with Václav Havel.

There's little to see in the town hall. Its noisy offices and corridors are filled with researchers, teachers, discussion groups, and an unusual number of old men and women boiling kettles. However, it houses a small information centre and shop on the ground floor, as well as the kosher restaurant.

> *Walk into the narrow alley between the town hall and Old-New Synagogue. This part of the Jewish quarter is not run by the State Museum but by the community, and you'll need another entrance ticket*

> *for the next two stops on this walk. Buy it from the **High Synagogue** (Vysoká synagóga), next to the town hall.*

The synagogue was built in 1586, but its interior dates from the 19th century. It now contains a small museum of Jewish textiles, some from the 16th century, but most far newer; almost all were confiscated from families and synagogues during the war.

> *From the High Synagogue, enter the **Old-New Synagogue** (Staronová synagóga), one of the oldest to survive in Europe, and still used by Prague's Orthodox Jews.*

There are two explanations for the synagogue's name. One very prosaic offering is that it was coined when the building was newly constructed on an older synagogue; but Jewish legend springs to the rescue with the claim that *Alt-Neu* ('Old-New' in German) is actually a corruption of *Al-Tenai*, or 'with reservation' in Hebrew. Angels and/or outriders of the Diaspora are said to have constructed the synagogue from the rubble of the last Temple in Jerusalem, which they carried over in about AD 135. The name stands as a reminder that when the Messiah finally arrives, Prague's Jews have to take it back.

Unless the legend is true, the synagogue appeared around 1270. The date was about a decade before the level of the Old Town began to be raised; and as you enter, you sink several feet to the level of (not quite) antediluvian Prague. The first chamber is the vestibule, and through the door on your left is the section where women are segregated during services; the slits through which they watch the goings-on are set into the northern and western walls of the interior. Men are asked to cover their heads before entering the main hall, and you can buy a cardboard *yarmulka* with your ticket. The gorgeous Gothic tympanum over the portal, a stylized vine, is divided into sections that represent the twelve tribes of Israel and the three continents of the world then known to Europe.

The splayed chinks of light, and the pillar supports, show how much the synagogue owed to Romanesque building techniques; but the vaulted naves, and the slenderness of the octagonal pillars themselves, represent the beginnings of Gothic architecture in Prague. The simplicity of the new features shows the influence of the Cistercians, who like their very different Baroque successors, the Jesuits, were tireless monastic messengers of an austere early Gothic style throughout the Continent. The Order had a masonic lodge in Prague, and architectural experts claim that the monks hewed and toiled with the Jews to build this synagogue. It sounds an unlikely scenario, particularly since the fifth rib of the vault, a feature unique in Bohemia, is thought to have been installed specifically to avoid the defiling symbol of the cross.

In the centre is the *almemar* (pulpit), surrounded by a 15th-century wrought-iron grille. Rabbi Loew apparently fought his final and most heroic battle here, when, alerted by a dream, he hurried to the darkened synagogue and found an apparition waving swords, dripping with gore, and ticking off a list of all Prague's Jews. 96-year-old Loew realized that this was Pogrom personified, and lunged for the beast. He ripped the scroll from Death's bloody grip, saved the ghetto from extinction, and missed only a scrap containing his name.

The banner above the *almemar* was a present from Emperor Ferdinand III, after Prague's Jews, preferring the devil they knew, fought off Protestant Swedes in 1648; they had been honoured with flag rights by Charles IV over 200 years earlier. On the eastern wall is a screen covering the Torah (the scrolls containing the Pentateuch, i.e. the first five books of the Old Testament), in front of which are four messy cushions, where the rabbi used to circumcise wailing infants. The Hebrew psalms on the walls date from 1618 and were recovered in the 1960s, after the neo-Gothic restorer Josef Mocker (whose aesthetic sensitivities often recall those of the Communists) had obliterated them during restoration in 1883. Among the other features that ham-fisted Mocker restored to oblivion were the bloodstains of those who barricaded themselves in the synagogue during the 1389 pogrom. For 500 years the unwashed walls had been a memorial to those elegized by Avigdor Kara, 'destroyed in the House of God by the bloody sword of the enemy'.

> *After leaving the synagogue, make a minor detour to the small adjoining green. It contains* **Moses** *(1905) by the Czech sculptor František Bílek, one of the few Baroque-influenced works by the artist; and from here you can contemplate what lies behind the 14th-century bricks of the Old-New Synagogue's roof.*

Rabbi Loew's golem (whose full name was Joseph Golem according to Jewish legend) eventually ran amok, as man-made creatures do, and went on a rampage through the synagogue. Loew was holding a service in the synagogue when he heard the news; and after consulting the scriptures to work out whether golems could be deactivated on the Sabbath, he went stalking Joseph and eventually turned him back to clay. Suitably chastened by his dabblings with the laws of creation, he announced that he would never make another golem; lifeless Joseph was taken up to the steep brick roof, and has apparently been there ever since.

Interweaving mysteries still shroud the loft. Several curious rabbis are said to have sneaked up during the 19th-century, all, needless to say, returning white as sheets and dumbstruck; the journalist Egon Erwin Kisch audaciously claimed to have been up and found nothing during the 1920s; and yet synagogue officials now make the mysterious claim that the keys were lost 200 years ago.

> Go back to Maislova and turn left. Cross Široká and on the left you'll find the **Maisel Synagogue**.

This was another of the mayor's gifts to the ghetto, but it was dully remodelled in neo-Gothic style at the end of the last century. The hall contains a collection of silverware—goblets, spice boxes, Torah pointers and burial implements—and is due to accommodate a new exhibition devoted to the long history of Prague's Jews.

> When you leave the synagogue, retrace your footsteps to Široká, and turn right.

For most of the rest of the walk you'll still be in the area of the old ghetto, but little more remains. Under the streets are reputed to be hundreds of passageways and rooms, silent oubliettes and medieval refuges, but if they exist they now form the cellars of the airline offices, French perfumers and antique stores that have taken over the area. With its central location and august feel, post-Communist Josefov is likely at last to develop into the bourgeois district of boulevards and avenues that its Paris-inspired designers always wanted it to be. But as you walk through the quiet streets, under the sculptured façades of fantastic neo-Gothic strongholds and Art Nouveau citadels, you can't help but hear whispers from the past.

> Cross Pařížská and continue along Široká to the junction of Vězeňská and Dušní. On the corner to your left is the last of the synagogues to survive the great tidying-up of 1897–1917—three were destroyed, along with some 30 smaller prayer halls. It's the **Spanish Synagogue** (Španělská synagóga), the arabesques and keyhole-shaped windows of which are the last reminder of the Sephardic Jews who settled in this part of the Old Town after their mass expulsion from Spain at the end of the 15th century. They commandeered an ancient synagogue on this site, but this neo-Moorish structure dates from the end of the last century and is now a very closed repository of the Jewish museum.

> Turn left down Dušní. On the corner with U milosrdných is the deconsecrated Church of SS Simon and Jude, with a net-vault that's an example of Prague's tenacious use of Gothic motifs into the early 17th century. Mozart and Haydn played on the organ in its heyday, and nowadays it regularly hosts chamber concerts of the Prague Symphony Orchestra. The Baroque front, along with that of the one-time hospital next door, dates from the 1750s—follow the apricot façade as it sprawls unevenly along the street to your right. As you cross Kozí, you enter one of the loveliest parts of the Old Town. The small houses and cobbled lanes, bathed in a sleepy hush, are a tantalizing glimpse of what a restored Josefov might have become. On your left you'll come to the entrance to

St Agnes's Convent *(Klášter sv. Anežky), which houses the National Gallery's collection of 19th-century Czech painting. (Open Tues–Sun 10–6; adm.)*

The oldest remaining Gothic building in Prague, the former convent was founded by King Wenceslas I in 1233, on the urging of his sister Agnes (Anežka) who had just signed up with the Order of the Poor Clares. In 1235, she became the first abbess of the new convent. The Poor Clares were a sister-community to the Franciscans; and like bees to a honeypot, the friars arrived next door in about 1240. The nuns happily cohabited with the monks for some 500 years, until stern Joseph II demanded that Prague's religious orders show what purpose they served. Poor Clares and Franciscans were mendicants, and as a result entirely useless. They left in 1782, and over the next century, hundreds of stray families moved in along with a fair proportion of Prague's tortured-artist community—until in the 1890s, slum clearance loomed. Patriots declared that it was a matter of national pride that the convent be restored, and set up a fund for the purpose. The occupants were swiftly ejected; restoration was completed in 1980.

Agnes was canonized as recently as 12 November 1989. The 750-year delay was occasioned by the fact that, despite years of hopeful pottering, her body was never found—a serious impediment to sainthood in a Church that has sanctified mythical characters a few too many times. The long wait meant that by the time she got the papal thumbs-up, the inevitable legend had arisen that her canonization would be accompanied by great marvels—a prophecy duly fulfilled when the Velvet Revolution began five days later.

> *Walk clockwise around what was the convent's cloister, dating from about 1360. The first vaulted arcade is the best preserved, but throughout the convent the modern restorers have struck a happy balance between non-intervention and confident reconstruction where necessary. After you've walked three sides of the court, turn left through the narrow passage into the oblong nave of the convent's **Church of the Holy Saviour** (Kostel sv. Salvátor), dating from 1240.*

King Wenceslas I's wife is buried under a slab in the centre, and on the right is a fake tomb for St Agnes, installed to keep up appearances after her canonization. Ahead is the presbytery (1270–80). On the capitals of the arched entrance are miniature heads of Bohemia's Přemysl kings (left) and queens (right). The building was the first in Bohemia to take up the lessons of French Gothic cathedral architecture—on a tiny but sublime scale. Light floods in through tall arched windows with simple tracery, under a high and graceful ribbed vault.

*Walk back through the arch. On your left is the presbytery of **St Francis' Church**; it was built some 70 years after the Holy Saviour, but the nuns had no time for the grandeur of late Gothic and stuck with the simple formula of their pocket presbytery. King Wenceslas I (not the Good one) is buried here. A door leads to a heavily restored hall, now used for concerts despite being covered by a wooden canopy that muffles all the best notes.*

*Return to the cloister, turn right and take the marked staircase to the first floor, which houses the **National Gallery's collection of 19th-century Czech painting**.*

The nationalist revival of the last century produced some terrible art. The subject matter tended to be noble peasants and the more specific myths of Bohemian history; the techniques were those of a country that had been a province for too long. The collection is worth a brief visit; the period is an important one in Czech history, and you've already paid your admission fee.

The first room is devoted to the greatest names of the national revival movement. The Mánes family dominates—as well as lifeless landscapes, father Antonín produced a brood of artistic offspring. Josef Mánes (1820–71) represents the pinnacle of patriotic striving, blending vegetable matter, folksy motifs and the disingenuous simplicity of neo-Gothic art into sub-neo-Raphaelite cartoons that even the most illiterate patriot could feel warm about. While whizzing through the collection, pay your respects to the strangely out-of-place talents of Josef Navrátil (1798–1865), represented by a number of accomplished still-lifes and luminous lakeside scenes. The next few rooms are piled high with the work of the 'National Theatre generation'. These heroes of the movement were firm believers in the unity of art and architecture, and many worked on the Municipal House (*see above*). Mikoláš Aleš (1852–1913), whose cartoons and sketches get a whole room, was particularly prolific, and his work defaces almost every turn-of-the-century public edifice in Prague. The last rooms contain works of other Czech painters active at the end of the century.

By now, you'll probably need a stiff drink. There's a vinárna *next to the convent's entrance, with a quiet terrace and a long tradition of abusive service. Alternatively, you could walk a few metres up Anežská to either the small wine bar on the right (with offerings from spaghetti to snails) or the full-blown luxury of* U čeverného kola *(see p. 294) on the left. And when you're sated, just roam through the dreamy streets until you find yourself on the way back to the hurly-burly of the Old Town Square.*

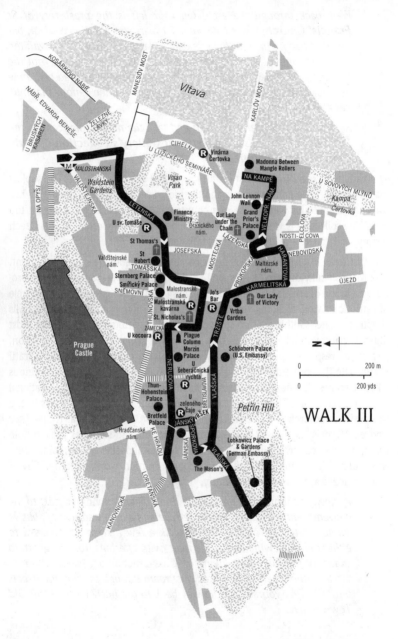

WALK III

Start: Ⓜ *Malostranská (line A), or trams 12, 18 and 22.*
Finish: *the Charles Bridge.*
Walking time: *2 hours, at an average idling pace.*

III: Malá Strana

Sloping from the castle to the left bank of the Vltava, Malá Strana's swirling canopy of orange tiles and chalky-green domes covers one of the finest Baroque preserves in Europe. The quarter was founded way back in the 13th century, but a fortuitous fire and the Thirty Years War cleared out the rotundas and Gothic clutter just in time for the arrival of the carpetbaggers of the Counter-Reformation. This walk explores their schemes and dreams: from the Jesuit church of St Nicholas to the gardens of General Waldstein, all glorious tributes to the power of money and architecture. You'll follow Catholicism on the march, tracking down the apparently ceaseless interventions of the Virgin Mary and the *Bambino di Praga*, a miraculous effigy that's now venerated by millions in Latin America. The walk takes you through the hills and gardens of a quarter that can have an almost spooky beauty, with all the luscious and peculiar flavours that you'd expect of a Baroque chocolate box. It's the best of all the walks in this book for a Monday, as it contains no museums.

---

lunch/cafés

Some of Prague's most exclusive, most discreet and most delicious restaurants are scattered along this route, and if you fancy a quail's egg or a snail you could turn to the listings in the Food and Drink section. The following is a cross-section of some of the more informal stops. One pleasant alternative on a warm summer afternoon is to prepare a picnic and unpack it in the silent woods behind the Lobkowicz Palace.

U sv. Tomáše (St Thomas's), Letenská *12. 3 pm–11 pm.* One of Prague's most best-known and oldest beer halls, with all that that entails—crooners, bassoonists and droves of homesick Germans. The walled garden is open in the summer.

Malostranská kavárna (Malá Strana Coffee Bar), in the middle of Malostranské nám. An ideal spot from which to watch Malá Strana in action. This Prague institution was for years the shabby haunt of Malá Strana's dissidents and diplomats, but it's currently under restoration. With luck, by the time you read this lunch and history will have been resumed.

Jo's Bar, Malostranské nám. 7. *Mon–Sat 12 noon–2 am, Sun 12 noon–1 am.* An island of ex-pats, presided over by the enigmatic son of a Canadian paper magnate. Irrepressibly convivial and filled with people from every background and place of origin, except Prague. Offers a tasty range of Mexican dishes from chewy quesadillas to crunchy nachos.

U kocoura, Nerudova 2. *12 noon–11.30.* For years this was a favoured tavern of the ranters, writers and guitarists of the underground, but as prices climb Czechs are going elsewhere. Still a lively spot for a beer and sausage.

U šeberačnická rychta, Tržiště 22. *11–11.* A beer hall hidden in a passage off Nerudova, and a gritty survivor of old Malá Strana, down to the stand-up gravy and dish-hurling waiters. That said, you'll probably find that it's been privatized and turned into an oyster bar.

U zeleného čaje (Green Tea), Nerudova 19. *10–7.* A sort of Body Shop for tea freaks. Brews you can choose range from camomile to strawberry; pick up an iced tea or tea-bag to go; and munch pizzas amidst pot-pourris and wholemeal surroundings. No smoking.

Vinárna Čertovká, U lužického semináře 24. *11–11.* A cool terrace next to the surging Devil's Stream. A drink here, as you gaze across the river to the Old Town, is the perfect way to slip into a Prague reverie after a hard day's walk. Pizzas, steaks and sundry snacks.

The name Malá Strana translates roughly as 'Lesser Quarter' or 'Little Side', and is a reminder that the district is something of an upstart compared to the rest of town. Until the 13th century, it was little more than a collection of isolated villages, tucked between the Old Town of Prague and the Romanesque castle. A monkish band of the Knights of St John kept themselves to themselves in the area around Prague's stone bridge; further south in Újezd, a Jewish settlement worshipped and buried its dead at a cemetery and synagogue that have long disappeared; and a limpet-like community around a market on the lower reaches of the fortification walls eked out an existence from the wealth of the castle on the hill. A few more centuries of urban sprawl might have given birth to a natural town, but ambitious Přemysl Otakar II didn't have the time to wait. In 1257, he issued a general invitation to German merchants to set up shop in Prague, hoping to strengthen the economy and his claim to the crown of the Holy Roman Empire (*see* p. 41). With the exception of the monks of St John, the locals were rounded up and expelled, and an entirely new Gothic settlement was built. This 'New Town' became 'Malá Strana' a century later, when Charles IV needed its original name for his new urban development.

The German merchants couldn't avoid the religious shenanigans of their Czech neighbours in the Old and New Towns for long. Malá Strana was almost literally wiped out at the very beginning of the Hussite Wars in 1419; and by the time it had recovered in the next century, it had been drawn squarely into the politicking of central Europe. The Germans got Lutheranism, nobles moved in to be close to the castle, and in 1541, a huge fire raged through the left bank. Property-hunting vultures of every faith descended onto the smoking plots, and Renaissance palaces and houses rose from the ashes.

A century later, Malá Strana's second mass expulsion took place. The Habsburg victors of the Thirty Years War ejected thousands of heretical losers from their new domain, and handed over vast tracts of confiscated land to the soldiers, monks and flunkies who were to complete the Bohemian Counter-Reformation. Fanatics and time-servers turned the winding and hilly streets into one of the most splendid towns of 17th- and 18th-century Europe. For 300 years, Malá Strana was the provincial playground of the Viennese nobility—and then the toffs lost out as the result of another war. The palaces were snatched in the name of the working class by the Communists in 1948, and many were indeed partitioned into apartment blocks; others were turned into embassies. The last twist in the tale was the restitution law passed in 1990. Exiled merchants, impoverished nobles and long-lost relatives have all tramped back, statute in hand, to reclaim their properties.

No one really feels for the embassies, and there's considerable sympathy for at least the humbler victims of the thieving Communists, but many fear that the *restituce* will be a deathblow to the community. The Communist housing policy, if not egalitarian, was at least random and over the years schizophrenic sculptors, war-widows, and orange-jacketed street cleaners have all found themselves allocated crumbling Baroque apartments in Malá Strana. In addition the quarter became a hive of opposition activists and artists, who took over the leaking, gorgeous rooms while more fastidious folk moved away to the warm sterility of suburban high-rise *paneláks*. Amidst the tourists and the diplomats, children played on the cobbles, corpulent men gazed out of 18th-century attics, and each evening, the pubs would fill with the gossipy, doleful, laughing and pensive world of non-Communism. It's all changing as the wine bars and antique shops move in. The area is becoming one of the most desirable residential districts in Prague, and as rents rise and multinationals buy up Baroque blocks the exodus to the suburbs has begun. However, the eclectic community remains one of the tightest-knit in town. Even if it's doomed, the nobles et al. will be hard-pressed to transform it by the time you start this walk.

> *The walk begins in the modern fountain courtyard of Malostranská metro station. At the far end, on the left, is the Riding Hall of the Waldstein Palace, which hosts temporary art exhibitions. Leave the courtyard through the door leading into busy Klárov. Under the weeping willows of the green in front of you are two reminders of the most recent violence to have touched Malá Strana. One is the grave of a fighter who*

died during the 1945 Prague Uprising, one of thousands of similar memorials dotted around the city. The other marks the spot where an engineering student, Marie Charousková, was shot by a Soviet soldier in 1968 for refusing to open her tool-box—one of about 100 Czechoslovakians killed during the Warsaw Pact invasion.

*Walk to Letenská and turn right. About 100 metres along, the rumbling street sheers off to the left, diverted by a 10-metre high blank wall. The screen is the first hint that you're about to enter what was once a very exclusive place indeed. Through the wooden arch are the **Waldstein Gardens** (Valdštejnská zahrada), a majestic maze of beech hedges, gravel paths and gurgling fountains lazing under the silhouetted spires and halls of Prague Castle. They're now an idyllic summer retreat from the overheating city, as well as a monument to **General Albrecht Waldstein** (1581–1634)—the most epic megalomaniac that Prague has ever produced. (Open May–Sept 9–7.)*

Waldstein belongs to the dubious band of men whose influence on Europe is difficult to exaggerate. Friedrich Schiller turned his life into *Wallenstein*, a three-act tragedy, and the general himself was one of the first to recognize his genius. According to his earliest biographer (1643), from the moment when, at the age of 21, he fell off a window ledge in Innsbruck and found the Virgin Mary swooping to the rescue, he 'made it the study of his life to penetrate the future and to discover the high destiny that awaited him'. At its peak, that destiny took him to the command of the combined Catholic armies of the Thirty Years War; and at its end, it left him bedridden with gout, declared a traitor by the empire he had saved twice, and ignobly dispatched by the dagger of an Irish dragoon.

Waldstein made the most of his opportunities. The first came when he landed the widow Lucretia in 1609. She was so hideous that his hagiographer anxiously had to explain that she had slipped the general a love potion. Although that was a gallant attempt to silence the rakish whispers aroused by the general's lifelong lack of *affaires de cœur*, it seems clear that Waldstein was firmly in control when he popped the question. Lucretia was seriously rich—and when she did what wealthy widows should, and caught the plague five years later, the general buried her in style and scooped up a windfall. A second big break came in 1618. While his countrymen were lobbing Emperor Ferdinand's men out of Prague's windows, Waldstein threw in his lot with the imperial cause. The defenestrators were executed; Waldstein snapped up confiscated lands for a song, and was put in charge of the imperial army, which he led through a decade of almost continuous victories over motley Protestant forces. But he was no employee. He provided the army to Ferdinand under a series of lucrative contracts, and with the help of an inflated currency scheme and manic organizational skills, Waldstein soon became the largest creditor of the Habsburg empire. Without the money to pay his general, Ferdinand had to reward him with other assets. Lands and honours poured through his hands, culminating with a princedom in 1627. To his already formidable powers, only the least of which was the right to legitimize bastards, he could now add the privilege of handing the emperor a napkin after he had used his finger bowl, and all but unlimited control over a vast fief in northern Bohemia.

Ferdinand's Jesuit advisers already loathed Waldstein for his pragmatic attitude to a war that they saw as a crusade, and to many, the fact that he could now keep his hat on while chatting to the emperor was the last straw. The intrigues intensified, until in 1630 Waldstein was relieved of his command. It was too late—his superbly run army had become indispensable. When Saxon Protestants retook Prague the following year, Ferdinand hastily recalled his champion, and appointed him generalissimo of the imperial forces. An almost omnipotent Waldstein finally decided to slip the leash. He began to negotiate with the enemies of the empire, and in January 1434, launched open mutiny against Ferdinand. Historians have spent the last three centuries discussing his reasons. Few doubt that he wanted to be king of Bohemia, but the riddle is whether he had been a Bohemian nationalist all along, whether he grew into one, or whether he was a power-mad traitor. The nuances didn't really matter to Ferdinand, and the *dénouement* unfurled. As Waldstein crossed northern Bohemia in a crimson litter, looking for the allies who were suddenly and mysteriously fading away, Vienna's churches were put on alert and ordered to pray, for 'a matter of the first importance'. Four days later, placards appeared across the city blaring that the legendary Waldstein was to be taken dead or alive. The noble renegade's game was up, and he and the commanders who remained loyal to him were finally done to death by Scottish and Irish officers in the town of Cheb. Assassination without trial was still considered rather outrageous, and the crocodile emperor did his best to distance himself from his dastardly deed. As Waldstein's Golden Fleece was returned to him, he murmured: 'They painted him blacker than he was'; and the general's name echoed into history with the 3000 requiems that Vienna's overworked churches were now commanded to say for his errant soul.

> *Waldstein's character oozes out of both his garden and his palace. When this complex was built between 1623 and 1629, on the site of 23 houses, three gardens and the municipal brick kiln, he supervised every stage of the work. A man who laid down dietary rules for his army's sick chickens wasn't likely to leave his Milanese architects to their own devices.*

*From the entrance, turn left and then right towards his magnificent ter-race, or **sala terrena**, through the **avenue of sculpture** by Adriaen de Vries (1545–1626).*

These green-streaked deities were among the last works to be produced by Netherlands-born de Vries, who died before completing his master's commission. The sculptor studied in Florence under Giovanni Bologna, the master of Mannerist sculpture, and the figures here show the refinement and elegance typical of both men's work. The themes were inspired by the Italian Renaissance's rediscovery of the classics; but the Mannerist fascination with graceful movement appears throughout. It's most evident in de Vries's version of *Laocoön* on the left, which shows the punishment inflicted on the Trojan family by the Greek contin-gent on Mount Olympus, after Laocoön Snr. had threatened to spoil the gods' fun (he had warned that the big wooden horse outside the gates wasn't to be trusted). The work was inspired by a late-Hellenistic antique that had set Europe's artists a-twittering ever since its rediscovery in a vineyard in 1506. The Italian Renaissance had approved of the ineffable grandeur with which those characters had struggled with their snakes, and the Baroque was to seize on the work's emotion and gore—but this sophisticated composition, twisting and straining with a stylized anguish, stands neatly between the two approaches. Waldstein particularly favoured de Vries's work; not only did it give his palace a distin-guished touch, but the man who would be king savoured the fact that de Vries's last, and very proprietorial, Prague patron had been Emperor Rudolf II, until his abdication in 1611.

None of the statues are original. Waldstein's former subordinate and fellow turncoat, Hans von Arnim, left the palace untouched when his Saxon army occupied Prague in 1631–32; but the Swedes were less respectful when they took the city 17 years later. The removal men of rapacious Queen Christina carted the sculptures to Drottningholm Palace, where they remain today, and these works are copies, dating from the beginning of the 20th century.

The path of sculptures ends with a fountain of Venus, cast by a Nuremberg sculptor in 1599, beyond which is Waldstein's terrace.

De Vries's sculptures represent the transition between the harmony of the Renaissance and the dynamism of the Baroque. In a very different way, the terrace (1623–30) also shows the beginnings of the new style. Its Milanese architect, Giovanni Pieroni, followed the 16th-century rules of proportion to the letter; but the sheer size of these gaping arches and doubled Doric pillars left their spirit far behind. Waldstein clearly appreciated the triumphal possibilities of Baroque architecture, but his greatest tribute to his own genius lies under the stucco vault, in the **frescoes of the Trojan Wars** (1629–30) by Baccio Bianco. Apart from Aeneas, staggering off to found Rome with his father on his back, the assembled heroes and damsels are dressed in the contemporary dress and armour of Waldstein's war. The capricious gods lounge around on the cloudy ceiling, but the general had more faith in himself than in any humdrum deity. He is a dead ringer for ginger-haired Achilles, and on the ceiling of the main hall of the palace, he had Bianco paint him as Mars, riding to war under a dark star.

In a small salon on the left as you face the sala terrena, *the general and his second wife (the reputedly less ugly Isabella von Harrach) would dine in the summer, under more heroic frescoes of the Argonauts' quest for the Golden Fleece. The courtyard now contains a café, which serves remarkably good ice cream. A grotto on the opposite side (closed at the time of writing) contains a door leading to what was once Waldstein's observatory. The general's astrological obsessions were another part of his fatal flaw, and an essential component of his elevation to tragic hero by Schiller. The best place to contemplate them is at the **grotesquery** on the southern wall of the garden. It runs behind a cage containing a pride of **peacocks**, which are often claimed to be descendants of Wald-stein's collection. They are probably a 20th-century introduction, but the aviary is original, and used to house 400 songbirds.*

The general would stare at this wall and listen to the warbles when the pressures of devastating Europe became too much. Grottoes had become popular across the Continent during the later 1500s, and this pendulous foliage, growing tumour-like into a mass of hidden faces and shapes, reflects Waldstein's mystical pursuits. He had spent some years studying in Padua, a hotbed of the quasi-sciences of the day, and his unorthodox interests were well known even during his lifetime. He had converted from tepid Lutheranism to lukewarm Catholicism, a fairly conventional step for the social climbers of the day, but many of his enemies muttered darkly that he had long since pawned his soul to the devil—a rumour fuelled by reports of a large black hound that he apparently consulted prior to major military manoeuvres. The general took any diabolical secrets he may have had to the grave, but his astrological mania was public knowledge. He had mundane stargazers scattered across his dominions, and seemed to have hit the jackpot in 1628, when Ferdinand asked him to look after the imperial mathematician, Johannes Kepler (*see* p. 105). The emperor had little use for the Lutheran son-of-a-witch, to whom he owed 11 years' back pay and who had fled his proto-Counter-Reformation in Styria back in 1600; but Waldstein hoped that the scientist would be a particularly reliable source of inside information as he planned his future. Unfortunately, it wasn't to be. Kepler had long been nagged by doubts as to how powerful planetary aspects really were, and his only comprehensive analysis of the general's fate was something of a deconstruction of astrology. It contained the news that 'the applicant is full of superstition' and warnings that to act on a horoscope was 'arrant nonsense', even though all that the general wanted to know was whether he would die of apoplexy and the star-signs of any enemies that he might have. However, the imperial mathematician was still sufficiently impressed by something that he saw to mention that March 1634 boded ill; the comment turned out to be an over-cautious reference to Waldstein's murder in February of that year.

> *At the opposite end of the garden is the Riding Hall mentioned above and a pool around a sculpture of Hercules, another copy of a work by de Vries. When you leave the gardens, turn right down Letenská, past the Finance Ministry on your left. The suitably granite façade is an extension of a complex that belonged first to the Barefooted Carmelites and then to the Order of the English Virgins. On the right is U sv. Tomáše (St Thomas's), once owned by the beer-drinking hermits of the friary that you are about to see, and still serving the descendant of the dark concoction that they first brewed in 1358. After the road bores through a building, turn right and you'll come to the entrance of the **Church of St Thomas** (Kostel sv. Tomáše), built for the friary of Prague's Augustinian hermits, whose one-time **cloister** is next door.*

> *The friars arrived in 1285, and left five centuries later when Joseph II purged the empire of its 'unproductive' elements, which included most religious orders and all hermits. The entrance to their hidden cloister is on the left as you face the church. It's now an old people's home, but non-geriatrics are welcome. The door is usually open during the day, but if not, have a word with the porter, through the window on the left of the vestibule.*

The present courtyard was built in the later 1600s, but several of the tombstones that line the first arcades date from the reign of Emperor Rudolf II, a century earlier. St Thomas's was the favourite church of the thinkers and drop-outs who hovered around his court, although the emperor himself steered clear of the friary, having developed a general fear of cowls ever since stargazing Tycho Brahe warned him that Death would come in the form of a knife-wielding monk. Among those buried here is an Englishwoman, Elizabeth Jane Weston, whose slab is at the end of the first arcade. She was just one of the more permanent of the colourful English contingent who drifted through Rudolfine Prague. Weston had personal contacts with most of the ex-pat community, and was apparently educated by Elizabethan England's most outlandish contribution to the city, the earless necromancer and alchemist Edward Kelley (*see* pp. 102–4). Little Elizabeth seems to have escaped his more baleful aspects, and by the time of her early death in 1612, at the age of 30, she was widely regarded as one of the most talented humanist poets in central Europe. Her fame has withered since, perhaps because she wrote all her verse in Latin. A better remembered English visitor was the poet Sir Philip Sidney, who returned to warn the Virgin Queen that Rudolf was 'few of wordes, sullein of disposition & extreemely Spaniolated'; and the most spectacular was Sir Anthony Sherley, swashbuckling emissary of Shah Abbas. His camel train rolled into an awestruck Prague three times, giving rise to folk legends that would last for generations, as Rudolf mulled over his proposal for a Habsburg–Persian alliance.

> *The two Renaissance portals (1596) in the next arcade lead into a Gothic hall that was once part of the friary, but they're closed to the public. Return to the street and take a brief look at the late Baroque façade. It looms over the tiny cul-de-sac, demanding a level of respect that the humble alley can't muster. The church's architect, Kilian Dienzenhofer, had begun to think in epic terms, and both its front and interior are grandiose trial runs for his later works. If the church is closed, try sweet-talking the sacrist; the bell is near Weston's tombstone.*

The powerful nave of the church, its stucco arches driving towards a sunlit chancel, is decorated with frescoes (1728–30) by Václav Reiner. They show Reiner's typical use of blocks of colour and monumental figures, and depict the life of St Augustine, formerly Bishop of Hippo, from his late baptism to his ascension. The hermits' hero made important contributions to early Christian thought, notably that Original Sin was transmitted through sexual intercourse. (He had the benefit of hindsight, having had a son by a mistress of 15 years' standing.)

Stern Augustine once said that 'beauty cannot be beheld in any bodily matter'. It's something that even confirmed hedonists might stop to contemplate under the third set of piers, where you'll find the skeletons of St Just and the Blessed Boniface crammed into glass cabinets, topped with two happy cherubs, and gripping the Augustinian emblem of a flaming heart (religious passion).

The brighter side of Prague Baroque returns under the **dome**. It dates from the late 1720s, just before Kilian Dienzenhofer was to start work on the eastern end of the Church of St Nicholas (*see below*). Light floods through the hidden windows around the dome and down from the cupola, illuminating more frescoes by Reiner. Produced later than his frescoes of St Augustine, they show a deliberate attempt to limit the exaggerated proportions of his earlier work. The fresco inside the dome seems to be of the *Resurrection*, and at the base are the *Four Corners of* *the World*: dark Africa, censer-waving and sensual Asia, crowned and learned Europe, and a shimmering, savage America with her then-traditional severed head and reptilian cayman. The easternmost frescoes are of St Thomas, whose legend culminates with the painting of his murder by savage Madrasis above the high altar. That, and *St Augustine* above, are copies of works by Rubens; the originals are in the National Gallery (*see* p. 217).

> *A small vaulted passage from the northern aisle is a remnant of the Gothic basilica that was replaced by the present church. It contains some delicate Gothic frescoes, and leads to the sacristy (which is closed to the public). From the church, return to Letenská and turn right. The next street on the right (Tomášská) is haunted by the best-known of Malá Strana's many ghosts, the skeleton of a cuckolded ironmonger who is still looking for someone to remove the nail that his wife drove into his head one night. At No. 4 is an example of Prague's Baroque sculpture at its most melodramatic, F. M. Brokof's St Hubert, kneeling above the doorway.*

Hubert was a huntsman before he became a saint, and converted when he spotted a crucifix between the antlers of a deer that he was stalking. The passion of the legend sounds difficult to convey, but Brokof was undaunted, and has invested the eyeball-to-eyeball meeting of man and stag with an emotion that's almost unseemly.

> *Retrace your steps the short distance to Malostranské nám. (Malá Strana Square).*

This area has been at the centre of left-bank life for a millennium. Prague's first market is thought to have stretched from here in the direction of Tomášská street to the outer bailey of the castle, and when the Jewish merchant Ibrahim Ibn-Jakub sang the praises of the bargains to be found in Prague in 965, it was the stalls here that he had seen. A rotunda in the middle of the square confirmed its growing importance, and with the foundation of Malá Strana in 1257, the square assumed full municipal functions. A parish church (consecrated to St Nicholas) and a town hall joined the rotunda, and for 300 years the most exciting things to happen in the square were ritual humiliation (the pillory stood on this corner) and strangulation (gallows on the next one up the hill). However, its history hotted up, quite literally, after 1541. The fire that destroyed most of Malá Strana and Hradčany in that year began in the **Sternberg Palace**, the second building over the arcade rising up the hill; and less than a century later, an even more far-reaching conflagration was sparked off in the **Smiřický Palace**, next along. On 22 May 1618, Albrecht Smiřický invited his noble friends around to discuss what to do with Ferdinand II's hated Catholic governors. They plumped for a defenestration, carried it out the next day, and the Thirty Years War began. Albrecht himself died in the same year, and in a good example of the convolutions of Malá Strana title deeds, the eventual recipient of the traitor's estates was traitor-to-be General Waldstein, whose grandfather was a Smiřický. The generalissimo is recorded as having said that the worst mistake that the nationalists ever made was to throw the governors out of a window instead of stabbing them. It's a mysterious comment, but it is interesting to note that he had survived one of these fates, and was to perish by the other.

> *On the corner of Letenská is a Renaissance building over an arcade, known as the **Beseda** ('Meeting Place'). It's now a rather sorry music club, the haunt of hairy drinkers and lost trendies; but between the late 1400s and 1784, it was Malá Strana's town hall. Towering over the square is the Baroque mass of the **Church of St Nicholas** (Kostel sv. Mikuláš) and adjoining one-time **Jesuit College**. All of Malá Strana now revolves around the odd couple of the tower and dome of the church. The Jesuits would have appreciated the compliment, but their enjoyment of their masterpiece was sullied by endless problems, of which their conflict with the town hall over the **tower** is a case in point.*

The Jesuits were given the old church of St Nicholas in 1623 by fanatical Ferdinand II, who was dishing out newly-vacated places of Protestant worship to almost any monkish zealot who was prepared to fight the good fight, and with particular alacrity when it came to Spaniards, who infested his Viennese court. The Order planned to build a new church and college from the outset, but this complex took years to get off the ground. The first problem was that the overstretched Order was impecunious. With the long-term vision of good monomaniacs they clung to their dreams, until in 1653 they were able to present the town hall with firm plans. Serious dispute then arose about who owned precisely which pieces of the architectural jungle in the centre of the square. The crucial stumbling block was an old Gothic tower, standing roughly where the present one is today. The Jesuits hoped to turn it into a belfry, but the councillors angrily claimed that it was Malá Strana's venerable fire post (and a useless one, judging from the blaze that had started a few feet away in 1541). Work stalled for another 20 years, until in 1673 the cunning clerics promised to build the town an even better watchtower if they could start work on their church. The council agreed and the Jesuits swiftly set about destroying the tower, school, vicarage, former town hall, two churches and street full of cobblers that had occupied their land. Eighty years later, this tower rose almost as an afterthought to the completed church—and the mendacious missionaries connected it to the church and planted saints on it. The sculptures briefly stood on the now empty pedestals on the corners of the tower. An aggrieved citizenry removed them, locked the door, and until 20 years ago, the tower—which looks to be part and parcel of the church—was one of the most unusual flats in the capital.

The Jesuits' tribulations didn't end there. They put the finishing touches to their church in the 1750s, and had hardly settled in when their Order was placed under a worldwide ban by the pope in 1773. It had served its purpose, and was becoming a little too powerful for the European establishment's liking. The Society found a refuge in Catherine the Great's Russia, but although the Holy See let them start up again in 1814, they were never to return to Prague. In a neat little turn, St Nicholas's then became the parish church of Malá Strana.

> *Make your way to the church, which exudes the confidence and ideology of Prague Jesuitry at its height. Cross the square and turn right just past the Malostranská kavárna. The front door of the tower is at No. 29 (556 according to the older system of numbering), and is marked by the crest of the jealous town. Walk along the southern side of the church, and then cross over to see the façade. The Jesuits put so much thought into this, the pinnacle of Prague's religious Baroque architecture, that it deserves a moment.*

The Order had a glacial appreciation of human psychology, which you can begin to appreciate by comparing the grim west front of the former Jesuit College (and now maths faculty of the Charles University) on the left, with the seductive face of the church itself. Although there was a 20-year gap between the two façades, and a church might be expected to be grander than a school, the contrast also had a deliberate purpose. The General of the Order, Father Oliva, warned the architects in 1673 that the lay house mustn't have the sumptuousness of the west front of the Clementinum (*see* p. 250). With their own building the Jesuits thrust their humility and austerity into the face of the heathens; the richness of the later church façade was all the more inviting as a result.

But the Jesuits were no aesthetic puritans. Following the example of their fervent Spanish founder, Ignatius of Loyola, each novice had to go through a month of 'spiritual exercises', during which he progressed from contemplation of sin and damnation to, *inter alia*, a mental munching of 'the loaves and the fishes with which Jesus feeds the multitude'. Ignatius' teaching that God was to be known through all five senses was instrumental in the development of later Baroque architecture, which was given an added punch in Bohemia, where the Jesuits had to seduce a population that had fought Catholicism for 200 years.

> *The façade was the work of Munich-born Kristof Dienzenhofer, and was completed around 1710. It's a development of the undulating rhythm used by Borromini in 1667 for his church of S. Carlo alle Quatro Fontane*

in Rome. But it is when you enter the church—which now charges admission fees and calls itself a museum—that the mobility of Prague's late Baroque architecture finally overwhelms you. (Open Nov–Feb 9–4, Mar–April 9–5, May–Sept 9–6, Oct 10–5; adm.)

All of the city's churches built during this period sought to capture hearts and minds for the Church Militant; but none other has the potency of this Jesuit cocktail of illusion, threat and promise. Even hardened cynics are momentarily stopped in their tracks; and it's relevant that this was one of the few churches to be given a full restoration in 1955, at a time when the Communist government's policies of Scientific Atheism were at their height. Inspired by the work of Guarino Guarini, who carried the idea of expressing movement through curves to an extraordinary degree, the decoration and structure create a space that pulls you in every direction. The nave's piers jut out at a diagonal, dragging your attention upwards; while the balconies sway forwards from pier to pier, over vast saints urging you onwards to the high altar. The vault adds to the intoxicating confusion, flowing almost imperceptibly from the pillars into three central bays, while the *trompe l'œil* extravaganza of the 1500-square metre **fresco** (1760) makes it almost impossible to say where construction ends and illusion begins. The fresco was the work of Johann Lukas Kracker, an Austrian who is thought to have trained under Franz Maulpertsch (*see* p. 74), and wasn't intended to be viewed from any single point, adding even more to the church's fluidity. It opens the vault into the dark drama of the life of St Nicholas. Better known to pagans as Father Christmas, Nicholas was a 4th-century bishop from Asia Minor and the patron saint of perfumers, pawnbrokers and sailors in distress.

> *The east of the church, from the third vault onwards, is the work of Kristof's son, Kilian Ignaz Dienzenhofer, home-grown and educated by the Jesuits themselves in the Clementinum.*

From the nave, the choir and altar seem almost irrelevant, a result not of an unsuccessful union between the work of father and son, but of the overpowering effect of the church as a whole. But by the time you're standing under the diffuse light of the painted dome, it is the nave that has become an appendage. The size of the dome caused terror; no one would enter the church until a commission of experts certified in 1750 that it wouldn't collapse. The painting, by Franz Xavier Palko, is the *Celebration of the Holiest Trinity* (1752–53).

God moves in mysterious ways while you keep your eyes heavenward—but there's little room for doubt when you notice the colossal statues (1755–57) stationed above and around you. The venerable Doctors of the Church standing at each corner of the stunted transepts have physiques more often associated with steroid abuse than religious devotion. Their brutality was no accident. SS Basil, John Chrysostom, Gregory of Nazianzus and Cyril of Alexandria are all associated with the early Christian struggle against heterodoxy in the East, and the Jesuits were drawing a parallel with their own cause in Bohemia. There are equally gargantuan statues of the Order's heroes, SS Ignatius and Francis Xavier, flanking the copper St Nicholas on the high altar. The analogy was clear but the Jesuits hammered the point home: Ignatius and Cyril are each coolly plunging a crozier into the throats of jug-eared heretics.

After the initial shock of the church, as you walk back, the trickery reveals itself. As in almost all Prague's churches, the marble is actually scagliola, a painted mixture of plaster and glue; the intimidating saints are plaster casts; and the chapels contain little decoration that stands up to a brief examination. The Jesuits knew that by the time their prey had got as far as the entrance, they were willing victims—and all eyes would soon have been on the equally fake, but splendid, **pulpit** at the end of the nave. It dates from 1765, and is decorated with reliefs of John the Baptist. The shell on which it stands was one of the favourite motifs of the Rococo, but this swirling mass of cream and pink still belongs in spirit to the Baroque.

> *As you leave, take a look at the last chapel on your left, the **Chapel of the Dead**.*

It was the first to be completed and, with its oval plan, it is the only one to stand outside the scheme of the church. The fresco is *The Last Judgment*, and the chapel contains one of the church's better paintings, a *Crucifixion* by the Czech Karel Škréta (1646).

> *Turn right past the plague column, one of Prague's many tributes to the saints who called off Bohemia's epidemic in 1715, and then left into **Nerudova**. The street is named after Jan Neruda (1834–91), a 19th-century Czech poet and journalist who lived here. His name was later filched by the Chilean writer and 1971 Nobel Laureate, Pablo Neruda, who apparently chose it at random, although he deposited flowers outside Jan's birthplace after finding out who he was. More a chasm than a street, its Baroque and Renaissance façades cling onto the incline. As you grapple with it, spare a thought for the assorted beasts and heralds who once had to lug the paraphernalia of the coronation procession along here, en route to the castle.*

The street has more **house signs** than any other in Prague—multi-coloured beasts, birds and apparently random objects which sometimes date back 600 years. They originally followed, in a lowly way, the strict rules of heraldry, but matters slipped out of control as the city grew. House-owners, desperate for an original name, resorted to zoological monstrosities (a house in the Old Town used to be called the 'Stag with Two Heads'); people adopted their property's name and took it with them when they moved; and streets were sometimes consumed by a counter-productive craze for a particular sign. Another grave problem was that people began to forget their significance altogether. Golden geese became white swans, Magi were transformed into musketeers, until in 1770 city fathers called a halt to the collective madness by introducing numbers. At No. 6 on the right is the narrow 18th-century façade of the **Red Eagle** (U červeného orla), one of the innumerable variations of the 26 avian species that adorned Prague's houses. The sign, surrounded by an intertwining Rococo cartouche, may have begun life as a vulture, which was the only creature allowed to perch on rocks by the heraldic guilds. The plaster decoration swirls into two less apparent images, sinister faces with dark tadpole eyes gazing out from the stucco above the first-floor windows. There's another sign at the **Three Little Fiddles** (U tří housliček), a small restaurant at No. 12. Three generations of violin-makers lived in the house, but legend insists that the sign has more to do with satanic fiddlers who gather here when the moon is full. Other signs to decipher as you walk up the street include a golden goblet (No. 16) and a golden key (No. 27), both from the 17th century, when castle goldsmiths used to heat and beat their metals along Nerudova; and a golden horseshoe (No. 34), recalling the days when steep Nerudova used to be the site of several humbler smithies. No. 34 is now marked only by a painted sign of a staid St Wenceslas on a bridling stud, but until the 1950s a large shoe used to hang under the picture, which some said had fallen off the hoof of the saint's white horse.

*On the left at No. 5 is the Baroque **Morzin Palace** (1713–14), now the Romanian Embassy, and the first of several embassies on this walk.*

The palace is an example of the inventiveness of Giovanni Santini, another of the greats of Prague's late Baroque. It was an adaptation of three older houses, and rather than go to the trouble of putting an entrance through the middle building, Santini put a balcony in the centre and had both sides of the façade thrust outwards towards it, making the asymmetry almost unnoticeable at first glance. The tension is thrown into even higher gear by the two atlantes, sombre Moors (the Morzin family emblem) who carry the balcony with ease and make a good job of supporting the rest of the façade. The other sculptures (all by F. M. Brokof) reinforce the illusory balance, both by their position and theme. The balcony is flanked by sunny Day and starry Night, and up on the roof, the Four Corners of the World are back to hold the building under their feet.

> Atlantes became fashionable during the 18th century, but if you look at the portal of the Italian Embassy (Thun-Hohenstein Palace) across the road at No. 20, you'll see that they didn't always work. It was built in 1721–26 for the Kolovrats, very soon after the Morzins had moved into No. 5. The newcomers liked the idea of having the family emblem supporting the portal. Unfortunately, the Kolovrats' was an eagle, and Matthias Braun duly sculpted these two preposterous creatures. Jupiter and Juno are left to perch above.
>
> Next to the embassy a set of stairs burrow up the hill to the New Castle Steps (see Walk I). Continue the climb up Nerudova, until you reach another set of steps to the left. The house to the left as you face the staircase is said to conceal the walled-up Kuzmack Tunnel, built by an imperial stooge in the 18th century to provide an escape route from the castle in case of siege. On the opposite side is the Rococo façade of the former **Bretfeld Palace** (1765), now a greying and blue-rinsed set of private apartments, but a centre of merriment in its youth.

The first Count Bretfeld threw balls that were renowned across central Europe, one of which Mozart attended in 1787. He wrote to a friend in Vienna that 'the cream of the beauties of Prague flew about in sheer delight to my *Figaro*', which was played repeatedly in his honour; and according to legend, he also rubbed shoulders with Giacomo Casanova on the dance-floor. The story sounds a little too neat, given that Wolfgang was in town to conduct the premiere of *Don Giovanni*—but it's not impossible. The ageing lover had been invited by one of General Waldstein's descendants to pen his kiss-and-tell memoirs in the family castle in 1785, and he lived in Bohemia until his death in 1798.

If you have the energy, a detour to the top of the street will take you past the remnants of two mutant signs (the Red Lion at No. 39 and the now very peeled and not-at-all Green Lobster at No. 43) to Jan Neruda's birthplace at No. 47, itself marked by two very sorrowful suns. There's also a serene and very normal white swan at No. 49. A final climb up the lane to the castle leads to a postcard view across the roofs of Malá Strana. As you retrace your steps, you'll walk past *Toileta* opposite Jan Neruda's house. It's a charming sculpture by the Czech Jan Štursa, whose work was marked by a particular affection for the female form until he blew his brains out during a burst of creative angst in 1925; but generations of snapshooters have predictably been more impressed by the fact that its name is plastered across the base.

> *Return to Mozart's ballroom, walk down the adjoining stairs, and turn right into the sudden hush of Šporkova. The lane narrows and then opens into a junction. At the end of the cul-de-sac on the right is **The Mason's** (U kameníka), remodelled with rich stucco decoration in the late 1720s. The mason himself, one Ondřej Kranner, used to stand on the empty pedestal over the door. The statue has mysteriously disappeared, but he was responsible for the façade, the theme of which is the Holy Trinity. Conspiracy-theorists could ponder the gable's eye in a triangle, which is both an old Trinitarian symbol and a sign of the strange-handshake society. It also appears on the mid-18th-century façade of the Sporck Palace, at the foot of the cul-de-sac. Coincidentally—perhaps—both Mozart and Casanova were active masons.*
>
> *Continue along Šporkova to the left. On the right is the one-time **Italian Hospital**. It's now the cultural centre of the Italian Embassy; film-screenings and an excellent library continue the work begun four centuries ago, when north Italian craftsmen settled around here to look for jobs during Prague's half-hearted foray into the Renaissance. The street drops you into a quiet square in front of the **Lobkowicz Palace**, now the German Embassy. The building dates from the early 18th century, and the stately aspect that it presents to the street conceals a beautiful garden and a much more charming façade at the rear of the palace. Turn right past the ravaged* Good Samaritan *(c. 1710) painted onto the Italian Hospital, and walk towards the whitewashed walls of the route leading up to the Strahov Monastery (see pp. 202–6). Turn left opposite the medical school-cum-church, and left again along the leafy path that runs behind the palace. The wood that appears out of nowhere is the foot of Petřín Hill. (You can clamber all the way to the summit from here, but you'd be kissing this walk goodbye if you did—and in any case, it's more fun to take the funicular railway to the top and zig-zag down here instead. See p. 280). On the left are the **Lobkowicz Gardens** and the rear façade of the palace.*

The top floors of the side wings were added in the later 18th century, and have disrupted the scale originally intended for the building. The elliptical plan, inspired by the work of Fischer von Erlach, originally bore a close resemblance to a 1665 project by Borromini for the rebuilding of the Louvre in Paris. Louis XIV rejected the design in favour of the grandiose colonnade that survives today, and if you imagine this prior to the alterations, you'll see why Borromini's plans lacked the required pomposity. The English layout of the gardens dates from the late 1700s, but they're still recuperating from the most momentous event in their sheltered history. In September 1989, thousands of East Germans arrived in Prague, dumped their Trabants, and clambered over these railings in the hope of being allowed to go west. They lived on the flower beds for a fortnight until permission was granted—and the rumble of their sealed trains, which President Honecker strangely insisted should pass through East Germany, were the final tremors before Europe's revolutions of 1989. In honour of the fleeing Ossies, a whimsical tribute by the Czech David Černý now stands in the garden: called *Quo Vadis*, it's a gold Trabant on four long legs, complete with an almost hidden scrotum.

> *Retrace your steps to the front of the palace, and continue along Vlašská. Just beyond the embassy is a restaurant that the Lobkowiczes opened to sell wine from their estates in Mělník; with the restoration of the noble: family's property after 1989, it has now resumed the task. The **Schönborn Palace** is on your right just past a police station, which the thoughtful Communists installed after the palace became the United States Embassy.*

The palace was built in 1643–56 and remodelled by Santini at the beginning of the 18th century, but its most glorious feature is its garden. The sight of Old Glory, fluttering from the tiny summerhouse half-way up Petřín, will bring a catch to the throat and a hand to the heart of any red-blooded American. You can't see it from here, and US citizens should head for Hradčany Square. During the 19th century, the palace crumbled into disrepair, and, no longer fit for noble habitation, it was rented out. Among the tenants was Franz Kafka, for a few months in 1917. The location made him uncharacteristically and dangerously jolly. He told his fiancée that it was 'the most marvellous apartment I could dream of', but his priorities were unfortunate in view of his weak constitution. 'I have electric light, though no bathroom, no tub, but I can do without that', he claimed; five months later, he suffered a massive haemorrhage that heralded terminal tuberculosis. Until recalled in 1992, a modern cultural hero of a different stamp lived here. Ambassador Temple-Black was older, and almost certainly wiser, but still the same Shirley who told the world about the Good Ship Lollipop.

> *Walk to the end of Tržiště and turn right into Karmelitská. On the right at No. 25 are the **Vrtba Gardens**, laid out in 1720. The observation terrace at the top of the gardens, lined with lonely Baroque gods*

sculpted by Matthias Braun, is one of the most still and secluded parts of Prague. It has been closed for years, but do as the locals do and see if there has been any change—the entrance is through the gate at the end of the courtyard.

From the gardens, continue along Karmelitská to the **Church of Our Lady of Victory** *(Kostel Panny Marie vítězně) on the right, which sits on the site of Prague's first Baroque church (1611). That was built by German Lutherans—a paradoxical start to religious Baroque architecture in Prague. (Open 8.30–4.)*

After the Battle of the White Mountain in 1620, Ferdinand II gave their church to the Order of Barefooted Carmelites, who had trudged into the city as part of the Catholic squad. The friars, who actually wore sandals, renamed it in honour of the Virgin (their protectress) and, more specifically, in commemoration of her role at the White Mountain where she had rained down destruction and smites on the enemy. The discalced crew took to their heels again when Saxon troops looted the church in 1631, and the present edifice is a rebuilt version dating from 1640. The Carmelites were finally expelled in 1784 as a result of Joseph II's anticlerical policies; and the church was taken over by the Knights of Malta, whose base was near by and whose cross now adorns the façade. The Knights were themselves expelled in turn by the Communists.

The structure is unimpressive—an ugly development of the façade of the 1568 Gésu in Rome (only the portal on the right remains from the Lutheran church) and an interior that retains much of the Lutherans' rigidity and austerity. The striking late-Baroque gold-on-black decoration is denied the play of light and motion that it deserves, since the church's few windows are obstructed by altars. These weren't planned for when rebuilding began, and were only made possible as a result of the miraculous financial assistance of the *Bambino di Praga*, in the illuminated altar on your right.

Rome's Barefooted Carmelites put Bernini's *Ecstasy of St Teresa* in their church. The showpiece of the Prague friars was this 1-foot-high wax effigy of the Infant Jesus. It's hardly less famous. Italians gave it the name by which it is best known, and the Bambino is venerated throughout the Hispanic world. In Central America, there's said to be a tribe that worships it as a god, and has very confused notions about what *Praga* involves. Intercessory prayers are now provided in over 10 languages, and during high season coach-loads of more-or-less credulous pilgrims arrive daily.

The Bambino's rise to stardom began when Polyxena of Lobkowicz, one of many Spanish brides taken by Czech Catholics during this period, gave the figure to the friars in 1628. It had belonged to Polyxena's Habsburg mother, and had been known to work the occasional wonder in the old country, but its big break came in 1637. The new abbot, picking through the debris of the church (which had remained untouched since the Saxons had swept through) found that the trinket had been tossed behind the high altar, and was missing only its arms. He declared it a miracle. Equally incredible was the discovery, made while the Carmelites were drumming up funds for a new church, that the Bambino would do anything in return for a small sum. After Countess Kolovrat touched it and had her sight and hearing restored, there was no looking back. Cripples and imbeciles poured in, and in 1741 enough money had been made to buy the doll its silver altar; during the early 1700s, it was granted the rights of a Count Palatine; while the most mysterious (some say miraculous) tribute came in 1958, when an official delegation from Communist North Vietnam stepped off the plane with a set of silk clothes for the Bambino. To this day, no one knows why. It's been bought and given scores of other costumes; after the Carmelites were expelled, the Order of English Virgins was allowed to continue dressing it, and even through the Communist era, a prelate of St Vitus's Cathedral continued changing the Bambino regularly. Look out for outfit No. 5, an apple-green number with gold embroidery, which was handed over personally by Queen Maria Theresa in 1754.

Above the altar, there's a dim celebration of the Battle of the White Mountain, but the church's other main attraction is now inaccessible. The power of the Bambino meant that few friars wanted to stray too far during the interval between death and resurrection, and the most fortunate had their corpses put into a catacomb, where they were blow-dried into mummies over the years. Privileged benefactors were also let in. Everyone's still there, but a spot of putrefaction has set in and the smelly chamber is now closed.

*From the church, continue along Karmelitská, and then turn left down Harantova. You emerge in front of the imposing Baroque façade of the Nostitz Palace, now the Embassy of the Netherlands. Turn left. The dainty Turba Palace on your left is the Rococo home of the Japanese diplomatic corps. Over the sunken arcade on your right is the Prague Conservatoire, and during term-time a walk past the building can be accompanied by anything from a sublime recital to a series of threatening grunts, groans and squeals. At the end of the street is a group of saints around John the Baptist—another example of Malá Strana's gratitude for having been only partly eradicated by the plague. The 16th-century restaurant on the corner (**U malířů**, or The Painter's) is one of Malá Strana's best-known. Until it was taken over by French gastronomes in early 1991, it was even popular with the locals. Nowadays,* *the nearest most Praguers get to a meal is a wry glance at the menu by the door and the calculation that it would take them a week to earn the turtle soup.*

The square that you're in is Maltézské nám. (Maltese Square), named after the title adopted in the 16th century by the crusading Knights of the Order of St John. They set up a self-governing enclave here in 1169 and were allowed to stay when everyone else was expelled in 1257. Turn right, and you'll see the two much-restored 14th-century Gothic towers of their **Church of Our Lady Under the Chain** *(Kostel Panny Marie pod řetězem).*

The Virgin has performed innumerable functions in Malá Strana over the years, and here she helped the knights guard the first bridge across the Vltava. That bridge has gone, but the chains still hang over Karel Škréta's painting on the high altar. The church is usually closed, which is no great loss. The monks knocked down their first Romanesque basilica in the 14th century, and only had time to replace the towers and chancel before they were chased out of town by anti-clerical Hussites. The chancel was remodelled in Baroque style in the 17th century, but as with Our Lady of the Snows (*see* p. 233), no one ever got round to building a nave. The open forecourt is where it should have been; if the gate is open, you can see remnants of the first church in the wall on your right.

Turn right. The Grand Prior of the Order (which was expelled by the Communists and reinstated in 1990) lives through the gate next door, marked by their Maltese Cross and dating in its present form from the early 18th century. Turn left into the leafy shade of Velkopřevorské nám. (Grand Prior's Square). Opposite the very proper charm of the apricot and white French Embassy (the Buquoy Palace) is the polyglot scrawl of the **John Lennon Wall**, *a colourful tribute to the Beatle-saint.*

The singer was a powerful symbol of nonconformity throughout Communist-ruled Europe after his murder in 1980, and this wall became the site of a surreal struggle between Prague's youth and the police. The former would daub it with pictures and slogans; the VB responded with regular pots of whitewash and, at the height of the subversion, video-surveillance equipment. When a fair proportion of Prague's hippies became government officials after December 1989, it was expected that moody adolescents would be able to doodle at will, but battle was rejoined against new meanies for a few tense months. However it all seems to have settled down now, and the debate continues: whether peace should necessarily be given a chance, whether love is *all* you need, and so on. If you're around on 8 December come and join the dreamy types who spend much of the night imagining no possessions, greed or hunger. Bring a guitar and brush up on your Lennon lyrics.

While deliberating, ponder the tree behind the wall.

It's said to be the oldest plane tree in Prague, and was carried back from Jerusalem by the gallant Knights of St John. They planted many more, but none of the others are thought to have survived a frenzied tree-slaughter that occurred in 1420, when Malá Stranites were apparently seized by the fear that Emperor Sigismund's invading army would otherwise hide in them.

> *Follow the wall onto the bridge over the **Čertovka** (Devil's Stream), an arm of the Vltava which is either named after a sprite who lives in it, or as a commemoration of the diabolical temper of a washerwoman who lived nearby. Next to the bridge is the descendant of a late-16th-century mill-wheel that the Maltese Knights used to make their bread. Adjoining the other side of the stream is a sky-blue 18th-century summerhouse, which is generally agreed to be the most desirable residence in Prague. From the bridge, walk over onto **Kampa Island** (from the Latin campus, i.e. field).*

Like most of Prague's romantic spots, the island has had its ups and downs. A long-standing border dispute with the Vltava river saw its shape change regularly, and despite being strengthened by imported debris from the 1541 fire, the deluges continued until the damming of the river in 1954. The abundant supplies of water meant that Kampa was particularly favoured by Prague's washerwomen, who are commemorated both by the stream and by the small early Gothic church of St John at the Laundry, just off the southern tip of the island on Říční.

> *Walk through the narrow passage ahead of you and just to the right. It takes you into a beautiful tree-filled square, crossed at one end by the rough Gothic arches of the Charles Bridge and lined with quietly decaying Baroque houses. It's one of the gentlest patches of Prague, and a spot in which to meander as you contemplate two final house signs. On your right at No. 1 is a sweet blue fox chomping a twig, under the* Bambino di Praga. *The juxtaposition is puzzling, but as nothing compared to the **balcony** on the top-floor window of No. 9, overlooking the Charles Bridge.*

The assemblage of objects here makes up one of the best-known signs in Prague, and a perfect example of a Prague myth that is still in the making. It comprises a Madonna between carved mangle rollers fronted by a lantern. An old-timer who lives in the house claimed that the painting floated past during a flood, and was recovered by a Mr Rott, who installed the lantern after the Virgin saved the life of his daughter. The icon proceeded to perform sundry other miracles, including the healing of a pair of hands that had been mangled by the rollers of the house laundry. The rollers were then piously removed and placed alongside. The tenant confidently asserted that she had known all the parties concerned, and added the convincing details that Mr Rott was murdered across the road in 1945, and that the mangle was used as a barricade across the Charles Bridge in 1968; but she was mysteriously silent when asked why the rollers are stylized carvings. Another mildly suspicious circumstance was the fact that she was only 84 years old, while a 1911 guidebook could already state that the lantern (now electric, and apt to switch off) was an eternal flame for all those in the throes of death. To confuse matters further, many Praguers warn that if the light goes out while you are watching it, within a year you'll have snuffed it too.

> *To end this walk, you could pick up a drink from the tiny Bistro Bruncvík across the square and take it to one of the two remaining gardens of Malá Strana. The first stretches across the south of the island, with a shady embankment over the swan-filled Vltava which is a favourite spot for canoodling couples. Even more secluded is the **Vojan Park** (Vojanovy sady); like the Waldstein Gardens, it's locked behind a wall and watched by the castle high above. It's on the way back to Malostranská metro station. Walk under the Charles Bridge, and then along U lužického semináře; the entrance is set into the blank wall on your left. (Open 8–7 summer, and 8–5 winter.)*

The almost hidden park is the oldest in Prague, laid out in 1248 by the Carmelites, taken over by English Virgins and now an integral part of the Finance Ministry. Modern sculptures regularly swing and squat under its willows and fruit trees nowadays, and even if no exhibition is being held, the park has a few notable curiosities. To the far left from the entrance is a grotto-chapel to the Old Testament prophet Elijah, who, the Carmelites insisted, had founded their Order, and somewhere in the gardens is rumoured to be a masterful Baroque sculpture of an impassioned St John Nepomuk standing on a fish.

Start: *Statue of Kepler and Brahe, Keplerova; tram 22.*
Finish: *Royal Summer Palace.*
Walking time: *3 hours, although the National Gallery of European Art could extend that considerably.*

IV: Hradčany

The shadow of the castle has always fallen between Hradčany and the city below. The district was founded in 1320 as a set of hovels in which the royal serfs could sleep and breed—and although it slipped out of the castellan's personal control in 1598, it never grew into a normal town. Locked into a slowly turning backwater, monks and nobles indulged their peccadilloes here for centuries; today, its cobbles and courtyards are a silent suburb of the castle which many visitors never see. This short walk takes you through the magnificent libraries of the Strahov Monastery, Prague's collection of six centuries of European art, and tours the Baroque miracles of Prague's Loretto shrine. It skims across the castle and ends in the royal gardens, where the Habsburgs grew their tulips and built the most splendid Renaissance palace north of the Alps.

Any day except Monday (closing day for most attractions) is fine for this serene stroll, and you can take regular shelter if it's raining. It ends near the castle; you could combine it with Walk I if you were up bright and early.

There's only one convenient way to **start** the walk if you're staying in the centre—luckily it's the ubiquitous 22 tram, which slithers all over town. Two easy points to pick it up are Malostranské nám., and Národní street. You can take the 22 again at the **end** of the walk; alternatively, Malá Strana isn't far if you retrace your steps to Hradčany Square.

---

lunch/cafés

There aren't many lunchstops in this dozy part of town, but everyone should find something to their taste in one of the places listed below.

U dvou zlatých hvězd (The Two Golden Stars), Pohořelec 3. *10.30–8.* Indonesian fast food from satay to nasi goreng. Tasty and convenient, but pickings are paltry for vegetarians.

U ševce Matouše (Matthew the Cobbler), Loretánské nám. 4. *12 noon–4 pm (lunch).* Recognizable by the copper boot that hangs in the vaulted arcade outside. Specializes in producing countless varieties of very thick steak.

U černého vola (The Black Ox). *10–10.* Velkopopovické beer and all the meat and dumplings you could hope for. Still popular with the locals.

U Lorety, next to Loretto. *11–3 pm (lunch).* Tranquil summer terrace with pastas, salads, steaks, cheeses and hams.

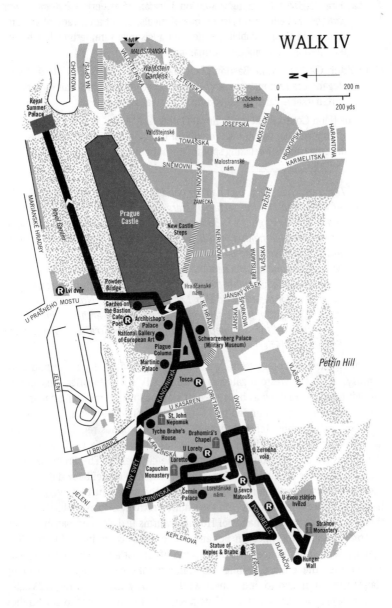

WALK IV

N ← ⊕

| 0 | | 200 m |
| 0 | | 200 yds |

CHOTKOVA

NA OPYŠI

VALDŠTEJNSKÁ

MALOSTRANSKÁ Ⓜ

Waldstein Gardens

LETENSKÁ

Dražického nám.

JOSEFSKÁ

MOSTECKÁ

PROKOPSKÁ

HARANTOVA

Royal Summer Palace

Valdštejnské nám.

TOMÁŠSKÁ

KARMELITSKÁ

MARIÁNSKÉ HRADBY

Royal Garden

SNĚMOVNÍ

THUNOVSKÁ

Malostranské nám.

TRŽIŠTĚ

Prague Castle

New Castle Steps

ZÁMECKÁ

NERUDOVA

BŘETISLAVOVA

VLAŠSKÁ

Ⓡ Lví dvůr

Powder Bridge

Hradčanské nám.

JÁNSKÝ VRŠEK

SPORKOVA

U PRAŠNÉHO MOSTU

Garden on the Bastion

KE HRADU

JÁNSKÁ

Petřín Hill

Café Poet Ⓡ

Archbishop's Palace

National Gallery of European Art

Schwarzenberg Palace (Military Museum)

VLAŠSKÁ

Plague Column

JELENÍ

Martinic Palace

KANOVNICKÁ

Tosca Ⓡ

LORETÁNSKÁ

ÚVOZ

U KASÁREN

U BRUSNICE

🏛 St. John Nepomuk

Tycho Brahe's House

Drahomíra's Chapel 🏛

U černého vola Ⓡ

KAPUCÍNSKÁ

U Lorety Ⓡ

Loretto

Ⓡ

NOVÝ SVĚT

Capuchin Monastery

JELENÍ

Černín Palace

Loretánské nám.

U ševce Matouše Ⓡ

U dvou zlatých hvězd

ČERNÍNSKÁ

POHOŘELEC

KEPLEROVA

Statue of Kepler & Brahe

PARLÉŘOVA

DLABAČOV

🏛 Strahov Monastery

● Hunger Wall

201

Tosca, Hradčanské nám. 5 (entrance on Loretánská street). *12 noon–3 pm (lunch).* Excellent (if pricy) range of meals, under an arcade of ancient arches and sloping cobbles. Perfect for a leisurely summertime lunch, but the interior is too gloomily formal for some tastes.

Café Poet, Garden on the Bastion (Zahrada na baště), *Tues–Sun 10–6.* In an elegant castle courtyard and on the edge of a ravine, this otherwise unremarkable café can fill you up with steaks and soups.

Lví dvůr (Lion Court), next to the Royal Gardens. *11–11.* Once the home of the Habsburg cats. Lobster is the wildest thing on the menu these days, but the courtyard is a relaxing spot to finish the walk.

---

*The tram snakes through hairpin bends to the top of the castle hill. Get off when you see the statue of stargazing Tycho Brahe and Johannes Kepler on your right, a 1983 sculpture that invests the squabbling duo with a calm that neither would ever have shown in the other's company during their lives (see p. 224). Cross over into Pohořelec, a triangular eyrie of Baroque houses nestling high over the glistening city. It earned its name—which roughly translates as 'afterburn'—after being razed to the ground for the third time in 1741. Cross over to No. 8, where you'll find a stone portal in the salmon-pink façade. The arched staircase carries you into the wooded forecourt of the **Strahov Monastery** (Strahovský klášter).*

The name Strahov comes from *stráž* ('guard'), and dates from the mid-14th century, when the western gateway of Charles IV's new fortifications around the left bank of Prague was built here. It's an unsuitably militaristic name for the monastery. When founded in 1140, it was called Mount Sion; although fires and armed mobs stormed through with monotonous regularity until the later 18th century, in spirit the monastery has always been a world apart from the bloodshed and religious tomfoolery of the city below. The Premonstratensian canons were an austere order—their insistence on celibacy didn't make them popular among the licentious monks of the day—but they were also an honest and hardworking crew. On their hilltop retreat, they assembled a library that, despite sacks at the hands of Hussite swarms in 1420 and oafish Swedes in 1648, became the finest in Bohemia. The books came in useful in 1782, when Joseph II announced the dissolution of almost all the monasteries and convents of the empire. While nuns and monks everywhere were being clapped in jail or told to find honest work, the wily abbot at Strahov, Václav Mayer, saved the day by turning it into a research institute for scholars. Strahov was one of very few monasteries to survive in Bohemia. The Communists were tough cookies—in 1950 they mounted a night-time raid, sent the canons to concentration camps, and turned their cloisters into the national literary museum—but the Premonstratensians proved even tougher. Eight hardy survivors shuffled back after the 1989 revolution, and Strahov is once again a functioning monastery.

The canons have been reproducing steadily since 1989, and about 20 now live here. They like their privacy and you're unlikely even to glimpse the flash of a white cowl. On the other hand, you may see any number of things that you wouldn't expect from a monastery. When the buildings were returned to the Premonstratensians in 1990, they were simultanously told to stump up £3 million (about $5 million) for restoration. After a moment of soul-searching they launched a ruthless investment drive. An Italian family firm now runs a disco in the 12th-century beer cellars, a restaurant will open opposite the copper-lidded towers of the church; and future developments that the canons are considering include an art auction hall, a patisserie and a brasserie.

> *At the time of writing, the courtyard is an ominously busy building site. Assuming accessibility, walk to the gate some 75 metres in front of the steps. It leads to the **Museum of National Literature** (Památník národního písemnictví). (Open Tues–Sun 9–12.15, 1–5; adm.)*

A museum devoted to Czech literature won't appeal to many English-speakers, but it's worth a brief visit simply to look around the monastery. Its architectural history is Prague's usual *mélange*—18th-century Baroque on top of tenacious Romanesque and Gothic details. The cerebral canons also had an evident fascination for illusionistic art: along the cloister are several two-dimensional altars to St Norbert (who founded the order and whose body Prague's Premonstratensians acquired in 1627), and one particularly curious green door, painted for unknown reasons onto a corner of the far wall. On the same side is a flight of steps creeping between the walls of the Romanesque heart of the monastery, which contains the museum itself.

Highlights include two ancient tomes of Glagolitic scrawls, and some rather more accessible illuminated manuscripts. They include the *Kunigunde Passional* and the *Kunhuta Passional*, mystical prayer books produced for the delectation of well-heeled nuns (who did much to advance Bohemian art and literature during the 14th century); and examples of Hussite illumination, glorifying the chalice and the rebel himself. The museum has another floor devoted to the 19th-century national revival of Czech literature—but you might want to go on to the highlight of Strahov, its magnificent **libraries**.

Work your way back to where you bought your ticket, turning left into the main courtyard. Ahead of you to the right, you'll see the **Church of St Roch** *(Kostel sv. Rocha).*

The church was built after Rudolf II had promised the plague-resistant saint a church if he protected Prague from the approaching pestilence. Roch accepted the offer—the bacilli screeched to a halt a few kilometres from the city walls—and although Rudolf took no chances and moved to Plzeň for the duration, he was as good as his word. The peculiar church dates from 1603–12. Gothic architecture lingered late in Bohemia, and the Renaissance influence of the blank niches and pedimented door is almost lost among the tenacious buttresses and tall, tracery-topped windows climbing the façade. St Roch didn't share the luck of the rest of the monastery; once the Strahov parish church, it was closed down by Joseph II in 1784, and now hosts sporadic exhibitions.

Turn left past the Church of the Annunciation (Kostel Nanebevzetí Panny Marie), a Baroque edifice built over hidden layers going back to the Romanesque origins of the monastery. Face the neo-classical façade of the **Philosophical Hall.**

The library was built frantically between 1780 and 1782, after Abbot Mayer got wind of the new Emperor Joseph's plans. Designed to provide room for a wider range of books and readers, it was intended to persuade the emperor of the quarter-truth that there was no conflict between rationalism and what the canons had been up to for centuries. Mayer also resorted to a prudent cringe: the haughty figure in gold above the stark façade is the scourge of the monasteries himself.

Buy a ticket at the entrance below. (Open 9–12, 1–5; adm.)

After climbing the staircase, you'll find yourself in the anteroom. It contains a few illuminated manuscripts and monkish doodles, but it's hard to resist being dragged into the opulence of the hall beyond. Walnut bookcases, strung with overripe gilt Rococo decoration, push through two levels. Any sensible library would stop at the gallery, but here the tomes march on, climbing 15 metres in all to the ceiling. When the cabinets arrived, the plan for the half-built room had to be changed to accommodate them. There are over 40,000 books, comprising works that Strahov had picked up from benefactors and less fortunate monasteries than itself, all lined up to prove to Joseph that it was providing a useful social service. The emperor seems to have been convinced—he bought the shelves for the monastery, after driving down their market value by abolishing the previous owner. The late 18th-century library represents the very end of the dream, as old as antiquity but restored during the Renaissance, of collecting all wisdom in one place. Humanity was on the verge of knowing too much—but at the organ-grinder desks, scholars could do their best to keep up by spinning through four books at once.

The ceiling fresco, rising from the sombre stacks into a celestial blue, was the last work of the Viennese Franz Maulpertsch, and dates from 1794. It's called *The Struggle of Mankind to Know Real Wisdom*, but there's also another struggle going on, between the sacred and the profane, which owes as much to Joseph II's threat as to the rationalist bent of the Strahov clerics. Christianity gets an honourable mention at both ends, but the woman in the cherubic supernova is not the Virgin, but Providence; and along both sides antiquity's truth-seeking heroes hog the stage. Alexander the Great and pensive Aristotle on the left face Plato on the right; Socrates welcomes his hemlock on the far right; and even Diogenes the Cynic has moved in, lock, stock and barrel, on the far left. Five years after the French Revolution, neither emperor nor Strahov had any sympathy for the troublesome Encyclopaedists—Diderot et al. are tumbling into an abyss next to the pillar on the right—but the nefarious Rational Dictionary still found its way onto the stacks, inexplicably filed under reference AA.1 by the canons.

> *Strahov's Premonstratensians didn't just bury their heads in books. They also stared at their collection of curiosities, now in the cabinets outside the hall: monstrous creatures of the deep, a sad crocodile, and cases of shining beetles and butterflies. Walk past the musty, dusty leather-bound books along the corridor. The display case at the end contains a replica of the oldest manuscript in the library, a 10th-century New Testament bound in fussy 17th-century encrustations, and on the right is the* **Theological Hall**.

This library was built in 1671, during the restoration of the monastery after the Thirty Years War. It doesn't have the solemn majesty of the later Philosophical Hall, but its stucco-laden barrel vault is even more sumptuous. It is decorated with ceiling frescoes, extolling the virtues of True Wisdom. They were painted by a member of the Order in 1723–27, and although Grecian philosophers don't crowd out the scenes, the secular nature of the allegories shows that the Enlightenment hadn't passed Strahov by. Favoured lay-scholars could work here along with the canons—all were prodded along by the frescoes' Latin inscriptions, dully insistent reminders that 'it is better to acquire knowledge than to make money', 'knowledge is difficult but fruitful' *et cetera ad nauseam.*

The clerics were liberal—but to a degree. They observed the prohibitions of the Vatican's Index, but kept choice selections dangling tantalizingly in the cabinet above the far door. If a prurient canon wanted to flick through one of Galileo's potboilers or a diabolical Hussite tract, he'd have to explain his reasons in detail to the abbot—a cumbersome process that was swept away during the glasnost of the 1780s, when the books were removed into the profanity of the Philosophical Hall.

> *When you leave the libraries, take a look at the heavy fortifications around the gate to your left as you re-enter the courtyard. They make up the end of the* **Hunger Wall** *(Hladová zed'), which was built by Charles IV in about 1360 to enclose the entire left bank of Prague, and which still crawls unevenly across the length of Petřín Hill. The name comes from a legend that Charles didn't really need a new wall and built it to create jobs for peckish Praguers after a failed harvest (although this project seems neither more nor less functional than all the other walls, churches, castles, bridges, cathedrals and towns then being built by the emperor). Walk back towards the Literature Museum, and you'll see a gate ahead of you leading into the Strahov gardens. To your right is Petřín—walk along the path on the left until you come to Úvoz. The view of Prague from here is one of the best in the city. The unmistakable dome of St Nicholas's dominates the foreground; across the river on the right are the twin towers of the Týn Church; and the Soyuz launch pad on the horizon is Prague's television and radio tower (see p. 275).*

> *When you get to Úvoz, turn right. The steep street careers down to Malá Strana, but jump off when you see a set of stairs to your left. Turn left at the top. To your right is a curious cubby-hole looking like the stranded remnant of a little-lamented church. In fact it's a chapel celebrating the spot where Good King Wenceslas's bad old mother, Drahomirá—a pagan, and a murderer to boot—was dragged into Hell. In front of you is Loretánské nám., with the 30 Doric half-columns of the 500-foot long* **Černín Palace** *ranged like riot police against the boisterous mob of cherubs and green onion-domes of Loretto (Loreta) to your right.*

The palace is the largest in Prague, and it's a beast: in form, its façade is still Renaissance; in its scale and deliberate repetition it belongs to the Baroque; and with its awesome pomp it has the timeless stamp of distant power. Humprecht Černín was one of the wealthiest of the *arrivistes* who moved into the jobs and properties left vacant by Protestant exiles after the Catholic victory at the Battle of the White Mountain in 1620. From his sojourn in Venice as imperial ambassador, he returned in 1664 with money to burn and a handful of half-baked architectural ideas—and this behemoth was the monstrous offspring of his appetites. He tried out plans by Rome's Bernini and rejected them; he tirelessly argued with his Prague architects who tried to endow his baby with some human features; and when he died in 1682 the palace remained unfinished. The family frittered away their fortune to complete it; and they had barely moved in the furniture before they decided to sell it in 1779, only to find there were no takers. In the end, the government moved in. It became a barracks in 1851, and since 1932 the bureaucrats of the Ministry of Foreign Affairs have stalked its desolate corridors. In 1948, Prague's fourth (and so far, last) defenestration occurred here, when the Foreign Minister, Jan Masaryk, fell from his office window. No one knows whether he jumped or was pushed. On the one hand, he was the popular son of Czechoslovakia's first president, and the Communists had good reason to bump him off; on the other, he was a manic depressive—but it's always a useful subject to bring up in Prague if the conversation starts to flag.

Černín's builders excavated a pagan cemetery full of headless skeletons, and hundreds of tons of earth. The fate of the bones is unknown, but the earthworks lay around in the centre of the square for a couple of centuries, and were only properly patted down in the early 1900s to form the embankment that divides the square into two levels. Turn left towards the bell tower of **Loretto.** *(Open Tues–Sun 9–12.15, 1–4.30; adm.)*

The original Loretto in Italy was a medieval Lourdes, one of the most visited shrines in Europe. It was the house where the Archangel Gabriel told Mary the good news, rescued from pagan hands and flown over from Nazareth by a flock of angels in about 1291.

The cult was wildly popular, and hundreds of imitations appeared across the Continent in the following centuries. After the Battle of the White Mountain, 50 were built in Bohemia as part of the miracle-culture being constructed to re-Catholicize the country. The Prague Loretto wasn't the first, but it became the grandest. The shrine was begun in 1626, only six years after the Catholic victory, and three generations of architects spent a century perfecting it.

The façade (1716–23) was the work of both Kristof Dienzenhofer and his son Kilian (see p. 72) and it's a charmer: bouncy cherubs and dinky tower cheerfully taunting the armed might of the Černín palace opposite. The atmosphere inside is altogether less sunny. The Loretto was established by Benigna Kateřina of Lobkowicz, one of the minor relatives of the Spanish Habsburgs who found their way to Prague; it was owned and run by an order founded by a Spanish warrior-saint; and it speaks the unearthly language of Spain's Counter-Reformation, the mixture of fanatical cruelty and sensual mysticism that spawned both an Inquisition and the art of El Greco. Pleasure and pain are part and parcel of any shrine, but in Prague the new cult was being thrust onto a people who had fought against Catholicism for two centuries: it worked, but only by tapping a morbid superstition and voyeurism that permeate it still.

> *Walk around the cloisters, built in 1661 to protect the hundreds of homeless pilgrims from heavenly deluges. They are lined with rows of painted saints in recently renovated pine cabinets. The Capuchins knew their audience—suffering and penitence were out, and the cloister is a department store of useful intercessors. Under this one roof, suppliants could get rid of toothaches (Apollonia), sore throats (Blaise) and gallstones (Liborius); if they had lost something, Antony of Padua would find it for them; and Sebastian inoculated them against the plague. You'll find plenty of others here, with their specialities helpfully inscribed underneath.*

Half-way round the cloister, you're led into the **Santa Casa**, a replica of the Nazarene hovel itself, complete with rich Baroque stucco reliefs. As you walk through the pedimented portal, you may feel that it's all slightly at odds with your understanding of the Gospels, but have faith—the exterior is the work of mid-17th-century Italians, but inside is what it *really* looked like. The brick room is something of an anti-climax: a sombre box, with a cedar Virgin on the altar, surrounded by smiling silver cherubs who look as though they were put together with tin foil. Set into the bricks on the left are two beams from the original Loretto.

> *Walk from the Santa Casa to the **Church of the Nativity**, taking a look at the relief on the back, which shows the story of the angelic*

transportation. Christians are slaughtered below—but there's room on the house for two. Madonna and child sit elegantly on the roof, before being whisked to safety over a rolling Tuscan landscape.

The church fits the cruel and surreal spirit of the shrine well. On the far right is a painting of the tortured martyr St Agatha—the patron saint of women with breast complaints—handing her own severed breasts on a dish to a welcoming angel. Even more macabre are the dummies in the glass cases on either side of the altar. The wax masks and dusty costumes shroud the skeletons of SS Felicissimus and Marcia, another Spanish addition to Loretto's box of tricks.

The most preposterous Iberian introduction to the shrine is yet to come. Continue round the cloister to the chapel on the corner before the entrance.

The figure with the Castro beard, on the cross to your left, isn't Christ (as you'll probably realize from the sky-blue dress with silver brocade) but the unfortunate Portuguese **St Wilgefortis**. She prayed on the eve of her wedding to be saved from her heathen suitor, and God in His mysterious way decided that the best remedy was facial hair, which she sprouted overnight. The prospective groom was suitably awed, and hastily withdrew from the wedding. Her father was less impressed—he crucified her. She's the patron saint of unhappily married women, and it sounds like the kind of story that should have done a roaring trade in Loretto, but apparently it was a flop. According to one of the workers here, 'a woman with a beard was alien to the traditions of Bohemia'.

*From the chapel, walk on and turn left up the stairs just before the entrance. The steps lead past a blood-drenched sculpture of the Crucifixion to the **Loretto Treasury**, a priceless collection of glittering monstrances and reliquaries.*

Most of the jewels behind the reinforced-glass cases were gifts from the quislings and newly rich who now made up Bohemia's aristocracy, and they smell less of pious duty than anxiety that the propaganda machine of Loretto should remain solvent. The Vatican understood the shrine's importance: in 1683 Emperor Leopold I received permission to sell off the precious metals of the empire's churches to finance his war with the Turks, but the Prague Loretto was granted a blanket exemption. There's some superb silver filigree work, but the most impressive bauble is at the far end—the **diamond monstrance**, over 6200 of the stones sprayed out like the quills of a horror-struck hedgehog. It was designed by Fischer von Erlach in 1699, and formed part of the gift of Ludmilla Eva Franziska of Kolovrat, who left her entire estate to the Madonna of the Santa Casa.

Walking around the shrine, you may have heard the appealing but cacophonous chimes of Loretto's carillon, 27 mechanical bells that have been urgently trying to learn a recognizable tune every hour for three centuries. They were among the few to survive a central European bell holocaust in the First World War, when the Austro-Hungarians turned most of the metal they could find into cannons (Prague's 267 bells were all rung for the last time on St Wenceslas's Eve in 1916). They're synchronized, for want of a better term, by grooved cylinders; their current effort is apparently called 'We Greet Thee a Thousand Times'.

> *From Loretto, turn right and walk diagonally across the square. The compact tiled roofs to the north cover the low-lying* **Capuchin Friary**.

The Communists turned this complex into the library of the Czechoslovakian Army, but the Capuccinos are back. The brown-robed friars now spend their days praying and contemplating, but it was not always so. The monastery was founded in 1600 by the Spaniard St Laurence of Brindisi, who had been sent from Rome. Laurence had the honest qualities of a fanatic: at Rudolf II's request, he took time out while in Prague to rally the empire's anti-Turkish troops, and ended up leading them into battle armed only with a crucifix. He survived; the Turks were massacred. But Prague's first Capuchins were a sneaky bunch. As well as maintaining the perverted pleasure palace of Loretto, the monks let General Waldstein's Catholic army clamber over their garden wall in 1632. The Saxons then occupying Prague were caught napping, and the balance of the Thirty Years War was swung.

> *Follow the perfidious wall into Černínská.*

The little mess of cottages sinking into a dell of grassy cobbles is ridiculously dreamy. In any other town it would have been turned into a warren of wine bars and poster shops long ago. It's not a good idea to say anything vaguely favourable about the Communists in Prague these days, but at least here you can whisper silent thanks for the rigor mortis of their iron grip.

> *Turn right down* **Nový Svět**, *which is also the name of the whole hamlet.*

It means 'New World'; Dvořák's symphony has a certain appropriateness, although it is Hovis commercials rather than the Land of the Free that come to mind. The quarter grew up during the 1500s as a set of ramshackle hovels for workers to trudge back to after a hard day's work at the castle. The Capuchins cleaned them up after moving in, and they're 17th-century cottages at heart, despite modifications made over the following 200 years.

As you wander along the street, you'll pass a notorious studio to your right, containing piles of air-brushed spacescapes that make up what several Praguers feel to be one of the most atrocious art collections to be found in the capital. The last house on the right was the home of **Tycho Brahe** during his stay in Prague as imperial mathematician to Rudolf II (1599–1601). Brahe was never really at ease in the house, and had incessant problems with his Capuchin neighbours. He complained that the monks had begun to ring their bells in a manner calculated to unnerve him—which sounds like the kind of thing that the Spaniards would do, but Brahe was little better. The Dane had the ear of the emperor throughout 1600, a year in which the rest of Rudolf was plumbing new depths of mental instability, and it's thought that it was Brahe who convinced the monarch to expel the Capuchins a few months after he had invited them in. As the monks packed their bags, Rudolf had another turn and commanded them to remain; and the seesaw of intrigue continued for another year until Brahe set off from this house on the fateful journey to the banquet at which his bladder would implode (*see* pp. 156–7).

> *Turn right at the end of the street. On the right is the* **Church of St John Nepomuk** *(Kostel sv. Jana Nepomuckého), the first of Kilian Dienzenhofer's works in Prague to be built independently of his father. It dates from 1720–28, roughly the same time that he was finishing the more elegant façade of the Loretto. Follow Kanovnická to your left, with luck avoiding the crazed drivers who occasionally swerve around at death-embracing speed, until you emerge into* **Hradčanské nám.** *or Hradčany Square.*

When a part of Prague can be described as tranquil, it often means that its history is steeped in gore or grinding poverty, but this square has less to hide than most. Many of the grand buildings that line it predate the Battle of the White Mountain; and although it had the standard pillory and gallows, the most impressive judicial murders took place in the Old Town Square where a larger audience could be guaranteed. It never even really had the hurly-burly of a marketplace—a few groceries and trinkets were sold here over the centuries, but the kings and nobles preferred to do their shopping downtown.

> *On the corner of the square is the façade of the* **Martinic Palace,** *plastered with cream-on-brown scratchings.*

The palace was built by the count of the same name in 1620, two years after his defenestrated descent into a dungheap had plunged him into the footnotes of history as one of the minor causes of the Thirty Years War (*see* p. 52). The *sgraffito* decoration was rediscovered during restoration in 1971. It's a merry Renaissance retelling of Old Testament stories. On the front is Joseph (of Technicolor Dreamcoat fame). The wife of his master Potiphar is eagerly trying to lie with him, but he doesn't want to know her. The artist seems to have had a penchant for men wronged by the treachery of the fairer sex; in the courtyard, there are fragments from the story of Samson, wrestling with his lion and tossing a Philistine pillar. Tucked away on the opposite side of this corner of the square is a house that cinema buffs might recognize. Miloš Forman chose it as Mozart's house for *Amadeus*, which was largely filmed in Prague.

> *On the opposite side of the square is the eye-catching façade of the* **Schwarzenberg Palace**, *endless* sgraffito *triangles crawling in diagonal formations across its Renaissance splendour. Walk towards it—you'll pass a* **Plague Column** *in the woody centre of the square; F. M. Brokof sculpted it in 1726. Unlike Rudolf's gift to St Roch, this was an ex post facto offering to appease the fickle saints, who had just done nothing as the pest had stormed through for the second time in 50 years. The palace was built by a member of the ubiquitous Lobkowicz family, who took advantage of the property slump after the 1541 fire to buy up the site. It now houses a* **Military Museum** *(Vojenské muzeum), containing exhibits from the dawn of warfare up to 1918. (Open May–Oct Tues–Sun 10—6; adm.)*

Those of a bloodthirsty bent will find plenty to enjoy here; and even pinko peaceniks should take a look, out of respect for Bohemia's savage history. A language that has given little else to the world provided it with the word 'pistol' (from the Czech word *píšt'ala*, meaning flute), and the Bren machine-gun, named after Brno where it was originally made. You'll find a millennium's worth of global killing represented here: merciless corkscrew daggers, crescent scimitars and pencil rapiers, terrifying wind-up crossbows, and more artillery than you can shake a stick at. The fraternal peace-loving propaganda of the old regime that used to be on the top floor has been cleared out, and the space now hosts exhibitions of modern art—often on anti-militaristic themes.

> *Walk across the square from the museum. Just next to the castle gate is the* **Archbishop's Palace** *(Arcibiskupský palac), built in Renaissance style but given the present Rococo façade in 1763–4 to keep up with Queen Maria Theresa's revamp of the castle. Next to the palace is an arch, through which a lane winds down to the* **Šternberk Palace**, *housing the* **National Gallery's Collection of European Art.** *(Open Tues 9–7, Wed–Sun, 10–6; adm.)*

Although this excellent gallery has long been one of the great pleasures of Prague, the years since 1989 have thrown up some unexpected problems. The first is that the property restitution law of 1990 has resulted in the loss of several important paintings. Although many of the rightful owners have reloaned their works to the gallery for insurance and tax purposes, that means that the displays are in something of a state of flux. Art theft has also hit the gallery: $30 million worth of Picassos were stolen in 1991, and although they were soon recovered, it's becoming apparent that Prague's *babičky*—watchful though they are—will not be able to hold off the international art theft mafia for ever. Security guards now help them out, but the relaxed atmosphere of the gallery still makes it feel like a heist-of-the-century waiting to happen.

> *The collection is divided into two parts. Across the courtyard is the collection of modern French art, but for now walk up the stairs to the first floor, where you'll find 14th- and 15th-century Italian art, ancient and classical art and icons, and 15th- and 16th-century art of the Netherlands.*

The triptychs and diptychs that make up the bulk of the work on this floor are no great shakes, but there are a few paintings worth noticing in the Netherlandish section. One that you can't avoid anyway is *St Luke Drawing the Virgin* (1513–16) by Mabuse (Jan Gossaert), which once adorned the altar of St Vitus's Cathedral. Ever since the 16th century, there has been strong support for the view that Mabuse was too clever for his own good, and this famous painting shows why. A stint in High Renaissance Rome had rather overwhelmed him: not only did he set the legendary painting session in a classical temple (rather than the more conventional studio or cloudy vision), but he cluttered the building with most of the mental baggage that he had picked up during his stay. It's unclear whether you are inside or outside—pillars, balustrades and arches are joined in a way that only perspectival trickery knows how—and the unassuming figures of Mary and Luke are watched over by a hotchpotch of antiquarian heroes and mythological symbols. To confuse matters further, Mabuse has painted another Virgin and Apostle outside a mutant late Gothic construction in the distance. Another painting worth noticing on this floor is Pieter Bruegel the Elder's *Haymaking* (1565), a happy landscape of rural harmony which originally formed part of a cycle; only four other Months survive, but they are now in Vienna and New York. Finally, have a quick gaze at the exquisite *Bunch of Flowers with Tulips* (1607–08), by Jan Brueghel, flower-painter *extraordinaire*.

> *Walk up to the second floor, which contains the rest of the gallery's European collection other than its modern French art.*

The first rooms contain work by German artists of the 14th–16th centuries, including several works by Lucas Cranach the Elder. At the beginning of his career, Cranach was an important representative of the 'Danube School', the first European artists to paint landscape for its own sake, but the works here come from his comfortable stint as court painter to Saxony's Frederick the Wise. There's barely a shrub to be seen, although the deciduous twig covering the pudenda of *Adam and Eve* (*c.* 1538) has a certain Danubian feel about it. That work is an example of the way in which Cranach (and others working in the stern atmosphere of proto-Lutheran towns) used religious themes to conceal his Renaissance-minded experimentation with nudity. As it and several other works show, the Gothic traditions of northern European art had some way to go before the proportions of the human form would be mastered, but despite some excessive deformations, most notably, the rather tragic *Christ Child—Emanuel* (*c.* 1530), the work here also shows the artist's characteristic realism and refusal to idealize beauty. A notable example is his *Old Fool*, showing dirty codger and wily wench locked into a cold transaction of fumbling and theft. (Incidentally, the theme of the mismatched couple was a favourite of Rudolf II, a man who sank into melancholy or insanity when the subject of marriage was raised, and Cranach was one of his favourite painters.) Despite his humanist leanings, Cranach, who was living in Wittenberg while Martin Luther nailed his theses to the door and became a close friend of the man himself, produced endless propaganda for the new religion. His *Suffer the Little Children to Come Unto Me* (*c.* 1540) represents a theme that left his studio in many versions and became one of the most popular in early-16th-century northern European art. The Gospel gobbet was seized upon to bolster the dour reformer in his bitter struggle with the even grimmer Anabaptists, who insisted that, until voluntarily dunked, infants were damned. However, commercially-minded Cranach had no objections to lucrative Catholic commissions, represented here by *SS Catherine and Barbara* and *St Christina* (1520–5) (the Calvinist iconoclasts of a century later were rather more strict, and both are fragments from a destroyed altarpiece painted for St Vitus's Cathedral).

In the next room is Albrecht Dürer's **Feast of the Rose Garlands** (1506), regarded as one of the most important paintings of the northern Renaissance. It represents Dürer's deliberate attempt to marry his country's late Gothic art with the technical tricks and new visions of the south, and this work—with its shimmering colour, noble proportions and beauty, and use of perspective—was an attempt to beat the Venetians at their own game (Dürer painted it on a visit to the city). It shows Virgin, Child and St Dominic handing out rosy honours to kneeling worthies, and is also one of the first group portraits in northern art. Those attending the outdoor ceremony (any excuse to stick in a landscape) include Pope Julian II and Maximilian I, plenty of bourgeois bigwigs, and, hopeful and hairy on the far right, the notoriously arrogant Dürer himself, clutching a small C.V. Rudolf II was obsessed by the artist's work, and had a special yearning for this painting— his father is the character being crowned by the Virgin. When the emperor eventually procured this, 'four stout men' were hired to carry it by hand over the Alps. In 1782, no-nonsense Joseph II put it under the hammer; it was sold for a gulden, but Strahov's monks bought it for a hundred the following year, and although it's been restored and re-restored far too often, it's still the National Gallery's pride and joy.

France and Spain are represented by a handful of minor works, the least unremarkable of which is Goya's *Portrait of Don Miguel de Lardizábal* (1815). The next wing continues with Prague's collection of Italian Renaissance art. The biggest names disappeared when the Swedes pilfered Rudolf II's massive collection in 1648, but a few delights have found their way here over later years. Lorenzo Lotto's *Portrait of a Musician* (pre-1530) is a typical portrait by the Venetian, who dug deep into the individuality of his subjects and imbued them with a sense of transience and melancholy more often encountered in the art of the north than in that of his less troubled home. The effect here is achieved with characteristic sense of detail—a sideward glance, a hand hanging listlessly over a (16th-century) musical score. An interesting footnote is that contemplative Lotto went off to die in Italy's Loretto. Sebastiano del Piombo's *Madonna with Veil* (1520) is of an altogether more heroic nature, produced after he had moved from Venice to Rome, and exuding the statuesque grandeur developed through years of studying antiques and chatting with Michelangelo. The room also contains two works by Agnolo Bronzino, *Cosimo de Medici* (1560) and *Eleanor of Toledo* (1540–3), examples of the many portraits produced by the artist for his Florentine patron. Bronzino's relentless accuracy was often a cruel unveiling of the weaknesses of his subjects, but at least here, Eleanor is more than a match for his piercing eye. The painting commemorates the birth of one of four little Medicis that she produced during the three-year period, and she exudes a cool but almost sensual triumph. Bronzino was to have richer pickings in later portraits, capturing her pain as she spent 12 years dying of tuberculosis.

Prague's Mannerist collection was unmatched in northern Europe until the Swedish heist of 1648, but it's thought to have contained few if any works by El Greco. However, the gallery has one acquisition by him, a *Head of Christ* (1595–7), in which the artist's fervour is reflected in the damp eyes of the Messiah, gazing at a light that only the lucky few are likely ever to see. As usual,

El Greco plays havoc with the artistic conventions of an age. Christ the Man, somehow combining humility with an almost superhuman nobility, is framed by a flaming rhomboid, taken from the figure of Christ the Judge in the rigid iconography of Byzantine art. The painting is one of the most unforgettable in the gallery.

Baroque light effects fill the next few rooms. The works include the scrawny and chiaroscuro-lit frame of *St Jerome* (1646) by Lo Spagnoletto (Jusepe de Ribera), much influenced by the realism of Caravaggio; the no less harsh but far more polished classicist tinge of Simon Vouet's *Suicide of Lucretia* (1625–6); Guido Reni's similarly idealized *Salome with the Head of John the Baptist*; and Domenico Fetti's masterful *Christ on the Mount of Olives* (1615), convulsed by rippling movement and illumination. Take a look also at the tempestuous and faintly macabre *Penance of Mary Magdalene in the Wilderness* (1710) by Il Lissandrino (Alessandro Magnasco), the flickering light and nervous brush strokes of whose work make it instantly recognizable. The gallery's Italian collection ends with Canaletto's *View of London from the Thames* (1746), painted from the balcony of Lambeth Palace at the beginning of his 10-year stint in England. The artist had painted too many of his gay Venetian waterscapes to change his ways by then, and this work transforms the Thames into a festive lagoon, with barques and rowing boats messing about on the river while the launch of the Lord Mayor-cum-Doge cruises past. The unfinished Westminster Bridge stretches across in all its pristine glory. The painting is placed next to a painted snapshot by Francesco Guardi: *(Palace Courtyard)*. It's a rather minute example of Guardi's work, but his almost Impressionistic views of Venice are often contrasted with the detailed deliberation of Canaletto.

The next wing of the gallery contains its collection of Flemish and Dutch art from the 17th and 18th centuries. The first room has two works by the Flemish Roelandt Savery: *Paradise* (1618) and *Landscape with Birds* (1622). Each is an excellent showcase for Savery's claim to art history fame as Europe's first painter of exotic animals. He developed his skills during the decade he spent at Emperor Rudolf II's court, and more particularly, during the time he spent in the imperial menagerie (which is coming up soon on this walk). Although these works were painted after he had left the capital, the subjects are almost certainly accurate likenesses of early 16th-century Prague beasts. A further Prague connection may exist in the case of *Paradise*. The tranquil scene—in which camels, cows and cats, beagles, bucks, boars and birds laze around in prelapsarian innocence—can be seen as an idealised allegory of the religious stalemate Savery had seen in Bohemia. As you contemplate the blissful scene, it's interesting to reflect that in the same year as it was painted, Prague's defenestration threw the continent into 30 years of throat-slashing carnage. The room also contains several works by Rubens, including the superb *Expulsion from Paradise* (1620), a preliminary sketch for one of 39 scenes commissioned by the Jesuits for their church in Antwerp. None was used, but even in its stillborn form the study shows the swirling brushwork and the ability to conjure up an instant of dramatic movement that set Rubens apart from every other European artist of his day. The room also contains a set of the clammy oysters with which part-time cork-seller Osias Beert made his name.

In the next room are works by Rembrandt, landscapes by Salomon van Ruysdael, still lifes by Jan Jansz den Uyl, and a number of notable minor works. They include an oddly spooky *Parliament of Animals* (1629) by Cornelis Saftleven, who spent his life perfecting such satires in the days before they became the stuff of wrapping-paper. Look out also for the *Raising of Lazarus* (1640) by Leonaert Bramer, a powerful work sunk in darkness by an artist who is thought to have been the teacher of Vermeer.

The oval heart of the palace that you enter next contains the grandest Dutch and Flemish painting in the gallery. Rubens holds centre stage with his *Martyrdom of St Thomas* (1637–8), showing the dramatic skills of the artist at their larger-than-life best. The Madras saint-killers are caught in mid-hatchet job, while the speared apostle heroically stretches for a palm of martyrdom being proferred by a squadron of exhilarated cherubs hovering overhead. Frans Hals is represented by a masterful *Portrait of Jasper Schade van Westrum* (1645). Like Rubens, the Dutchman didn't waste a brush-stroke, and he's captured the brashness of his 22-year-old subject with a typical economy of expression that's made him a perennial favourite among artists (and rich American buyers) in the hurried 20th century. The very different portraiture of Rembrandt, kneaded from the palate and laboriously formed on the canvas, is reflected in his *Scholar in his Study* (1634)—an unknown character painted early in the artist's career, but showing the quizzical mystery of facial expression that was to obsess him in later life.

The art of the Low Countries ends with some minor gems in the next room, including the eerie monochrome of *Lighthouse in the Estuary* (1646) by Jan van Goyen, whose lifelong fascination with moody clouds placed him (along with Salomon van Ruysdael) at the forefront of Dutch landscape painting of the 17th century. There are three notable still-lifes: *Still Life with Lemon* by Willem Kalf, sparkling glasses and glistening fruit set off against a dark rug, showing both the contrast and sumptuous display that typifies his work; Jan van de Velde's *Still Life with Smokers' Effects* (1647), a strikingly simple example of Dutch still life, lighter glowing and beer unfinished to bring to mind the absent presence of the puffer concerned; and Jan Davidsz de Heem's *Still Life with Fruit* (1652), which exemplifies the more opulent Flemish still-life tradition, dripping with moisture and very active life forms.

The gallery's 20th-century art begins with a dreamy *Water Castle* (1909) by Gustav Klimt, next to his luscious *Virgin* (1913). Klimt's celebration of feminine fecundity is mocked by Egon Schiele's nightmarish *Pregnant Woman & Death* (1911), the cadaverous couple dolefully contemplating life's bloody terror. Schiele visited Bohemia the same year, but the trip didn't lift his spirits judging from his holiday snap: in *Town (Český Krumlov)*, he transformed one of Europe's most beautiful spots into a Pittsburgh of the soul. Another tortured spirit, Edvard Munch, is represented by three paintings. His *Dancing on the Shore* (c. 1900) dates from the height of his creative powers, and is one of the works that was probably intended for his loosely-planned 'Frieze of Life', a liquid, musical and utterly beautiful contribution to what he called his 'poem of life, love and death'.

German Impressionism is represented by a couple of earlier works by Lovis Corinth, including his *Self Portrait with Glass* (1907), snatched with an urgency unusual even for Impressionism, in a state of undress and half-way through a drink. The social concerns of Expressionism take over with two unnerving portrayals of the powers-that-be. Wilhelm Thöny's *Verdict* (pre-1929) is Kafka in monochrome, while the excellent *Operation* (1912) by Max Oppenheimer takes the form of an indictment of the medical profession—a turbulent sea of white coats surround the all-but-hidden patient, fingers grasping for the jagged wound, and Mephistophelian doctors fascinate themselves with everything other than their charge's wellbeing. The late works by Max Pechstein (*Bridge on the Elbe* —1922) and Karl Schmidt-Rottluff (*Village Green*—c. 1920) turn German rural landscapes into tropical outposts of thunderous colour, reflecting the primitivism of which they were so fond. The deliberate restraint more typical of German Expressionism in the 1920s is shown by Karl Hofer's *Boy with Ball* (1925), as well as the Flemish Constant Permeke's *Peasant Woman with Bared Breast* (1942).

Oskar Kokoschka is represented by several works, most painted during his stay in the Czech capital between 1934 and 1938. Over the previous decade he had painted a series of city views, always surging away from an elevated viewpoint, and there are three panoramas of Prague here; his *Charles Bridge and the Hradčany Castle in Prague* (1935) is one of the finest examples of such works. Imbued with the powerful subjectivism of all the artist's creations and with the love that he felt for the city where his father had been born, they are all visions of a magical island of peace in a continent that was slipping into insanity. The idyll didn't last—the Nazis put Kokoschka on their aesthetic blacklist, and he left shortly before they rolled into town. He spent the war years in London, and his *Red Egg* (1941) is a powerful attack on the common enemy, with a typically Czech stab at appeasement and the Munich sell-out.

> *Walk back down to the ground floor and cross the courtyard to the collection of 19th- and 20th-century French art. Prague discovered Impressionism, Post-Impressionism and Cubism within a few years of each other during the first decade of this century, and French culture profoundly affected its artistic life right up to the German invasion in 1938. The collection is small, but you have to give credit to the city for its taste.*

The gallery contains several sculptures by Rodin, who attended an exhibition of his work in Prague in 1902. He called Prague 'the Rome of the north', but the city didn't mind and bought his seminal *Age of Bronze*. Critics accused him of using a live model to make the original cast in 1875, paradoxically affronted by the fact that the work was so realistic that it lacked the idealism they still required in a nude. Rodin was undaunted, and 10 years later, those detractors that remained were confronted with the open sensuality of *Martyr* (1885). By the time he produced *Iris (Study for a Figure in Flight)* (1890–1), he was dabbling in soft-porn. The far end of the room contains a patchy collection of early-19th-century work, a portrait by Degas and one by Manet of Proust, and a summery set of hazy Impressionism. The last group includes works by Camille Pissarro: *Countryside at Eragny* (1880) and *In the Greengrocer's Garden* (1881); the idyllic *Lovers* (1875) by Auguste Renoir; and a verdant *Ladies in Flowers* (1875) by Claude Monet. There are also two nautical pieces of pointillism by Seurat and Signac, and a gay *Moulin Rouge* (1892) by Toulouse-Lautrec.

The two romantic heroes of Post-Impressionism come next. Gauguin's lifetime preoccupation with colour is reflected in his *Bonjour, Monsieur Gauguin* (1889), as well as the hopefully-named *Escape*, dating from 1902, by which time he had settled in Dominica and left everything behind except the syphilis that killed him the following year. Gauguin's erstwhile friend, Van Gogh, is represented by the swirling undercurrents of *Green Rye* (1889), created from the lunatic asylum that he entered after his failed knife attack on Gauguin and his notoriously more successful assault on his own ear.

Cézanne is represented by a handful of works. His *Portrait of Joachym Gasquet* (1897) creates a rare intensity of expression with the studied and extraordinary use of colour and tone on the subject's face, and is particularly remarkable given that the artist at this time was generally less concerned with the mood than with the spatial location of his human subjects. With the two other works—a small but juicy *Fruit* (1882) and his *House in Aix-en-Provence* (1885-7)—you see the beginnings of that preoccupation with volume that was to consume his career. Indirectly it would also come to concern much of Europe: after two memorial exhibitions of his work in Paris in 1907, many French artists became fascinated by the artist's constructive and compositional skills. The most dramatic results come up soon, but you can see a definite turn towards wonkiness in the works by Maurice Vlaminck (*Landscape with Poplars* and *Grey House* (1914)) and André Derain (*Cadaqués* (1910), *Montreuil-sur-Mer* (1910), and *Still Life with Jug* (1913)). But the fancy experimentation didn't affect everyone: Pierre Bonnard was having none of it, and his *Conversation in Provence* (1912–13) is a serene memory of Impressionism, while Henri Matisse floated through through it all with timeless works such as the stunning *Joaquina* (1910).

> *Although the representation of artists in the gallery is generally limited to one or two paintings, its collection of early Cubist works is the most impressive in central Europe. The director of the National Gallery during the 1920s, Vincenc Kramář, lived in Paris during the early years of the century and had an unerring appreciation of the emerging style. The works that he assembled were profoundly to influence the coming generation of Czech artists and the 30 that he himself bought and then bequeathed to the gallery are now the subject of what promises to be one of the most bitter Czech restitution battles of the decade. Kramář's children claimed in 1992 that he was threatened and cajoled on his deathbed; the gallery points to the Communist ideals he maintained for a lifetime and his deep commitment to securing public access to art collections. With luck, the kids won't yet have won by the time you read this; but with price tags of $200 million being plucked out of the air by mischievous observers, nor are they likely to let the matter drop.*

The work by **Pablo Picasso** forms the core of the collection (and the forthcoming lawsuit). The prize is the artist's *Self-Portrait* (1907), painted while he was still thinking his way out of the world of appearances. It dates from the same year as his *Desmoiselles d'Avignon*, and like some of those well-known characters, the black-rimmed eyes and stylized features of the painting borrow heavily from the primitive sculpture then being studied by the artist. From the same period, the gallery contains his *Woman* (1907) and *Nude Woman* (1908). Picasso is clearly dabbling with perspectives and planes in all those works, but as you can see in his *Landscape with a Bridge* (1909), still predominant is a post-Cézanne interest in the way in which space can be used to define objects. But matters start to become very odd with the first truly Cubist piece of the collection, *Woman in an Armchair* (1910). Here volume is finally turned into space alone, Picasso having torn apart his subject and reconstituted it in an entirely new visual language. No one has ever been quite sure to what extent you are meant to reconstruct the puzzles, an exercise that tends to defeat the point of the artist's endeavours, but you certainly wouldn't want to dispense with the titles when looking at the rest of the Analytical Cubist paintings. *Cadaqués Harbour* (1910) shows how far Picasso's experimentation had advanced: if you go back to Derain's view of the same town (*see above*), produced in the same year, it's quite startling how orthodox the latter now looks, compared to when first seen. Picasso turns Derain's solid roofs, towers and blocks into a series of angular hints, nautical clues and a dash of sea blue. The style develops through *Mandolin and a Glass of Pernod* (1911) and *Woman with a Guitar at the Piano* (1911), and explodes into particular obscurity with *Clarinet* (1911) and the murky mystery of *Toreador Playing the Guitar* (1911). By the following year the high-water mark of Picasso's Cubism had passed, and three works here—*A Souvenir of Le Havre* (1912) and the excellent *Boxer* (1912) and *Absinthe and Cards* (1912)—show how, with colour and two-dimensional texts, Synthetic Cubism returned to less recondite expressions of space and form. The room also contains a copy of Picasso's *Woman's Head* (1909), the first ever Cubist sculpture. Later works by the artist are fairly representative snapshots of his career separated by 20-year intervals. The statuesque *Standing Woman* dates from the period of married tranquillity and his classical phase (1921); the grim *Woman's Head (Head in Grey)* is from the war years of bulls and horses (1941); and by the time of *Abduction of the Sabines* (1962), the artist had finally reached entirely uncategorizable status.

The co-creator of Cubism, Georges Braque, is less comprehensively represented, but his *Violin and Glass* (1910–11) is a particularly interesting still life. The assembly of objects is classically balanced but the depiction falls somewhere between the voluminousness of Cézanne and the broken and opened planes of Cubism. There are also a number of Synthetic Cubist works by the artist.

There follow four paintings by Maurice Utrillo, and a pretty *Flowers* by Suzanne Valadon, mother of Utrillo and active lover of plenty, including 'Teapot' Toulouse-Lautrec. The room also contains works by Raoul Dufy (including *Still Life with Sea in Background* (c. 1926)), Georges Rouault (*In the Bar* and *Three Naked Women*—both 1914), and an example of would-be proletarian art by Fernand Léger (*Two Lovers in the Country*). There's a song in the heart of Marc Chagall's joyful *Circus (Equestrienne, Danseuse)* (1927).

The final room contains Le Douanier Rousseau's *Moi-même, portrait paysage* (1890), the only known self-portrait by the artist, painted with typical charm against a Gallic backdrop of flag-bedecked boat, floating balloon and the year-old Eiffel Tower. But the work that dominates the room is a copy of one of Rodin's best-known sculptures—*Balzac* (1898). As Rodin mulled over the meaning of genius, he transformed the novelist into this epic, which he called 'the sum of my whole life'; when it was unveiled, others called it 'a toad in a sack'. With one-liners like that, the detractors have predictably joined the ranks of the fall-guys of art history. It has to be said that on the purely visual level, the work bears a more than passing resemblance to a toad in a sack, but the psychological mystery and almost Expressionistic power of the sculpture make it perhaps the most original ever produced by the artist.

> *Turn left when you leave the gallery and enter the gate to the left of the castle's main entrance. Continue leftwards through the* **Garden on the Bastion** *(Zahrada na baště). Now a peaceful little spot, redesigned in the 1920s with deft elegance by Jože Plečnik (see pp. 82–3), it was once a defensive ditch and later an artillery emplacement. At the end of the garden, turn right and walk alongside the chasm that plummets downwards in front of you. At the end of the path, turn left along the* **Powder Bridge** *(Prašný most). It's now firmly supported on a solid bank of earth, but until the rebuilding of the castle in the 18th century, it was a wooden bridge over the ravine below. Ferdinand I built it and in his weirdo Habsburg way, included a not-very-secret tunnel underneath, so that he could sneak off to his newly-built Royal Summer Palace without anyone seeing him. His grandson Rudolf II liked the idea and built an entire warren under the castle. The Communists, on the other hand, couldn't make up their minds: after constructing even more escape routes and hideaways, they suddenly got cold feet and filled the castle tunnels with concrete blocks just in case anyone tried to invade through them.*

> *Far below to your right is the* **Stag Moat** *(Jelení příkop). At first, it was a useful natural ditch, but with the invention of artillery, Vladislav II sensibly decided to rely instead on the powerful fortif ations that you can see on the right. The Habsburgs filled the fissure with stags, who multiplied and gambolled here until 1743. In fact, they had a rather rough time—not only did Rudolf II occasionally include his pet lions and tigers in the hunting parties, but they also suffered regular epidemics from the slop poured over them by the residents of the Golden Lane (see p. 141). Over the bridge, to your left is the Riding School of Prague Castle*

*(Jízdárna Pražského hradu), home to temporary exhibitions of the National Gallery, and on the opposite side of the path is the **Royal Garden** (Královská zahrada). (Open April–Oct Tues–Sun 10–5.45.)*

The garden was founded by Ferdinand I in the mid-16th century, and until the Habsburgs left for Vienna after the Thirty Years War, it was their Prague play-ground as well as a laboratory for their explorations of the natural world. Shrubs and plants were grown in greenhouses (tulips stopped off for several years on their way from Turkey to Amsterdam, obtained thanks to the untiring efforts of Ferdinand I's ambassador to Constantinople) and on the slope down to the Stag Moat, Rudolf II grew figs and oranges. The park was laid out as an English garden in the 19th century, after having been devastated during the 17th and 18th centuries; the Swedes and Saxons bombarded the figs, and the rest of the blooms were blown up by the Prussians in 1757. Only the French showed some refinement. They occupied the garden in 1743, but agreed not to obliterate it after the head gardener offered them 30 pineapples.

The gardens were strictly off-limits to the general public until 1989, due to the fact that the adapted 18th-century summer house on your right was the **President's residence** until that year. Most rulers develop odd phobias eventually, but the Czech Communists elevated paranoia to an impressive level. By the mid-1970s Gustáv Husák had installed a reinforced concrete slab above his Baroque study here, to thwart the rocket attacks and air strikes that he had begun to fear. The garden's spooky associations meant that Václav Havel's wife, Olga, refused to move in when he was elected president. As a result the presidential couple still live in their shabby tenement overlooking the Vltava at Rašínovo nábř. 78.

> *Beyond the house but on the same side of the gardens is the* sgraffiti-*covered **Ball Game Hall** (Míčovna), dating from 1567–9. It resounded with the rackets of the Habsburgs and favoured guests for some 50 years, until the family deserted troublesome Prague for good. The sculpture in front is an* Allegory of Night *by Antonín Braun. Examine the monochrome façade closely. When restoring it after the war, the author-ities, in a fit of Communist whimsy, added a few new details to the Renaissance decoration—such as the hammer and sickle discreetly tucked away next to the figure of Justice.*
>
> *The one-time **Orangerie** stretches along the slope below the garden, which is closed by the graceful splendour of the **Royal Summer Palace** (Královský letohrádek), also known as Belvedere.*

The palace was built between 1538 and 1564 for Ferdinand I. More particularly it was built as a token of love for his wife—although he unfortunately loved her too much, and she died while giving birth to their 15th child before the palace was completed. It's the purest example of Italian Renaissance architecture in Prague. Slender Ionic columns swing up and down in happy harmony along the arcade running around the palace, and there are none of the alien Mannerist growths that infected the city's later explorations of the Renaissance (although its roof, an upside-down ship's hull of sea-green copper sheets, defies categorization). The **Singing Fountain** in front of the palace dates from 1568 and tinkles slightly when the water's on. Ferdinand and his entourage would trot through his tunnel to the palace when life at the castle became just too dreary, perhaps to have a ball in the room upstairs. His grandson Rudolf II was less given to revelry; according to Prague's papal nuncio he smiled once during his 26-year reign, when confronted by a diplomatic delegation from Persia scurrying towards him on all fours to kiss his feet. In 1600, he installed an observatory for Tycho Brahe inside the palace. Johannes Kepler also worked here, but his short-lived collaboration with Tycho was fraught with difficulties. Kepler had accepted the Dane's offer of a menial assistant's post only after he and his fellow Lutherans in Styria had been given 45 days' notice to quit by Catholic Archduke Ferdinand; and despite his respect for Tycho's mathematical wizardry, he had already begun to doubt the latter's necessarily ever-more complex model of the universe, in which five planets circled the sun in a flotilla that hurtled around the earth at different speeds. From the moment that Kepler arrived, he tried to double-check Brahe's evidence. In a series of unhappy letters he reported that the tetchy astronomer would only mention the occasional apogee or planetary orbit over dinner, that he had had to promise to keep all the morsels to himself, and more generally that 'Tycho philosophizes rather queerly'. Brahe's unfortunate death was a stroke of luck for the German astronomer. Although Brahe's heirs guarded his work with equal jealousy (the notation of observable facts was widely regarded as an artistic creation) Kepler managed to weasel them out through disingenuous flattery, and was appointed Brahe's successor as imperial mathematician. As the title suggests, Kepler was subject to Rudolf's occasional quirk, but he got on well with the tolerant emperor, who was correspondingly fascinated by his astronomer's outlandish vision of a heliocentric universe. It all bore fruit in 1609, when he published his first two Laws of Planetary Motion based on the work he did here, with an effusive dedication to the emperor.

> *You could end this walk in the Chotek Park (Chotkovy sady), one of the favourite retreats of Franz Kafka. It's on the far side of the palace from the Royal Gardens, and as well as a queer grotto peopled by life-size marble characters from the works of a Czech Romantic poet (Julius*

*Zeyer), it commands a panoramic view over Prague. Alternatively you could remain with the Renaissance. Like fruits and flowers, animals were an important part of the life of any self-respecting 16th-century monarch, and if you leave the garden and turn right, you'll see the **Lion Court** (Lví dvůr). Now a restaurant, it was once the Habsburg zoo.*

Lions were kept here as early as the 14th century, simply as a heraldic emblem, but when Rudolf moved the imperial court to Prague in 1576, they were joined by wolves, leopards, lynxes and a host of other beasts. Ivan the Terrible's son brought three leopards for the emperor on his visit in 1585. The cats were often taken a-hunting, and would line up like kittens behind the horses, ripping the stags apart only on command. The court favourite was Muhammad the Lion, and Tycho Brahe once cast his horoscope. He solemnly announced that the beast and Emperor Rudolf were bound by the same fate. Rudolf died a day after Muhammad—a mystery to chew over while eating your steak.

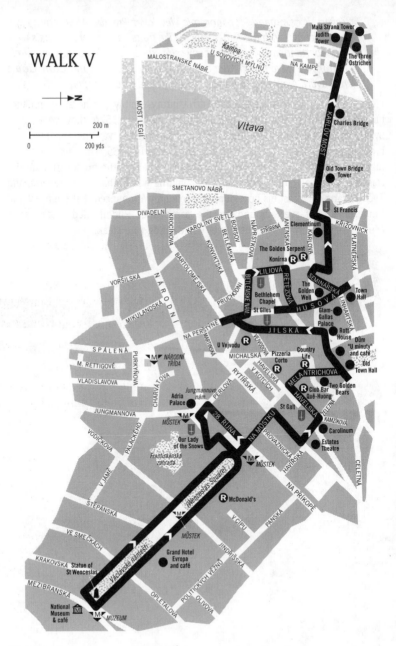

WALK V

N

0 ————————— 200 m
0 ————————— 200 yds

Malá Strana Tower
Judith Tower

The Three Ostriches

Kampa
MALOSTRANSKÉ NÁBŘ.
U SOVOVÝCH MLÝNŮ
NA KAMPĚ

Vltava

KARLŮV MOST

Charles Bridge

Old Town Bridge Tower

MOST LEGIÍ

SMETANOVO NÁBŘ.

St Francis

DIVADELNÍ

KROCÍNOVA

KAROLÍNY SVĚTLÉ

BORŠOV

NÁPRSTKOVA

STŘÍBRNÁ

ANENSKÁ

KARLOVA

KŘIŽOVNICK

PLATNÉŘSKA

Clementinum

The Golden Serpent
Konírna ℝ ℝ

VORŠILSKÁ

MIKULANDSKÁ

KONVIKTSKÁ

BARTOLOMĚJSKÁ

BETLÉMSKÁ

PRŮCHODNÍ

LILIOVÁ

BETLÉMSKÉ NÁM.

RETĚZOVA

HUSOVA

SEMINÁŘSKÁ

LINHARTSKÁ

The Golden Well

Town Hall

Bethlehem Chapel
St Giles

NA PERŠTÝNĚ

JILSKÁ

Glam-Gallas Palace

Rott House

Dům
"U minuty"
and café

SPÁLENÁ

M. RETTIGOVÉ

PURKYŇOVA

CHARVÁTOVA

NÁRODNÍ
TŘÍDA

MICHALSKÁ

U Vejvodu ℝ

PERLOVÁ

VEJVODA

MARTINSKÁ

HAVELSKÁ

V KOTCÍCH

Pizzeria Corto

Country Life ℝ

MELANTRICHOVA

Old Town Hall

Two Golden Bears

VLADISLAVOVA

Adria Palace

Jungmannovo
nám.

RYTÍŘSKÁ

NA MŮSTKU

Club Bar
Qué-Huong

TÝNSKÁ

JUNGMANNOVA

28. ŘÍJNA

St Gall

Kamzíková

VODIČKOVA

PALACKÉHO

MŮSTEK

M

Our Lady of the Snows

Františkánská
zahrada

NA PROVAZNICKÁ

HAVÍŘSKÁ

Carolinum

Estates Theatre

V JÁMĚ

MŮSTEK

M

ŠTĚPÁNSKÁ

VE SMEČKÁCH

MŮSTEK

(Wenceslavské náměstí)

ℝ **McDonald's**

V CÍPU

PANSKÁ

NA PŘÍKOPĚ

CELETNÁ

KRAKOVSKÁ

Statue of St Wenceslas

Václavské náměstí

Grand Hotel Evropa and café

JINDŘIŠSKÁ

POLITICKÝCH VĚZŇŮ

OLIVOVA

MEZIBRÁNSKÁ

National Museum & café 🏛

M MUZEUM

OPLETALOVA

Start: *the top of Wenceslas Square.*  *Muzeum (lines A and C).*
Finish: *the Charles Bridge.* **Ⓜ** *Malostranská and*

V: Wenceslas Square – Charles Bridge

Ⓜ *Staroměstská (both line A) flank the next bridge north. Trams 12 and 22 stop at Malostranské nám. just beyond the end of the walk; and trams 17 and 18 follow the embankment on the Old Town side of the river.*
Walking time: *about 3 hours.*

This walk is a whistle-stop tour back through the centuries. It begins in Wenceslas Square, the clamorous boulevard where four decades of Communism died in November 1989; and ends on the Charles Bridge, the vortex of the capital for 600 years. On the way, it passes the mechanical marionettes of the ancient Astronomical Clock, descends to the level of Romanesque Prague, and stalks the royal coronation route through the labyrinth of the Old Town. Its streets, fading into a peeled and pastel charm, are swamped by tourists, but as you explore its silent back-alleys and cloisters, you'll encounter the evidence of a past that most never see.

Start this walk by lunchtime at the latest. Although the museums on the walk have no more than curiosity value, there are several galleries, courtyards and interiors that tend to close by 6 pm. Choose a clear day. You could hop from café to café in the rain, but you'd miss most of what's on offer. The sprawling Old Town is divided between this walk and Walk II, and you may want to explore the Old Town Square as you skim across its edge. On a warm summer evening, you could cross the few hundred yards that separate the Charles Bridge and Walk III, and begin a twilight exploration of Malá Strana.

---

lunch/cafés

There are scores of dining possibilities along this route, including an inordinate number of vegetarian cafés. The following represents a cross-section of what's on offer, and you'll find a number of other places listed in the Food and Drink section.

Muzeum Café, National Museum, Václavské nám. 68. *Wed–Mon 9–5.* Fresh sandwiches and salads under the Hollywood-meets-Paris Opera staircase of the National Museum. Opinions differ as to whether you have to pay admission charges simply to eat here—argue forcefully and you should get through.

Evropa Café, Václavské nám. 25. *7 am–12 midnight.* Service is usually abysmal, only cheesy and hammy dishes are available, but the Art Nouveau decor almost makes up for everything. At least stop for a coffee.

McDonald's, Václavské nám. 9. *8 am–1 am.* A cheerful hamburger restaurant, popular among Czechs.

Club Bar Quê-Huong, Havelská 29. *Mon–Sat 11–8.* Delicious Vietnamese food amidst the slovenly kitsch of the country's cultural centre.

Pizzeria Corto, Havelská 15. *10 am–12 midnight.* Wine and fluffy pizzas under the arches of a Gothic arcade.

Country Life, Melantrichova 15. *Mon–Thurs 8.30–7, Fri 8.30–2 pm, Sun 12–6 pm.* Stand-up vegetarian café with some of the tastiest and healthiest sandwiches in town.

Dům 'U minuty' (House at the Minute), Staroměstské nám. 2. *10 am–11 pm.* Over 30 teas and about 40 coffees, blended with spirits and liqueurs in ways both tasty and revolting. Also pancakes, sandwiches and strudels.

U Vejvodů, Jilská 4. *10–10.* Age-old beer hall that has somehow survived without quadrupling its prices. Offers the usual range of stodgy Czech delicacies and Pilsner lager to help get them down.

Konírna (The Stable), Anenské 11. *Mon–Fri 12 noon–12 midnight, Sat 6 pm–12 midnight.* Vegetarian café, serving beans and pasta salads in a converted, secluded and extremely pretty stable. Prague's animal liberators often gather here to plot, so leave your furs at home.

U zlatého hada (The Golden Serpent), Karlova 18. *11–11.* Spacious but cosy restaurant, serving a renowned fish soup and well-cooked meals from steak to plaice.

There's an odd connection between the beginning and end of this walk: both Wenceslas Square and the Charles Bridge were founded almost simultaneously by Emperor Charles IV in the mid-14th century. The square, actually a half-mile boulevard, was the horse market that Charles needed for his New Town (*see* p. 268 *et seq.*), and you could have followed the route of this walk 600 years ago. It's not something that's apparent any more: Wenceslas Square itself is now the commercial centre of the city and significant for its recent political history rather than for any lingering remains of its horse-trading days. But as you leave the square, you sink ever deeper into streets that are simultaneously an accretion and detrition of centuries of architecture, and petrified testimony to the history that has raged through the Old Town.

> *The walk begins at the head of Wenceslas Square. Whether you're walking or emerging from Muzeum metro station, you'll have no problems finding the first stop. It's the grandiloquent **National Museum** (Národní muzeum; open Wed–Mon 9–5; adm.) which now seals Prague's central avenue with all the half-pillars, pilasters and pomp that the brown and solemn architecture of the Czech national revival was able to muster.*

A museum of Bohemian history was a dream of early 19th-century patriots. They launched an appeal for objects, but as the domestic appliances and folk art poured in, it became apparent that Bohemia's traditions needed a home more glorious than the temporary accommodation that was so far available. In the 1870s Prague's council stepped in with this rent-free site. The grandeur of the neo-Renaissance building (1885–90) was meant to express the confidence of the Czech national revival movement; the effect was to shatter the balance of old Wenceslas Square. It encouraged the almost complete renewal of the street's architecture over this century; and paradoxically, the symmetry of the museum, its bulk set off by a golden central dome, now makes it an almost elegant point on the 20th-century exclamation mark that Wenceslas Square has become.

The museum is worth a visit just for the open staircase that greets you beyond the entrance—three floors of veined marble pillars and banisters, globular lamps and swaying palm fronds. Under the glassy dome, on the first floor, is a **sculptural pantheon** of some 60 national heroes gazing down from the walls and plinths: an eclectic and eerie collection of work by most of Prague's leading early 20th-century sculptors. Wait for a very, very rainy day before exploring the rest of the building, which houses a stupefying collection of stuffed animals and anthropological knick-knacks. Even the mammoth is fake.

> As you leave the museum, you'll be faced with a view of the former horse market, rolling towards the hidden Old Town. The image is one that you may recognize: in November 1989, this was the site of one of the hardest-fought battles of the Velvet Revolution, between the cameramen of the world's press. Silhouetted against the panorama is the rump of one of the symbols of Prague, the **equestrian figure of St Wenceslas**. Make your way to the figure, crossing the main road by the subway around the corner on your right.

Although a familiar name to English carol singers since the 1850s, Good King Wenceslas ruled as a prince rather than a king, until murdered by his notoriously cruel brother, Boleslav the Cruel, in 935. Just to confuse matters, there were eventually four *King* Wenceslases and the country is now ruled by another (Václav = Wenceslas). The saint's reputation for goodness arose from an obsessive and harmless Christianity, but over the years, Wenceslas has metamorphosed from religious to national hero. The legends have followed him; and this figure will apparently gallop into life at Bohemia's moment of greatest need.

The symbolic importance of the statue came to obsess its designer, J. V. Myslbek. The grand old man of 19th-century Czech sculpture, Myslbek began work in 1887 with the idea of Wenceslas as a shaggy Slav; but as the reality of a national state grew closer, he transformed the Dark Age prince into the serene and noble leader you see today. Ardo the stallion had to take weeks off his military duties to pose in the sculptor's studio; and when his work was finally unveiled in 1912, Myslbek sighed, 'Now I see it could have been still bigger.' Perhaps—but he needn't have worried. Ever since it was unveiled, it has been a public rallying point: in 1918, Czechoslovakian independence was announced at Wenceslas's feet; after 1948, Communist May Day parades goose-stepped along the square; and after the Soviet-led invasion of August 1968 the monument was the focus for Prague's desperation. In that month, an 11-year-old boy was shot dead as he stood on the steps and pushed a Czech flag down the barrel of a Soviet tank; and on 16 January 1969, next to the fountain of the National Museum, **Jan Palach** burned himself alive. A week later, 800,000 Czechs followed his coffin past the statue. The happiest moment of the monument's recent history came in November 1989, when Wenceslas and Ardo made it onto millions of television sets across the world, at the head of the demonstrations that finally saw off the shoddy dictatorship.

> *Directly in front of the statue is a round pedestal, which became an impromptu memorial to victims of Communist oppression after the revolution.*

Among those commemorated by the candles and pictures is Jan Palach. Every year on the anniversary of his death, police would come out in force to protect public order; in February 1989, Václav Havel was sentenced to nine months in jail for having attempted to place flowers here. Another of those honoured is Professor Jan Patočka, a 70-year-old spokesman for the Charter 77 movement (*see* p. 60), who died of a brain haemorrhage while being questioned by the police. The authorities paid their respects by sending a helicopter to the funeral, which hovered a few metres above the open grave as the oration was read.

> *Stroll on down the street. You'll probably run a gauntlet of moustachioed chaps whispering 'Cambio?' or 'Moneychange?'; you respond at your peril. Men should also beware of women in tight leather skirts. On the right just before the central crossroads is the glorious Art Nouveau façade of the **Grand Hotel Evropa** (1903–06).*

The hotel café is a favourite spot for the same prostitutes and money-changers to compare notes, and a subtle variation on a clichéd theme of central European elegance. The interior looks the part—revolving doors spin you into a shabby and beautiful room of mirrors and mahogany, crystal chandeliers and carriage lamps—but the clientele is a motley crew indeed. Alongside oblivious tourists and gossiping *babičky* are gum-chewing rent boys, one of the city's most confident transvestites, and a self-proclaimed gipsy king. During the winter, a table is often occupied by an animated discussion group of deaf and dumb people. The café has recently taken to charging admission fees throughout the day: the intention is presumably to ensure that deviants are priced out, but there seems little danger of that. Come back in the evening, when the house trio add their cacophonous touch to the ambience.

> *When you leave the Evropa, turn right. As you cross Jindřišská, you'll see on your right the Polish Cultural Centre, which once housed the insurance company where Franz Kafka began his first job in 1907.*

Kafka never quite settled in to the Wenceslas Square location. A week after starting, he was already dreaming of 'someday gazing out of an office window upon sugarcane fields or Muslim cemeteries', and within a year he had moved on. However, he went nowhere more exotic than nearby Na poříčí street and would work in the field of industrial injury for the rest of his life. It was a surprisingly distinguished career: Kafka visited factories across the country, he drafted elegant reports on workplace accidents that he proudly sent to friends, and was even recommended for a national medal in 1918, failing to receive it only because the Habsburg empire collapsed shortly before the papers could be processed.

> *The next half of Wenceslas Square is a hotch-potch of Prague's early 20th-century architecture; while between the Functionalist Alfa and Tatran buildings on your left is the Hotel Adria, one of the last Baroque façades on the square. The Air India offices on the right (No. 13) used to house Aeroflot; some older Praguers still fondly remember the night in 1969 when Czechoslovakia beat the Soviet Union at ice-hockey and they made a bonfire of the furniture.*

As you gaze at the façades, you can now safely consider one of the more surreal rumours of the November revolution: that after June 1989, the jittery authorities had a cardboard copy of the entire square constructed somewhere in Slovakia, in which their troops could practise Tienanmen-inspired crowd-control techniques. It has never been found.

> *Walk on. On the far side of the street, at No. 8 is the **Peterkův dům**, perhaps the most elegant Art Nouveau façade in the capital; it was designed by a 28-year-old Jan Kotěra (see pp. 76–7) and shows the precision that would later inspire some of the finest Czech Constructivist architecture (one example is the neighbouring Baťa shoe shop). At the foot of the square is the so-called **Golden Cross**, a junction of shoppers and idle youth which—along with Ardo's tail—is Prague's most widely-used meeting point. Turn left along 28. října. At*

the end of the paved precinct, you'll see the bizarre crenellations and turrets of the **Adria Palace** *on your left across the street.*

The building is a striking example of the Rondocubist architecture that Pavel Janák, the designer, was trying to develop into a Czechoslovakian national style fit for the 20th century. Modern Prague would have been an architectural curiosity of titanic proportions had he succeeded, but this urban citadel (1923–5) is one of only a few examples that got off the ground.

The Adria used to house the Magic Lantern Theatre, which was the press centre of the Civic Forum during the first hectic days of the 1989 revolution. That movement, now defunct, was set up after the clash between police and students on Národní street (running to the west) which set off a six-week earthquake. There's a memorial a few hundred metres down the road on the left, but save that for another day. Make a U-turn to your left, and in the wall ahead of you is a doorway leading into the forecourt of the **Church of Our Lady of the Snows** *(Kostel Panny Marie Sněžné), one of the last remnants of Emperor Charles IV's New Town.*

Charles founded the church in 1347, five years before the 1000th anniversary of its Roman namesake, better known as Santa Maria Maggiore. The latter was built after the Virgin appeared in a wintry flurry one August afternoon and showed Pope Liberius a snowy model of what was required. Construction of Prague's version proved less straightforward. The open courtyard was to be the body of a vast triple-naved church, but the Hussite Wars and lack of money put paid to that idea, and the blank wall in front of you closes the only part of the project to be completed. It's the cavernous Gothic chancel (1397), which at about 33 metres matches the height of St Vitus's Cathedral. The buttresses and narrow arches of the stump towered over the left bank of Prague until the redevelopment of the New Town locked it behind a wall of modern architecture and turned it into the best-concealed church in the capital. The interior is dominated by a splendid early Baroque high altar, climbing in three black-and-gold storeys to an aerial Crucifixion scene; Christ is pinned to a net-vault, which dates from the 17th century, built after its predecessor found the weight too much and collapsed.

Leave the forecourt of the church through the door to the right. Walk towards the curious Cubo-Expressionist lamppost on your right (1912)— try its built-in seat—and then through the passage in front of you, which returns you to the Golden Cross. The broad street opposite is **Na příkopě**—*the name means 'on the moat', and true enough, it was a muddy ditch separating the Old and New Towns until 1760. Following the example of its Viennese namesake,* Der Graben, *Prague's Germans* *turned it into a weekend promenade during the 19th century. Their cafés lined what was then an elegant avenue, and by the early 1900s when duelling scars were the latest thing, it hosted regular Sunday afternoon battles between proud German thugs and their Czech counterparts.*

Take Můstek, the narrow route to your left, running on from Wenceslas Square and beginning the journey into the heart of the Old Town. The stone bridge over the moat used to stand here; a chunk of arches was unearthed when the metro was built, and now sits sadly in the vestibule wall of Můstek (Little Bridge) metro station. Turn right at Rytířská. The neo-Renaissance lump across the road used to celebrate the life and times of Klement Gottwald, the loathed postwar leader of the Communist Party, and was the dismal destination of generations of school outings. Its unexpectedly splendid interior, an atrium watched over by buxom caryatids and lying under an expansive sheet of red and grey glass, now houses the most comfortable savings bank in Prague, with sofas and café for weary investors (open Mon–Thurs 8–6, Fri 8–4). When you reach the corner of Železná, on your left, you'll see the pale green and white façade of the **Estates Theatre** *(Stavovské divadlo).*

Its pediment and pillars flow from the body of the building in concave curves, with all the elegance of neo-classical architecture at its best. It was a bastion of German opera for 150 years until 1945, and its early history has made it a minor place of pilgrimage among Mozart-groupies for two centuries. With two tiers of boxes and a capacity for over 1000 opera-buffs, the theatre was already the finest in central Europe when its curtain first rose in 1783. In 1786, it saw the performance of Mozart's *The Marriage of Figaro*. The opera was panned by the snooty Viennese, but Prague's critics couldn't praise it too highly. Wolfgang came to town and had a ball, literally (*see* p. 191) and metaphorically. Fêted by the city's bourgeoisie and nobility, he merrily wrote back to Vienna that 'Nothing is played, sung or whistled like Figaro. No opera is drawing like Figaro. Nothing, nothing but Figaro.' The management knew a box-office success when it heard one and collared the composer. Commissioned to write another opera, he returned with the score of *Don Giovanni*, which he conducted here for the first time in October 1787. The theatre's place in the minutiae of musical history was assured.

The building next to the theatre, the **Carolinum**, *is the core of the Charles University, founded by Emperor Charles IV 1348. It was the first university in central Europe, as Prague's guidebooks proudly state, and the 35th in the rest of the Continent, as they generally forget.*

That said, 1348 was not a good year for the rest of Europe. The Black Death was in the process of wiping out a third of its population—along with several universities—and Charles was concerned to do his bit to maintain educational standards. Like all imperialists he also appreciated the subtle advantages of educating potential enemies. In its early years, budding prelates and princes enrolled from across Europe, but Prague soon showed that it wasn't ready for the hurly-burly of medieval contemplation. As the city's politics polarized in the later 14th century, the melting pot boiled over. The heretic-to-be Jan Hus (see pp. 45–6) became rector in 1402 and declared his support for the writings of the Oxford reformer John Wycliffe; the university's German Catholics rallied to the defence of their rotten Church. A noisy stalemate ended in 1409, when the Czech Hussites persuaded feeble Wenceslas IV to triple their voting power, and 5000 Germans packed their bags and left to found Leipzig University. For the next two centuries the Carolinum was a think-tank of anti-Catholicism, and when Bohemian Protestantism was trounced at the Battle of the White Mountain in 1620, its fate hung in the balance. The cruel Spanish generals on the Habsburg team murmured that the building should be obliterated, but the cunning Jesuits, who understood the power of education, persuaded Ferdinand II to give it to them instead. To keep the Spaniards happy, the notoriously eloquent tongue of ex-rector Jessenius was sliced off before he was quartered in 1621.

> *The building was gutted by retreating Nazis in 1945, and its front almost entirely destroyed—but through the large windows, arched by restorers to retain a Gothic touch, you can see the vaulted arcade of the original building provided by Wenceslas IV in 1383. The cloister and rooms sometimes host exhibitions, but otherwise the only reminder of the Carolinum's former glory is in the lane next to the Estates Theatre, where you'll find an oriel window (1370), decorated with crests, pinnacles and a small set of Gothic nightmares. Retrace your steps, and turn left down Havelská, the street facing the entrance to the Carolinum, which takes you past the green onions and quivering Baroque façade of* **St Gall's Church** *(sv. Havel).*

Like most of Prague's churches, St Gall's is built on layers of earlier buildings. It dates from the 13th century when it was founded as the parish church of St Gall's Town, a German community invited to set up their laws and markets in an enclave of the Old Town. The church was reconstructed in the late 1600s and the present façade, plastered on in 1723, is a *tour de force* of Prague's late Baroque architecture. The architect was Giovanni Santini, who, like contemporaries across northern Europe, fell under the spell of Borromini's undulating works in Rome. With the asymmetry and interweaving elements of this work, he created the most energetic exterior of all the churches in central Prague (with the extremely honourable exception of St Nicholas's in Malá Strana—*see* pp. 186–9). The façade shimmies across the street, with sculptured saints, reproachful and violent, glaring at you from the roller-coaster roof.

> Walk along until you get back to Melantrichova. Havelská continues across the road with a picturesque set of Renaissance and Baroque façades, veering distantly over a broad stone arcade left behind from Gothic days. St Gall's Germans were a business-minded bunch and market stalls filled their town, which stretched back as far as Celetná street along the bow-shaped Ovocný trh ('fruit market'). That area, behind the Estates Theatre and Carolinum, has recently been restored and is a sparklingly clean expanse of nothingness; but the barrows around Havelská, laden with fruits, flowers and acrylic sweaters, are the reviving descendants of a tradition that pulled through Communism and dates back 700 years.
>
> Turn right down Melantrichova, past the plaque of rumbustious Jan Marek Marci, until you come to Kožná on your right. On the corner are two brutes padding through the arched entrance to **The Two Golden Bears** (U dvou zlatých medvědů). The Renaissance doorway (1590), saturated with the twirling vegetation more characteristic of late Gothic art, is one of the most sumptuous portals in Prague, and was understandably kept in place when the rest of the house was rebuilt in around 1800. The corridor through the door winds into a tiny arcaded court. On the other side of Melantrichova is an arch leading through to the shattered Baroque **Church of St Michael** (c. 1740) (Kostel sv. Michal). Deconsecrated in 1786, then used as a warehouse, and now utterly ruined, the crumbling masonry is yielding up a 15th-century archway from the Gothic church it cannibalized when built.
>
> Go back to Melantrichova, and continue until it spits you out from a buttressed bottleneck into the Old Town Square. You'll find yourself in front of the **Old Town Hall** (Staroměstská radnice).

The privileges attached to town life in medieval Europe were immense. Peaceful coexistence and fortifications had always been a way for decent folk to protect themselves against rapine and pillage; but a town charter also gave them a degree of political power that was potentially more or less independent of the monarch. The dilemma for a king was that to declare war on uppity subjects could strain resources (although it was still often judged worth while); and when a community had reached critical mass, monarchs tended to cut their losses and hand over a town charter. The Old Town got fortifications and a royal charter in the mid-13th century, and Wenceslas II grudgingly let Praguers have a clerk in 1296; but Wenceslas put his foot down when they asked for a town hall to put the clerk in. The townspeople had to wait until 1338, when they were able to take advantage of blind King John of Luxemburg. The errant king was too busy being gallant to fret over the trivia of municipal affairs, and waved the plans through—but commanded that the town hall be funded from a new tax on wine. That threw the thrifty burghers; but they were able to make a humble start later that year when they bought a house and turned it into the tower in front of you. As the receipts poured in, they were slowly able to add all the buildings on your left. It was a piecemeal process, involving the destruction of spinners' sheds and the roofing-over of the lane to the goose market, but the maroon and white 18th-century façades—encrusted with Gothic and Renaissance survivals from earlier days—now house a single interior, stretching from the tower to the end of the block.

*On the tower is the town hall's pride and joy, its **Astronomical Clock**, or horologe* (orloj).

Prague woke up late to the idea of clocks—by the time this one was installed in 1410, every other major city in Europe had one—but they were still exotic devices, and the city's burghers were apparently concerned that things should stay that way. Legend has it that when it was remodelled by a certain Master Hanuš in 1490, the Municipal Council took the precaution of blinding him to protect its copyright. A peeved Master Hanuš scaled the building, tossed a medieval spanner in the works, and promptly died. Prague's timepiece was out of joint for almost a century; but since 1572, it has ticked away without interruption, the occasional fire and artillery blitz notwithstanding.

The arcane clock is a reminder of an age when such machines were regarded as very powerful creatures indeed. Only in the 19th century did the industrial world really begin to operate on the assumption that clocks simply recorded the hours—as far as medieval thought was concerned, it was just as plausible that they created them, and even into the 17th century, the connected notions of clocks, clockwork and perpetual motion were imbued with a mystery that is hard to imagine today. This one purports to tell the time, but that's only the beginning. Its astronomical symbols, pointers, and interlocking circles also register the phases of the moon, the length of the day, the equinoxes, Babylonian time, and the dates of innumerable mobile feasts; and all the cogs and wheels whirr with added complication, according to the orbit of the heavens around the earth. Mechanical magic also treated awestruck spectators to a morality play, all but unchanged for 500 years. Every hour two cuckoo-clock windows open and statues of the 12 Apostles mince past while bony Death tinkles his bell. The great leveller is pooh-poohed by preening Vanity, and those bugbears of 15th-century Europe, the Turk and the Jew. The latter now lacks his beard and horns, and is politely referred to as Greed, having been sanitized following the town hall's bombardment in 1945. The post-Holocaust decision was understandable; but the paradoxical effect was to whitewash the bloody feature of central Europe's history that had just reached its culmination. A cock, and delighted children, screech when the ceremony is all over.

The temporal theme is taken up by the painted calendar below the clock showing the monthly labours of rural folk. It's by Josef Mánes, a prolific artist of the 19th-century Czech national revival movement. Bucolic subjects were favoured by Romantics everywhere, and especially so in Bohemia where Germans were popularly seen as an unhealthy brood of urban lounge lizards. Again, the stereotype had connotations that stretched back to darker times; by the early 20th century, some 85 per cent of the German-speakers in Prague were of Jewish origin.

> *A wooden door on the right as you face the clock conceals one of Prague's stranger tourist attractions. This detour is a highly optional one; as keen noses may already be able to tell, the door leads into a small section of **Prague's sewer system**. (Irregular opening hours; adm.)*

In modern Prague, no space is safe from the spirit of free enterprise. Young entrepreneurs have leased this section of the drains from the municipality, and for a small sum you're invited to stare at the capital's waste as it roars under the Old Town Square. The group seems to think that it is on to a winner, and now has plans to organize guided tours of a sewage works in northern Prague. Further information from the cash desk.

> *The Gothic arch on the left as you face the clock, engulfed in foliage and 16th-century cats, is the formal entrance to the Town Hall. If it's Saturday, you'll probably stumble across a marriage here, as this is a popular spot for tying the knot. Behind it is a foyer containing work by one of the most ubiquitous of the 19th-century patriotic artists, Mikoláš Aleš: cartoon-like mosaics of Libuše founding Prague (see pp. 38–9) and*

*an all-purpose Bohemia, showing the noble personification herself,
enthroned between various symbols and architectural pinnacles of 19th-
century nationalism. Walk to the modern **entrance of the town hall**,
under the Renaissance window (1520). The Latin phrase means 'Prague,
head of the kingdom', and was a motto extracted by the burghers from
devil-may-care John of Luxemburg.*

*Open Tues–Sun March–Oct 9–6, Nov–Feb 9–5; adm. At the time of
writing you pay separately for the chapel and the tower, and a guided
tour takes you around the rest of the rooms. However, thorough reconstruction and reorganization of the building is imminent; all that can be
said with certainty is that things will either be simpler, or much more
complicated, by the time you read this.*

The small Gothic **chapel** on the first floor dates from 1381. A Nazi tank shelled it
to smithereens at the height of the Prague Uprising, but it has been restored well,
using as much of the original rubble as could be identified. The delicate cross-ribs
of the presbytery frame starry cobalt vaults and 19th-century paintings of the
Evangelists; the 15th-century crests on the walls belong to once-privileged
families and trade guilds. Under the stained glass of the oriel (now a serene
modern design from 1987), kneeling unfortunates would take their leave of life
before being done to death next door (*see below*) or in front of the hoi polloi in
the square. The chapel's main attraction is up on your right as you face the oriel:
through a glass door, the **figures of the 12 Apostles** wait on the spokes of two
wheels for their moment of glory. Chains clunk, cables twang and sprockets tense
nervously throughout, and if your timing is right, you can be here to see the
windows open and the figures twirl into life when the hour strikes.

*From the chapel, begin the trek to the top of the **tower**. After gasping—
and gasping—at the view, descend again for the **guided tour of the
town hall's rooms**.*

The tour leads past a **memorial cross** made from two charred wooden beams.
At least 14 men died in the building during the Nazi assault; it was the headquarters of the committee that led the Prague Uprising. The resistance fighters holed
themselves up in the network of late 12th-century **town hall cellars**, which are
due to be reopened to the public soon. The clammy warren comprises a number
of halls, a well and a dungeon for those women who were thought to talk too
much. There are plans to link the town hall cellars with those of its neighbours
and turn the whole into a restaurant, which should make for a novel dining experience, not least because the network stretches as far as the (originally Gothic)
lavatories in nearby Malé nám.

The rest of the tour takes you under painted Renaissance joists on the first floor; on the second, faded Gothic murals and a turn-of-the-century drawing of Prague from Petřín Hill, minus the housing estates on today's horizon. The next two rooms contain four works by Václav Brožík (1851–1901), whose speciality was portraying turning points of Bohemian history with a turgid solemnity. Until 1526, the country's king was chosen in the town hall, and *The Election of King George of Poděbrady* shows Hussite George being given the nod by the country's nobles in 1458. The equally monumental *Jan Hus's Trial at Constance* is one of several versions churned out by Brožík for the nationalist movement. Among those watching Hus's doomed attempts to present a defence to charges that included the allegation that he believed himself to be a fourth member of the Holy Trinity are the great men of 19th-century Bohemia, including Smetana, Dvořák and none other than Václav Brožík himself. The two canvases in the next room are *Charles IV Founding Prague University* and *Comenius in Exile in Amsterdam.*

The **Old Council Chamber**, dating from about 1470, does most to conjure up the years when municipal powers were at their height. Councillors would hammer out policy at the broad table, supervised by the solemn Gothic sculptures. The haunting figure of Christ (*c.* 1410) implores them in Latin to 'Judge Justly, Sons of Man'—a fair plea, since it is here that Master Hanuš's fate would have been decided; summary execution was the norm in politically sensitive cases, when last rites would be swiftly administered in the neighbouring chapel. The councillors found themselves at the receiving end of some rough justice in 1483, when a Hussite mob threw the Catholic mayor and several cronies out of the window in the second of Prague's four defenestrations. The reformers then continued the good work with a pogrom in the Jewish Quarter—eradicating Judaism was widely thought to be a precondition of the Messiah's expected return in 1500. The scene of the first crime is no longer known; the Renaissance window through which light now trickles into the chamber was installed 40 years later.

> *Turn right from the Town Hall. In front of you is the striking cream and brown façade of the **House at the Minute** (Dům U minuty), one of Franz Kafka's many childhood homes in Prague (1889–96).*

No one knows how the house got its name—the only explanation that has been offered is that 'minute' doesn't refer to time, but to the apparently very small bric-a-brac that was once sold here. The scenes that cover the building date from around 1610. The direct influence of the Italian Renaissance on the city was limited, but *sgraffito* decoration was a remarkably popular Italian import to the capital. The rediscovery of classical myth was another Italian innovation that found its way to Prague, and here centaurs and assembled deities brush shoulders with Biblical worthies. The more coquettish of the Seven Virtues who adorn the lowest set of windows, swathed in diaphanous *sgraffiti* and displaying pounds of statuesque flesh, would have raised eyebrows in the puritan Old Town even when the plaster was first peeled away in 1610; and they disappeared after the arrival of the Counter-Reformation, only to be uncovered again by accident during the 1920s.

> *Continue into Malé nám. (Small Square), no more square than any of Prague's misnamed* náměstís.

The triangular junction, the historical haunt of French merchants and fruit-sellers, is dominated by more Aleš-inspired paintings on the 1890 neo-Renaissance house of connoisseur, patriot and ironmonger, Mr Rott. Tatra and Škoda exhaust pipes have done their best, but the façade, entirely swamped by organic growths and rustic heroes, is still a smoky blaze of crimsons, oranges and greens. On your left is a quaint pharmacy full of empty mahogany drawers and phial-filled shelves. The noble torsos at the door are the classical friends of apothecaries everywhere: ancient Asclepius, Greek myth's first physician, eventually struck off by Zeus for resurrecting a corpse; and his youthful father, Apollo. Under the arcade opposite Mr Rott's shop, you'll also find the Gothic toilets mentioned above.

> *Walk down Karlova. You're now entering the riddled core of the Old Town, with lanes and passageways crawling through the gaps left by the architectural undergrowth of centuries. Follow the road as it turns to the left. The solemn drummers, carriages and grinning yokels that made up the royal coronation procession used to advance precariously around this corner and then lunge to the right, where Karlova continues its tortuous progress to the Charles Bridge. The road ahead of you forks; continue along the left prong (Jilská). The street uncurls between huddled Baroque and Renaissance houses and the backside of a monastery that you'll see soon. Continue past the Esperanto society on your left. The street opens into a square, and then narrows and twists again. You'll suddenly emerge into a grim 20th-century junction. U-turn to the right into Husova, and then take the first road to your left. This leads into Betlémské nám. where, on the right, you'll find the twin peaks of the* **Bethlehem Chapel** *(Betlémská kaple).*

True to Prague form, this calm square has had a tumultuous history. The trouble began in the mid-14th century, when Prague's spellbinding ascetic and resident fanatic, Jan Milíč, stumbled upon the peaceful hive of prostitution that existed here. One of the leading chiliasts of his century, his personal way of preparing for Heaven on Earth was to take the harlots under his wing and rename the brothels Jerusalem. Milíč himself fell foul of his apocalyptic visions before long, clapped in jail by Emperor Charles IV after he accused the monarch of being the Beast, but Jerusalem became established as sanctified turf. In 1391, reformers chose to build a church here in which services could be held in the vernacular. The idea was never popular in the medieval Church, which only approved a chapel and began to monitor events closely. Bohemians rose to the challenge and built the largest chapel in the land; with panache, they centred it around the pulpit rather than the altar; and with the protestant preference for scripture to saints, they, like Milíč, thumbed through the Bible for a name. Jan Hus began to preach in the Bethlehem Chapel in 1402, the same year that he became rector of the Carolinum. His sermons filled the 3000-capacity chapel, which set alarm bells ringing in the Church. Prague's archbishop warned him to pipe down; Hus was excommunicated; and an exasperated pope finally had to have him roasted in 1415. The second Vatican Council retrospectively voided the sentence in 1965.

The building is a modern copy of the original, which was all but demolished in 1786. Its historical significance had little to do with the destruction; rational despot Emperor Joseph II rarely saw the point of religious organizations. Neither did his ideological heirs, the Communists, but in 1949, they began faithfully to rebuild the chapel according to the original plans. President Gottwald, a stalwart of Scientific Atheism, was asked why. He patiently explained that '500 years ago, the people of Prague were already fighting for Communism'. The fanatical excesses of the more extreme Hussites make that a tenable view; but Gottwaldian historiography no longer being in favour, the exhibition that used to expound it has been evicted. As a result, there's little to see inside other than daubed sermons preserved on three walls. Preachers have begun to deliver sermons here again, but the attempt to revive the tub-thumping tradition usually goes badly wrong. About 40 people attend a chapel that once held 3000, the minister gets nervous and starts to stutter, and when the congregation tries to conceal its embarrassment by singing a hymn, 40 years of Scientific Atheism telescope into a moment and no one can remember the words.

Continue past the chapel. If you're in the mood, you could pop into the fascinating museum at No. 1, a monument to the ever-wider obsessions of a Mr Náprstek—intended as a tribute to Europe's machine age, but now full of tomahawks, mummies, masks and boomerangs (see pp. 263–4). Otherwise, turn right at Liliová, and right again at Řetězová. The narrow cobbled alley, with its cast-iron green lanterns and line of Prague brownstones (i.e. 18th-century cottages) is a short and sweet plunge into the picturesque days of rats and slums, and—like the similar streets around nearby Anenské nám.—has been a favourite location for foreign film-makers for years. After about 20 metres, you'll find, on your left, the

House of the Lords of Kunštát and Poděbrady *(Dům pánů z Kunštátu a Poděbrad).*

This Renaissance building stands over part of an even older Prague. The cellar dates from around 1200—about a century before the burghers buried the town in protest at the incessant floods of the Vltava river. It was an extreme step, and not one that was tried again (although the river didn't give up); most of the city's Romanesque architecture was lost for centuries.

> *Open May–Oct, Tues–Sun 10–6; adm. Pay at the room to the left, which houses temporary exhibitions, usually of broken pottery. Retreat to the other door.*

The ground floor (the first floor of the Romanesque building) has a permanent display devoted to George of Poděbrady, who lived here until promoted to king in 1458. At the end of the main room, a staircase descends to the damp odours and street level of 13th-century Prague. The sepulchral chambers, with the cracks of their windows peering into the emptiness of a buried outside world, were built several decades before even the hints of Gothic architecture had begun to arrive in the city. Later centuries would use ribs to carry weight to the walls—here, central pillars have to support the massive roof, and the rough curves of the vaults and portals are a world apart from the arches then leaping skyward in the cathedrals of Paris. The house is still one of the grandest of the period to have been found in Prague, but no one knows who the first owner was; it lurked in damp subterranean isolation for 600 years, until the beginning of this century.

> *Continue along Řetězová, taking a look at the grass-skirted chaps on the façade of No. 7 as you go. The house is known as the Three Wild Men* (U tří divých mužů)*; the late-17th century noble savages are thought by art historians to be touched-up adaptations of an earlier and earthier band of satyrs, but Prague folklore disagrees. Picaresque legend has it that a mysterious tanned trio moved into the house, and grunting only enough Czech to charge admission fees, enthralled the capital with their unusual dances and dietary habits until a startled south Bohemian farmer recognized them as his fugitive swineherds. Walk to the end of Řetězová and turn right along Husova. A small door to your left at No. 8 leads into the* **Dominican Friary and Church of St Giles** *(Konvent řádu bratři kazatelů Dominikanů u sv. Jiljí), founded in the mid-17th century. (Open Mon–Fri until about 6 pm.)*

Irreligious Communists turned the friary into a technical institute in 1954, but the brethren are back. Their small cloister is ethereal, filled with rambling rose bushes and creepers. Its southern arcade is connected to the Order's adjoining Church of St Giles. Friars wander through, but you have to use the street entrance.

Apart from the northern tower, stunted by fire in 1432 and never the same again, the triple-naved church has retained its 14th-century structure. However, the gloomy Baroque interior is caged off and is only worth a brief visit to see the ceiling frescoes. The church vault has three, all by the Czech Václav Reiner (1733–4). On the left is *The Legend of St Thomas Aquinas*; on the right *The Legend of St Giles*, a sympathetic character who patronizes lepers, cripples and, most helpfully, anyone who needs forgiveness but won't tell him what they did wrong; but the most exciting, in the centre, shows *The Foundation of the Dominican Order*. Here, Rome's Lateran Church is on the verge of collapse and being stabilized only thanks to Dominic himself. Pope Innocent III woke up from this nightmare scene while Dominic was in town hoping to get papal sanction for his Order; he hurried the papers through the next day. Innocent was a worried man; the dream apparently recurred eight years later, when Francis of Assisi had just arrived with another monkish scheme.

> *Retrace your footsteps along Husova. On the left is a well-known beer hall,* **The Golden Tiger** *(U zlatého tygra). Among those who regularly quaff Pilsners here is Bohumil Hrabal, one of the Czech Republic's best writers, whose respect for alcohol is legendary. The street on your right, and that further to your left are the zig-zagging Karlova again—another traumatic intersection for the royal procession to conquer. Just beyond the bustling junction is a flood-marker, showing what the Vltava was getting up to in 1845, and next to it are the colossal atlantes of the* **Clam-Gallas Palace** *(Clam-Gallasův Palac), built in 1713–19 and designed by one of the masters of Austrian Baroque, J. B. Fischer von Erlach.*

The tense powerhouses, straining to hold the balcony, are one of the most characteristic motifs of Austrian and Bohemian Baroque architecture. They're the work of Prague's Matthias Braun, who, showing both humour and the Baroque love of illusion, gave one of the giants a loincloth which turns into a lion's head if you stare shamelessly enough. The rough sandstone figures were intended to set off the cool façade; as it is, they command the little junction, and manage to overwhelm the palace itself. Fischer von Erlach's design for the building is extremely impressive on paper, structured around a triangular pediment with a sense of proportion and balance that is almost neo-classical, but it's easy to walk along the narrow alleyway without really registering the palace's existence. That wouldn't have surprised either the Austrian or Count Gallas. Both assumed that the entire block opposite would be knocked down and turned into a square, a plan that was scuppered by protests when Gallas let the occupants know.

Under the sculptures are two more heroic scenes: Hercules astride the Nemean lion, and clubbing an unidentified centaur. The interior of the palace contains a magnificent four-flighted staircase, crowned with an illusionistic fresco (*The Triumph of Apollo* by Carlo Carlone 1727–30); and two small archivists' rooms, filled with scholars, two peeling ceiling frescoes, and Baroque stoves and wallpaper. If you're curious, you can get past the porter and librarian on most weekdays.

> *Otherwise, continue along the façade. You'll pass a second set of atlantes and Herculean reliefs, and emerge into Mariánské nám. On your right is a niche containing a fountain. It's the neo-classical* Vltava *(1812: copy), a jug-bearing nymph popularly known as* **Terezka***.*

Terezka has been a Prague talking-point ever since the turn of the century, when a pensioned dragoon made her the sole beneficiary of his will. He was upset that she had been painted green by unknown assailants. His greedy relatives were no less perturbed, and had him posthumously declared of unsound mind. Fortunately, the city authorities took up the case, and she's been dribbling ever since.

> *On the eastern side of the square is Prague's modern Town Hall. The façade and roof are decorated with relaxed nudes peering down at the street, and reliefs representing various virtues, the most rarely honoured of which have to be Control and Accounting on the right-hand cornice. On the corners of the building are sculptures to two of Prague's legendary figures. Go first to the one on the right, a 1910* **statue of Rabbi Loew***, the Jewish mystic of 16th-century Prague (see pp. 105–7).*

The sculptor, Ladislav Šaloun, also sculpted the Monument to Jan Hus in the Old Town Square (*see* p. 154); and he intended this to be no less solemn a tribute to a man who represented 'everything noble which was produced from the ghetto'. In fact, the hook-nosed and slovenly figure, grasping his robes with gnarled fingers, looks rather like an extra from that classic of the Nazi screen, *Jud Süss*. (The Nazis themselves didn't think so, and removed the figure during the war.) The lion to the left represents Loew's name in German; the rest of the work portrays one of the legends surrounding his demise. Death shied away from a direct confrontation with the fearsome rabbi, and pounced on the 96-year-old after hiding in a rose being given to him by his granddaughter; Šaloun's freestyle adaptation omitted the rose, and transformed the granddaughter into a voluptuous nude flinging herself at his cloak (which may have been what the sex-obsessed fascists objected to most).

To the left of the Town Hall is a **stone knight**, Šaloun's tribute to an iron knight who hung outside Prague's armourers' guild until 1908. The original is now in the Museum of the City of Prague. Legend has it that he was flesh and blood until cursed for murdering his lover, and now clanks these streets once a century, trying to kiss a virgin and break the ferrifying spell.

> *Opposite the Town Hall is the eastern entrance of the Clementinum, which you'll see soon. Walk along Semínářská, to the left. The street winds into Karlova. The junction is filled by* **The Golden Well** *(U zlaté studně), its bow windows and angled façades ploughing through the block like an icebreaker.*

This Renaissance building is covered with Baroque decoration. The lower figures are St Roch, with his faithful canine provider (looking rather like a pig here), and St Sebastian, punctured with his traditional arrows. Both characters are guardians against the plague: Roch, because he helped victims, eventually succumbed, and recovered—thanks to prayer and the loaves of bread brought daily by his worried dog; Sebastian, only because his arrows reminded the symbol-minded of Apollo's poison-tipped weaponry (the god caused as well as cured disease). The saints appear incessantly in monuments around Prague and Bohemia, almost all built around 1715, when the pest had just paid one of its periodic visits.

> *Continue along Karlova. On the corner with Liliová is* **The Golden Serpent** *(U zlatého hada), marked with a sign of its hissing, glistening namesake, and once the home of an Armenian named Deomatus Damajan, who opened Prague's first café here in 1708.*

The deed has ensured him an honourable place in Prague folklore, but he actually left the city under something of a cloud. Damajan had the odd habit of distributing calumnious tracts with his cups of coffee, and once went too far by accusing a leading Prague Jew of embezzling charitable moneys. His victim sued, Damajan fled, and returned only very briefly to collect the 130 gold pieces that he was awarded by an extremely generous pardon granted by Emperor Charles VI (the troublesome Jewish community had to come up with the cash). As the birthplace of Prague's café society, you might expect The Golden Serpent to exploit its background ruthlessly, but it does nothing of the sort. Half of it is a restaurant, while the rest, in a frustratingly near miss, has been turned into a garish take-away coffee bar. With luck, someone with more historical sense will soon take over and install the incense holders, hookahs, chess sets and mule-headed management that Damajan's heritage demands.

> *Opposite The Golden Serpent are two porches, built to follow the bend in the road, and nestling under the domes, tiles and steeples that hang over the final stretch of Karlova. They form the entrance to two chapels associated with immigrant communities: in front of you is the oval Italian*

*Chapel (Vlašská kaple), built by and for the Renaissance Gästarbeiter of the 1590s; and to your right, embedded within the sheer wall, is the 18th-century **Church of St Clement's** (sv. Kliment). The latter is now used by Prague's small Greek Orthodox community, refugees from the colonels' coup in 1967, and is worth a very discreet visit when priests clad in green mumble services according to the Old Slavonic liturgy.*

*Retrace your steps and go through the doorway on your left, which leads into the **Clementinum** (Klementinum), the first Jesuit college in Bohemia and the nerve-centre of the country's Counter-Reformation.*

The Society of Jesus was founded in 1540 by St Ignatius of Loyola. Waved off by Pope Paul III, members scattered across Europe to confront the Antichrist of reform. Organized on military lines and headed by a general elected for life, the Order made up the advance platoons of the Counter-Reformation. Setting up Baroque base camps and barracks as they moved, the missionaries penetrated deep into Protestant Europe; and during the uneasy peace that preceded the Thirty Years War (1618–48), the Clementinum relit the Catholic flame in a city that had become 90 per cent Protestant.

One of the most successful weapons in the Order's armoury was education. While Jesuits themselves lived on an austere diet of mysticism and martyrdom fantasies, their schools became known throughout Europe as solid centres of excellence. Jesuit pedagogues showed an ever greater open-mindedness as the scale of their task became apparent. The extremely useful and excellently-named theory of Probabilism was developed (nothing heretical unless manifestly absurd); many went the whole hog and subscribed to Laxism (absurdities not to be condemned out of hand); and the clerics would also lead their charges in singing and dancing lessons to hone their sensual skills, and thus, their ability to feel God.

Prague's Jesuit college took shape after 1556, when a 40-strong squad was invited into Bohemia by Emperor Ferdinand I. The Jesuits' rivals watched hamstrung as the singing, dancing clerics seduced their pupils away and even let them titter at the occasional heresy; all that Prague's dour quasi-Calvinism had to offer curious boys was a sound thrashing. The Clementinum's success was such that, by the 17th century, non-Catholic families were queuing up to enroll their little ones; and after a short-lived expulsion on the eve of war, the Society returned in force in 1620 to supervise a century of militant reconversion. The Clementinum swallowed up its arch-rival, the Protestant Carolinum, two years later, and only in 1773 did it lose its religious nature. It's now the Czech State Library.

The Jesuits took their architecture seriously. They moved into this site in 1556, but the present complex was built in protracted stages between

1653 and 1723, on the site of 30-odd houses, three churches, 10 court-yards and several gardens. The central tower, topped with a Baroque Atlas, was the last part to be built (1721–3, and remodelled in 1749); it was the college observatory, and as late as 1918, a flag would be waved from the balcony when its sundial struck noon, and a cannon would thunder across the city from distant Letná Park. The once graceful ground plan isn't easy to appreciate any more, paved in asphalt and disrupted by the chunk of modern concrete on the left, but its rooms and walkways are filled with surprises. Turn left, and walk through the door marked 'Národní kníhovna' (National Library). Turn right down the corridor. Stride past the porter's lodge silently and without flinching, and bear in mind that the building is crawling with sensitive scholars.

About half-way along, the passage becomes what was once the vaulted cloister of the monks. The sides have been glazed but the drowsy courtyard to your left has remained untouched. The ivy-drenched enclave is a stunner, its gables painted with sections of a solar clock and a Baroque fountain spraying happily in the centre. Just opposite the entrance to the court is the way into the main reading room. Under the crisp stucco and dangling putti of what used to be the Jesuits' refectory, you'll find what some claim to be the largest Rococo stove in central Europe. The swirling reliefs are filled with Jesuit motifs, including their device— IHS, the abbreviation of the name Jesus in Greek—and the conventionally-balding head of Ignatius himself. The monolith kept the Order warm for only 11 cosy years until its abolition in 1773.

Return to the corridor and turn left at the end. Go up the staircase (along on the right), and turn right at the top. You'll be led to the beginning of a 100-metre long barrel-vaulted passage, a lonely tunnel lined with 34 stucco cartouches containing scenes from the hectic life of St Francis Xavier.

Francis, proto-Jesuit and the Order's second saint, spent the last ten years of his life in Asia on a one-man baptism drive. His achievements were considerable. On his first stop, he curbed the activities of Goa's syphilis-spreading Portuguese set-tlers; and in 1549, he gave the Mikado a clock and a music-box and swiftly immersed Japan's first 2000 Christians, which proved to be something of a mixed blessing when later and less liberal Mikados gave the country its first several hundred martyrs. He died on the way to fresh pastures in China and now lies incorrupt back in Goa, minus an arm (nabbed by the Vatican in 1615) and a toe (swallowed by an ecstatic pilgrim some years before). The scenes here were painted by an unknown Jesuit. They are of no artistic merit, but—in this case at least—the Order clearly believed that subject matter alone would be enough to inspire and prepare the hopeful novices. Those who mastered their spiritual exercises could aspire to levitation and resurrections; disasters, savages and lonely death were what all should prepare themselves for in heretical Bohemia.

Ignatius's life-story is in the corridor immediately below. Unfortunately, it's been sliced down the middle by prefabricated offices: they're called temporary; at the time of writing, they look increasingly permanent.

There's one more stop to complete your Jesuit experience. Follow the corridor running off the centre of Francis's parade. At the end, you'll see a sign marked 'Hudební Oddělení' (Music Library) on your right—walk through the door and head right around the passage. The small reading room, with its cherub-topped Rococo bookshelves, contains the Jesuits' fascinating tribute to astronomy: models of the universe, diagrams of eclipses, and on the vault, a Baroque parade of approved thinkers. (Open Mon and Thurs 2–7; Tues and Fri 9–7.)

The Jesuits did their best to keep abreast of new learning, but as the Enlightenment advanced, astronomy became very tricky territory. The pantheistic philosophy of Giordano Bruno had shown where outlandish speculations could end: in his own case, frying on a Roman stake in 1600, and more importantly for the Jesuits, to a nasty question mark over the first line of the Bible. They soon accepted that there was more to the heavens than met the eye, but although they were among the more intellectually honest clerics of their day, they never stopped looking for a compromise.

Prague's Jesuits built their observatory in 1721, and the fresco was painted at some point between then and the tower's remodelling in 1749, as shown by the fact that the original building is part of the background. On the left are seven pretty Mathematical Disciplines including Gnomonics, the once-popular spirit of sundial construction; and under the Latin inscription 'God Gave the World to be Comprehended by Discussion', astronomy's heroes are gathered. Aristotle, doodling in the sand, is in front of Appolonius of Perga, Hipparchus and Ptolemy; on the far right Tycho Brahe, wearing his false nose (*see* pp. 156–7) is holding full and frank discussions with Giambaptista Riccioli (1598–1671), the Jesuits' black-robed representative. Riccioli's last-ditch attempt to keep the earth at the centre of the universe is on the right of the wall in front of you. A century after Galileo and Johannes Kepler had suggested alternative proposals, the Clementinum's scientists still regarded it as the pinnacle of astronomical achievement.

Walk down the stairs at the entrance to the room. You'll emerge back at the porter's lodge. As you leave the building, turn right and then right again. The dapper student in the next courtyard, sporting goatee and banner, is Josef Max's 1847 tribute to the pupils who dashed across the road in 1648 to fight the last battle of the Thirty Years War (see below). As you leave the complex, on your right is the western wing of the Clementinum, the section containing the paintings of SS Francis and Ignatius and the oldest part of the college (1653).

The almost martial façade, with its relentless alternation of pilasters and windows, was one of the trailblazers of the Baroque in Prague. Pollution and erosion have taken their toll, and it now takes some imagination to picture it in its prime—but it certainly impressed General Oliva, the then head of the Order in Rome, who let it be known that it was too ostentatious. Coming from a Jesuit, that's saying something.

Turn left. The Church of the Holy Saviour (Kostel sv. Salvátor) next door was the first church built by the Jesuits in Prague (1593–1601). Take a brief look back up Karlova—Kepler lived behind the ill-maintained sgraffiti of No. 4 between 1607 and 1612, five fertile years during which he produced inter alia *the principles of planetary motion and* Somnium, *a short description of life on the moon. In the courtyard is a tower-like construction, which was allegedly the site of his observatory.*

Walk back to the main street and cross over. The oval-domed St Francis's (sv. František) (1679–89) on your right is Prague's only church to make extensive use of real marble; everyone else had to make do with scagliola, *but the rich Knights of the Cross owned a quarry. Follow the tide of people flowing towards the **Old Town Bridge Tower** (Staroměstská mostecká věž), designed by Peter Parler (see below), and completed in the 1390s during the reign of Wenceslas IV. (Open April–Oct 10–6 ; adm.)*

As part of the fortification walls, this titan has had both symbolic and practical functions. After the execution of Bohemian nationalists in 1620, 10 heads putrefied from its first floor for a decade; and in 1648 the final hours of the Thirty Years War raged around the tower, when Sweden's army went on a last-minute looting spree and the Old Town was saved by a motley alliance of bearded students and Prague Jews. A Europe-wide peace had already been negotiated, but another truce was clearly necessary. It was signed on the middle of the bridge, in a wooden cabin specially partitioned to keep the opposing factions from each others' throats.

The battle destroyed most of the decoration on the western façade of the tower. The east still has its original 14th-century decoration, with sculptures of SS Adalbert and Procopius at the top, Charles IV and Wenceslas IV enthroned below, and St Vitus in the centre. More intriguing are the minor details, which show the whimsical and irreverent spirit that was abroad in the late Gothic art of Wenceslas's court. On the corner to your left is a figure running his hand up a nun's habit, a scene that is sadly eroding into non-indecency; and one of Wenceslas's dalliances is directly commemorated by the birds and scantily-clad female figure which appear all over the sides and golden-ribbed vault of the tower. The birds are probably kingfishers, but possibly halcyon birds (creatures of yore that were said to calm waves and wind in order to copulate more comfortably), both of which are symbols of bathkeepers. According to legend, it's all in honour of one Zuzana. In 1394, the feckless king was temporarily locked up by disgruntled nobles in the Old Town, and she rowed him to the safety of Malá Strana after he persuaded his captors to let him have a bath. She was only a bathkeeper's daughter, but the king's gratitude knew no bounds—not only did he bed her, but he also raised her hitherto shady profession to the status of a guild. The situation seems to have got out of hand by 1561, when male bath-attendants were reminded, on pain of death, of the need to wear loincloths when attending female customers.

The view along the bridge from the first floor is impressive—so much so that Communist buggers used to sit here and point eavesdropping equipment and lenses at particularly suspicious conversationalists down below. The listening post was only dismantled in 1990. Just before the viewing gallery at the top is a stone hunchback who guards the tower from evil spirits. Unfortunately, the medieval inscriptions that once used to help him have mysteriously disappeared. Demons were known to read everything they came across in case it contained a curse, and the tower used to contain two Latin phrases—*Signatesignatemeremetangise-tangis* and *Romatibisubitomotibusibitamor*—which it was hoped would delay them more than usual. They seem to mean, respectively, 'Take note, take note, you are touching and torturing me' and 'Rome, love overcomes you with sudden force', but more importantly, they are both palindromes. With luck, puzzled fiends would never be able to tear themselves away.

> Through the vault of the tower lies the **Charles Bridge** (Karlův most), a curving, swerving ley line through Prague. For centuries the city's energy has squeezed through this narrow channel; and the coronation processions and fairs of yesteryear find their modern equivalent in the scores of musicians who turn every evening into a fiesta during the summer. Ominous rumour has it that the bridge is soon going to close for thorough and drawn-out restoration; if you're unlucky, you'll have to make do with reading, staring and imagining.

There was a wooden way over the river over 1000 years ago, if Cosmas the chronicler is to be believed; an incidental detail of his account of the murder of St Wenceslas is that the bridge was damaged in 932, requiring a spot of Divine Intervention to fly the pallbearers across. Nothing is left of that structure, but remnants of the Judith Bridge, built in 1158 and Europe's second stone bridge after Regensburg, survive in the piers of the present work. The Judith Bridge was destroyed by floods in 1342, but the civic pride of Charles IV, who ascended the throne four years later, ensured that Prague didn't remain bridgeless for long. Astrologers were asked to find a suitably auspicious celestial configuration, and in 1357 Charles's architect, 27-year-old Peter Parler, got to work. No expense was spared—when the masons asked for eggs to strengthen the mortar, an egg tax was imposed on every hamlet in the land—and in the early 1400s, construction was complete. For over 400 years, the bridge was Prague's only river crossing. This feat of medieval engineering has survived centuries of deluges and, until 1950, the trundle of motor traffic.

The stark structure of the bridge is perfectly complemented by the 30 sculptures that now line it. The 14th century saw a simple wooden crucifix placed on the bridge; the Counter-Reformation knew a propaganda opportunity when it saw one, and during the late 1600s and early 1700s an entire avenue of Baroque saints was added to the bridge, inspired by Bernini's 1688 work on the Ponte Sant'Angelo in Rome. The hapless commuters of Prague were a captive audience to what would then have been an awesome array of swooning and gesticulating saints. According to the autobiography of a Prague old-timer, even into the early years of this century, pious souls would doff their caps 30 times as they made the crossing. Many of the works have now been replaced by copies, and there is some lifeless neo-Gothic statuary from the 19th century, but the overall effect of the sculpture is still superb.

The oldest work is the bronze **Crucifixion** (1657), third on your right, flanked by 19th-century work. The figure hasn't met with universal approval: the Hebrew inscription on the statue was the compulsory contribution of an outspoken Jew, who apparently wandered past in 1695 muttering blasphemies; while English-born Queen Elizabeth is said to have been horrified by the sinuous manliness that she glimpsed somewhere in the Messiah on her arrival in Prague in 1618. The fifth statue to your left shows Francis Xavier being borne aloft by grateful coolies. It's a copy of a 1711 work by F. M. Brokof which was swept away by a flood in 1890. The river also destroyed three arches around where you're standing, and was dammed, not before time, in 1954. Ignatius used to stand on the opposite side of the bridge; after sinking in 1890, he was replaced by the youngest statue here, Karel Dvořák's 1938 sculpture of SS Cyril and Methodius.

About halfway across on the right is a small bronze Lorraine Cross embedded in the wall. According to rumour, the Dalai Lama recognized this point as the centre of the universe during his visit to Prague in 1990; and it also marks the spot where **St John Nepomuk** was hurled into the river. Put your hand on it, make a wish and then go to his statue, the eighth on the right. John was a Vicar-General of Prague who was put in a sack and dropped into the Vltava in 1383 by Wenceslas IV. Two explanations for the king's act exist: the boring truth is that John appointed an abbot against the king's wishes; far better is the jolly tale put about three centuries later by the Jesuits when they were casting around for a wholesome Catholic rival to Jan Hus. The story is that Wenceslas asked John what the queen had told him during confession. (He had little time for his first wife. If contemporary chroniclers are to be trusted—which, fortunately, they aren't—she was eventually devoured by his dog after the king had drunk himself into a stupor.) Honest John supposedly replied from the rack that he'd forgotten, and wouldn't tell even if he could remember. Five stars appeared above the bobbing corpse (hence the unusual headgear that you'll see on all the saint's monuments in Prague). The Jesuits erected the statue in 1683; but John's canonization had to wait until 1729, after the Order had exhumed his coffin and claimed to find his tongue (*see* p. 129). A chapel used to stand around the the saint, and the rubbing of a million fingers has meant that tumbling John is still a glittering dot on the oxidized reliefs at the base of the figure. He will get you across any bridge safely, despite his own misfortune; and he's the saint to turn to if someone suspects you of doing something that you just didn't do. He also gets women pregnant.

SS Vincent Ferrer and Procopius on the left deserve a mention; among the feats noted on their statue are the salvation of 100,000 souls, the conversion of 2500 Jews, 70 exorcisms and 40 resurrections. A downcast devil, Turk and Jew support the saints. If you look over the bridge here, you'll see the statue of **Bruncvík**, a chivalrous character linked to the legend of Roland. The latter was a sanguinary epic of crusading Christianity, but Bruncvík has become enmeshed in a pot-pourri of mythological motifs and Prague legend. Various versions exist, but the most complex is that his invincible sword, buried in the Charles Bridge, will be unearthed in Bohemia's moment of greatest need by a stumbling white horse belonging to St Wenceslas; the saint will be at the head of the lost Hussite heroes who fell asleep in Blaník Mountain in 1434.

Of the petrified melodramas that remain, take a look at Matthias Braun's **St Luitgard**, fourth from the end on your left. Generally agreed to be the best-crafted sculpture on the bridge, it shows Christ letting the blind saint nuzzle His wounds, a vision she enjoyed late one night. Two statues along is F. M. Brokof's pantomime-like tribute to the **Trinitarian Order**, established for the age-old purpose of ransoming Christian hostages from infidel clutches. The founders of the Order stand above a little grotto full of captives, guarded by a pot-bellied pasha and a mad dog.

> *The Baroque hubbub subsides as you near the end of the bridge. An arm of the Vltava separates the island of Kampa (see pp. 197–8) from the mainland, and on your right are all 13 houses of Prague's so-called 'Little Venice'. The end of the bridge is punctuated by the **Malá Strana Bridge Tower** on the right, which was built in the early 1400s (open March–Dec 10–6; adm), and the stumpy **Judith Tower**—which despite the Renaissance decoration, belonged to the 12th-century predecessor of the Charles Bridge. The inseparable duo, wearing tiled top hats and forming the parapet and arch into Malá Strana, frame St Nicholas's Church and one of the most tempting photo-opportunities in Prague.*

> *Just to your right is **The Three Ostriches** (U tří pštrosů), a Renaissance house (the scrolled top-floor is a later Baroque addition) with paintings of the creatures on the façade. Jan Fux, purveyor of novelty plumage, bred and plucked the beasts here at the end of the 16th century. It's now a hotel and overrated restaurant and not the place to end this walk. If you are feeling energetic you could go on a final tower climb; if you're not, you could just sit back and watch life pass you by on the bridge, which is a favourite promenade for the capital's poseurs. Another possibility is to look for **Tonda**, the longest-established of the many picture-sellers on the bridge.*

You should be able to find him nearby, shirtless, surrounded by his art, and wearing a confused scowl. For a decade he has been drawing self-portraits and trying to sell them to tourists, who generally accelerate in alarm as they walk past. The result is that he has become a Charles Bridge institution, and visitors returning to Prague after some years sometimes find themselves buying his picture simply out of nostalgia. But he remains an enigmatic character. In 1992 he began to draw himself with horns and a lolling tongue, but will only laugh nervously when asked why. Indeed, he rarely speaks at all, except to wail 'Portrait, Deutschmark, dollar?' at passers-by. However, he was prepared to reveal that his ambition is to buy a dolphin and keep it in his bath.

> *A final way of winding up the walk is to pick up a coffee and cream cake in the cosy café just past the towers. As you walk through the gateway, cast your head up to the grooves on the wall to the left: they're the scars of years of axe-sharpening, from the days when Malá Strana's executioner's rostrum used to stand here.*

Galleries and Museums

The biggest museum and art gallery in Prague is the city itself, and many visitors never set foot inside the collections scattered across the capital. However, there are some curious and beautiful things behind its doors, and this section will help you decide what may be worth a visit. Prices are still lower than in many western countries, and most museums offer a 50 per cent reduction for students, children, pensioners and disabled people. The standard closing day is Monday, with a couple of maverick collections shutting down on Tuesday instead, and you can never count on being allowed into *any* building in Prague if its advertised closing time is less than half an hour away. Otherwise there's really no best or worst time to pay your choice a visit. In some cities you almost have to queue to see each painting or exhibit, but you can usually roam free in Prague's repositories, and in more obscure museums your very arrival may represent the largest crowd of the day. However, there's one minor obstacle to free movement that you'll face in almost every one of the city's museums and galleries. It's the dreaded and legendary *babička* posted in each room, whose veins tense the moment you trespass on her turf, and who is poised to snap or spring if you move into a very vaguely-defined security zone around the paintings. Particularly suspicious-looking coves may find themselves being stalked, and passed from *babička* to *babička* like a relay baton as they walk through a gallery.

Since the 1989 revolution, tremendous changes have been taking place in all of Prague's museums and galleries. The opening of the country's borders has brought international art theft to the capital, and a spate of audacious heists has meant that many museums and galleries are having to buy costly new alarm systems or conversely, to hide away some of their most outstanding holdings. Prague's grandest 20th-century art theft, the confiscation of religious and aristocratic collections by the Communists, is having even more dramatic repercussions. Laws passed in 1990 have granted a right of restitution to all those who can prove ownership of seized goods, and although the cockroaches and meteorites of the National Museum remain safe, some exceptional works in the National Gallery and the Museum of Decorative Arts have been lost. The time limit for nobles to reclaim their furniture is over, but monasteries and churches are continuing to pick at the city's public collections. To their credit, several are contemplating opening museums of their own.

One final point is that the country's postwar history is underrepresented in Prague's museums. You probably won't be surprised to hear that the V. I. Lenin Museum and the Klement Gottwald Museum ceased to exist some time ago. Despite occasional rumours, there is still no appropriate post-revolutionary commemoration of the years of Communism.

Art Galleries

The first four collections in this group all form part of the National Gallery. There is still no permanent venue for its huge collection of 20th-century Czech art. The bulk of the collection is scheduled to move into the Tradefair Palace (on Veletržní street in Prague 7), but administrative questions—including whether the gallery is to set up as an entirely independent institution—have delayed the transfer. Contact one of the galleries below for further information.

As well as the permanent exhibitions listed below, there are innumerable temporary displays being held in Prague at any given time. The National Gallery has two regular venues: the **Riding School of Prague Castle** at U Prašného mostu 55 and the **Goltz-Kinsky Palace** in the Old Town Square at Staroměstské nám. 12, the second of which specializes in exhibitions of graphic art. The Czech Ministry of Culture runs another long-established exhibition space, the Waldstein Riding Hall (Valdštejnská jízdárna) next to the Malostranská metro on Valdštejnská 2. The graceful Renaissance palace of Belvedere (see pp. 223–5) is home to shows organized by Prague Castle; and one of the best independent public galleries is the Stone Bell House (Dům U kamenného zvonu) at Staroměstské nám. 13. Details of what's on display at all the above venues can be found in any listings magazine. Prague's best commercial galleries are mentioned in the Shopping section (pp. 344–5).

National Gallery's Collection of European Art to the 20th century, Šternberk Palace, Hradčanské nám. 15, ℂ 35 24 41–3. (*Wed–Sun 10–6, Tues 9–7.*) This excellent gallery achieves the impossible, and takes you through six centuries of European art, almost ignoring the High Renaissance and often having artists represented by only one work, and yet leaving you momentarily at a loss to think of anything that you missed. Its acknowledged masterpieces are few (Dürer's *Feast of the Rose Garlands* and Bruegel's *Haymaking*), but the works here by Cranach, El Greco, Goya, Rubens, Rembrandt and a host of others leave few disappointed. The 20th century is represented by Klimt, Schiele, Munch, Kokoschka and others; and another section of the museum runs through French art from Impressionism through to Chagall, including a valuable collection of works by Picasso (*see* pp. 212–22).

National Gallery's Collection of Czech Gothic and Baroque Art, St George's Convent, © 53 52 46. (*Tues–Sun 10–6.*) The Gothic painting of this collection represents a unique period of Bohemia's artistic history. Some of the extraordinary panels by Master Theodoric are on display, and even those who generally shudder at the thought of endless Crucifixion scenes and Madonnas with Children will find some of the painting and sculpture here sublime. The same can't be said for the Baroque collection, but the statues lose none of their power to fascinate when seen at close quarters. There's also a small selection of work from Emperor Rudolf II's court (*see* pp. 136–9).

National Gallery's Collection of 19th- and 20th-century Czech Sculpture, Zbraslav Monastery. *16* (*April–Nov Tues–Sun 10–6.*) This gallery is a 30-minute journey from the city centre, and as a result, although it is among the capital's finest collections, it is only visited by a determined and well-informed minority of visitors. If you have the time, you should try to be one of them. To get there, take any of the following buses from the terminus outside Smíchovské nádraží (metro line B): 129, 241, 243, 255. Get off at Zbraslavské nám., a quiet suburban square just past the second bridge you cross, and the grounds of the low Baroque monastery are to your right.

The ground floor is dominated by the work of J. V. Myslbek, the country's most influential 19th-century sculptor. His work teeters between classicist restraint and the sweeping Romanticism demanded by his patriotic times, a conflict evident in his early studies for the *St Wenceslas Monument.* In the finished version at the head of Wenceslas Square (*see* pp. 229–32), Myslbek synthesized the struggling tendencies. There are many more of his later works here, including the startling larger-than-life *Crucifixion*, wrapped in an almost Art Nouveau arrangement of thorns and hair.

The mainstream of Czech Art Nouveau is represented by Ladislav Šaloun, and a gentle series of small copper and bronze reliefs by Stanislav Sucharda. Upstairs, the belated influence of Rodin, who exhibited in Prague in 1902, is reflected in the earlier works of Josef Mařatka and Bohumil Kafka, both of whom spent a couple of years working in the great man's studio. Kafka's sculpture pays the less heavy-handed debt, with the spontaneous and dark Impressionism of *Mummies*, inspired by the sight of desiccated Peruvians whom he had seen on show in Paris. There's a broad selection of the exceptional work of Otto Gutfreund, which begins with some of the first and most original Cubist sculpture in the world, and ends with the beautiful simplicity of the painted wood and terracotta figures he produced in the 1920s. The social realism of Gutfreund's later work influenced the whole of the next generation of Czechoslovakian sculptors, including Karel Pokorný, Jan Lauda, Karel Dvořák and Karel Kotrba; and their tributes to the humble and the meek pepper the gallery. There's also a broad collection of postwar sculpture, including an ever-expanding selection of work by contemporary artists. The gallery has also set up a tactile exhibition for visually-impaired and blind people, made up of copies of some twenty of its exhibits. Braille catalogues are available. Even if you are fully-sighted, the wood, bronze and steel make for an interesting feel. Shut your eyes or bring a blindfold.

National Gallery's Collection of 18th- and 19th-century Czech Art, St Agnes's Convent, ✆ 231 42 51. (*Tues–Sun 10–6.*) The convent itself is a tranquil retreat on the edge of the Old Town and one of the first examples of Gothic architecture in Bohemia. The romantic and nationalistic art that it contains is junk (*see* p. 172).

Bílek Villa (Bílkova vila), Mickiewiczova 1. (*15 May–15 October Tues–Sun 10–12, 1–6.*) A superb collection of the powerful work of František Bílek, one of the most isolated and extraordinary sculptors in modern Czech history (*see* p. 77). The well-laid out museum is in the house that he designed for himself, which apparently represents a cornfield.

Central Czech Gallery (Středočeská Galerie), Husova 19. (*Tues–Sun 10–12, 1–6.*) Exhibitions of Czech and foreign art from the 20th century. Regular displays of work by young contemporary Czech artists are held in the basement of the gallery, a pillared Romanesque house from the 13th century.

Picture Gallery of Prague Castle (Obrazárna Pražského hradu), Second Courtyard of Prague Castle. *Opening times undecided.* A small collection of art from Renaissance to Rococo, which lay around unrecognized for some 200 years. Contains paintings by Tintoretto, Titian, Veronese and Rubens, but although the gallery is worth a brief visit, it's less exciting than the hit-list might make it sound (*see* pp. 121–3).

Prague House of Photography (Pražský dům fotografie), Husova 23. (*Daily 11–7 May–Sept, 11–6 Oct–April.*) Temporary exhibitions of Czech and foreign photographers.

Troja Chateau, U trojského zámku. (*Tues–Sun 10–6.*) This Baroque palace to the north of central Prague houses a collection of 19th-century Czech art, but it's the decoration of Troja itself that makes the journey here worth while. It was built in the 1600s by an ambitious Czech nobleman, who was so anxious to please Bohemia's new masters that he submerged his main hall in an apotheosis of the Habsburgs. Painted by the Flemish-born and Roman-trained Abraham Godyn from 1691–1697, it is the richest illusionistic painting in the capital. Austrian triumphalism is the order of the day, and as well as innumerable scenes showing the wisdom, prudence and bravery of the kooky clan, the gaudy masterpiece heaps scorn on the Turks, who had just overplayed their hand for the last time. With the relief of Vienna in 1683, the Sublime Porte had begun its relentless metamorphosis into Sick Man of Europe, and there are cringing infidels dotted throughout, and one particularly impressive turbanned loser, with *trompe-l'œil* shadow, tumbling from the wall. The simple theme returns as allegory in the chateau's small grounds, littered with scenes from a Baroque battle of the gods and giants, and including a series of sculptures cascading down both sides of a stone staircase.

Music Museums

Prague's collection of musical instruments, the second largest in Europe after that in Brussels, was evicted from its former home by a posse of returning monks and is temporarily homeless. Keep your ears open for any future relocation. Until then, the following collections should soothe all but the most savage breast.

Mozart Museum (Bertramka), Mozartova 169, © 54 38 93. (*Daily 9.30–5.*) This charming villa is one of the few houses of the suburban gentry to survive the dark advance of industry into Smíchov during the 19th century. Mozart stayed here on three of his visits to Prague as a guest of the musically-minded Dušeks, to whom he was close—so close that his relationship with Josefina has caused Praguers to smile knowingly ever since. Legend has it that he once found himself at a loss for what to compose next, and she decided to inspire him by locking them both into one of Bertramka's rooms. Quite how she loosened his creative block isn't made clear, but he apparently emerged clutching either an aria dedicated to her, or the overture to *Don Giovanni*, depending on whom, if anyone, you believe. The story is a gift to the museum owners, who dramatize it in period costume every night during high season, and once a week during the rest of the year.

The building was seriously damaged by fire in 1871, giving the exhibits a certain speculative feel; no one's *quite* sure whether Wolfgang really slept, studied or was incarcerated in any of the rooms that escaped. If you ask sweetly, the cashier can usually be persuaded to play the English taped guide as you walk through the rooms. The rapid-fire commentary is interspersed with snatches of the composer's greatest hits. Cult-followers might appreciate the collection of 13 hairs, a rare relic of the body that notoriously got lost somewhere under Vienna's St Mark's cemetery. Summer evening concerts are held on the outdoor terrace, and at the far end of the garden is a stone table at which the composer is said to have mused.

Prague has two small museums devoted to its two great 19th-century composers (although none to the Moravian-born Leoš Janáček). Both have small collections of scores, photographs, diaries and the like, and again they lay on greatest-hits tapes.

Antonín Dvořák Museum, Ke Karlovu 20, ✆ 29 82 14. (*Tues–Sun 10–5.*) This museum is housed in a charming Baroque villa designed by Kilian Dienzenhofer, and the surrounding streets make up one of the least visited but most tranquil parts of the New Town.

Bedřich Smetana Museum, Novotného lávka 1, ✆ 26 53 71. (*Wed–Mon 10–5.*) Located in an adapted water-tower very close to the Charles Bridge, just above a nightclub that is perhaps the most musically uninispired in the capital.

Military Museums

Prague maintains an impressive array of mothballed weaponry in its military museum, housed in three separate locations. All will quicken the pulse, but the two devoted to modern killing have the added thrill of political contentiousness. The purge of the Czech armed forces since 1989 has only been a partial success, and the military retains a very equivocal view of the country's recent history. The head of the museum personifies the turbulence that the armed forces have seen in the last few decades: a colonel in 1968 and now a general, he spent 21 years between ranks working as a bricklayer after he refused to back the Warsaw Pact invasion of his country. Innumerable issues are still up for grabs, and the modern exhibitions often provide fascinating insights into the mental struggle between old and new that is still taking place in the Czech Republic.

Military Museum (to 1918) (Vojenské muzeum), Hradčanské nám. 2, ✆ 53 64 88. (*May–Oct Tues–Sun 10–6.*) No political angst in this place, which is devoted to the pure joy of olde worlde warfare, from flails to cannons (*see* p. 212).

Military Museum (1918 to the present), U památníku 2, ✆ 27 29 65. (*April–Oct Tues–Sun 9.30–4.30, Nov–March Mon–Fri 8.30–5.*) Contains exhibits on the Czech Legion, the Palestine- and England-based anti-Nazi forces and, interestingly enough, the anti-chemical unit that stood around in the Gulf during 1991. There's talk of reorganizing the collection around the theme of 'Resistance', with exhibits from 1968 and the years of Charter 77; a band of militaristic patriots are said to be waging low-intensity warfare against the dirty dissident idea. You could also keep your eyes open for any mention of Semtex, the nation's most recent contribution to mass destruction.

Military Museum—Exhibition of Aeronautics and Cosmonautics (Exposice letectva a kosmonautiky), just off Mladoboleslavská in Prague 9, ✆ 82 47 09. (*May–Oct Tues–Thurs and Sat–Sun 9–5, Fri 2–5.*) This museum lies miles from the centre of town, but it's well worth a visit. It comprises three hangars filled with a superb collection of propellers, ack-ack guns, jet engines, Spit-fires and Tiger Moths, and just about every plane the Warsaw Pact produced until the mid-1960s. As you wander among the sleek silver MiGs and dumpy Suchoi bombers, you can't help but contemplate the aerial death they might have delivered had Europe's Cold War ever warmed up. Times are changing: the museum's newest acquisition is a cobalt-blue Phantom, handed over by Britain in early 1992. The museum also contains several requisitioned Panzers, lines of Soviet tanks and a couple of tactical rocket launchers. Mili-tary parking lots and a still-functioning airfield surround the museum. They're off-limits, and an accidental meander through them is the kind of diversion that would probably have got you deported before 1989. Among the planes and personnel carriers are partially dismantled Warsaw Pact rockets, helicoptor gunships and, sitting incongruously pretty in the middle of a hardware graveyard, Prague's notorious Pink Tank (*see* p. 279–80). That will probably have been repainted by the time you read this, but for the latest information contact the museum's director, Colonel Vladimír Remek—Czechoslovakia's first and last man in space, with 161 hours of cosmonautical floating to his name.

General Museums

Alois Jirásek and Mikoláš Aleš Museum (Muzeum Aloise Jiráska a Mikoláše Alše), Letohrádek Hvězda, © 36 79 38. (*Tues–Sun 10–5.*) The exhibits, minutiae from the lives of two very patriotic Bohemians (writer and artist respectively), are self-explanatory and dull—but their home, in the Hvězda (Star) Summer Palace, merits a visit if you find yourself near by. The six-pointed structure was designed in 1555–6 by the son of Bohemia's first Habsburg emperor, Ferdinand I, and the ground floor of his folly is entirely covered with some superb Italian stucco work. The crisp decoration is centred around the piggy-back duo of Aeneas and Anchises, off to found Rome (and, as Habsburg lore would have it, the empire that the family had taken over), and scores of other deities, satyrs and crazy chimeras dance across the rest of the ceilings. The cellar of the palace has a small exhibition on the Battle of the White Mountain. Although Czechs commemorate their mammoth defeat with peculiar zeal in every historical museum in the country, it has a special relevance here: the White Mountain is about a kilo-metre from Hvězda; the sanguinary last stand occurred about half that distance away; and when it was all over, the tired but happy Catholics came to the palace to celebrate.

Anti-Nazi Resistance Memorial in the crypt of the Church of SS Cyril and Methodius, Resslova 9, © 29 55 95. (*Open Tues–Sat 9–11 am; no entrance fee is charged, but the church badly needs donations*) Admission is via the sacristy, on your right as you face the memorial on the wall. A small, dramatic and moving exhibition at the site of the pitched gun battle fought between the Nazis and the assassins of Reinhard Heydrich (*see* pp. 269–70).

Jewish Museum (Židovské muzeum), Jachýmova 3, © 231 06 34. (*Sun–Fri April–Oct 9–5, Nov–Mar 9–4.30.*) This state-run museum covers most of what remains of the Prague ghetto, and includes several synagogues, the 12-layer Jewish cemetery, an exhibition devoted to Prague's Jewish history, and collections of thousands of Jewish artefacts (predominantly textiles, books and silverware) from across Europe. The artefacts were assembled by the Nazis, who planned to transform the quarter into an 'exotic museum of an extinct race'; another memorial to the Holocaust is an almost unbearably painful set of drawings and paintings from the Terezín ghetto. The Jewish community itself maintains two more synagogues and the Jewish Town Hall. (*See* p. 164 *et seq.*)

Kafka Museum, U radnice 5. (*Tues–Sat 10–6.*) A small collection of photos, quotes and snippets from the author's life.

Museum of the City of Prague (Muzeum hlavního města Prahy), Na poříčí 52, © 236 24 50. (*Tues–Sun 10–6.*) The highlight here is a 1:480 model of most of Prague minus the New Town. It's the work of an obsessed amateur artist called Langweil (which translates roughly as 'Boredom') who spent some 10 years completing it, almost, before dying in 1837. It answers those questions that begin to niggle once you've been in Prague for a while—what the Jewish ghetto once looked like, how many spires the City of One Hundred has really got, and so on. The rest of the exhibits form an interesting collection of Romanesque and Gothic decorations rescued from the attentions of rapacious bulldozers over the years.

Museum of Decorative Arts (Uměleckoprůmyslové muzeum), 17. listopadu 2, © 232 00 51. (*Tues–Sun 10–6.*) A colourful display of the decorative arts from the late 16th century onwards. The massive holdings of the museum also include a unique collection of Cubist furniture, one of the best glass collections in the world and tens of thousands of modern posters and photographs—but it doesn't have the space to show any of it. If you're lucky, a generous benefactor will have bought it a spare warehouse by the time you read this; if you're not, this is still the most beautiful collection in the capital. It also contains an excellent 150,000-volume library, open to the public (*Mon–Fri 10–6; see* p. 162).

Náprstek Museum of Asian, African and American Cultures (Náprstkovo muzeum), Betlémské nám. 1, © 22 76 91. (*Tues–Sun 9–12, 12.45–5.30.*) Mid-19th century Mr Náprstek intended to set up a museum devoted to the wonders of industry, but assembled so many primitive objects while pondering the superiority of technology, that his wife persuaded him to put them on display as well. In the end, his machines were hived off to form the beginnings of the National Technical Museum, and there's no longer a flywheel or spring to be found. Náprstek's first artefacts came from Milwaukee, but the museum now contains shaking sticks, boomerangs, ponchos and peace-pipes from the entire non-technical world.

National History Museum, Lobkovický palac, Jiřská 3, © 53 73 06. (*Tues–Sun 9–5.*) Rather too small to encapsulate Bohemia's history, but it neatly wraps up a trip to the castle and is covered at the end of Walk I (*see* pp. 143–4).

National Literature Museum (Památník národního písemnictví), Strahov Monastery, © 53 88 41. (*Tues–Wed, Fri–Sun 9–4.30.*) A perusal of Bohemian literature from Cyrillic bibles through to the literary efforts of the 19th-century national revival movement. However, it's the opulent libraries that make a visit to Strahov essential (*see* pp. 203–6).

National Museum (Národní muzeum), Václavské nám. 68, © 26 94 51. (*Wed–Mon 9–5.*) The splendid neo-Renaissance interior is worth seeing, and the exterior is unavoidable, but otherwise this is a natural history museum with few of the features that generally make such places tolerable. The skeletons are of small and humdrum creatures, and it's hard to be impressed by the museum's claim to own every mineral known to man. It apparently contains a collection of very rare meteorites (*see* pp. 229–30).

National Technical Museum (Národní technické muzeum), Kostelní 42, © 37 36 51. (*Tues–Sun 9–5.*) Tremendous fun. The colossal main hall is a Grand Central Station of transport, with infernal steam engines, Bugattis and Mercedes, and long lines of motorbikes dating from 1887. The first car Karl Benz ever sold (in 1893) is here; there's also a 1900 railway carriage, the mahogany trimmings and upholstered sofas of which were designed for the comfort of Habsburg monarchs on the move. Sailing over everything are 13 aircraft (14 if you include the balloon that's apparently rising through the roof), an impressive assortment of translucent dragonflies and vintage biplanes. Another hall is filled with hundreds of still and movie cameras, including some of the earliest doomed attempts at stereoscopic photography. The history of chronography is recorded in another ground-floor room. Most of the devices are calm enough (look out for the Renaissance pocket sundial), but several of the dropping balls and swinging pendulums tick mercilessly throughout, and erupt into pandemonium at random intervals. No less unnerving is the acoustics exhibition on the first floor, an interactive cacophony of screaming children and every noise from feedback to bird warbles. On the top floor is a small astronomical collection, which includes sextants and astrolabes used by Tycho Brahe and Johannes Kepler in Prague. If you arrive at 11 am, 1 pm or 3 pm, you can follow a guided tour down to the belly of the building, a tremendous mock-up coal mine far underground.

Physical Training and Sports Museum (Muzeum tělezné výchovy a sportu), Újezd 40, © 53 45 51. (*Tues–Sun 9–5.*) Physical culture has assumed mass proportions in the nation's past, but this is a low-key homage to the temple of the body. Highlights are limited to three boneshakers and an eight-person sled.

Police Museum (Muzeum policie), Ke Karlovu 1, © 29 52 09. (*Sept–June Tues–Sun 10–5.*) Once devoted to the activities of the National Security Corps, this museum has been cleaned up since the revolution and is now intended to laud the acceptable face of authoritarianism. It's still a rather ominous place, with video surveillance equipment operating throughout,and unexplained photos of ski-masked paramilitaries bursting in on sad punks and gipsies.

Postage Stamp Museum (Muzeum poštovní známky), Nové mlýny 2, © 231 20 06. (*Tues–Sun 9–4.30.*) A very small museum in one of the New Town's oldest houses, next to an early 17th-century water tower. The staff are shocked if someone stops by, and all the more friendly as a result. Philatelists can peruse 300 pull-out displays, and the ignorant can have a quick stare at the Tu'penny Blues and Penny Blacks in the UK section. Upstairs, there are some pretty 19th-century lithographs concentrating on the pleasures and perils of a postman's life, and a series of wall paintings, entirely unrelated to postage, by the 19th-century Czech artist Josef Navrátil.

GREATER PRAGUE

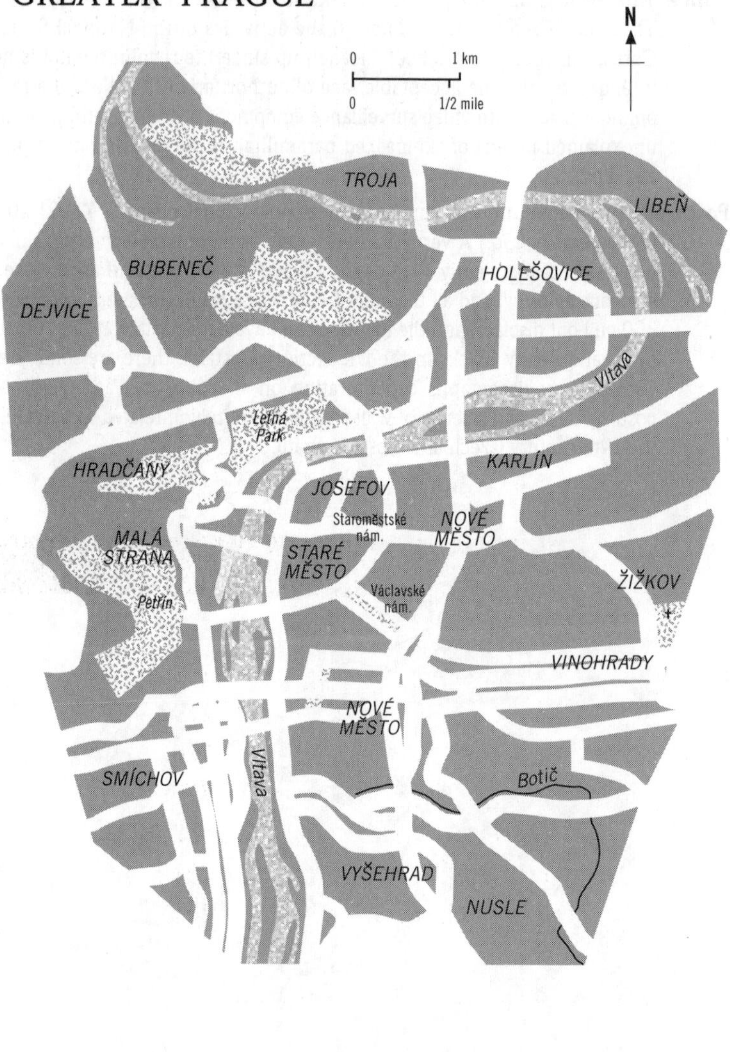

N

| 0 | | 1 km |
| 0 | | 1/2 mile |

TROJA

LIBEŇ

BUBENEČ

HOLEŠOVICE

DEJVICE

Vltava

Letná
Park

HRADČANY

KARLÍN

JOSEFOV

Staroměstské
nám.

NOVÉ
MĚSTO

MALÁ
STRANA

STARÉ
MĚSTO

ŽIŽKOV

Petřín

Václavské
nám.

VINOHRADY

NOVÉ
MĚSTO

SMÍCHOV

Vltava

Botič

VYŠEHRAD

NUSLE

Peripheral Attractions

The few square miles covering Hradčany, Malá Strana and the Old Town contain more than enough to keep most visitors busy, but there's a ragbag of attractions further from the beaten track. Explorers and romantics should all find something to their tastes in the sights listed below, and there are particularly rich pickings for cemetery ghouls. There is also an inordinate number of memorials to Prague's troubled 20th-century history: as well as reminders of genuine tragedy, several spots demand a quiet chuckle in honour of the more ridiculous aspects of totalitarianism. All the following districts are easily accessible by public transport, and are included in the roughly clockwise order in which they circle the Old Town.

Nové Město/New Town

The New Town rises in a crescent from the south-west to the north-east of the Old Town, which it locks into the river-bend. It's actually not very new, having got its name back in 1348, when Emperor Charles IV established it to cater for the monks and merchants flooding into his new capital. Charles was also worried that the cacophony of Prague's cobblers, wheelwrights, smithies and the like would disturb the repose of his new university in the Old Town, and over the next century the quarter came to have a higher concentration of workers than any other section of the city. They, and the vagabonds and riffraff who joined them, turned the area into a centre of radical Hussitism during the early 1400s. The 1420s was a tense decade, during which the New Town vied for supremacy with the relatively moderate Old Town, but it lost and for several centuries the quarter was little more than an appendage of Prague proper.

Over the last century, however, the New Town has become the commercial and administrative centre of the capital. It's only listed as a 'peripheral' attraction because its sights are scattered over too wide an area to be covered elsewhere in this book. With the help of only a handful of modern roads, the broad boulevards, squares and streets have carried Prague's traffic unchanged for over 600 years. Paradoxically, the area's ability to adapt has meant that it's suffered from the 19th and 20th centuries to an incomparably greater extent than the other districts of medieval Prague. Most of its buildings are sooty blocks of every neo-variety possible, with an unco-ordinated mess of modernist architecture scattered throughout. However, if you have the time and muscle to spare, a trek takes you through a part of living Prague that most visitors never find.

Wenceslas Square is covered in Walk V, and most of the other sites worth seeing are near **Karlovo nám.** (Charles Square), which you can reach by metro (line B) or trams 4, 6, 16, 21, 22 and 24. The square was laid out as a park during the last century, but it was originally the hub of the New Town. As well as providing a site for the capital's cattle market, it was the spot that Charles IV used for his annual relic displays (*see* p. 44) and in the north-east corner is the **New Town Hall** (Novoměstská radnice). It was founded in the mid-1300s, but only the tower (1425–6) has any look of age about it; the rest of the building was completely rebuilt during the 19th and early 20th centuries. In 1419 its former windows were the venue for **Prague's first defenestration**. Jan Želivský, a Hussite firebrand of a priest, led a rabble to the building to demand the release of some heretics, and the Catholic councillors apparently lobbed stones at his monstrance. That proved to be a serious misjudgement. The crowd stormed the building, hurled the councillors from the windows, and then bludgeoned to death anyone who survived the fall. The times were violent ones, and Jan himself didn't escape: in 1421 the burghers of the Old Town invited him to their place for full and frank discussions, and beheaded him. The Communists always had a soft spot for radical John, and there's a monument to him here dating from 1960.

Halfway down the square, at the junction with Ječná, is the **Church of St Ignatius** (sv. Ignác), which along with the neighbouring college (now a hospital) formed the Jesuit encampment in the New Town. The powerful arches of the chapels and broad nave are laden with half-immured cherubs and angels, and the gold and creamy-pink interior has the usual ostentatiousness of Jesuit architecture. It was built in 1665–70, too early for it to display the fluidity and seductive power of later Jesuit churches such as St Nicholas's in Malá Strana (*see* pp. 186–9).

In Resslova, the main street leading off the opposite side of the square, is the Orthodox **Church of SS Cyril and Methodius** (sv. Cyril a Metoděj). It is recognizable by a pock-marked section of wall that commemorates one of the most dramatic events to occur in Prague during the Second World War. After the killing of Reinhard Heydrich (*see* p. 57), seven members of the group responsible holed themselves up here. They were betrayed, and during the early hours of 18 June 1942 over 300 SS and Gestapo soldiers took up positions around the building. Through the night, wave upon wave of machine-gun fire poured into the church, but only as dawn broke did the shooting from within stop. The Nazis entered to find that they had spent the night battling three men—four remained in the crypt. Gunfire resumed, and for another two hours the fighters held out in the catacombs against bullets, tear gas and hand grenades. *The gouged and battered crypt is open from Tues–Sat 9–11 am and it's one of the most powerful memorials to anti-Nazi resistance in Europe. To see it ring the bell at the* *sacristy, on your right as you face the wall. No admission fee is charged, but the church needs donations to keep the crypt open.*

You enter the crypt from the nave, through wooden floor panels that swing aside to reveal an 18th-century stone staircase. Catacombs line either side (they held the bodies of church priests until desecrated by the SS), and above you on the left are two in which the last fighters took their lives. They did so only after reaching the end of their ammunition: German troops had pushed a high-pressure hose through a vent, and with water flooding into the pitch-black crypt and the Nazis on the point of blowing open the long-disused staircase, the men blasted themselves with their final bullets. The gashes of the shots still mark the walls. The small exhibition includes photographs of the Nazi assault, taken by a Czech police officer with a camera in his lighter. There is also a series of pictures from the scene of the assassination itself, an event that has two interesting postscripts: Heydrich's chauffeur survived the clumsy ambush only to fall victim, 49 years later, to a Red Army Faction attack in Hamburg; while Lina, the wife of Heydrich and one of those who was instrumental in urging Hitler on to bloody revenge in 1942, now draws a war-widow's pension from the German government. At the far end of the crypt is a 1-metre-long hollow, smashed away with a pipe while the Nazis pumped gunfire and water through the ventilation hole overhead. Although hundreds of troops had been stationed at sewage outlets along the Vltava to forestall any escape, the crypt is actually next to a Grand Central of Prague sewers. Had they hit the drain, the men would have been home and dry. They were 30 centimetres away from doing so.

At the southern end of the square is the Baroque **Faust House** (Faustův dům). The name was conjured up during the 19th century and is only very tangentially related to Goethe's tragic diabolist. A student tenant left without having paid the rent, there was a hole in the roof, and Prague's overworked fabulists concluded that he had been abducted by the devil. However, the house's history is not entirely without mystery. One of Emperor Rudolf II's pseudo-scientists, the necromancer and would-be wife-swapper Edward Kelley (*see* pp. 102–4) lived in the original Renaissance building, and in the 18th century it was occupied by Ferdinand Mladota, another mystical trickster. Today the building is occupied by chemists rather than alchemists, and unless you have a prescription there's no point venturing within.

To the south of the square, on Vyšehradská, is the Baroque **Church of St John Nepomuk on the Rock** (Kostel sv. Jana Nepomuckého Na skalce). Effortlessly perched on a craggy curve, it's one of the most elegant of all Kilian Dienzenhofer's churches in Prague. The twin towers of the narrow façade are echoed by the bizarre peaks of the **Emmaus Monastery** (Klášter Emauzy) across the street. The roof of the Gothic monastery was obliterated during an Allied bombing run in February 1945, and the 1960s replacement, flowing into two spires, is one of the most distinctive pieces of postwar architecture in the capital. The monastery was founded by Charles IV in 1347 for Balkan Benedictines, who (thanks to a spot of pressure on the pope) were granted the rare privilege of being allowed to chant their dirges and liturgies in Old Slavonic here. Pope and emperor each hoped that their respective spheres of influence would thereby be extended eastwards, but the Croatians and Dalmatians played their own game. When the Hussites popped round to storm the monastery, the clerics audaciously informed the mob that they fully sympathized with the anti-clerical cause. It was a gamble, but it worked: the confused crowd slunk off and the cowled monks were left to intone in peace. In 1446 they consolidated their position by re-establishing themselves as the only Hussite Order in the world. The Spanish Benedictines recovered Emmaus from their wayward brethren after the Battle of the White Mountain in 1620, and the Order has ebbed and flowed through ever since. It was last evicted by the Communists in the early 1950s, and reinstated in 1990. The monastery's cloisters contain a somewhat battered cycle of Gothic mural paintings, commissioned by Charles himself. The scenes juxtapose incidents from the Old Testament with those that they allegedly prefigured in the new world order of Christianity. Their astrological and alchemical symbolism (as well as a healthy dose of sun-worship) provides a fascinating glimpse into the arcane depths of religious belief in 14th-century Prague. However, long and occasionally futile arguments with the Benedictine bouncer are now necessary before you can get in to see them. Try at the door to your left as you enter the monastery grounds. Just further along the street, where it rolls into Na slupi, are Prague's **botanical gardens** (Botanická zahrada), a sloping retreat of roses, rhododendrons and azaleas. *(Open 1 Jan–15 March 10–5, 16 March– 31 Oct 10–6, 1 Nov–31 Dec 10–4.)*

Although the New Town is riddled with some particularly thunderous streets, life slows to a standstill in the small island of hills, cobbles and educational institutes behind the gardens. On Viničná 7 you'll find part of the science faculty of the Charles University, where Albert Einstein lived between 1911 and 1912, when he taught as Professor of Theoretical Physics in Prague. The blank wall across the road conceals the gardens of the Neurological Institute—and fun-loving Einstein apparently once told a visitor, while gazing down at the pottering lunatics, that you'd have to be mad not to understand quantum theory. There are two worthwhile stops further up the hill on Ke Karlovu street. At No. 20 is the **Vila Amerika**, a gorgeous Baroque summerhouse designed by Kilian Dienzenhofer and set among sculptures by Antonín Braun. It houses the small

Dvořák Museum (*see* p. 261). The crimson dome of the **Church of Our Lady and Charlemagne** (Kostel Panny Marie a Karla Velikého) stands at the end of the road. The church was founded by Charles IV in 1358, for French Augustinians. Its unusual octagonal plan was loosely modelled on the Aachen burial church of Charlemagne, one of the many bigwigs adopted by Charles to bolster his political credentials. Like several other new churches, it was deliberately sited to command the horizon of the New Town, and towers over the vast Nusle valley.

The most awe-inspiring feature of the church is its remodelled interior, shaped like a single star, 24 metres in diameter. Legend has it that the architect was a novice who built it with the devil's help; others claim that it was designed in about 1575 by Bonifaz Wohlmut, court architect to Ferdinand I—but either way it's one of the grandest flourishes of (extremely) late Gothic architecture in Prague. *The church is open from 2–5.15 on Sundays and holidays.*

The neighbouring monastery houses the Police Museum which has a perverse appeal to some (*see* p. 265). Otherwise, there's little else left to see save the 14th-century fortification walls that stretch down from the church. You could wander down the grassy stone steps of Albertov street, which was the starting point of the candle-lit demonstration on 17 November 1989 that went to Národní street to meet the batons and last stand of a rotten government (*see* p. 60). Alternatively, contemplate the gargantuan **Nusle Bridge** (Nuselský most), leaping half a kilometre across the Nusle valley. Some Praguers still suspect that the bridge, which carries six lanes of scooting traffic and two tracks of tunnelling metros, was intended to facilitate any urban military manoeuvres that the Communist government or its fraternal foreign allies might have deemed necessary. It's probably not true, since construction began during the relatively liberal mid-1960s, but it's hard to believe that someone somewhere didn't check that a line of tanks could safely trundle across. The bridge used to be named after Klement Gottwald, Czechoslovakia's first Communist president, and has long been the most popular spot for public suicides in the country. The former regime never got round to releasing the annual figures, but a worker under the bridge made the assertion, fortunately rather unbelievable, that for several years at least one body a month had crashed to a halt outside her shop.

Žižkov and Vinohrady

These districts, sprawling eastwards from Wenceslas Square, are as old as the New Town—but while Charles IV was drawing up the plans of his Prague extension, they were being planted with vineyards (*vinohrady*), and remained little more than fields until well into the last century. Industrialization and urban fecundity gradually populated them, and in the late 1870s the northern area of Žižkov and Vinohrady to the south each received municipal charters. Their lives as towns were short—both were incorporated into the capital in 1920—but as suburbs, each has developed a distinct character over the years. Vinohrady, crisscrossed by broad boulevards and quiet cobbled avenues, is filled with dilapidated 19th-century mansions and forlorn hints of how bourgeois Prague would be, given half a chance. Through the lace curtains of grimy French windows, sparkling chandeliers illuminate vast high-ceilinged rooms; while the sinuous beauty of wrought-iron Art Nouveau balconies is sabotaged by lines of underpants and corsets hanging out to dry. However, the area is being rediscovered, not least by property speculators, and the cafés and restaurants of gentrification are already mushrooming across the district. The future of Žižkov is less clear. Although the hilly backstreets of its western half are peppered with the same Art Nouveau and neo-Renaissance architecture of Vinohrady, the area has always had a rougher edge than its genteel neighbour. Over the decades it developed a proud and self-conscious sense of community: until the 1950s the inhabitants even had their own accent, and 'Red Žižkov' was for years a stronghold of Communism. That eventually became a contradiction in terms in Czechoslovakia, but the district remains more blue-collar than any other in Prague. Even climatically, there's something peculiarly gritty about Žižkov: much of it is built in a smoky basin, and it can spend days doggedly sitting in a sulphurous haze while the rest of the capital basks in the sun. It all makes for a quarter that much of Prague would never choose to live in—particularly because of the number of gipsies who live there—but it has a bustle and life that is beginning to attract young foreign residents and estate agents who enjoy risk.

A walk through both districts is still an interesting way of finding out what Praguers get up to when tourists aren't around; and although your logistical skills (or legwork) will be tested, the tour will show you a scattered and eclectic collection of some of the most memorable 20th-century monuments in Prague. Start at U památníku, a steep lane running up from Husitská. If you follow the path past the modern **Military Museum** (see p. 261) to the top of the wooded hill, you'll reach the National Memorial at Žižkov (Národní památník na Žižkově)—one of the lesser-known marvels of the capital. This ridge was the site of an epic battle in 1420, during which the radical Táborites (see p. 384) saw off a papal crusade and set off the action-packed decade of the Hussite Wars. To commemorate that event, a nine-metre high sculpture of Hussite hero Jan Žižka now sits on the summit, mace in hand and surveying the railway tracks and decrepit housing of the district named after him. It's the largest equestrian statue in the world, but it slots almost discreetly into the scheme of the granite edifice that lies behind it—and it is firmly put into the shade by that building's extraordinary history. Although built in the early 1930s, it was the **Communist Party mausoleum** between 1955 and 1989.

As you walk along the windswept stone pavements, up broad grey steps and past immense and empty torch holders, refrains and newsreels from a past era might flash through your mind. Up here the Czechoslovakian lion survives, rampant under the Communist star, and cycles of bronze reliefs still celebrate the violent progress of the dialectic—through Hussite demagoguery and the class-consciousness-inducing whips of the imperial police—and the final glorious triumph of technician, worker and smoking factory. And inside the building, things become very chilly indeed. From a hall of grey-veined-marble walls, bathed in eerie purple light, red-carpeted steps lead down into the crypt. Brutal rectangular pillars and two lines of brown sarcophagi flank the central tomb of Klement Gottwald, Czechoslovakia's 'First Working-Class President'. All the graves are now empty. In 1989, to forestall an expected desecration, the Central Committee finally offered the urns (all were cremated) to the next-of-kin. Gottwald's family refused to accept his ashes, and his whereabouts are now unknown.

The strangest is yet to come. Underneath the crypt is an entire complex of rooms all constructed in the early 1950s for a single purpose—the mummification and display of Gottwald. That episode ended rather messily, and you might want to read the details on pp. 108–9 as you walk through the chambers. Under the yellowing tiles of the first room—a refrigerated morgue—the F.W.C.P. was pickled by a team of taxidermists from the Soviet Union, and it was here that the increasingly desperate attempts to keep him together were later made. A hydraulic lift in the nearby annexe used to raise and lower the besuited mummy from casket to slab. Next door is a bank of dials and knobs, regulating humidity and temperature, and manned continuously by ultra-loyal members of the Party. Finally, you come to the engine room. It contains an emergency generator and a maze of tanks, valves, and pipes—all installed in pairs, in order that no mechanical failure could ever threaten the immortality of the demigod upstairs.

At the time of writing, the complex is being renovated, and a series of bizarre plans has been mooted for its future. A rooftop restaurant is likely to open, exhibitions will be held, and a serious proposal has been made to install a waxwork of Gottwald's corpse as the centrepiece of a memorial to Communist kitsch. The young director of the halls pays lip service to the idea that it should return to its origins and become a national memorial—but even he can't suppress a burst of embarrassed laughter as he stands among the tombs and suggests that it could become a recreational centre for all the family. A visit here is likely to remain a suitably unwholesome experience for years to come.

About a kilometre due south of the monument is another grand project of Communism, the **Žižkov Tower** *(Žižkovská věž)* next to Fibichova street. You should have few problems finding it—at 287 metres, the futuristic silver steeple can be seen for miles around. At close range the tower is phenomenally impressive, almost ready to begin a sleek and fiery ascent from the broad and quiet square of pastel tenements in which it waits. Since 1992, it has been happily broadcasting TV and radio signals, as well as bouncing innumerable mobile phone messages from passing satellites, but its early working life was plagued with problems. From the moment construction began in 1984, awestruck locals began to whisper that it would be used to jam, beam and survey with hitherto unheard-of power. By 1989 most of Prague had become convinced that the *Pražský čůrák* (Prague penis) was emitting everything from subliminal propaganda to gamma rays, and under popular pressure the new government invited a team of international inspectors to check. The boffins prodded solenoids, waved Geiger counters, and found nothing. However, urban myth can still tell you about the many mutants born in the neighbourhood, and the strangely incongruous patter that occasionally crackles out of the mouths of passing *babičky* or their dachshunds. You can mull over the possibilities, and listen out for any odd humming, at a café on the fifth floor or a viewing gallery on the eighth *(open 10–12 midnight)*.

One of the genuinely more spooky things about the tower is that it is built over the ground that served as a **Jewish cemetery** between 1787 and 1891. The Communists destroyed it and turned it into a park in the early 1970s—well before they planned the TV station—for reasons that are either unknown or obvious, depending on your point of view. However, a small strip of the cemetery still stands to the north of the square, and it's a rather amazing sight. With tottering stones and crumbling inscriptions, it is powerfully reminiscent of the Old Jewish Cemetery, but here you're likely to be the only person wandering among the ivy-covered graves and haphazard piles of decommissioned slabs. As you stand under the shadow of the rocket, with the knowledge that the silent graveyard once stretched across the entire square, that can make for a disconcerting experience.

At the nearby nám. Jiřího z Poděbrad, you'll find the 1933 **Church of the Sacred Heart** (Kostel Srdce Páně)—a worthy addition to the modern masterpieces of Žižkov. Surrounded by tissue-tinted mansions and with the TV tower in the background, the view from this square is one of the more surreal to be found in Europe. The monochrome church, the eastern façade of which combines the pediments of classicism, the ornamentation of Art Nouveau, two obelisks and a mammoth glass clock, defies categorization. It's the work of Jože Plečnik (1872–1957), a Slovenian who studied in turn-of-the-century Vienna and spent most of his life teaching and designing in Ljubljana. By adapting historical motifs, Plecnik attempted to create a modern architecture that retained the beauty and spirituality of the past; but paradoxically, although that made his work suspect to many of the cube-lovers of the day, it was Prague's hidebound conservatives who eventually had him run out of town (*see* pp. 82–3). Despite that, it's since the dubious triumph of the concrete block that this church has come back into its own. It now looks not only more human, but also more new-fangled than the Constructivist and Functionalist designs of most of Plečnik's contemporaries.

The final attraction in this part of town is the necropolis that stretches from Flora to Želivského stations on line A of the metro. It's less haunting than the Malá Strana cemetery (*see below*) but more suited to a lazy graveyard stroll. The **Olšany cemeteries** (Olšanské hřbitovy) began life in 1680 as a repository for plague victims, but since 1784 they have made up Prague's main cemetery, and the 500,000 square metres are still being filled (*open Nov–Feb 9–4; Mar–April 8–6; May–Sept 8–7; Oct 8–6*). The complex comprises 13 different sections, and its tombs range from the stoic neo-classicism of Prague's golden age of tombstone design to the bourgeois wealth of marble obelisks and granite sarcophagi. Rows of white crosses mark the dead of central Europe's endless wars, and there's an entire plot filled with the odd crucifixes of the Russian Orthodox Church. The eastern wall is lined with thousands of urns, arranged in stone display cabinets and counters that look rather like a line of quaint chemist shops. The grounds become a fearsome sight between All Saints' Eve (31 October) and All Souls' Day (2 November), ablaze with candles and filled with silent mourners.

Just to the right of the main entrance on Vinohradská is the **grave of Jan Palach**, the young man who burnt himself alive following the Warsaw Pact invasion in 1968 (*see* pp. 59–60). Some 800,000 people followed his coffin here from the Old Town in January 1969, and Alexander Dubček, still clinging to power, ordered that black flags be flown from every public building in the capital. One of the most sordid acts of the profoundly shabby regime that followed was to disinter Palach in 1973 and rebury him outside Prague. He was replaced by an unknown woman, Marie Jedličková, but for 16 years determined mourners decorated her tomb with flowers and candles on the anniversary of his death. In 1990, Palach was returned to his original resting place.

Near the Olšany cemeteries, on the other side of Jana Želivského street is the **New Jewish Cemetery** (*Sun–Thurs Sept–Mar 8–4, Apr–Aug 8–5; men are* *asked to cover their heads*). It has been used by Prague's Jewish community since the end of the last century. You'll find the **grave of Franz Kafka** here, at the end of plot 21, about 300 metres along the path to your right. The writer spent the last months of his life in Berlin and then in a Viennese hospital, but as he once claimed, his home town had claws. Dr Kafka—he had studied law—is buried with his mother, and the father he reviled. All his novels remained unpublished (and incomplete) at his death, and he was mourned only by some close friends. The notice penned two days after his death by his former lover Milena Jesenská is suitably dramatic food for thought as you stand in front of the tomb:

'He wrote the most significant works of modern German literature, [which] reflect the irony and prophetic vision of a man condemned to see the world with such blinding clarity that he found it unbearable and went to his death.'

The halo of martyrdom settles rather too easily over artists who die young, but uncompromising and screwed-up Kafka, who called writing 'a form of prayer' and completed his last story on his deathbed, probably merits it as much as any cult hero of modern times.

A memorial at the grave commemorates Kafka's three sisters, all of whom died in Nazi concentration camps, and other victims of the Holocaust are recalled throughout the cemetery. As the number of professing Jews in Prague sank even further in the postwar years, the graveyard became one of the loneliest in the capital. No old ladies came to tend the tombs, few came any longer to mourn, and the stones were slowly lost under a riot of dandelions and buttercups and ivy. Restoration has begun, but it remains to be seen if Prague's Jewish community can reverse its decline and take root again. If not, the graves still being dug mark the protracted conclusion to a story that lasted a thousand years.

Church of the Sacred Heart and Žižkov Tower

This ancient crag over the Vltava has spawned a thick web of nationalistic lore and legend. Most Praguers will still be able to reel off the myths, but its romantic heyday was a century ago, when it was infested with poets and painters in search of patriotic inspiration. It's now little more than a pleasant retreat on a lazy afternoon. *The easiest way to get here is on line C of the metro to Vyšehrad station—walk away from the Hotel Forum. Alternatively, you can scale the rock from the stone steps on the embankment (Podolské nábř.), linked to the centre of town by trams 3, 17 and 21.* There's a superb view over the river, but huffers and puffers might appreciate it more on the way down.

The area was probably settled way back in the 9th century, and according to the city's oldest legend, soothsaying Princess Libuše was standing here when she came over all funny and prophesied Prague (*see* pp. 38–9). In the later 11th century, Vratislav II moved to the rock, prompted by dislike of his brother, who insisted on living in the castle; the change of royal address lasted almost a century, but the only remaining evidence is the heavily restored Romanesque **Rotunda of St Martin** (Rotunda sv. Martina). Near it are remnants of the fortification walls built by Charles IV around the New Town in the mid-14th century. The area's landmarks are the twin towers of the **Church of SS Peter and Paul** (Kostel sv. Petra a Pavla), founded in the late 11th century but entirely rebuilt in dull neo-Gothic style a hundred years ago. To the north of the church is the **Vyšehrad Cemetery** (Vyšehradský hřbitov). Established at the end of the last century to accommodate the cultural heroes of the Czech national revival, it forms an impressive gallery of modern Czech sculpture. Among the 600-odd corpses of the great and good are those of Smetana and Dvořák. At the far end is a **pantheon** (*slavín*), a mass grave of 50 artists (last count) and still the final destination of the *crème de la crème*.

On the other side of the church are the **Vyšehrad Gardens** (Vyšhradské sady), small but peppered with a selection of strapping sculptures from Czech myth. They are all 19th-century works by J. V. Myslbek (who also sculpted the St Wenceslas monument—*see* pp. 230–1). Enraptured Libuše is here next to moody Přemysl the Ploughman, and nearby you'll find another duo from the prehistoric battle of the sexes that informs early Czech folklore—*Ctirad and Šárka*. Faithless Šárka belonged to a bunch of Bohemian Amazons, and tied herself to a tree to attract Ctirad's attention. The gallant prince stopped to woo her, but came to a sticky end when he blew his horn at Šárka's request and her lady friends charged to the rescue. There's also a strange old column, which is thought to have kept track of the solstice in the days when Vyšehrad was still a glorified pagan mound.

Before leaving the area, be sure to see the **Cubist houses** designed by Josef Chochol (*see* p. 78) between 1911 and 1913. There's a little triplet on the embankment below Vyšehrad (Podolské nábř. 6–10), one on Libušina 3, and most impressively, the prismatic apartment block jutting outwards and upwards from the corner of Přemyslova and Neklanova.

Smíchov

This is one of Prague's most intriguing suburbs, minutes from the centre but a world apart from the golden city. In the 19th century it became the capital's industrial powerhouse and brewery, traditions that continue today. Factories and traffic seem to belch out more greenhouse gases than the rest of the city combined, but the uniqueness of the atmosphere now owes more to the large concentration of gipsies living here. You won't find tinkers' stalls or caravans, but on warm evenings the streets can have the liveliness of an extremely tranquil and central European New York City. Gangs loaf, music blares from apartments, and no-good kids yell obscenities or invitations (or both) from their tenement windows. If you want action, pop into one of the lively bars around here. You won't get blown away, but leave your credit cards at home.

The best streets are those around the macabre **Malá Strana Cemetery** (Malostranský hřbitov), *open from May–Sept 9–7. Trams 4, 7 and 9 will get you there*. Founded during the 1680 plague epidemic, it's been disused for over a century, and the only evidence of many of its tombs is the rise and fall of the ivy sheet that has inundated it. It has one of the most impressive concentrations of late Baroque and neo-classical sculpture in Prague, centred around the monumental cast-iron tomb of Bishop Leopold von Thun-Hohenstein; but it's the ruin and disrepair that somehow makes this one of the most extraordinary cemeteries in Europe. Decapitated angels teeter from pillars; crucifixes lie in pieces on the ground; and yawning tombs leave you in little doubt that everything here is slowly crumbling into nothingness.

Although the cemetery can envelop you, it's tucked between two (very) main roads. If you need a break from the rumble of traffic, even the tone-deaf will appreciate the tranquillity of the nearby **Mozart Museum at Bertramka** on Mozartova (*see* pp. 260–1). Finally, when you leave Smíchov you could pick up a tram from nám. Kinských. Between the flagpoles here, there used to stand a Soviet tank, T23, which enjoyed a brief moment of worldwide fame in 1991 as Prague's **Pink Tank**. T23 was (probably) the first to enter the capital during liberation in 1945—but although that intervention by the Soviets had been no bad thing, the dubious role of Red Army tanks in the city's subsequent history threw T23's future into question after 1989. For two years the city argued whether the tank was anti-fascist or pro-Communist: a debate that was more important than it might sound, and a test of the mettle of post-revolutionary Prague. T23 clung onto its podium with remarkable dignity throughout—until David Černy, well-known wit and prankster (see p. 85), wandered along, painted it pink and surmounted it with a large papier-mâché penis. The gesture had its effect: Černy was briefly arrested under a catch-all law that had been a favourite of the Communists and the tank was repainted, only to be splashed pink again by a group of parliamentarians, outraged at how government-like the government of Václav Havel had become. After a few more weeks of official embarrassment and deep protests from beetle-browed veterans at the Soviet Embassy, the tank was finally removed. It's now at the Museum of Aeronautics and Cosmonautics (see pp. 261–2). As of early 1993 it was as luminous as ever, although it had hidden under a tree next to its new friend, a dismantled rocket.

Petřín Hill

Petřín is the green and wooded hump on the left as you cross the Charles Bridge from the Old Town. The forest that once used to stretch for miles to the south has disappeared, and vineyards no longer clamber up the hill, but its patchwork of gardens still makes for a perfect retreat as temperatures rise in the hazy city below. *The best way of getting there is the funicular railway which slides up and down between about 5 am–midnight. It leaves from a station just above Újezd street, about 100 metres north of the junction with Vítězná.* Alternatively, the Strahov gardens (see p. 206) are linked by paths to Petřín; there's a gate into the Kinský gardens on nám. Kinských; and one of the loveliest walks in Prague is along the path to the north of Nebozízek restaurant, which turns from asphalt to forest as it slowly sinks into Malá Strana's sea of olive domes and orange tiles.

The first stop on the funicular is Nebozízek, marked by a terrace restaurant standing on what used to be a vintner's cottage (see p. 299). In the woods to the south is a monument to the Romantic poet Karel Mácha near which generations of wistful Praguers claim to have necked and spooned for the first time. At the summit is a rose garden and several minor spectacles. On the left is the Baroque St Lawrence's Church, and the Prague Observatory and Planetarium (*open Tues–Sun, but the hours vary wildly from month to month—call 53 55 51/3 if you're set on a visit*). Across the lawns to the right is a **model of the Eiffel Tower**, built in 1891 (two years after the original) by the Club of Czech Tourists, and used as a TV transmitting station until 1992. The globetrotting club was apparently very proud of its tower, but at 60 metres it falls laughably short of the

Gallic symbol. 1891 was the year of Prague's Jubilee Exhibition, and the kooky Czech Tourists also contributed the nearby **maze** (*bludiště*), full of wibble-wobble mirrors and a diorama depicting the Swedish attack on the Charles Bridge in 1648. Finally, look out for the remnants of the 14th-century **Hunger Wall** (Hladová zed') (*see* p. 206), the crenellations and battlements of which crawl unevenly across Petřín as far as Strahov.

Letná Park

This expanse of greenery was landscaped in the mid-19th century, and though it doesn't have the rolling splendour of Petřín, it offers another enjoyable stroll. One way of entering the park is by climbing the set of stone steps opposite the Svatopluk Čech Bridge (most Svatopluka Čecha), which fork and then rejoin at the graffiti-drenched **plinth of the former Stalin statue** (*see* p. 109). Uncle Joe was blown up in 1962, but some of his rocky remains are still in the chambers below which were also used to store potatoes for many years. With due disrespect, young Praguers used to break in regularly before 1989 to hold parties in the warren of underground passageways, a tradition of intermittent clubbing that continued until Prague's municipal council put its foot down in late 1992. Surveyors had warned that it was only a matter of time before the hillside fell on someone's head. After canvassing a number of options, the councillors decided to grow mushrooms in the space. There's a more conventional dance-floor in the nearby **Hanava Pavilion** (Hanavský pavilón) to the west, an Art Nouveau exhibition piece that was moved here in 1898. To the north is the barren expanse of **Letná Plain**—which is entirely devoid of interest, save that it used to host the speech days of the Communists (1 May), and that on 25 November 1989, it was the site of the demonstration that marked the death of the old régime, when a million people watched Václav Havel shake hands with Alexander Dubček. The nearby **National Technical Museum** on Kostelní is filled with venerable one-time miracles of modern technology and is great fun (*see* p. 264).

Holešovice and Troja

These two areas of northern Prague contain the city's largest and wildest park, its most quirky one, and the Baroque chateau at Troja, next to the tragic city zoo. The two districts are separated by the Vltava, an island and a railway line, but it's possible to make your way on foot from one to the other along a route that runs from Stromovka Park to Troja. *To get to the area, go to Holešovice nádraží, on line C of the metro. Výstaviště and Stromovka are a short walk from the station (or a stop away on trams 5, 12, and 17); and bus 112 will take you to Troja.*

Výstaviště, or Exhibition Park, was the site of the Jubilee Exhibition of the Kingdom of Bohemia in 1891, and its original iron and glass structures have all the cranky charm of seaside piers and crystal palaces. Some claim to detect the beginnings of Prague's Art Nouveau in the buildings, but only the thirst for novelty links these crazy hybrids to the style then being developed in England and Belgium. A suitable addition to the eclectic atmosphere of the park was made in the centenary year of 1991, when a new generation of postmodernist follies was constructed, including a circular theatre, a big blue pyramid, and a canopy of metal rods and girders. Pride of place goes to the **Křižík Fountain**, set within an amphitheatre of white steel, which looks rather like the passenger deck of an ocean liner. Its 50 pumps and 3000 jets rhythmically squirt to the accompaniment of classical music and an underwater light show on summer evenings. The park is filled with other attractions, including a funfair, adventure playground and a three-dimensional circular diorama of the Battle of Lipany, a 1000-square metre painting complete with weapon-strewn foreground and the clatter, clamour and clip-clopping of a very unconvincing soundtrack. Finally it contains the **Sculpture Collection of the National Museum** (in the building on your right as you enter the main gates), which includes many of the original statues, now replaced by copies, that used to stand on the Charles Bridge.

You couldn't get much further from the spirit of the Výstaviště than in the wooded wilderness of neighbouring **Stromovka**, founded back in the 14th century as a royal enclosure by King John of Luxemburg. Nevertheless, its lake is the product of an earlier age's fascination with mechanics. Rudolf II had it created in 1593, and it's fed by an underwater canal running from the Vltava river nearly one km to the south. The entrance to the tunnel is near the lake, but Rudolf II's chateau has disappeared, as have the 4000 creatures with which he stocked the park. It's still Prague's finest spot for an urban ramble.

Troja is north of the Vltava, and opposite the splendidly-decorated Baroque chateau on U trojského zámku (*see* pp. 259–60), you'll find **Prague zoo** (*Oct–Mar 9–4, April 9–5, May 9–6, June–Sept 9–7; adm*). The attractions here are extremely limited. Some of the 2000 beasts are apparently extinct in the wild, but judging from these often insane specimens, it might have been preferable to let them all die out in peace. The zoo's best features have nothing to do with its *raison d'être*: the first is a wonderful hilltop location (it was once a vineyard); and the other a stupendous chairlift which scoops you up and carries you hundreds of metres over an aviary far below. The seat harness is optional and useless—perfect for children, horrifying for anyone beyond the age of reason.

Food and Drink

Eating out in Prague is no longer the mediocre chore that it used to be. With new restaurants opening all the time, ingredients improving, and the arrival of immigrant *restaurateurs* from as far afield as Iceland and India, a Prague meal can sometimes even be exciting—the first time that can honestly be said in decades. Even so, many restaurants still offer little more than a list of steaks, but this section should ensure that your culinary experience of Prague doesn't leave a bitter taste in your mouth.

Food

The specialities of the Czech kitchen represent the culmination of centuries of serfdom and peasant experimentation. Favoured vegetables are the turnip, cabbage and potato, and although meat of every description finds its way onto the table, offal is treated with unusual respect. There's a robust suspicion of most herbs other than marjoram and all spices save garlic, and matters are only mitigated by the influence of the hot-blooded Slovaks and their Hungarian neighbours.

The most distinctive delicacy of the Czech kitchen is the *knedlík*, or dumpling. Praguers treat it as the highest expression of the country's cuisine—and if you say that you recently ate an unexciting one, you're almost certain to be told that *you have to know where to go*. Unfortunately, only the most discriminating foreign palate can truly tell the difference in most cases. The main distinction is between the floury *mouka knedlík* and the *bramborova knedlík*, made of mushy potato. Both are usually served with a lump of flesh in a thick gravy, and are staple fare in beer halls. *Špekové knedlíky* are marginally more interesting, mixed with bacon; while *kynuté knedlíky* are downright wild in comparison, centred around lumps of stewed fruit.

You're on tastier ground when it comes to cold meats. Prague ham (*šunka*) is of high quality, but it's generally agreed that the best salamis are the harder Hungarian-tinged varieties, particularly the flat *lovecký salám*, and both *Oherský salám* and *salám alékum*. Sausages are much loved, and you can pick up a *párek* (two long porkers) in stands across the city. The frankfurter-like *Liberecký parky* and the paprika-flavoured *čabajka* are the best varieties; and if you avoid pork, you can safely eat *hovězi parky* and *drubeží parky*, made of beef and chicken respectively.

Decades of acid rain and toxic leaks have left their very dirty mark in the food chain, and you might want to consider the alternatives to red meat. Czech chickens aren't factory-farmed, and with an average lifespan of 42 days, few of them have as much time as they might want to absorb background carcinogens and contaminants. Freshwater fish are another healthy possibility: carp and trout are bred in the lakes of southern Bohemia and, along with the pike and eel that are occasionally found with them, they are widely available in Prague.

Soups (*polévky*) are often delicious, and in cheaper beer halls and cafés they are often the most likely winners on the menu—but among the standard meats and vegetables, there are a few Czech peculiarities of which you should be aware. Broths are often served with a raw egg yolk bobbing along the bottom of the bowl, and the done thing is to puncture it and swish it about before eating. *Dršťková* is one of the most popular soups and comprises floating pieces of a cow's stomach, while *zabijačková polévka* is a pungent concoction made largely of pigs' blood. The name, roughly translated, means 'slaughter soup', although it's also known by the mildly obscene term *perdelačka*.

There are a few other snacks that you'll probably encounter. *Vafle* (waffles) are everywhere, and to find one of the squashy pieces of sponge and cream, you generally need do no more than follow your nose. There are also stalls across the city selling *bramborák*, a garlicky potato pancake that is delicious if not greasy. *Ďábelský toust* is a fiercely tasty mixture of meat (usually beef) on toast. *Smážený sýr* is fried cheese, which is more appetizing but no less unhealthy than it sounds. The most common cheeses are tasteless copies of Edam (*eidam*) or Brie (*Hermelín*), but native creations are usually of the most malodorous kind. If you can stand the whiff, they go well with the rich wine. One of the most fetid is *olomoucké sýrečky*; and if you're drinking beer, ask the bartender for some *pivní*. It isn't designed to be eaten by itself—pour some of your drink onto the plate, add chopped onions while kneading gently, and offer the rank concoction around. In the summer, you'll also see hawkers selling bags of Slovakian sheep cheese (*gorbáč*), which looks like stringy pieces of fresh pasta. Prague's sweetmeats are fairly unremarkable, although Viennese-style cream cakes are making a comeback to meet the expectations of tourists. Sweet teeth may enjoy *koláče*, tasty tidbits topped with curd, and *palačinky*, pancakes that can be atrocious or scrumptious depending on the tosser.

Drinks

Czech food may often be nothing to write home about, but the **beer** is world famous. Plzeň is the home of Pilsner Urquell, the first lager and the father of a thousand German imitators, while the brewing town of Budweis (České Budějovice) has become part of the American dream. In fact, the American company Busch actually borrowed little more than the name, and the potent concoction produced in the Czech Republic puts the US slop to shame. (Perhaps realizing that, Busch prevented Czech Budweis beer from being sold legally in the west for decades, and has now begun to move in on the Czech operation.) Both beers are chock-full of alcohol and sugar, all created naturally during the brewing process unlike that in their additive-laden western rivals. You may already like sweet beers, and if not you should acquire the taste—look out for beer halls and bottles marked *Plzeňské prazdroj* and *Budvar*. Prague produces several beers of its own (such as *Staropramen*, *Braník* and *Smíchov*), which are slightly more bitter. They taste fine to most people, but some of the capital's own beer bores disavow them, and you may hear it claimed that the Vltava is pumped directly through the brewery. Most beer is 12° proof (i.e. about three per cent alcohol), but 10° beer is also sold. A dark alcoholic treacle is served at the beer halls U Fleků (14°) and U sv. Tomáše. When you have your first draught in a *pivnice*, Praguers claim that you should stick a matchstick into the head to test the quality. The only danger is that if it doesn't stay erect for at least ten seconds, you may be accosted by a staggering drunk who'll suggest that you all go elsewhere.

Wine connoisseurship is a game that is played by waiters in the swankier restaurants in Prague, but it is even less merited than usual in the case of Czech wine. Moravia has the best grapes, but you'd have to have your tongue embedded in your cheek before you could describe any of the wines as cheeky, playful or vintage. Most of the whites tend to be as sweet and thick as a bottle of red plonk. The driest is probably *Rulandské*, but in most cases, robust reds slip easier down the throat, and *Frankovka* and *Vavřinec* are two of the better labels. Bohemia's only worthwhile wines come from the Mělník vineyards, and have a rather pleasant woody fragrance–try *sv. Ludmila*. A glass of Czech wine is twice the size of a regular measure in the UK and US, and if you're a moderate sort you should ask for a *deci*. The quality of the wine makes it particularly suitable for mulling, and during the winter most cafés have a permanently bubbling pot of wine, cloves and cinnamon—ask for *svařené víno*. One other speciality is *burčák*, which is sold and drunk across the capital from late September onwards. It is the first wine of the year, Prague's semi-fermented Beaujolais Nouveau—and it's an impudent little rascal which masquerades as a soft drink until it knocks you senseless. Bohemia also produces sparkling wine *(sekt)*, which is good for popping and conspicuously wasting, but it seems to make many people feel very queasy if they drink much of it. Russian *sekt* is marginally less sickly, and widely available.

The Czech Republic produces no vodka worth the name. However, Russian *Stolichnaya* and *Moskovskaya* can be found everywhere for a fraction of the price in the UK or US, and they're both rather excellent when cooled to semi-viscosity. Czech rums and whiskies are little better than hogwash, but on your alcoholic reveries through the city, you should look out for three **native liquors**. The first is *Becherovka*, the 20-herb recipe of which is one of the world's many distilling secrets supposedly known only to two men. The mystique surrounding the ingredients, along with the manufacturers' only-too-garrulous bumph about every other stage of the drink's creation, sells about 10 million of the flat green bottles worldwide, and you'll find it sold in every single bar and pub in Prague. It comes from the spa town of Karlovy Vary and is said to calm an upset stomach, as Prague's dipsos are fond of telling foreigners as they drink their way into double figures. Two other spirits, eclipsed by the fame of their cousin but nevertheless popular are Slovakian *Slivovice* (plum brandy) and *Borovicka*, a native form of mother's ruin made from juniper berries. Finally, couples dining in the more expensive restaurants may want to relish a cognac, which is usually provided in huge glasses, sometimes bigger than your face. Men usually get balloon-shaped ones, and women are given tall and curvaceous vessels. The waiters love the ceremony, and may come to your table with a selection of glasses before warming your choices over a portable stove.

Eating Out

There are several types of eating and drinking establishment in Prague: beer joints (*a pivnice*, *hostinec* or *hospoda*), wine bars (*vinárny*), cafés (*kavárny*), and restaurants (*restaurace*). In the days of central planning, each had its prerogatives and permitted menus, but nowadays the only significant difference is between those places devoted to beer, and everywhere else. The former tend to be cheap, smoky, male and unfriendly to outsiders, with the menu restricted to the more humble Czech dishes. The general rule is riddled with exceptions and you should try making a meal out of a pub crawl at least once, but in most cases the city's best food is to be had in the city's wine bars and restaurants.

The dining culture in Prague is still extremely underdeveloped. The growth of a postwar dinner-party circuit was stymied by rabbit-hutch flats, mediocre ingredients and a lack of foreign cookbooks; while only the dedicated few made a habit of eating out. A sociologist might explain the stay-at-home culture in terms of the social atomization engendered by 40 years of repression; another reason was atrocious service and identical menus. Although the culinary outlook is now improving hugely, price increases are often equally dramatic. As a result, it's still the case that in many of the city's best eateries, the only Czech diners that you will hear will be those speaking English, loudly, to their nodding and serious business partners. Lack of tradition and experience also means that the typical ambience of a Prague restaurant is rather different from that in its western equivalent. Floodlights and dazzling chandeliers are still common, and waiters often insist on tuning in to their favourite FM station: candlelit dinners are punctuated by advertising jingles and news bulletins, while power lunches might be conducted to a soundtrack of thrash metal and Europop.

Reservations

In Prague more than many other cities, the more attractive a restaurant sounds, the more advisable it is to make an advance reservation. The large number of high-rolling foreign residents, many of whom have discovered the joys of restaurant-hopping for the first time in Prague, has added to the demand that has always been placed on the city's best eateries. During the summer call at least three days in advance to be absolutely sure of getting a table.

Dress and Etiquette

In the smartest restaurants, men are expected to wrap a tie around their throats, and women should make the appropriate equivalent gestures. Most places also insist that jackets be either worn or handed in at the cloakroom, and some of the surlier waiters and waitresses studiously ignore you if you have anything draped over the back of your chair. Prague eats early—often before 8 pm—but there are no major dining quirks. Traditionally, Czechs say nothing while eating a meal, but although you should still think twice about accepting an invitation to a village dinner party, the custom has thankfully died out in the capital.

Service

Recent years have seen a general improvement in waiters' table manners, often the result of crash courses in charm instituted by desperate new owners, but it's still too often the case that only the *concept* of politeness has been grasped by Prague's restaurant staff. The theory that the customer is always right runs directly contrary to the convictions of most Czech waiters, and although they usually maintain the pretence, in moments of candour or crisis their superiority complexes will win through.

As a result, handling Prague's waiters demands self-discipline and confidence. The most important skill is a willingness to give as good as you get. Don't wait to be seated unless there's a physical obstruction in the way, and never be afraid to accost a member of staff who has walked past you twice. If your course doesn't arrive for some time, always assume that you have been forgotten. Paying your bill can be an art in itself. The first stage is to say *za platím* (may I pay?) to someone. He or she will probably nod, mumble *koleg* (colleague), and walk away, never to return. What that means is that the man with the purse has to be tackled. He'll often be hiding in the kitchens or sharing a joke with friends, and although he can get fairly upset if interrupted, the best thing to do is to present him with your bill and cash. Alternatively, you could make as if to do a leisurely runner, which may or may not draw some attention in your direction. A final possibility is to leave your money on the table, and walk out—which usually causes consternation, and may lead the man with the purse to deliver a mini-lecture on the fact that they do things differently in Prague.

Tricks

Even assuming that you eventually find someone who is prepared to give you a bill, you aren't clear yet. A secret government survey in 1985 found that deliberate overcharging accounted for 3 per cent of total restaurant turnover, and some waiters still regard theft as a perk of the job. Check your bill carefully and question any strange notches and ambiguous squiggles that you find. At worst, the man with the purse will treat you like a moron as he deciphers his hieroglyphs, and at best, he will shrug, smile and reduce your bill by half.

Another scam that has become institutionalized in many older restaurants is the canapé con. It involves presenting a tray of unidentified snacky objects to your table shortly after your arrival, and inviting you to make a selection. If you're peckish, the natural impulse is to scoop up a plateful… which is just what they want you to do. When the bill arrives, you'll find a big number that you didn't expect; and when you question it, the happy waiter will inform you that the lumpfish roe sandwich that you chomped while finishing your cigarette was actually Malossol caviare on toast.

Tipping

A tip of 10 per cent is usual in the most expensive restaurants; in others, anything over a couple of crowns is OK and 5 per cent will startle your waiter or waitress. In most places, your bill is totted up in front of you, and you're expected to say a figure that you want to pay in total, rather than the amount of change you want returned. How much you actually leave depends on your theory of the tip, but given the variable standard of service in Prague, you'll be doing your bit for future generations of visitors by strictly linking the amount to your level of satisfaction.

Breakfast

Although the best you'll get in most places is an omelette and coffee, and occasionally *hemenex* ('ham and eggs'), breakfast is becoming more common in Prague. **Velryba** on Opatovická 24 has a range of suitably light snacks on its menu, and another calm spot to start the day is in the Art Nouveau **Evropa Café** at Václavské nám. 25. The meal there is deeply uninspired, involving watery coffee and piles of bread, cheese and ham, but it's been a Prague institution since the days when you would eat it while perusing one of the café's several copies of the *Morning Star*. Weekend brunch is slowly becoming established in the city. On Sunday afternoons at **Jo's Bar** (Malostranské nám. 7) you will find hordes of the city's English-speaking ex-pats ruminating, regretting or piecing together the events of the night before. Strangers are welcome, and as well as making friends you can munch through a tasty Mexican mish mash of tortilla pies, salsa and fried eggs, fruit juices and generous coffee refills (*Sunday 12–3*). Less jolly, more refined and far more expensive is the stylish brunch at **Parnas** at Smetanovo nábř. 2. As well as cereals, freshly-squeezed orange juice, yoghurt and innumerable fruits and meats, a trio of jazz swingers and an expansive view over the river smoothly set you up for a splendid day.

Vegetarians

Vegetarians have a rough time in Prague, where central Europe's meat fetish still exerts a tremendous power. You'll be confronted with slabs of flesh and bloody carcasses everywhere you go, and even when you order an apparently meatless meal you run the constant risk of being slipped a sausage. However, restaurants are slowly adapting to the new-fangled fads of western stomachs, and a number of exclusively vegetarian cafés now exist, notably **U Govindy**, **Country Life** and the **FX Café**. To ask whether there are vegetarian dishes, say *máte bezmasé jídlo?* Vegans will have as grim a life in Prague as they have everywhere else. Country Life and the **Vacek Bio-Market** on Mostecká 3 carry a large selection of lentils, beans and seeds, and bread is of course widely available.

Restaurants

Apart from a handful of overrated restaurants, which have been listed simply to warn you to avoid them, the following places offer some of the tastiest, best value and most interesting meals currently available in the capital. The selections are divided into three categories: expensive, moderate and inexpensive. Estimates can only be very rough, but you should expect to pay the following for a **three-course dinner for two, including a bottle of Czech wine**:

> Expensive—£30–60 ($45–90)
>
> Moderate—£15–30 ($23–45)
>
> Inexpensive—up to £15 ($23)

Several of the places below don't serve full three-course meals, but they have been put into whichever category they would be in if they did. Most foreign visitors will still find eating out to be extremely good value in all but the most exclusive restaurants, but remember that many Czechs would regard even the top end of the 'cheap' category as a luxury. If you've asked a friend to join you, you can avoid a lot of embarrassment by asking him or her to choose a place, or insisting that you pay. You'll find menu terms and other useful vocabulary at the back of this book. *Dobrou chut'!*

Credit Cards

AE=American Express

DC=Diners Club

MC=Mastercard/Eurocard/Access

V=Visa.

Nové Město

expensive

U šuterů, Palackého 4, ☎ 26 10 17. *Mon–Sat 11.30–3, 6.30–11.* A glorified steakhouse run by Belgians, the distinguishing feature of which is that patrons cook their own food on lumps of superheated lava on each table. The management claims, with a straight face, to have thus introduced Prague to the latest concept in dining; the next concept will presumably be to leave a cow, an axe and a bill in the restaurant and go home. That said, the informality and conversational possibilities inherent in handling and frying a piece of meat make this a perfect spot to bring a nervous first date or truculent business contact. AE, MC, V.

moderate

Adria, Národní 40, ☎ 26 17 47. *11.30–11.30.* A large menu, undistinguished save for its *gazpacho* which is never, by all accounts, disappointing. But the real reason to eat here is to sit under the sculptures and Rondocubist battlements of the Adria palace and watch Prague scurrying around beneath you. AE, MC, V.

Crazy Daisy, Vodičkova 9, ☎ 235 00 21. *11 am–11.30 pm.* Ordinary but filling steaks and vegetarian dishes among old tin signs, red telephone boxes and other standard curiosities. A swing pianist is here most evenings, failing which the greatest hits of Elvis the King are usually played. No cards.

Klášterní vinárna, Národní 8, ℂ 29 05 96. *11.30–3.30, 5.30–12 midnight.* Rather gloomy restaurant in a former monastery, useful if you're going on to the Magic Lantern or National Theatre next door. AE.

Mayur, Štěpánská 61, ℂ 236 99 22. *12–11.* A slightly Indian restaurant. The food is prepared and served (very politely) by Czechs, but the seekh kebabs and tandoori chicken are just about tasty enough to bring back happy memories of the local takeaway. Vegetarian choice is limited, and Czech handiwork is unmistakeable in the watery dals. There is also an **Indian snack bar** next door, with a truncated and mildly cheaper version of the same menu and daringly nonchalant service. DC, V.

Na rybárně, Gorazdova 17, ℂ 29 97 95. *12 noon–12 midnight. (kitchen open until 10.30 pm).* A fish restaurant serving everything from whale to eel, under nets, lanterns and a quease-inducing briny scene. Václav Havel lives near by and occasionally brings his friends. They have taken to scrawling their names on the walls as the hilarity increases; in the back room are shaky mementoes of the Havels, Mick Jagger, Keith Richards, Paul Simon and numerous no-hopers. Try your luck with a lipstick. Make a reservation on the same morning as you plan to eat. AE, V.

Palace Hotel, Panská 12. *10–10.* A salad bar made out of wood, plastic and mirrors that's useful for vegetarians and anyone in a hurry. It introduced the 'as-much-as-you-can-eat' principle to Prague but cheats by providing saucers, so you should cheat back by piling the red and greenery high. It also has school-dinner-type hot dishes. The bar once plugged a crucial gap in Prague's cuisine, but now that other establishments have taken up the veggie gospel and property prices are skyrocketing, it may be turned into an up-market grocery store. No cards.

Pezinok, Purkyňova 4, ℂ 29 19 16. *11–11.* One of the best places for Slovakian food in Prague. Stuff yourself on sheep's cheese, shashliks, and tasty charcoal-grilled steaks called things like Tinker's Pocket and Robber's Delicacy. AE.

Šumická vinárna, Mikulandská 12, ℂ 29 15 68. *12 noon–3, 6–12 midnight.* A popular underground restaurant, with Czech food and red-jacketed gipsies wandering among the tables from 7 pm. No cards.

U bilého slona (The White Elephant), Soukenická 4, ℂ 231 19 93. *11–11.* Prague's first Thai restaurant, with an imported chef and a range of basil-, ginger- and chilli-flavoured dishes. They are an unadventurous selection so far, and the management is hedging its bets against Prague culinary conservatism by also providing a Czech menu. Nevertheless tasty, and improving. Try the lemongrass shrimp soup. MC, V.

U kalicha (The Chalice), Na Bojišti 12, ℂ 29 07 01. *11–3, 5–10.* Only mentioned because you might hear of this beer hall and think that it sounds interesting. It was mentioned in *The Good Soldier Švejk*, and it's milked the fact dry. No cards.

inexpensive

Country Life, Jungmannova 1, ℂ 22 53 78. *Mon–Thurs 8.30–6.30, Fri 8.30–3.* A vegetarian shop and small café. It's run by Seventh Day Adventists, but the only evidence is its odd hours, a few pieces of good news scattered among the cookbooks, and abnormally friendly service. Delicious and fresh sandwiches, pizza-ettes, soups, salads and juices. No cards.

Grill Restaurant Pepino, Jugoslávská 11, ℂ 236 73 38. *9 am–10 pm.* Prefabricated, with motorway-service-station decor, but the food is excellent value. Delicious soups, fresh and perfectly cooked chicken, beef and pork steaks, and amiable speedy service. The small, wet and vinegary salads are the only disappointment here. No cards.

Kavárna Velryba (Whale Café), Opatovická 24, ℂ 20 39 91, 20 41 07. *11 am–2 am (kitchen until 11 pm).* Extremely popular among literary types and time-wasters. You have to eat twice to fill up here, but there are several tasty snacks, including scrambled eggs with mushrooms and a cheesy Pasta chez Velryba. Food served until 11 pm. No cards.

U Fleků, Křemencova 11, ℂ 29 32 45/6. *8.30 am–11 pm.* Prague's best known beer hall, which has brewed the same 14° beer on the premises since 1459. 500 seats—most of which are occupied by Germans—and simple Czech food. The shady garden is a pleasant spot for raucous summer drinking, but commercial pressures, *i.e.* the desire for easy money, mean that a fee is now charged to sit there. No cards.

Staré Město

Eating Out

expensive

Canadian Lobster, Husova 15, ℂ 225 72 40. *12–3, 6–11.* Delicious imported food, including shrimps, snails, Parma ham and melon, and grilled salmon with wild rice. AE, V.

Opera, Karolíny Světlé 35, ℂ 26 55 08. *7 pm–2 am.* Intimate, exclusive, and exorbitant. Those who have eaten here claim that the pianist is excellent and the food sublime, but that the minuscule portions are liable to evaporate unless eaten quickly. No cards.

Parnas, Smetanovo nábř. 2, © 26 12 50, 26 57 60. *12–2.30, 6–10.45.* Grab a
window seat with a riverside view of the castle and settle down to a
superb meal. The fish-and-fruit appetizers (which include salmon and
papaya and shrimp and kiwi) will appeal to radical palates, and less daring
diners will find plenty of entrées to their taste. Try the excellent spinach
tagliatelle with cream and mushrooms. AE, DC, MC, V

U červeného kola (The Red Wheel), Anězská 2, © 231 89 41. *11–3, 5–11.* An
intimate spot for supper, tucked away in a sublime corner of the Old
Town near St Agnes's Convent. Smoked tongue and smoked eel are
among the tasty starters; the 20 or so steaks on offer are consistently
excellent; and service is faultless. The wine list is fun: few other places in
the world would dare to use words like 'reminiscences', 'bouquets' and
'linden blossom fragrances' to describe Moravian wine. AE, DC, MC, V.

U Sixtů, Celetná 2, © 236 79 80. *12 noon–1 am.* Superb Czech and French
cuisine in a centuries-old cellar on the edge of the Old Town Square.
The red meat and poultry dishes are rich and well flavoured, and the
restaurant's Icelandic fish menu is a lodestar in Prague's culinary firmament. AE.

V zátiší (In Seclusion), Liliová 1, © 26 51 07. *12–3, 6–11.* Some of the most
satisfying food in Prague in simple and elegant surroundings. Dishes are
fresh, light and international in inspiration, ranging from poached salmon
in dill sauce to steamed chicken on fresh spring vegetables. There are
several (home-made) pasta dishes, and a number of vegetarian choices. AE.

moderate

Košer Restaurant Shalom, Maislova 18, © 231 89 96. *Sun–Thurs 11.30–2,
6–9, Fri 11.30–2 pm.* Prague's last Jewish restaurant in the former town
hall of the ghetto. The strange atmosphere veers from clattering liveliness
when the locals are around, to all-foreign evenings with piano music.
Since 1989, it has realized its tourist-trap potential, and non-Czechs are
now surcharged just under 100 per cent; the restaurant only just creeps
into this price category and will probably hop out of it before long. The
food is certified kosher and imported from Vienna, but unless you're an
Orthodox Jew it doesn't justify more than a lunchtime stop. No cards.

Obecní dům (Municipal House), nám. Republiky. *11–11.* Steak and chips-type
meals, all served with a snarl. But things are changing, and one day a meal
here might be as pleasurable as the Art Nouveau interior already is. AE, V.

Red Hot and Blues, Jakubská 12, © 231 46 39. *11–11.* Attractive US-run
Cajun food restaurant in the rooms and courtyard of the ancient royal

stables, decorated with art that includes canvasses by the Australian naïve painter, Georgia Schaller. The still-evolving menu offers a delicious assortment of dishes, from a good-value chicken fillet in cream sauce, to salmon steak in mustard sauce and a piquant Shrimp Creole. The restaurant also offers a notable range of rich desserts, beignet brunches, mint juleps, zombies and hurricanes, and all to a soundtrack of jazz and blues. Take it easy. AE, V.

Reykjavík, Karlova 20, ℂ 26 57 76. *11–11*. The steakhouse decor of this place conceals one of Prague's finest fish restaurants, serving a daily range of scaly creatures freshly flown in from Iceland. The fish soup has become a legend in its own lunchtime, and it's impossible to go wrong when presented with a choice that includes poached salmon, plaice in camembert and cream, and—for the English—cod and chips. AE, MC, V.

U golema (The Golem), Maislova 8, ℂ 232 81 65. *Mon–Fri 11–10, Sat 5–11*. Standard meaty dishes in a dim restaurant within the confines of the old Jewish ghetto. AE, DC, MC, V.

U pavouka (The Spider), Celetná 17, ℂ 231 87 14. *12–3, 5.30–12 midnight*. This place has an inexplicably strong reputation among normally-cynical Praguers, who excuse its high prices as exclusivity, and its use of canned vegetables and overcooked meat as tradition. Positive features are the friendly service and the subterranean location. A resident pianist provides mood music every evening; the management should help him out by investing in a dimmer switch. AE, DC, MC, V.

U Rudolfa, Maislova 5, ℂ 232 26 71. *10–10*. A tiny modern restaurant filled with sizzling smells from the stove behind the bar, in the heart of the old Jewish ghetto. The menu of hams, cheeses and steaks is even more minuscule, but no one ever complains about a meal here. Reserve a day in advance. AE, DC, MC, V.

U 7 andělů (The Seven Angels), Jilská 20, ℂ 26 63 55. *12–3, 6–11*. A cosy Czech restaurant in a winding thoroughfare of the Old Town, serving duck, pork, goulash and dumplings to the accompaniment of jolly accordion music. AE, MC, V.

U supa (The Vulture), Celetná 22, ℂ 22 30 42. *11–11*. A spacious beer hall, serving as its speciality a rich dark brew called Purkmistr 12°, with a broad range of steak, duck and tasty game dishes. The most impressive item on the menu is the roast suckling pig, basted in beer and lard, which the proud chef will wheel out and slice in front of the drooling diners concerned. For a third of the price, he'll do the same with a goose. Perhaps sensing what might happen, children seem to love this place. MC, V.

U sv. Huberta (St. Hubert's), Husova 7, ℂ 235 36 11. *11.30–4, 5.30–11.* Tasty game dishes in a Gothic cellar. The entrance is just off the street, through a corridor lined with skulls and antlers. Not suitable for vegetarians. AE, MC, V.

U zelené žáby (The Green Frog), U radnice 8, ℂ 26 28 15. *12 noon–12 midnight.* A gloomy vault hung with blades and dripping with history, thanks to the fact that Prague's executioner ate here in the 17th century (*see* p. 160). Book yourself into his alcove. The snack-like menu is no great shakes, but the red version of the unusual Bohemian house wine (Velké žernosky) is a suitably juicy accompaniment to the bloodthirsty atmosphere. AE.

U zlaté konvice (The Golden Tankard), Melantrichova 20, ℂ 26 21 28. *6.30 pm–12.30 am.* A unique location in Prague, stretching through 600-year-old chambers and cellars and running a fair way under the Old Town Square. Food limited to sausages, hams and cheeses, but this is more a place to drink and dance among the tables, to the gipsy band who play here from 8 pm. AE, DC, MC, V.

U zlaté studny (The Golden Well), Karlova 3, ℂ 22 05 93. *11 am–12 midnight.* Long-established and popular among Praguers. The menu has some hit-and-miss poultry and game dishes, but otherwise the most exciting features of this place are its location in a 13th-century cellar and the bilberry pancakes. AE, V.

U zlatého hada (The Golden Serpent), Karlova 18, ℂ 235 87 78. *11–11.* Owned by the neighbouring Reykjavík (see above), and a place to try much of the same food in more attractive surroundings. Piano music in the evening. AE, MC, V.

U zlatého jelena (The Golden Stag), Celetná 11, ℂ 26 85 95. *11 am–1 am.* Set in the oldest Gothic banqueting hall in Prague, this is an enjoyable spot for an evening meal, serving steaks and venison to the nightly accompaniment of polkas and other peasant tunes. The waiters are particularly proud of their Moravian wines, and will think long and hard on the best one for your dish. You can find several of them in the meanest Prague supermarket, but let the boys earn their keep. AE, V.

V Dlouhé, Dlouhá 35, ℂ 231 61 25. *Mon–Fri 11–11, Sat–Sun 11–10 (kichen closes an hour earlier).* Tasty Czech cooking in a large and bright dining hall. Dishes range from rabbit to Rabbi's Purse. Try the chicken liver in wine and olives or chicken breast in honey and pineapple. The fish soup is cheap and excellent. No cards.

Blatnička, Michalská 6. *Mon–Sat 12 noon–12 midnight.* A standard steak menu with a comprehensive list of Moravian wines. After downing your flagon and finishing your meal, resume drinking with the scores of young œnophiles who lounge around Michalská street during the summer. No cards.

Café Bar Fano, Haštalska 10. *Mon–Sat 11.30–9.30.* Only a very small range of food dishes, but this is a hidden and cosy spot for a drink. The café doubles as a gallery for local talent, and paintings ranging from the mediocre to the atrocious cover most of the walls. No cards.

Decorative Arts Museum Café, 17. listopadu 2. *Mon–Fri 10.30–10.* Long and lively café, popular among students from the nearby Philosophy and Arts faculties of the Charles University. One of Prague's most exceptional museums is upstairs. Although sandwiches are available, this is more a place to drink and expound your philosophy. No cards.

Konvikt Klub, Konviktská 22, ✆ 26 56 63. *Mon–Fri 10 am–1 am, Sat 2 pm–1 am, Sun–2 pm–11 pm.* This spot combines the best of a beer hall with a friendly trendy crowd. No cards.

Mikulka's Ristorante San Pietro, Benediktská 16, ✆ 231 57 27. 1 *1.30–10.* Large plate-loads of pizza and pasta in a restaurant that's a foreigners' favourite. The spaghetti dishes are erratic—sometimes cold, sometimes from the bottom of the pot, sometimes old—but if you come on a good day, they're delicious. Of the pizzas, try the Fruti di Mare, crawling with crustaceans and squiddish objects, or choose from a range that includes anchovy, wild mushroom, and even apple and cinnamon. AE, V.

New York Pizza, Na Perštýně 4, ✆ 26 81 34. *Mon–Thurs 8 am–12 midnight, Fri 8 am–1 am, Sat 11 am–1 am, Sun 12 noon–12 midnight.* Another collection of pizzas, thinner, crispier and spicier than at Mikulka's. Choose from pepperoni, mushrooms, olives, spiced ham, egg, smoked cheese and plenty more. Also has heros, and a full and tasty breakfast. Pizza deliveries on the above number. No cards.

U dvou koček (The Two Cats), Uhelný trh 10. *11–11.* A beer restaurant located at the heart of Prague's extremely tame red-light district. Still patronized by a few shady ladies and dodgy men, but like most of central Prague's beer joints, it has become too expensive for most locals. Pilsner, and the standard meat and steak dishes. No cards.

U krkavců (The Raven), Dlouhá 25, ✆ 231 04 56. *Mon–Sat 4–midnight.* Cosy Gothic wine bar hidden under a courtyard some distance from the street.

Predominantly a place to come and court over a bottle of *Frankovka*, although the small range of aromatic pasta dishes is delicious. The polite staff are also more than happy to toss together a tasty vegetarian dish. No cards.

U medvídků (The Little Bear), Na Perštýně 10, ✆ 235 89 04. *9 am–11 pm.* Uncomfortably bright and incomprehensibly popular beer restaurant, serving Budvar beer and a set of uninteresting Czech dishes. No cards.

U.S. Burger, Masná 12. *10–10.* Popular haunt among no-good schoolkids playing hooky or taking very extended lunch breaks. The name conceals what is a strangely Czech café, and burgers form only a small part of a menu that includes fish fillets, chicken livers and a tasty salad bar. Very close to the Old Town Square. No cards.

Viola Trattoria, Národní 7, ✆ 26 67 32. *12 noon–12 midnight.* Italian food under empty gourds and on red, white and green tablecloths. The dishes often betray traces of Czech paternity, such as the veal, steak and livers in wine and olives, but the menu is a large and tasty one. This is also one of the few spots in town where you can buy Lambrusco and Chianti, if you want to. AE, DC, V.

Malá Strana · Eating Out

expensive

David, Tržiště 21, ✆ 53 93 25. *12–3, 6–11.* Terribly exclusive restaurant set in a former living room, favoured by diplomatic types and all those with expense accounts to inflate. If that sounds like you, you're in for a delicious meal, from the gratinated asparagus to the fresh fruit salad. AE, V.

Lobkovická vinárna, Vlašská 17, ✆ 53 01 85. *12–3, 6.30–12 midnight.* Set up by the Lobkowiczes in the 18th century to sell their Mělník wines and recently returned to the 30-something aristocrat at the end of the line. Intimate atmosphere and excellent menu, loosely French-inspired, which includes snails in garlic butter, homemade ravioli and an excellent set of seafood and poultry main courses. When drinking, the done thing is to splash out on the sparkling Chateau Mělník, although you should grab the chance to sample the hard to obtain *sv. Ludmila.* When it's all over, you'll be proferred a cigar box and invited to puff on a Havana six-incher. AE, MC, V.

U malířů (The Painter's), Maltézské nám. 11, ✆ 53 18 83. *7 pm–2 am.* Not a place to go Dutch with a Praguer. Since being taken over by a group of very serious French *cuisiniers* in 1990, the ingredients here have been imported by lorry from Paris each week, and the resulting prices are the highest in Prague. One set menu costs about £65 ($97), or just over two weeks' wages for the average Czech, and drinks could bump that up to the full month. But if you can afford it and enjoy French food at its most sumptuous, you won't be disappointed: recent offerings on the ever-changing menu have included truffle and foie gras soup, baby pigeon, and venison and hazelnuts in pepper sauce. The pretty interior is another reason to dine here: the wall paintings aren't too old, but this has been a restaurant ever since the original 'painter' moved here in 1541. AE, DC, MC, V.

moderate

Nebozízek, Petřínské sady, ℂ 53 79 05. *11–6, 7–11.* A meal here is pure romance from the moment you step into the funicular railway up Petřín Hill (get off at the first stop). The gleaming white villa, halfway up the hill-side, offers a mesmerizing view over golden Prague; and its menu offers some of the tastiest, healthiest and best-value food to be found in Prague. Reservations are absolutely essential here; be sure to ask for a window seat. Walk back down to catch the winking city at its heartmelting best, and try to avoid the canoodlers who congregate on the hillside as the sun sets. AE, V.

Rybářsky klub, U sovových mlýnu 1, *Mon–Sat 3–9.30.* An anglers' club tucked away in the park on Kampa Island, with food prepared by the fishwives themselves. It seems to spend about half the year closed 'for hygienic reasons', but those who have managed to get a meal here swear that it's a tasty experience. Carp and trout are the standards, but pikes, perches and eels sometimes get a look in. No cards.

U čerta (The Devil), Nerudova 4. *11.30–11.* Cosy, quiet and unassuming restaurant on pretty Nerudova street, serving steaks and little else. AE.

U mecenáše (Maecenas'), Malostranské nám. 10, ℂ 53 38 81. *Mon–Fri 5–11.30, Sat–Sun 12–3, 5–11.30.* An interior structurally unchanged for almost 400 years and filled with pieces of gallows, firearms and swords amassed over the centuries. Mydlář the Executioner used to pop across the river regularly from the Green Frog, and his scrawled signature is pre-served behind a piece of glass in the front room (although it's the homely back room that you should reserve). The menu offers an excellent range of starters, from wild mushrooms to caviare, a less exciting series of chicken-and-fillet main courses, and a set of flambéed desserts served with panache and concealed glee by the waiters. One of the most comfortable places in town to pursue a romance. AE, MC, V.

U tří pštrosů (The Three Ostriches), Dražického nám. 12, © 53 61 51. *12–3, 6–11.* Part of the beautiful Renaissance hotel at the end of the Charles Bridge, but the gloomy interior and mediocre standards of the restaurant have got a long way to go before they catch up with its reputation. No cards.

inexpensive

Café-Bar bíly orel (White Eagle). Malostranské nám. 28. *9 am–4 am.* Black and silver bar popular among young Praguers, with steaks, omelettes, salads and a long list of cocktails. The late hours are worth noting, although after 11 pm a short emergency menu takes over. No cards.

U kocoura (The Tomcat), Nerudova 2. *12–11.30.* Grubby beer rooms serving Pilsner and an assortment of simple and smelly dishes, including sardines and the putrid *pivní* (*see* p. 285). A favourite of Malá Stranites for decades, but rising prices mean that few Czechs come here any more, unless they want to ponder the meaning of change. No cards.

U šebaráčnická rychta, Tržiště 22. *11–11.* A Staropramen beer hall and restaurant hidden away in an alley in the heart of Malá Strana. Its survival is little short of a miracle: while its neighbours have been washing the tablecloths and adding noughts to the menu since 1989, this place still attracts scores of Czech regulars and remains authentic all the way down to the sausages and surly service in the beer hall. Come here while you still can. No cards.

U vladaře (The Prince's), Maltézské nám. 10. *11–11.* Only the dietetically perverse would eat here more than once, but this *vinárna* is a useful corrective after you've spent a while staring at the exorbitant prices being charged by U malířů next door (*see above*). For approximately one-tenth of the cost, you can stuff yourself on pickled gherkins, cabbage soup, bean salad, carp, veal and beefsteak, and, to end it all, a set of fruit dumplings. No cards.

Hradčany

Eating Out

expensive

Peklo (Hell), Strahovské nádvoří 1, © 53 32 77. *7 pm–2 am.* An extraordinary dining experience, in the 12th-century beer cellars of the Strahov monastery, which the monks have leased to an Italian firm for five years. The dishes are as delicious, minimalist and expensive as you might expect from such an exclusive location, but the kitsch decoration to which the firm has stooped is astounding. Fairy lights line the steps that sweep down from the entrance, and one whole chamber has been made into a disco, complete with mirror-ball and overhead glass booth for the DJ. AE, DC, MC, V.

Tosca, Hradčanské nám. 5 (entrance on Loretánská), ℂ 53 18 97. *12–3, 6–1.* Pop in here to have a peek at the wine bar in the two colossal cellars. They are far more impressive than the overpriced internationalist cuisine and arrogant service, but the café in the outdoor arcade (10–10 pm) is a cheaper alternative, and a pleasant summertime stop. AE, MC, V.

U labutí (The Swan), Hradčanské nám. 11, ℂ 53 94 76, 53 69 62. *Mon 7–12 midnight, Tues–Sun 12 noon–3, 7–12 midnight.* A former stable with intact water-troughs in tranquil Hradčany Square. The returned owner is currently revamping the menu and interior; the changes she will institute remain unclear, but with a long tradition as one of Prague's most exclusive eateries, U labutí is unlikely to plummet too far into the realm of fried cheese and dumplings.

U zlaté hrušky (The Golden Pear), Nový Svět 3, ℂ 53 11 33. *11.30–3, 6.30–12 midnight.* Wonderful Czech and French food and excellent service in the most romantic alleyway in Prague. So smart that it raises its eyebrows a fraction and murmurs an apology if you try to pay with a credit card.

moderate

U Lorety, Loretánské nám. 8/10, ℂ 53 13 95. *11.30–3, 6–11.* Cosy and quaint, serving some tasty Czech dishes including venison. The outdoor terrace is a splendid spot for long evening meals in the summer, next to the madly tinkling belltower of Loretto and opposite the ludicrous Černín Palace. No cards.

U ševce Matouše (Matthew the Cobbler), Loretánské nám. 4, ℂ 53 35 97. *12–4, 6–11.* Look for the copper boot hanging over the door. A footwear theme used to pervade this place, with a shoesmith available to provide a while-U-eat cobbling service. Unfortunately, he was sacked by the nine people to whom this restaurant has been restituted. Register your protest and with luck he'll return; meanwhile this is a cosy and dependable enough place with 13 types of beefsteak, and various trouts and chicken breasts. No cards.

Vikárka, Vikářská 39, ℂ 53 51 59. *11–10.* Steeped in the shadow of St Vitus's Cathedral and heir to a long line of hostelries originally set up to satisfy the appetites of the local vicars. The walk through the empty echoing castle after your meal can be magical, but the (Czech) food and service here never transcend the mundane. The lack of atmosphere is typified by the fact that the walls of its wine cellar were once signed by most of Prague's early 20th-century artists, until the management decided to repaint them. No cards.

inexpensive

U cerného vola (The Black Ox), Loretánské nám. 1. *10–10*. Basic food and 12° Velkopopovické beer, brewed just outside Prague. Still popular among the locals. No cards.

U dvou zlatých hvězd (The Two Golden Stars), Pohořelec 3. *10.30–8*. Indonesian fast food from Migoreng to Meat Mixture à la Martin. No vegetarian dishes. No cards.

Žižkov and Vinohrady — *Eating Out*

expensive

Myslivna, (The Gamekeeper's Lodge) Jagellonská 21, ☏ 627 02 09. *11–4, 5–12 midnight*. The gamiest game in Prague. If you have the cash, come and bag a pheasant, deer or boar and taste Czech food at its best. AE. V.

moderate

Fenix (Phoenix), Vinohradská 88, ☏ 25 03 64. *11–3, 6–11*. Large portions of tasty Chinese food, cooked and served by a family of recent immigrants. No cards.

Lucie, Dalimilova 5. One of Prague's most entertaining spots to sample gipsy food. A sense of adventure is essential: specialities include *halušky*, a starchy slime of cheese and bacon fat, and the marginally less repulsive *goja*, comprising sausage skins stuffed with potato. No cards.

Quido, Kubelíkova 22, ☏ 27 09 50. *11.30–11*. One of the best-value Czech restaurants in town, with a wide choice of tasty seafood, pasta and poultry dishes. The restaurant is next to Prague's incredible TV tower (*see* p. 275), and a post-prandial walk around it can verge on the hallucinogenic. No cards.

inexpensive

Demínka, Skřetova 1, ☏ 236 28 31. *Mon–Fri 9 am–12 midnight, Sat–Sun 11 am–12 midnight*. Basic fish, flesh and fowl dishes under the dusty chandeliers and plants of what has become a Prague institution. Shows worrying signs of smartening up, although the manager swears that nothing will ever change. No cards.

FX Café, Bělehradská 120. *11 am–6 am.* Excellent vegetarian snacks above a throbbing nightclub. Tofu, spinach and avocados make regular appearances on the menu, on top of (slightly crunchy) pizzas and useful toasted sandwiches. Also worth noting the late hours here. No cards.

Na zvonařce (seems to translate as On the Little Bell Founder), Šafaříkova 1, ℂ 25 45 34. *10 am–11 pm.* Crouched over the Nusle valley and under chestnut trees and peeling neo-Renaissance mansions. Popular among generations of Praguers: teddy-boys used to gather on the nearby stone steps, and the outdoor stone dance floor is still used at weekends. The food is very Czech—try the chicken livers, and (for its excellent curiosity value) the carp in aspic—as is the abysmal standard of service. You may have to wait an hour to eat: not a place to come if you have a plane to catch, but perfect for laid-back summer evenings. No cards.

Rebecca, Olšanské nám. 8, ℂ 627 69 20. *Effectively open all hours, all week, minus a few breathing periods around breakfast time.* One of Prague's longest-established all-nighters, popular among restless clubbers, wealthy sleazeballs, off-duty barmen and insomniacs. Video-games, satellite TV and a munchy-crunching menu as long as the granite bar. AE, V.

expensive

Čínský Restaurant CG, Janáčkovo nábř. 1, ℂ 54 91 64. *11–11.* Surprisingly good Cantonese food prepared by Czech chefs. No cards.

moderate

Café Savoy, Vítězná 5, ℂ 53 97 96. *12 noon–12 midnight.* An elegant airy café, horizontally partitioned by the Communists and only recently restored to 7-metre-high splendour. It tries hard to conjure up its *fin de siècle* past, but with no more than a handful of patrons each evening, the joint is not yet jumping. Still a pleasant spot for a quick steak or a quiet drink. No cards.

Secese, nám. 14. října 16, ℂ 54 72 01. *11 am–12 midnight.* An enormous pseudo-Art Nouveau restaurant in a neo-Renaissance building, owned by the Pilsner brewery and serving up a menu of Czech dishes that's almost as large as the place itself. As well as steaks, there's veal, hare and venison on offer, and the excellent dessert menu includes superb blueberry pancakes and a wide range of cheeses. The only problem with this hangar is that it engulfs anyone who enters. One interesting, if irrelevant, feature of this place is that the bathrooms have bidets. AE.

U Mikuláše Dačického, Viktora Hugo 2, © 54 93 12. *Mon–Fri 12 noon–1 am, Sat–Sun 6 pm–1 am.* Very attractive, very popular and very Czech hostelry, filled with lanterns and wall paintings. Although the dark interior looks ancient, it's the work of 1920s set-designers. Unexceptional food, but if you're more interested in wooing and wining, this is the place for you. No cards.

U vojáčků, Vodní 11, © 53 56 68. *12 noon–12 midnight.* Attractively dowdy fish restaurant, with beer on tap and every scaly creature you can catch in Bohemia on the menu. The only downside is the service, which is consistently appalling, but thanks to the delicious fishes the staff can get away with it. No cards.

inexpensive

Pizzeria Mačedonia, Kořenského 3, © 54 17 92. *Mon–Fri 11 am–12 midnight,* Sat–Sun 5–12 midnight. Pizzas that are usually the best in Prague, with an invariably excellent level of service. The salads are also delicious: try the Škopský salát, piled high with cheese and pungently dressed. Less appetizing, but apparently popular among extroverts, is the Pizza Erotica, topped with a sausage between two fried eggs. No cards.

Privat Restaurant Austria, Štefániková 25, © 54 98 79. *Mon–Fri 11–3, 4–10, Sat–Sun 11.30–3, 4–10.* Excellent Czech food. The chicken liver is delicious, and vegetarians can choose from a surprisingly broad range of dishes, including spinach, potato pancakes and trusty fruit dumplings. AE.

Southern Suburbs   *Eating Out*

moderate

Terasy Barrandov (Barrandov Terrace), © 54 53 09. *11–11.* A Constructivist eyrie, designed by Václav Havel's uncle and lodged on a hillside high over the sodium streetlights and snaking motorways of southern Prague. It was a popular spot for a swinging night out before 1989, but it's only just reopened after years of restoration. Václav's brother, Ivan, now owns it; he has leased it out, but the barman swears, rather unconvincingly, that the lads pop in regularly. Wicker chairs, plastic marble tables, cheap Czech food, stupendous views of urban nothingness, and a dance floor

(*9 pm–3 am*) that can be pulsating or stone dead. Stop by if you're in the area. No cards.

U pastýřky (The Shepherdess's), Bělehradská 15, ✆ 43 40 93. *5 pm–12 midnight*. A log cabin, serving steaks and kebabs grilled on the cast-iron stove that stands in the centre and housing a resident gipsy band who play from 7.30 pm every night. If you think it all sounds too authentic to be true, you'd be right: the restaurant charges a small admission fee and its fur-lined seats and long benches are usually filled with tour groups. Nevertheless it's all but impossible not to enjoy a evening here as the tunes and carafes of wine take their raucous hold. No cards.

inexpensive

Orient, Otakarova 1, ✆ 43 09 13. *Mon–Sat 11–3, 5–11, Sun 5–11*. This place has never had a non-Czech on the staff, and the food that has evolved from long years of hopeful but blind experimentation is a fascinating hybrid of Vietnamese, Cantonese and Indian cuisine. Friendly service, red dangling lanterns and strokeable velveteen walls add to the appeal of this place, and it's well worth a stop if you're local. No cards.

Northern Suburbs — *Eating Out*

expensive

Thang Long, Dukelských hrdinů 48, Prague 7, ✆ 80 65 41. *11.30–11*. A plush set of screens and fans, serving pseudo-Vietnamese food at extortionate prices. Far cheaper and more authentic food, as well as immeasurably more courteous service, is to be found at the Club Bar Saigon (*see below*). AE.

U zlatého rožně, (The Golden Spit), Československé armády 22, Prague 7, ✆ 312 10 32. *11 am–1 am*. Cosy underground restaurant, specializing in Icelandic fishy dishes from plaice and catfish to crab, as well as a set of tasty Chinese-type dishes. AE.

Moderate

Bali, Čechova 9, Prague 7, ✆ 37 03 42. *12–10*. Indonesian food, praised by those who have eaten here. AE.

Na ořechovce (The Walnut), Vychodní 7, Prague 6, ✆ 312 48 42. *12 noon–1 am*. Very large portions of duck, chicken and steak, accompanied by hit-and-miss soups and salads. A couple of favourable reviews in 1991 overexcited the staff, who now display unmerited airs and graces and occasionally veto your dining selections. However, if you live in the neighbourhood and have a cold, the food will do you good. AE.

U cedru (The Cedar), Na Hutích 13, *©* 312 29 74. Small but delicious selection of Lebanese dishes. The owner left the civil war behind in the late 1970s, but Beiruti shops still provide regular supplies. The menu includes several Czech entrées, but the done thing here is to order a couple of glasses of *raki*, a basket of fresh pitta bread, and then to work your way through the list of appetisers. They include a superbly seasoned *baba ghanoush*, a refreshing *tabbouleh* and innumerable old favourites from *falafel* to *houmos*. Honied *baklava* and intoxicating cardamom-flavoured Arabic coffee provide a perfect end to an excellent meal. Even the service here is faultless. Picnickers and locals could also note that the restaurant operates a take-away service. DC, V.

inexpensive

Club Bar Saigon, U vody 1, Prague 7, *©* 80 26 38. *Mon–Fri 11–10, Sat–Sun 4 pm–10 pm.* The Czech Republic has a population of many thousands of Vietnamese, but thanks to the rigidities of Communism none opened a restaurant before 1989. This family-run café, a shocking pink beacon in a wasteland of broad roads, railway sidings, wharves and cranes, is some distance from the standard tourist routes, but its small and tangy menu of duck, crab, chicken and beef dishes won't disappoint. No cards.

U Govindy (Govinda's), Na hrázi 5, Prague 8 (near Palmovka metro), *©* 683 72 26. *Mon–Fri 12 noon–6.* The Hare Krishna hangout, and a godsend for all vegetarians. Ingenious use of spices makes the set menu (lentils, watery soup, etc.) far tastier than its insipid appearance might suggest. If you're of a sociological bent, you might also be interested in watching your fellow diners. Buddhism is still a little-known discipline in Prague, and nervous piety is the order of the day, with no one quite sure what taboos they are breaking or what unnatural act they might be expected to perform after the meal. Only the Hare Krishnas, swanning ethereally from stove to shrine, let their hair down. Operates a pay-what-you-like system with a suggested donation, the latter having been added after too many people paid what they liked and the Buddhists did their sums. No cards (yet).

U tří hrochů (The Three Hippopotami), Bubenečská 8, Prague 6, *©* 32 52 56. *10–10 (and often later).* Young and cosy suburban hangout. Small but delicious set of home-made pizzas, and the chef can sometimes be persuaded to let you create your own—a gift for veggies, and anyone else who likes to play with olives, sheep cheese, asparagus and the like. Healthy starters too. No cards.

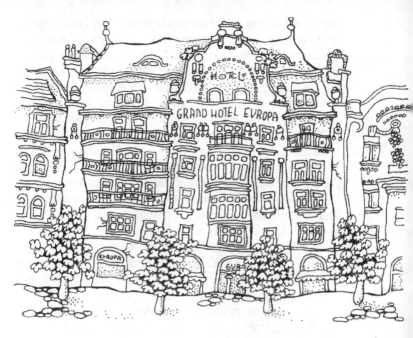

Where to Stay

For a city boasting one of the most extraordinary architectural preserves in Europe, the accommodation that Prague offers its visitors can be very disappointing. Only a handful of hotels can honourably claim to be more than a century old, and the genteel pensions and quirky cubbyholes that pepper most other European cities have yet to materialize. The situation can, not surprisingly, be blamed on the Communists. Hotels, along with almost everything else, were nationalized in the late 1940s, and many were given plywood partitions and turned into obscure institutes or cramped collective housing. For the next 40 years, the needs of the ordinary tourist were all but forgotten. Apart from a handful of five-star palaces, which served the needs of the seriously-monied, Prague's hotels degenerated into fleapits the colour of nicotine and rust, characterized by slovenly service and facilities that extended not much further than a toothbrush glass and bottle-opener. Stultification has now been restored by chaos. Scores of hotels have been returned to their pre-Communist owners; most others are in the throes of privatization; and across the city, thousands of workers with drills, masks and welding equipment are pounding together an entirely new generation of fit hotels for tourists to live in.

The offices of Čedok and AVE listed on p. 321 can make advance reservations for a large proportion of the following hotels. They charge a commission of about 10 per cent. You can also book directly. In either case, a credit transfer is usually required and the booking will take effect upon confirmation of payment.

Hotels in Prague have historically divided themselves up into a convoluted A/B/C/* division, which never bore much relation to observable facts and is entirely ignored in the list below. Note is made of those establishments that are classed **** and above, but otherwise the only classification used is cost. **The hotels below are divided into four price categories, according to how much they charge per night for a double room with bathroom:**

> Luxury—£130–240 ($200–360)
> Expensive—£70–130 ($100–200)
> Moderate—£35–70 ($50–100)
> Inexpensive—£18–35 ($30–60)

Except at the very bottom of the scale, rates are between 20 and 50 per cent lower out of season. Those places that take credit cards are marked as follows: AE = American Express, DC = Diners Club, MC = Mastercard/Eurocard/Access, V = Visa.

As a result of the tumultuous state of Prague's hotel industry, several establishments currently under reconstruction have been omitted from the following list simply because no information can be obtained about their likely appearance when the dust settles. However, those with particularly interesting features are mentioned, even if they currently resemble a bomb site. Although the hotels listed all meet minimum hygiene standards (hot water, no rodents, only household insects), some are particularly poor value or unfriendly and are included only as warnings to be considered if Čedok or some other agency offers you a room in them. Finally, before booking a hotel at all, it's worth noting that a private apartment may well be far more appealing and atmospheric than any hotel room. Accommodation agencies are listed towards the end of this section.

Nové Město and Vinohrady — *Where to Stay*

Little of these districts survived large-scale redevelopment over the last 100 years. The majority of Prague's hotels are now situated here, and range across the scale of noise and comfort. In most cases, you can expect shuddering and dirty streets, but you won't be more than a 15-minute journey from the peace of the Old Town Square. Parking is a problem in most of these areas, and you may have to leave your car some distance from your hotel.

luxury

Atrium, Pobřežní 1, © 284 11 11, fax 232 35 95, 232 37 91. A spectacular
★★★★ complex of glass and fibre-optic-type decoration, built around an atrium so expansive that some claim to have seen very small rainclouds occasionally floating across it. Fountains, a 25-metre pool, an indoor tennis court, transparent lifts and four restaurants make this the perfect hotel in which to lounge, but the orange and ordinary rooms are considerably less exciting. Certainly worth a visit, and at the very bottom of this price category, it's not quite as exorbitant as some of its fellow four-starrers. Strictly speaking it's just outside the New Town, but it's so close to the centre that to describe it as being anywhere else is misleading. Underground guarded car park. 788 rooms. AE, DC, MC, V.

Esplanade, Washingtonova 19, ✆ 22 25 52, 22 60 56–8, fax 26 58 97.
★★★★★ Sizeable simple rooms, modern and comfortable with lots of calm blue and gold tubing. Bright and spacious restaurant. Close to Wenceslas Square and the main railway station. Expensive and unexciting. 64 rooms. AE, DC, MC, V.

Jalta, Václavské nám. 45, ✆ 26 55 41, fax 22 63 90. Extremely central location
★★★★★ and comfortable enough, but otherwise a lacklustre redoubt of pre-1989 unprofessionalism. 86 rooms. AE, DC, MC, V.

Moráň, Na Moráni 15, ✆ 29 42 51, fax 29 75 33. Reconstruction has left
★★★★ this thoroughly modern, unsurprising, soulless and overpriced. 57 rooms. AE, DC, MC, V.

Palace, Panská 12, ✆ 219 71 46, 219 71 11 (reservations—219 71 20), fax
★★★★★ 235 93 73. Modern, central, comfortable, and the only hotel in Prague where the porter wears a topper and a turquoise cloak. Conference facilities and casino. The former Art Nouveau hotel has been completely remodelled, and apart from a whiplash bar and some crazy-paned glass there's no reminder of its past. Guests enjoy an unctuous level of service, superb facilities, and pay more than anywhere else in Prague. Has special rooms 'designed for lady travellers', which are pink, have more mirrors than usual, and come with a red rose. 125 rooms. AE, DC, MC, V.

Penta, V celnici 10. A grand 309-bedder between the Masaryk railway station
★★★★ and nám. Republiky, currently in the final stages of construction. For reservations call (081) 897 0551 or fax (081) 759 87 55 in the UK, and 1-800-225 3456 in the US. 309 rooms. AE, DC, MC, V.

expensive

Adria-Neptun, Václavské nám. 26. Once a set of matchbox rooms where prostitutes waited for business in the corridor showers, this hotel is currently in the throes of upheaval and total renewal. It's hard to tell what is going to emerge from the rubble, but judging from the large number of workmen it will be significantly different from the Adria of old. That has to be good, and with a location at the centre of Wenceslas Square, this will probably be one of Prague's better hotels before long. Its place in this category is based on pure speculation.

Ambassador, Václavské nám. 5, ✆ 214 31 21/4, fax 236 31 72, 22 33 55. A
★★★★ lively and bustling hotel—its lobby sometimes looks like an extension of Wenceslas Square—with ornate neo-classical furniture in several of its 103 rooms. The reception here also handles reservations for the neighbouring **Hotel Zlatá Husa** (Golden Goose Hotel) at No. 7, which has

another 98 rooms, generally slightly smaller than those in the Ambassador. AE, DC, MC, V.

Hotel Meran, Václavské nám. 27, © 26 68 95, fax 231 14 77. This hotel was tacked on to the neighbouring Evropa (*see below*) after the war, but following the restitution of each to its (different) owner a not-very-painful Siamese split has separated them once again. This tall and narrow building can't match the Evropa's effortless style, but it has its Art Nouveau trappings and atmospheric paraphernalia will probably be moved in soon. Until then, the 16 rooms are clean but unexceptional. Few facilities; bottom end of this category. MC, V.

Hotel Meteor, Hybernská 6, © 235 85 17, fax 22 47 15. One of the best-run mid-range hotels in Prague, with a proud owner recently returned from Australian exile and a friendly and professional staff. Clean and comfortable rooms, equipped with all mod cons including safes and hair dryers. Also contains a built-in underground car park, a restored Gothic restaurant, and a conservatory-cum-summer terrace. Bookings can be made through in the UK on (081) 541 0133, fax (081) 546 1638, and in the US on 1-800-528 1234, fax (602) 780 6099). 98 rooms. AE, DC, MC, V.

Pension Páv (Peacock Pension), Křemencova 13, © 20 46 30, 20 49 15, 20 51 62, 20 53 08, fax 20 17 13. Small and comfortable boarding house, no more than a stagger and crawl away from Prague's oldest beer hall. 8 rooms. No cards.

moderate

Albatros, nábř. Ludvíka Svobody, © 231 36 00/34/81. One of Prague's 'boatels', stably moored on the Vltava. Closer to the Old Town Square than Wenceslas Square, but the view as you wake up is just too far from the Charles Bridge to be dreamy. Two long corridors of clean cabins (all doubles, save for a few four-bedders), all with showers. Largely young crowd. 90 rooms. No cards.

Atlantic, Na poříčí 9, © 231 85 12, fax 232 60 77. Attractive, well-appointed
★★★★ and extremely reasonably priced at the time of writing, but it's about to be sold to an unknown buyer who has equally obscure plans for it. 60 rooms. AE, V.

Axa, Na poříčí 40, © 232 44 67, fax 232 21 72. This hotel is slowly being overhauled, and at present half the rooms are soothing blue and black bedchambers, with their own bathroom; the other half are prefabricated orange spaces with basins. They cost the same... so do the right thing. The hotel has a 25-metre swimming pool. 130 rooms. AE, MC, V.

Evropa, Václavské nám. 25, © 26 27 48/9, fax 236 52 65/74. Prague's legendary Art Nouveau hotel, and still a bargain for all those who like their atmosphere louche. The rooms themselves are a disappointment: although a handful are faintly redolent of a cheap turn-of-the-century bordello, most are unadorned plywood boxes (and less than half have their own bathroom). The secret is to spend your time cruising the broad corridors. They're filled with monstrous vases, dusty chaise longues and armchairs, mirrors, lanterns, and the fronds and leaves of a hundred scattered plants—all under a vast skylight and within the ovals, arches and wrought iron of the New Art at its most atmospheric. Try to make advance reservations 10 days in advance by fax; any other time period or method of communication generally fails to secure a place. 98 rooms. No cards.

Hotel Florenc, Křižíkova 11, © 236 26 04/20, fax 236 25 88 (reception on first floor). Fairly spacious mauve and white plywood rooms. This place is next to Prague's main coach station, and it has an appropriately transient and no-frills feel. 19 rooms. AE.

Hotel Harmony, Na poříčí 31, © 232 00 16, fax 231 00 09. A functionalist block on a busy street, thoroughly reconstructed in recent years. Clean, well run and close to the centre. 59 rooms. AE, MC, V.

Juliš Hotel, Václavské nám. 22, © 235 28 85–7, fax 235 52 47. Reconstructed hotel restored to its owners, above a well-known cake shop and two tacky nightclubs. Extremely ordinary but very central. Situated at the top of a set of stairs and entirely unsuitable for wheelchairs. 54 rooms. AE.

Hotel Luník, Londýnská 50, © 25 27 01, 25 66 17. Small, comfortable, clean and friendly. 35 rooms. No cards.

inexpensive

CKM Juniorhotel, Žitná 12, © 29 29 84. A very good value youth-orientated hotel, with showers in every room and particularly good prices for trios. Totally unsuited to wheelchairs. 22 rooms. No cards.

Juventus, Blanická 10, © 25 51 51, fax 25 51 53. For years this hotel has been a cheap spot for young travellers to exchange horror stories and backpacking tips, but the family to whom it has been returned plan to go up-market. Quite how far is unclear, but you can probably expect a comfy pension-type hotel. At the time of writing there is no lift, and the only showers are in the corridors. 21 rooms. No cards.

Opera, Těšnov 13, © 231 14 67 (reservations:231 56 09), fax 231 14 77. Small and clean rooms, only a third of which have their own bathrooms. A useful spot for penny-watchers, but light sleepers should beware—it's next to a flyover, which delivers a double-whammy of noise and smell during the summer when you have to open the double-glazed windows. 66 rooms. No cards.

Pension City, Belgická 10, tel/fax 691 13 34. Large, bright and clean rooms in a well-run and friendly pension. Get a room with a street-side view over the cobbled avenues; the alternative is to look over the neighbours' dingy courtyard. The reception desk is open from 8 am–11 pm, but if you call in advance you can arrive at any other time (guests are given their own keys). 15 rooms. No cards.

Staré Město   *Where to Stay*

This area is perhaps the most convenient location of them all, but only the Ungelt is actually part of its history (*see* p. 151).

luxury

Intercontinental, nám. Curieovych 5, © 280 01 11, 231 18 12, fax 231 97 91.
★★★★★ Reservations can be made on (081) 847 2277 (UK) and 1-800-327 0200 (USA). Five-star facilities, central location and comfy rooms. If only it didn't look like an ugly piece of concrete Lego. AE, DC, MC, V.

Paříž, U obecního domu 1, © 236 08 20, fax 236 74 48. The extraordinary Art
★★★★ Nouveau façade, turned into a fortress by neo-Gothic turrets and arches, lets you down with narrow dark rooms, and consistently lackadaisical staff. Otherwise a comfortable, attractive and central place to stay. 98 rooms. AE, DC, MC, V.

expensive

President, nám. Curieových 1, © 238 75 23, fax 231 82 47. Spanish-owned
★★★★ hotel with comfortable and larger than usual rooms. Relatively good value; one idea is to stay here and use the five-star facilities of the neighbouring Intercontinental. 97 rooms. AE, MC, V.

Ungelt, Štupartská 1, © 232 04 70/1, fax 231 95 05. A modernized Gothic house on the edge of the Old Town Square, with tiled floors and airy corridors that make it feel more like a chalet camp than a Prague hotel. Contains 10 spacious and pretty apartments, each with cooking facilities and capable of sleeping up to four people. Hotel facilities are limited to a fax machine and restaurant, but if that suits you and you can afford the top end of this price category, this place won't disappoint. No lift. AE.

Centrál, Rybná 8, ✆ 232 43 51, 232 42 40, fax 232 84 04. Dingy and forlorn, but the grim corridors open into small clean rooms and its name does not lie. Due to be reconstructed and every room will have its own bath. 76 rooms. No cards.

inexpensive

Penzion Unitas, Bartolomějská 9, ✆ 232 77 00/9, fax 25 73 47. Extremely cheap and central boarding house in a former monastery, opposite a police station that used to be the main interrogation centre of the secret police. Stark rooms; shared, clean and large bathrooms in the corridors. No lift. 30 rooms. No cards.

Malá Strana — *Where to Stay*

This picturesque quarter, filled with orange pantiled roofs and smoking chimneys, is the image of Prague you send home on a postcard. If you're happy to pay an arm and a leg, this is the place to stay. Anyone offered lodgings here by one of the accommodation agencies should count himself or herself very lucky indeed.

luxury

Hoffmeister, Pod bruskou 9, ✆ 53 83 80, 53 28 49, 53 79 14, fax 53 09 59.
★★★★ A Baroque house that's been disembowelled, extended and attached to its neighbour to form one of Prague's newest hotels. On a main road, but a short walk to the cobbled peace of Malá Strana proper. Expensive, but very well equipped. 44 rooms. AE, DC, MC, V.

U Ježiška, Jánský vršek/Břetislavova 6, ✆ 53 16 18. At the time of writing, this hotel consists of the shells of four Baroque houses in the historical heart of Malá Strana. They are due to be turned into a 70-bed hotel, which the new owner claims will be suitable for everyone except students. If that sounds like your kind of place, try calling the above number for booking details. Again, its position in this category is conjecture.

expensive

U páva (The Peacock), U lužického semináře 34, ✆ 53 22 51, 53 70 69, fax 53 33 79. An absolutely charming hotel, perfectly located and with courteous staff and tastefully furnished rooms. Prices vary according to the view; if possible, pay the premium to get one of the third-floor rooms looking up to the castle over the Vojan Gardens. It's a scene you won't forget. No lift. 11 rooms. AE, V.

U tří pštrosů, Dražického nám. 12, © 53 61 51–4, fax 53 61 55. Perhaps the most picturesque place to stay in Prague, in a 16th-century house about 15 metres from the Charles Bridge. Unfortunately, the staff are a supercilious and cringing bunch who deny the hotel the atmosphere and charm that it deserves. That said, waking up under the Renaissance joists and throwing open your windows on a warming summer morning looks to be an unbeatable yawn. No lift. 18 rooms. AE, MC, V.

moderate

Hotel Kampa, Všehrdova 16, © 53 90 45, 53 30 45, fax 53 28 15. Good value for the location alone, in an alley from which you can see the cathedral high above. Clean and bare rooms, all turned into L-shapes as a result of a rather hasty bathroom-installation programme. Has regular mass-bookings from travel agents; to make a reservation, send a fax just after the 20th of the month preceding your arrival. 85 rooms. AE, DC, MC, V.

Hradčany

luxury

Savoy, Keplerova 6. Save for its impressive façade, this Art Nouveau mansion
★★★★★ has just been entirely knocked down and rebuilt. It's due to reopen as a five-star hotel, and according to one of the cement-mixer operators on site here, it will have 'many machines for businessmen'. No further information is yet available.

expensive

Spiritka, Atletická 115, © 311 82 04, fax 53 64 22. An attractive low-lying
★★★★ complex perched on a hill high above Prague, on the site of a 17th-century fort, a slate quarry, a Baroque winery and a farm called Spiritka. The Interior Ministry built the hotel during the Communist era, and as you might expect of a place designed to let besuited thugs unwind, the large and irregularly-shaped rooms have an extremely attractive, understated and co-ordinated elegance about them. The staff are enthusiastic and friendly, and as the facilities improve, this is likely to become one of the city's better hotels. Travelling to the centre can be a bore; however there is a nearby bus service, the hotel operates a summer shuttle, and you can also hire a Tatra, Taurus or Cadillac limo if you're feeling lazy. 27 rooms. AE, DC, MC, V.

Pension U raka, Černínská 10, © 35 14 53, fax 35 30 74. A quiet stay in one of the drowsiest and most beautiful streets of Prague. The log cabin itself is a fairly offensive extension, but it's probably warmer and more comfortable than the mess of ancient cottages that surrounds it. Only five double rooms, and no meals, but the owner of this money-spinner is an efficient sort with a cordless phone, and he can sort out a string of dinner reservations once you arrive. AE.

U krále Karla (King Charles), Úvoz 4. A superb location at the top of steep Nerudova street, and a five-minute walk to the castle. The hotel remains under construction at the time of writing, but judging from its sister hotel, U páva (*see above*), it will offer an elegant and memorably pretty place to stay. Its position in this category is speculative; contact the reception desk at U páva for further information. 20 rooms.

moderate

Comenius Praha, Parléřova 6, © 35 20 10. Situated on the 3rd and 4th floors of a student dormitory, and at the inexpensive end of this price category. 126 beds. No cards.

Coubertin, Atletická 4, © 35 28 51-3, fax 35 40 69. Redbrick complex on a windswept section of Strahov. Sports-oriented, with a fitness centre that claims to be especially expert at soothing soccer players. Modern and comfortable. 24 rooms. AE, DC, MC, V.

Pyramida, Bělohorská 24, © 311 32 41 (reservations © 311 32 96), fax 311 32 91. A vast glass temple with clean if unexciting rooms. All have showers. Fitness centre below, and a short walk from Prague Castle, albeit one along a dusty main road. The poor man's Forum. 325 rooms. AE, MC, V.

Smíchov | *Where to Stay*

This area is industrial, and bustles. It's a smoky and spluttering jog away from the centre, and contains cheap restaurants and some of the liveliest pubs in town.

expensive

Vaníček, Na Hřebenkách 60, © 35 28 90, 35 07 14, fax 35 06 19. A custom-
★★★★ built hotel that clambers in five terraces up a steep hillside. It looks as ungainly as it sounds, a prefabricated kit of jagged edges and angular recesses around an interior maze of lifts and stairs, but the rooms are comfortable and service is excellent. A bus journey from the centre, with a shuttle bus in June and July. Garage parking. 24 rooms. AE, MC, V.

Admirál, Hořejší nábř., ✆ 54 74 45-9. Another boatel. All details are as for the Albatros above, except that it has a minuscule dance floor and a few more beds. No cards.

U Blaženky, U Blaženky 1, ✆ 53 82 66, 53 80 75. A small pension in a neo-Renaissance villa. Friendly, relaxing and suitable for anyone who wants a quiet life. 14 rooms. No cards.

inexpensive

Balkán, Svornosti 28, ✆ 54 01 96, fax 54 06 70. No lift, and only three rooms have showers. Sombre, basic, clean and cheap. Serious economies of scale apply if you are a group of three or more and don't mind sleeping on top of each other. 26 rooms. AE.

Praga, Plzeňská 29, ✆ 54 87 41. Situated on a main road in the heart of Smíchov. The management are at pains to make clear how safe guests are although their assurances can have a strangely counter-productive effect: why, you wonder, do they *need* an all-night guard equipped with handcuffs, truncheon and a Colt-45? No lift. 45 rooms, only three of which have showers. No cards.

Žižkov *Where to Stay*

A residential district ranging from hilly cobbled streets to busy Art Nouveau thoroughfares.

moderate

Bílý lev (White Lion), Cimburkova 20, ✆ 27 11 26, fax 27 32 71. Cheap, clean and small rooms in a quiet hotel on a side street. No surprises here. The very bottom of this price category. 22 rooms. No cards.

Ostaš, Orebitská 8, ✆ 627 93 86, fax 627 94 18. A recently modernized set of small, clean and slightly sombre rooms. 34 rooms. No cards.

Vítkov, Koněvova 114, ✆ 27 93 41, fax 27 93 57. A curving functionalist block, some distance from the centre, but the trundling trams that meet at the busy crossroads outside will get you into town. Comfortable, clean and well equipped. 62 rooms. AE, MC, V.

inexpensive

Hotel Kafka, Cimburkova 24, ✆ 236 81 92 (reservations). Brown doors and whitewashed walls opening onto a courtyard. The rooms are furnished in pine-and-linen style, and all have showers. Clean and very good value, even if it looks like the kind of place that rents rooms out by the hour. 23 rooms. No lift. No cards.

Nusle and Michle *Where to Stay*

Heavily damaged towards the end of the war, and not an area that you'll want to explore too much. However, the following hotels are all no more than a motorized hop, skip and jump away from the centre.

luxury

Forum, Kongresová 1, ✆ 419 01 11, fax 42 06 84. Reservations can be made on
★★★★ (081) 847 2277 (UK) and 1-800-327 0200 (USA). Over 1000 comfortable beds, well-equipped fitness centre, and an electronic revolving door that can take 15 at a time. Tremendous views over a very long bridge and a dull suburban valley; 50 metres from the metro platform; and a five-minute whizz along the motorway into the centre. Every facility imaginable, and the place to come if you're rich and fear risk. 531 rooms. AE, DC, MC, V.

expensive

Panorama, Milevská 7, ✆ 416 11 11, fax 42 62 63. A swanky tower block that
★★★★ has about 70 per cent of everything that the Forum has, except bowling and squash. 412 rooms. AE, DC, MC, V.

Union, Ostrčilovo nám. 4, ✆ 692 75 06, fax 692 72 98. Recently reconstructed in the Hygienic style, with white tiles, gold tubes, globular lamps, and pastel green themes. Entirely inoffensive, and linked to the centre by the convenient tram that stops outside. 52 rooms. AE, DC, MC, V.

Dejvice, Letná and Holešovice *Where to Stay*

These areas to the north of the Vltava stretch from the heartland of Prague's (ex-) Communist chattering classes, across a bustling residential district to the the city's best park (Stromovka) and the sad zoo.

luxury

International, Koulova 15, ✆ 33 19 91, 331 91 11, fax 311 60 31. A big granite tower built in 1954 for the Ministry of National Defence. At 88 metres, it's a relatively understated example of Stalinist phallophilia, but the friezes and paintings that adorn the building, honouring the onward march of labour and the joy of peasant life, always made this an enjoyable spot to contemplate Communism. Unfortunately, it's recently been bought by a band of Belgian businessmen, whose plans are unknown. One can only hope that they have a sense of history and humour.

Praha, Sušická 20, ℂ 333 8 1111, fax 312 17 57. A curving ribbon of glass
★★★★★ and concrete owned by the Central Committee of the Communist Party until retrieved for the international travelling class in early 1990. It's now owned by the Hyatt-Regency chain. The Party built itself unembellished but extraordinarily comfortable rooms, and half come with terraces that look out over rolling lawns and the best panorama of Prague that you'll ever see. If you have about £400 ($600) to spare, you can even book into one of the eight presidential suites (365 sq m) and unwind in the jacuzzis that may or may not have been used by Mikhail Gorbachev and/or Eduard Shevardnadze. Otherwise, there's a small pool, bowling lane, jogging tracks, and ever-expanding business facilities. Offers one of the quietest and most relaxing stays in the city. 124 rooms. AE, DC, MC, V.

Diplomat, Evropská 15, ℂ 331 41 11, fax 34 17 31. An unsurprising island of
★★★★ international comfort that prides itself on its business facilities. A good place to receive faxes, hold conferences and so on. 387 rooms. AE, DC, MC, V.

expensive

Parkhotel, Veletržní 20, ℂ 380 71 11 (reservations:38 15 26), fax 38 20 10.
★★★★ One of Prague's more venerable glass-and-concrete hotels, dating from 1968. The staff often seem abnormally distracted and confused, but otherwise you'll have few problems with a stay here. 234 rooms. AE, DC, MC, V.

moderate

Belvedere, Milady Horákové 19, ℂ 37 47 41–9, fax 37 03 55. Unexciting building, but the rooms are fine and the quality of service here has improved significantly in recent years. Particularly cheap out of season. 120 rooms. AE, DC, MC, V.

Splendid, Ovenecká 33, ℂ 37 33 51–9, fax 38 23 12. Comfortable and very clean rooms in a tranquil avenue of Art Nouveau buildings. Nothing exceptional, but friendly management and a hassle-free stay are almost guaranteed. 69 beds. AE, MC, V.

Although the following hotels are situated away from the centre of town, none is beyond the municipal transport system.

luxury

Villa Voyta, K Novému dvoru 124/54, Prague 4, ✆ 472 55 11, 472 88 38,
★★★★ fax 472 94 26. This rather extraordinary hybrid of neo-Art Nouveau kitsch and residential villa might appeal to some suburban off-the-wall types. Although at the very bottom of this price category, each room contains a safe, a hair dryer, a fax machine for anyone who wants one, and a level of luxury that extends to gold-plated bedsteads. Some distance from the centre, but the hotel has a limousine service and car-hire facilities. Pleasant restaurant and friendly staff. 13 rooms. AE, DC, MC, V.

expensive

Club Hotel Průhonice, on the E50 and E55 motorway, ✆ 643 65 01, fax 643
★★★★ 68 35. A modern sporty paradise, with 10 tennis courts, two squash courts, bowling, pool, gym and accessible horses. Lurks low on the edge of a motorway, and although the rooms are as well appointed as you'd expect, atmosphere isn't its strong point. 100 rooms. AE, DC, MC, V.

moderate

Golf, Plzeňská 215a, ✆ 52 32 51, fax 52 21 53. A dull motel, named after the facility that makes it unique in Prague. You'd have to be an obsessive putter to spend much time here. 171 rooms. No cards.

Karl-Inn, Šaldova 54, ✆ 232 25 51/2, fax 232 80 30. A plywood-and-lino hotel owned by Čedok. A place to sleep and shower; nothing more, nothing less. 168 rooms. AE, DC, MC, V.

Olympik II, U sluncové 14, ✆ 684 55 01–4. A busy tower block, slightly shabby but otherwise good value, that is popular among coach parties and within easy reach of the centre. Not to be confused with its four-star namesake next door, where unprofessional complacency reigns supreme. 255 rooms. No cards.

Accommodation Agencies *Where to Stay*

Prague's housing shortage is chronic. It is notoriously common for families to live together until the children marry, and the claustrophobia that ensues goes a long way to explain the mismatches, extramarital affairs, and early divorces that typify young love in the capital. The tourist explosion of recent years has exacerbated the problems, but rather than despair Praguers have risen to the lucrative challenge by moving in with each other and sending their parents to make marmalade in the country. As a result, you will have few problems in finding private accommodation, and the following agencies all have a variety of properties on their books. All offer the option of one room in a family flat, or a self-contained apartment. The former is rarely as constricting as it sounds, although your hosts may insist on waking you up with coffee and cakes and asking you polite questions about monarchs, presidents, football teams and the like. The agencies can reserve accommodation in the centre if you give them enough warning; specify that you want an address in Prague 1 (although parts of Prague 2 can be just as convenient). *Prices range from about £12 to £30 ($18–45) per person per night for a flat, and rooms cost from £8 ($12) a night.* If you are travelling from the UK, you can arrange accommodation in advance through the **Czechbook Agency**, 52 St John's Park, Blackheath, London SE3 7JP, © (081) 853 1168. With the Czech firms listed below, you should make reservations more than a week and less than a month before leaving home. English is spoken in all of them, but where a fax number is given, a faxed request should precede a confirmatory telephone call. Bookings are accepted on trust; credit-card payment over the phone is still not possible.

AVE, Hlavní nádraží, Wilsonova 8, © 236 25 60, 236 30 75, fax 236 29 56. *June–Sept non-stop, Oct–May 6.00 am–12 midnight.* The largest of the agencies, with a total of some 3000 beds in hotels, pensions, youth hostels and private flats. Co-operates with the Prague Information Service (PIS) and can therefore provide a range of sightseeing services. AE, DC, MC, V.

Čedok, Panská 5, © 22 56 57. *April 15–Oct 31 Mon–Fri 9 am–9.45 pm, Sat 8.30–6, Sun 8.30–4.30, Nov–April 14 Mon–Fri 9–8, Sat–Sun 8.30–2.* Has a choice of about 150 rooms, but no flats. A minimum stay of two nights is required, and advance booking is not possible. Just outside the entrance, you'll find a small throng of cocky chaps with their own list of accommodation offers, often far better value than anything Čedok has to offer. AE, DC, MC, V.

City of Prague Accommodation Service, Haštalské nám. 13, © 231 02 02, fax 231 40 76. *Daily 9–8.* Small and well-run, with a high proportion of centrally located properties. Provides minibus rides where necessary. V.

Hello, nám. M. Gorkého/Senovážné nám. 3, tel/fax 22 42 83. *Daily 9–10.* Established, efficient, and cheaper than many other agencies. Provides a lift to your room or flat. AE, DC, MC, V.

Stop City, Vinohradská 24, ✆ 25 78 40, fax 236 13 68. *April–Oct 10–9, Nov–Mar 11–8.* Located close to the railway station, and offering a range of prices and properties. No cards.

Top Tour, Rýbná 3, ✆ 269 65 26, 232 10 77, fax 232 08 60. *Mon–Fri 9–8, Sat–Sun 10–7.* A large number of properties, many in the centre, and a broad price range. No cards.

Hostels *Where to Stay*

The longest-established hostels are in student dorms up on Strahov hill around Chaloupeckého street, which you can (almost) reach by taking bus 176 from Karlovo nám. to the end of the line. The **Estec Hostel** in Block 5 (✆ 52 73 44, fax 52 73 43) is the largest, and there are also beds available in nearby Blocks 4, 7 and 11. They, and most of the city's other hostels, cost *between £7 and £10 ($10–15) per night.* Several of Prague's other college dorms open up to tourists between June and September, and if you contact AVE or one of the other agencies you'll be given plenty of addresses. There are particularly central dormitories at Platnéřská and Panská streets, both in Prague 1. IfB on Václavské nám. 27 often has very cheap hostel accommodation on offer, and Prague's widest selection of bargain beds can be found at **CKM** on Žitná 12, ✆ 20 54 46. *The office deals with personal callers only and is open between 9 am and 6 pm daily from April–Sept and Mon–Fri during the rest of the year.*

Camping and Caravanning *Where to Stay*

The following are among the least isolated and best appointed sites in Prague.

Caravan Camp, Plzeňská, ✆ 52 47 14. Well appointed and linked to the centre by quick and convenient tram routes.

Intercamp Kotva Braník, U ledáren 55, ✆ 46 17 12, fax 46 61 10. Caravans, camping and chalets (tents can only be pitched between April and October). Southern Prague comes to a noisy end around here, among a maze of asphalt bridges and flyovers, tram termini and signs for Vienna. However, this camp on the edge of the Vltava somehow escapes the hubbub and offers a cheap and quiet stay. Facilities include tennis, volleyball, badminton and bicycle rental; canoes can be hired and paddled several kilometres downstream.

Na Vlachovce, Rudé armády 217, ✆ 84 12 90. The chalets here come in the shape of large Budvar beer kegs. Particularly popular among Germans, and other people with a sense of humour.

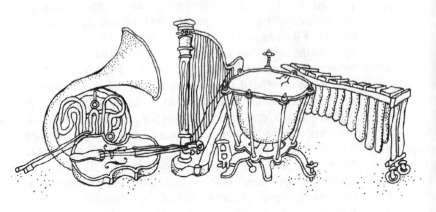

Entertainment and Nightlife

A city that was once among the saddest in the world has turned into one of the hedonistic capitals of Europe. While operas and symphonies resound from Prague's stages, a summer stroll will lead you past the whole gamut of tomfoolery, from sword-swallowing to didgeridoo-snuffling, and a night of clubbing could take you on to dance in a Romanesque cellar or a nuclear bomb shelter. It's a far cry from the barren years of yore, when the wicked witches of the bureaucracy often used to insist not just on being invited to the ball, but on drawing up the programme. Spontaneity was discouraged and occasionally criminalized, while the work of the country's best playwrights, directors and singers was regularly banned. But the energy that always used to be somewhere else is pouring back into the city: the sounds of poncho'd Colombians and passionate Barcelonista echo across its squares and alleyways, DJs from London and west Africa keep the city's turntables moving, world-famous conductors and orchestras attend the Prague Spring music festival, and an international babble of poetry and jazz seeps from its cafés. So long as you avoid the tourist-trap dross—the shoddy Kafka-itsch plays and Don Giovanni puppet shows—you need hardly yawn until you get home.

This section can only begin to outline what is one of the fastest-moving aspects of a rapidly changing town. Prague's English-language newspapers will provide a clearer snapshot. Advance booking information is on p. 36, but the general rule is that you should always aim to obtain tickets directly from the venue concerned.

Concerts and Opera

Following a bloody orgy of privatization, Prague opera acrimoniously split into two separate companies in 1992. The **National Opera**, based in the neo-Renaissance National Theatre on Národní 2, is the more splendid and staid of the two. It has taken very unkindly to the pretensions of its rival, which lives in the almost-as-ornate edifice on Wilsonova 8—once the Smetana Theatre and now cheekily renamed the **State Opera** (Státní opera). Prague opera is competent rather than inspired, and has always depended on vendettas and intrigue for its energy, and as a result the rivalry between the directors and staff of the two companies promises to invigorate it over the next few years. The State Opera has thrown down the gauntlet by announcing an all but impossible number of new productions; and a pained National Opera has responded to the gadfly challenge by ponderously starting to overhaul its conservative repertoire and shoddy props. Battle has been joined and, if public relations officers are to be believed, nothing is ruled in and nothing is ruled out. That may be true, but what you can hope for is imaginative innovation from the former company and dependable quality from the latter.

As well as Smetana, Janáček and other native composers, the work of Mozart is a favourite, thanks to Prague's insistence that his connection to Salzburg was no more than an accident of birth. His music still lilts across the city, honoured by enraptured buskers sawing violins and puffing out harmonica concertos. If you decide to succumb to what has become a Prague cliché and take in a Mozart opera, you may as well go the whole hog and attend it at the neo-classical **Estates Theatre** (Stavovské divadlo). Among those in whose footsteps you'll be following is Wolfgang himself (*see* p. 234), and a bonus is that most of its productions are dubbed into English and relayed through headsets.

The above venues all act as concert halls from time to time, as does the Art Nouveau **Smetanova sín Obecního domu** (Smetana Hall of the Municipal House) on nám. Republiky. The Czech Philharmonic Orchestra is based at the **Rudolfinum** on nám. Jana Palacha, which regularly puts on some of the best-value concerts in town. An important venue for **ballet** is the **Palác kultury** (Palace of Culture). A haemorrhage of asylum-seeking talent during the 1970s and 1980s has left Czech ballet in an unimpressive state, but if you want to make your own judgement you'll find the aforementioned palace, a block of concrete erected in the late 1970s, next to the Vyšehrad metro station (line C). There are also regular concerts and recitals in many of the palaces and churches in central Prague. The best acoustics are generally agreed to be in St James's (sv. Jakub), but listening to a symphony amidst the all-encompassing splendour of St Vitus's leaves most people feeling very small and rather overjoyed. There are concerts there (and virtually everywhere else in town) during the Prague Spring music festival, booking details for which are on p. 36.

Plays

The largest theatres are the **National Theatre** (Národní divadlo) mentioned above, and the neighbouring **Laterna Magika**, squatting under what looks like a very big piece of plastic bubble wrap. The first shows suitably unadventurous performances of Shakespeare, Molière, G. B. Shaw, Karel Čapek (*see* p. 91) and the like, while the second combines film, theatre and mime. The granddaddy of Prague's tourist traps, it has degenerated from radical beginnings and international plaudits at the Brussels Expo '58 to a candyfloss multi-mediocrity. The first dramatists to work at the theatre, who included Miloš Forman of Cuckoo's Nest fame, were soon edged out, and although it is perfectly inoffensive it has hardly changed since. In a similar vein is the Black Theatre, housed in the **Divadlo za Branou II** (Theatre behind the Gate II) at Národní 40. On the basis of one idea—that black-clad actors can move things against a dark stage without being seen—it sparked off an entire genre of gimmickry (called 'black light theatre') that you'll find across the capital.

It will probably come as little surprise that, with a playwright in the presidential office, Prague's smaller theatres have been experiencing a renaissance since 1989. However, the experimentalism of their broad repertoires has often had a floundering desperation about it, and a sense that the most important motivation is to make up for lost time. That said, two consistently interesting theatres are the **Divadlo na zábradlí** in Anenské nám., ✆ 236 04 49, and the **Divadlo Labyrint** on Štefánikova 57, ✆ 54 50 27. The first was where Václav Havel worked his way from stage-hand to literary adviser in the early 1960s, and had his first play premiered; the second saw the very beginning of the Velvet Revolution in 1989, when the actors of what was then the Realistic Theatre apparently suggested the general strike that was to ring the death knell of the old regime. The **Činoherní Klub** on Ve Smečkách 26, ✆ 235 23 70, is also highly regarded by many Praguers; however, its reputation rests on its long association with Oscar-winning film director Jiří Menzel, and it has stultified in recent years. Its former role at the vanguard of Prague drama is being assumed by the **Studio Ypsilon** on Spálená 16, ✆ 29 22 55, regarded by many as the finest acting company in the capital.

Finally, you just may want to attend a marionette show while in Prague. Puppeteering has a long tradition in Bohemia and, according to its disciples, it is an under-appreciated art form. You can judge for yourself at one of the street puppet theatres that dot the capital during the summer, or at the Divadlo Minor at nám. M. Gorkého/Senovážné 28, ✆ 22 51 41 or the National Marionette Theatre on Žatecká 1, ✆ 53 80 45. It may help to know that Prague's favourite puppets are the father-and-son duo of Špejbl and Hurvínek, whose plodding worry and agile impudence have enthralled generations of Czech children.

Poetry

Prague has a small poetry club, **Viola** on Národní 7, ✆ 235 87 79, tucked away at the end of an Art Nouveau corridor, which is sometimes worth a visit (*Mon–Sat 7 pm–12 midnight*). It has a long, if now tired, history as a dissident hang-out, and alongside the not-very-angry young men and women who use the club as their local wine bar you can still find a number of melancholy chaps with uncontrollable beards and poetesses guarding secret sheaves of thought. Events held here include one-man plays and sometimes very beautiful recitals of Czech lyrical poetry. *The box-office for advance tickets is open from Mon–Sat 4–8.15.* You could also look out for one of the many literary workshops regularly set up by English-speaking residents in the city. Recurring subjects include childhood traumas, Prague laments and deconstructionist pastiches of North American culture.

Cinema

One of Prague's best cinemas is the **Dlabačov** at Bělohorská 24, © 311 53 28, a club with an ever-changing set of flicks that span the range from Tarkovsky to Charlie Chaplin. The **Pražský filmovy klub** (Prague Film Club) at Sokolovská 1, © 231 57 05, is another interesting spot. *Both venues are popular and you should get tickets in advance.* Particularly intrepid buffs could also try the **Illusion** at Vinohradská 48, © 25 02 60, which specializes in films from the glory days of early Czechoslovakian cinema—meaning anything from prewar melodramas to the cinematic triumphs of Socialist Realism. Elsewhere in the capital, you'll find a hotchpotch of films, with all the Hollywood hits and soft-porn classics that you might expect. Many foreign films are left in their original language nowadays, with Czech subtititles added; however, that's something you may want to check before buying your ticket.

Jazz

Prague jazz has had a chequered history. As recorded by writer (and amateur musician) Josef Škvorecký, its savage rhythms were suppressed by Nazism and Communism in turn. The modern low point came in 1986, when members of the spiritedly independent Jazz Section of the Musicians Union were jailed on trumped-up corruption charges; but since 1989 the city's players have revelled in their new freedom. The scene is an eclectic one—ranging from smooth syncopators with oil-slicked hair to goggle-eyed corkscrew heads who have digested one Howlin' Wolf LP too many—but with a long musical heritage and centuries of folk melodies in the national back catalogue, Prague jazz can be surprisingly relaxed and innovative.

There are three notable venues in the centre of the capital. **Reduta** on Národní 20, © 20 38 25 (*Mon–Sat 9.30 pm–12 midnight*) is the longest-established. Although pricy and unusually popular among Scandinavians and Germans, it remains something of a Prague institution. It's oddly parochial—everyone whoops a little louder if a visiting black person appears on the stage—but its intimacy makes it a good place to fraternize with the band between sets. Look out for Martin Kratochvíl, music mogul, multimillionaire and mean jazz pianist, whose bald head and handlebar moustache are often to be found bobbing around on stage here. The **AghaRTA Jazz Centrum** on Krakovská 5, © 22 45 58, is another cosy spot: as well as being a small shop, it operates as a tranquil café during the day and has a small food menu (*Mon–Fri 1 pm–1 am, Sat–Sun 7 pm–1 am; music from 9 pm–12 midnight*). You can also snap your fingers and feel good in the sub-supper club ambience of **Viola** (*see above*) on Saturday evenings, when it usually hosts a live jazz act.

Café Society

In one of his many unpublished stories, Franz Kafka pondered the meaning and origins of café society. Lonely Franz explained to a friend that he imagined a man who wanted somehow to 'make it possible for people just to see others, to talk to them, observe them without getting involved in any relationships, without hypocrisy'. Prague's first café was actually opened by an irascible Armenian who was only looking for a captive audience (*see* p. 246), but by the early 1900s the capital's coffee houses had developed a vitality that would turn them into sepia-tinted legend in the grim years and decades that followed 1938. Although everyone from anarchists to anti-Semites had their favoured haunts, the culture transcended its localism and achieved Europe-wide fame. The best-known haunt was the **Café Arco**, the favourite of Kafka, Max Brod and the other 'Arconauts', which was a beacon for central Europe's writers, thinkers and shoulder-rubbers until the Nazi invasion. It survives—after a fashion—on Hybernská 12, but the garish assembly of mirrors, slot machines and pool tables that it has become is no longer a place in which you can comfortably struggle with your novel or harangue a few close friends. However, its long hours and proximity to the railway station make it a useful waiting room if you have a train to catch (*open 7 am–5 am*). Those with imagination could also ponder the past in the now soulless restaurant that sits in the former palace at Na příkopě 17. Until 1945, it housed the Café Continental, known affectionately as the Conti by the scarred Junkers, monocled Nazis and generally proud Germans who frequented it. *Untermenschen* entered at their peril.

The mosaic of cultures that made up prewar Prague was shattered by the Nazi invasion. Nostalgic myth subsequently asserted that the city's café-crawlers were always predominantly Jewish and German, but Prague's Czechs were never without their *kavárny*. They regularly reconnoitred at the now-destroyed Café

Union, and generations of Praguers have famously wasted time at the **Café Slavia**, on Národní 2 opposite the National Theatre. Under its green painting of a lonely absinthe drinker, the Nobel Prize-winning poet Jaroslav Seifert dreamed of meeting Apollinaire in his *Slavia Poems*; the 1920s avant-garde adjourned here whenever things became too stormy at the nearby Union; and until 1989, the unofficial opposition came to exchange ideas and typewritten manuscripts. In 1992, the café was leased to foreign investors who promptly closed it for renovation. All of Prague is nervously awaiting its reopening: the tacky decoration and proverbially terrible service of the old Slavia won't be missed, but if its regular clientele of bonnet-topped *babičky* and loafing film students are finally priced out, a Prague institution will have died. Other longstanding Czech cafés are the subdued Art Nouveau **Obecní dům** on nám. Republiky, and the immeasurably more lively **Evropa Café** on Václavské nám. 25—an essential stop on any historical tour of the city's coffee houses. The regulars here are an odd bunch: suitably enough for an Art Nouveau interior that teeters between elegance and sensuality, it has always attracted the highlife and the lowlife in almost equal numbers (*see* pp. 231–2). The best time to come is in the evening at weekends: service is so appalling that it's charming, and the same is true of the caterwauling musicians who torture their instruments through an unchanging repertoire of mini-symphonies, monochrome film tunes, and Slovakian folk tragedies. Finally, you could investigate the neo-Renaissance **Café Savoy** on Vítězná 5. The high-ceilinged hall dates from the end of the last century, but it hasn't quite recovered from the trauma inflicted by the Communists, who split it into two floors and turned it into a carpet warehouse and community propaganda centre. Though restored, it's too dainty, too fastidious and too empty. However, if the much-rumoured closure of the Charles Bridge takes place, the Savoy may come up trumps as waves of diverted pedestrians pour across the nearby Legion Bridge (most Legií).

Although the Slavia and a few other coffee houses (such as the **Malostranské kavárna** on Malostranské nám.) operated as opposition hang-outs and student sanctuaries throughout the Communist era, only since the revolution has café society in its true freewheeling sense returned to Prague. One of the new haunts with most character is the **Kavárna velryba** (Whale Café), a self-styled literary café sunk a few feet below street level at Opatovická 33. It hosts regular readings of Czech poetry, and is popular among the kind of man who regularly glances up from his copy of *Ulysses* to see who's watching. Although the more furtive pen chewers tend to be foreigners, the management makes deliberate efforts to prevent the café turning into an ex-pat ghetto (to the extent of sometimes excluding Americans). That said, anyone is usually welcome to join the people-watching; one sneaky viewpoint is through the large convex mirror at the bar.

The only reason *not* to come is the coffee, which tastes rather like a watery grave would. (*See* p. 293 for opening times.) Another popular modern café is the **Bunkr Café** on Lodecká 2, above the nightclub and bomb shelter of the same name. The clientele is hairier and more leather-clad than that of Velryba, but during the afternoon it can be a relaxing place to note flitting impressions or play silent games of chess with punk rockers. As dusk descends the atmosphere changes, and at 10 pm it makes the rather theoretical transition to a late-night bar: by then the only faraway stares among the clientele are likely to be drink- or drug-induced. **Kavárna Hogo-Fogo** (Hoity-Toity Café) on Salvatorská 4 is an unexceptional but pleasant hangout (*Sun–Thurs 12 noon–12 midnight, Fri–Sat 12 noon–2 am*). Finally, the lively and friendly **Konvikt Klub** on Konviktská 22 is worth a visit; although it is more a beer restaurant than a café, its role as an informal Prague melting pot lends it honorary coffee-house status for the purposes of this section.

Prague's new immigrant communities make up an essential component of the coffee house culture. One of the most gregarious groups are the refugees from old Yugoslavia, who—having left to escape conscription or ethnic killing—are bound together by their memories rather than ripped apart by them. The sometimes melancholy, usually friendly subculture is in evidence throughout the city: try the **Caffé Zlatá Ulička** on Masná 7. English-speaking residents are also great café-haunters, not least because of the common superstition among younger ex-pats that a great writer of the future is stalking the city unnoticed. Simultaneously, a few seem secretly to suspect that they are that great writer, and the net result is that Prague's cafés are teeming with literary tyros who debate, applaud and steal each other's ideas in roughly equal measure. One particularly good spot for observing the cross-fertilization is the **FX Café** at Bělehradská 120, where ex-pats often come to discuss literary technique before dancing in the club downstairs.

Beer Halls

Prague takes its beer as seriously as most other cities in central Europe, but to enjoy it as it should be enjoyed, your best bet is to scan the information on pp. 285–6 and then launch yourself on a *pivnice* crawl without too many prelimi-naries. Trial, error, and dubious drinking partners will soon help you assemble your own list of favourite watering holes. However, it's only too easy to get mired in the first stop—your glass is replaced and a notch added to your bill before you can say *už nepiju* (roughly, 'Enough drinking, already'), which soon becomes far too difficult anyway. The procedure reaches almost industrial scale and efficiency at **U Fleků**, where hundreds of people are intoxicated nightly by trained waiters who coast around with huge tin trays of brimming black beers. The only problem with that inn is that it's long been ceded to Germany by Praguers; if it's Czech company that you want, go down the local *pivnice* or look through the Food and Drink section of this book for an appropriately authentic oasis. Be warned that the more traditional a place is, the greater is the likelihood that your arrival will set off grim mutterings among the more florid of the regulars. If you enjoy a real challenge head towards **U zlatého tygra** on Husova 17, a ferociously exclusive hangout for literarily-inclined drunks, where the waiters won't serve you if you sit in the wrong place and no one will talk to you if you fail to observe any one of about 137 Czech drinking customs.

Outside the centre, Žižkov and Smíchov are both particularly good areas for an adventurous stagger, both peppered with gipsy pubs that occasionally erupt into fistfights and/or song. The **Bar Lucie** on Dalimilova 5 is a safe bet for a night of unpredictable and uncontrollable events. Clarinettist, double bassist, *cimbál-*tinkler and accordionist play through the night with ever-increasing fury, and by the early hours the tight-suited singer's crooned tributes to the ladies have turned into enraged and directionless tirades against the horrible futility of it all. That doesn't stop everyone from having a marvellous time, but be prepared for the table-dancing worst. Seedier but often no less fun is the **Hospoda na čečeličce**, on the junction of Na Čečeličce and Plzeňská. It has music at weekends, and you may well be whisked off your feet by a grinning crone or a sweaty man with swaying hands and bloodshot glaze. If you ask politely, the barman will give you a set of well-fingered cards (*filkovy*). They look rather like the tarot, and you can often find someone who's happy to break you into the game, so long as you're prepared to bet on winning each lesson. The rules change quite often. The pub edges onto Prague's most macabre and beautiful cemetery (*see* p. 279), and the temptation to scale the railings on moonless nights has been known to overcome heavy drinkers. That can lead to terrible accidents, most memorably in mid-1992, when a confused travel writer fell into a tomb.

Wine Bars

The best wine bars (*vinárny*) are also restaurants and are listed in the Food and Drink section. Outdoor drinking on summer evenings, preferably from a bottle on the slowly cooling cobbles of the Charles Bridge, provides an unbeatable vision of Prague. The string of wine houses along Michalská street is another traditional spot to have a glass al fresco; neighbours and weather permitting, scores of young drinkers spill out onto the street to compare the day's suntans and interrelate. Nearby is a pleasant gallery-café run by Bosnian refugees and serving wines from across eastern Europe: **In vino veritas** on Havelská 12 (*daily 8 am–12 midnight*).

Finally, serious socialites could head for **Jo's Bar** on Malostranské nám. 7. It's a favourite among the city's English-speaking foreigners; and although it sometimes feels like a bad college bar, when the crowd gels the place is little short of a party.

Ballroom dancing

One of the more specialized activities that you might consider while in Prague is balling a night away. Almost every single Prague adolescent takes dancing classes during a short but crucial part of his or her salad days, and around May and December the newly acquired skills are put to the test at graduation balls (known as *věnečky* or 'little garlands') across the capital. Anyone can buy a ticket and attend, although you're well advised at least to *look* like students. Be on your best behaviour: as well as dances, the youngsters are taught rules of etiquette, gallantry and deportment, and clodhopping or partner-swapping types are treated with all the cold fury that teenage angst can muster. Dress: black tie and white gloves (men); balldress, as trad. or as rad. as you dare (women). Dances: waltz, polonaise, jive, cha-cha, foxtrot. RSVP: SLUNA at Václavské nám. 28, where you can buy tickets for most balls; the grandest venues are the Lucerna Palace and the Obecní dům, and the summer balls on Prague's islands are also huge fun.

In the hope of reviving a grand tradition, the Czech Republic's bourgeoisie *manquée* has begun to organize some seriously swanky balls. So far their success has been limited, and not helped by a cabal of pesky anarchists who have insisted on throwing tomatoes at arriving guests. The well-known Czech speculator Ivana Trump hosted one of the first dances (and tomatoes), and numerous others now take place regularly in the capital's hotels and theatres.

Clubbing

Prague has finally learnt to party hard. Václav Havel set his compatriots an impressive example during his first presidency, with a range of clubbing partners who included Mick Jagger, Lou Reed and Frank Zappa; in the heat of the moment, he even appointed Zappa to be Czechoslovakia's cultural envoy at large, an appointment swiftly reversed by incredulous bureaucrats. Older and more sensible though he now is, the president still goes club-crawling occasionally, but with the exponential increase in venues your chances of stumbling into him are fewer than ever before. But even without Havel it's possible to have fun aplenty, and everyone can find a niche in the city's burgeoning nightclub scene.

In a city as protean as Prague, clubs can metamorphose overnight and a constant struggle is being waged for the fickle hearts and flickering minds of Prague's *jeunesse d'orée*. To discover the flavour of the moment, supplement the information below with the listings in the *Prague Post* or *Prognosis*. In particular, you could keep your antennae alert for news of raves, which were all the rage during the summer of 1992. Young foreigners made up the hard core, but the Aquarian aspects of acid-house culture were also welcomed by a significant minority of Prague's love children. In a city that never quite made the break with headbands and flares, that probably means that musical be-ins are safe for at least another decade. Reggae fans should also keep their ear to the ground; although there are several clubs in the capital at any given time, none has displayed much staying power and they are not listed below.

Avoid the discotheques of Wenceslas Square at all costs. They're prohibitively expensive for most Czechs and as a result teem with lonely businessmen planning to be unfaithful and Prague prostitutes eager to help. Unlike any of the places mentioned here, they may also operate dress codes, often changeable at will and used only to keep undesirables out.

Borát, Ujezd 18, © 53 83 62. *Tues–Thurs, Sun 6 pm–2 am, Fri–Sat 6 pm–6 am.* The first private club of post-revolutionary Prague, set in what looks like a short-term squat, and retaining some of the grungy diversity of the underground culture of Communist days. Against a backdrop of graffiti-covered walls, you'll find lots of dirty hair, smoke, beer, talk, and very loud music, with scarcely a posing opportunity in sight. Bands play in the ground-floor front room.

Bunkr, Lodecká 2, © 231 45 35. *8 pm–5 am.* The club that heralded the explosion in Prague's nightlife, set up in a bomb shelter and opened on the second anniversary of the Velvet Revolution. The decor is a rather gentle form of late 1980s industrial wasteland chic, and the music ranges from three-chord thrashing to the Beatles. If that sounds slightly like hell, this may not be the place for you; otherwise, you can expect a relaxed, young and mixed Czech and foreign crowd. When the pogoing and the puddles of drink become too much, have a powwow in the bar upstairs with the nocturnal oddballs who hold the fort until 3 am. There are constant rumours that this little Prague institution will close; but although it certainly seems too wild to live, it's somehow too young to die.

Futurum, Zborovská 7 (Prague 5). *9 pm–5 am.* A gloomy set of rooms blasting out a wall of punk and axe-attack death metal sound. You don't come here to make new friends, only to bang your head. Even that is difficult if there's no band on, when the club looks rather like a party that everyone just left. It's housed in an abandoned cinema, hence the queer dance-floor, which is actually an auditorium without the seats.

Gag, Národní 25, ✆ 26 54 36. *10 pm–2 am*. Little more than a theatre bar cluttered with dummies, pianos and telephone boxes, but singalong strummers turn it into a jolly dancing space. Very friendly crowd, predominantly young Czech student types.

Jo's Garáž, Malostranské nám. 7. This jazz and blues club, due to be located in cavernous chambers under the bar of a similar name, is not yet open at the time of writing. However its owner, a dynamo named Glon who rushes around clutching a bunch of keys, swears that it will be up and running by late 1993.

Klub 007, in Block 7 of the Strahov student dorms. *9 pm–4 am*. Extreme youth and tone-deafness are essential for this place, as is a willingness to nod angrily when told that punk is not dead. If dancing, the rule is jump or be pushed. There are two gentler school-disco-type clubs in Blocks 1 and 11 of the student dorms.

Lávka, Novotného lávka 1, ✆ 22 82 34. *9 pm–4 am*. Enticing location on an island just under the Charles Bridge, with a view of river, bridge and castle that can be hallucinogenic during a hard night of outdoor dancing. It's during the long hot summers that Lávka takes off, the holiday-romance scene of swooping pick-ups and hokey cokeys and unforgettable kisses, all to an unrelenting soundtrack of MTV/Europap at its worst.

Radost (Joy), Bělehradská 120, ✆ 25 12 10. *9 pm–6 am*. A late-night lighthouse for the Beautiful People, with video screens, halogen lamps and a small but active dance-floor kept moving by shifts of lithe podium-writhers. Music is poppy, though the DJs also toss on anything from techno to ragga to keep the punters on their toes. The club is popular among foreigners as well as trendier Praguers, and the sofas and seats are comfortable spots from which to watch the capital's club culture pass before you in dumb show: glamour and glitter, lonely money, shoulder-brushing encounters and the yelping of the ex-pat crowd. Be warned that the bouncers sometimes let in only favoured pass-holders; on busy nights you may find yourself held at the door while hipper folk breeze past, flashing their cards with grim pride. The vegetarian restaurant upstairs (colonized by foreigners) is open for pick-me-up peanut butter sandwiches, pizzas, conversations and coffees until 6 am.

Rock Café, Národní 20, ✆ 20 66 56. *Mon–Fri 10–7.30 pm and 8–3 am, Sat 11.30–7.30 pm and 8–3 am, Sun 8 pm–3 am*. Dull, overpriced and filled with the most unadventurous out-of-towners. A place to know to avoid.

U bílého koníčka (The White Pony), Staroměstské nám. 20, ✆ 235 89 27. *Tues–Sat 9 pm–2 am*. A spacious Romanesque cellar, attractively gloomy despite being hung with a mirror ball and spotted with rainbow lights. Its unfortunate history, however, is that it was once the place where the youth wing of the Party would come to make whoopee, and many of the tight-lipped hip-thrusting regulars have the distinct air of ageing Young Communists about them. Prague swingers now give it the cold shoulder, but you could at least wander down the steps to peek at the interior.

U zoufalcu, Celetná 12. *9 pm–4 am.* Another smoky and grimy corrective to the slickness of Prague's newer clubs. The music ranges from heavy metal to techno, while the young and largely Czech clientele either gaze blankly through the haze or flail around on the dancefloor.

Ubiquity/Fetish, Pařížská 9, © 232 62 82. *9 pm–5 am.* A British-run club that moves around a lot; if you don't find it here, ask around. Ubiquity's Prague reputation rests on a history of wild spectacles, ranging from dancing bears to female motorcyclists from hell roaring across the dance floor; the current fetishistic theme is limited to some soft porn and a few dismembered shop dummies, but if excessive hedonism is your cup of tea, come to investigate. On a good day the club can be one of the liveliest in town and the perfect place in which to dance until dawn. On a bad day, it can be like somebody else's school dance. It used to bar gipsies; the policy has probably been changed, but if you are dark and denied entry, you could always check.

Uzi, Legerová 44. As you might expect of a club named after a machine gun, this is not a place to stroll into by accident. It's racist and reactionary, with possibilities of bodily abuse that extend as far as, but are not limited to, a tattoo studio upstairs. The club is the haunt of Prague's sad bikers who look right, and act right, but lack one essential accessory—bikes. You'll find them here nursing beers and fidgeting with their leathers while they dream of abusing biker-chicks and riding through the wind. All that said, this is a good place to meet young Czechs, and so long as you don't mess with the bouncers' dumbbells, you'll probably avoid serious physical injury.

Gay Prague

Suppressed for several decades as an intrusive symptom of late capitalism, Prague's homosexual culture is finally beginning to throb again. The weekly listings magazine *Program* has a regular page of gay things to do, and there are now several clubs and bars in the city where you can meet like-minded folk. Although not yet open at the time of writing, the wildest is sure to be **Valentino's** on Londýnská 57, planned as a leisure complex of sauna, restaurant and disco. Its preincarnation, whose staff and management are going to run Valentino's, was popular among deviants of every description: big boys in leather, crop-headed ladies and hairy transvestites mingled with ordinary boys and girls, and even a handful of straights. To add to the friendly atmosphere, a gentle *babička* used to wander through, telling gossip and selling pornographic magazines to the regulars. The **David Club** at Sokolovská 77 (Prague 8), ✆ 231 78 82, is a cosy bar and dance floor outside the centre (*Tues–Sun 8.30–3 am*). The city has one gay pub, **U dubu** at Záhřebská 14 (*Tues–Sat 4–midnight*), and the **Evropa Café** is a well-known cruising parlour. Condoms aren't available everywhere, and gay men should be sure to pocket a wad before coming out.

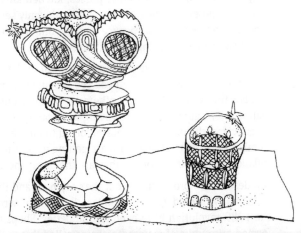

Shopping

The free market has finally hit Prague. As the formerly state-owned retail industry is privatized, the capital's malls and high streets are being transformed. Rusting corrugated shutters are being opened for the first time for years, interiors are being remodelled and relit, and shop windows that spent the last 40 years trying to sell the same dusty jar of gherkins now display Apple Macs and fax machines. In the city where a crate of olive oil could once set off a 20-strong queue you can now buy anything—from a mango to a MiG-50 fighter jet. The entire capital has become a marketplace. Wide boys line the tourist routes, hawking their Gorbachev dolls, totalitarian kitsch and fake antique watches, and on the boulevards a peculiarly Czech form of hustler—middle-aged housewives with microphones and an evangelical sales pitch—draw rapt crowds as they hold aloft their fake leather purses, kitchen knives and fluff brushes. And everywhere are the spotty, slovenly security guards, whose truncheons and arrogance lend a whiff of adventure to even the most prosaic shopping expedition.

Praguers themselves have so far adapted well to the changes. However, for every man or woman you see proudly lugging home the family's first video are several others for whom economic liberalization is bringing an often terrifying uncertainty. For the working housewives, the old and the infirm, forced to hunt an ever-shrinking number of bargains, the queues are getting no shorter; and if inflation spirals out of control they are the ones who will hurt most.

But despite the problems, all but the very poor and the very conservative would agree that so far, the changes wrought since the 1989 revolution have been for the better. Shops that once formed grim units of mammoth chains called things like 'Meat', 'Tobacco' and 'Fruit-Vegetable' now offer a broad variety of goods, including many home-produced items that are widely available for the first time thanks to improvements in the elephantine distribution network. Perhaps most importantly, the shortages once caused by centralized production are over. Never again should Praguers have to go through crises such as that of November 1989, when, with the Velvet Revolution at its height, the country's three largest toilet-paper factories seized up— leading, according to legend, to the largest-ever sales of the Communist Party daily, *Rudé právo*.

Nevertheless, there are still a few relics from the past which may puzzle you. The reflex of joining a queue just in case it leads to anything interesting still manifests itself on occasion; similarly, if you gaze into any shop window for some time you will usually attract a small knot of curious companions. In several places, you aren't allowed to enter without a basket (for which there is usually a queue). The fear isn't that you will pocket a pot of yoghurt, but that the number of people in the store would otherwise reach critical mass. Another time-honoured tradition is that you often order your goods in one place, pay in another and collect your carefully-wrapped purchases in a third. There are generally queues at all three spots. Finally, you can still expect a rather startling level of rudeness in most shops. Enquiries are usually met by abrupt gestures of disinterest, and supplementary questions will generally elicit sarcasm, incredulous pity, or mild abuse.

Shopping Hours

Standard shopping hours are 9–6 pm on weekdays, and 9–1 pm on Saturdays. Food stores reflect the early working day of many Praguers and usually open at 6 am. Many private shops are now staying open later and opening on Sundays, but on the other hand, hundreds of the capital's shops, offices and businesses still take an extended lunch-break at any time between midday and 2 pm. Quite how the siesta made it to Prague is intriguing, but if you don't have time to mull it over, head for a shop marked 'Nonstop'. Despite their go-getting name, Nonstop shops generally do little more than skip lunch, but there are now several useful late-night food shops. The small grocery at Spálená 37 stays open until midnight, and the larger Vacek Bio-Market at Mostecká 3 is open from Mon–Sat 6.30 am–10 pm and Sun 10–10 pm. There's a real non-stop shop at Roháčova 38 in Žižkov. Set in an urban wilderness, it's a bright oasis of coffee, ice-cream and potato salad, and a useful destination when the midnight munchies take hold.

Some of the best stops for any shopping spree are listed below. Those places that take credit cards are marked as follows: AE = American Express, DC = Diners Club, MC = Mastercard/Eurocard/Access, V = Visa.

Antique and Junk Stores

The years since 1989 have seen a huge increase in the amount of curiosities and antiques available for sale. They are often the knick-knacks and heirlooms of financially hard-pressed families, but there are sometimes even less pleasant forces at work. A wave of low-level looting has been stripping provincial churches and graveyards of their unguarded paintings and statuary, and an identifiable amount finds its way to Prague's antique stores. If you're tempted by a fishy object, you should ask about its provenance and remember that you're expected to declare anything that costs you over 500 crowns.

Antik Schwarz, Betlémské nám. 11. *Mon–Fri 10–1, 2–5.* A small selection of junky knick-knacks. Clocks, violins and costume jewellery.

Antiqua, Panská 1. *Mon–Fri 10–6, Sat 10–2.* Not cheap, but a real curiosity shop. Cigarette cases, clocks and watches, tea cups and cut glass, some lovely furniture, a rocking horse and a shabby spinning wheel.

Bazar, Blanická 12. *Mon–Thurs 9–6, Fri 9–5.* General junk, with some particularly attractive if battered furniture.

Eduard Čapek, Dlouhá 32. *Mon–Fri 10–6.* The granddaddy of all Prague's junk stores: this private firm survived 40 years of Communism in an enchanted house under the Týn Church, only to be moved to the present premises after 1989. Springs, wires and ratchets dangle from every corner, and although you occasionally find an attractive candlestick or lamp, the best reason to come here is to marvel at the fact that Praguers find a use for it all.

Hodinářství Václav Matouš, Mikulandská 10. *Mon–Fri 9–5.* Clocks in all shapes and sizes, from grandfathers to cuckoos. V.

Military Antiquities, Charvátova 11. *10–6.* A collection of Communist and Nazi memorabilia, military bayonets and sheath knives, some deactivated explosives and a small collection of knuckledusters.

Starožitnosti, Kaprova 12. *10–6.* A pricy and extremely tasteful set of watches, clocks, pewter, old marionettes and excellent Art Nouveau and Art Deco glassware. AE, MC, V.

Rudolf Špičák, Ostrovní 24. *Mon–Fri 9–6 pm, Sat 9–5 pm.* Three underground rooms of junk including busts, piles of plates, glass and crystal, and oddities such as moose skulls.

Vadamo Galerie, Na příkopě 23. *Mon–Fri 10–12, 1–6, Sat 10–4.* Contains some extraordinary Baroque statues and religious artefacts, and old Czech paintings that are rarely interesting and often terrible. Also sells watches, jewellery and turn-of-the-century Viennese arts and crafts. The price tags here are more frightening than in any other shop listed. AE, MC, V.

Arms and Ammunition

Brymová, Staroměstské nám. 8. *Mon–Fri 9–6, Sat 10–2.* Weapons are unlikely to be high on your shopping list, but it's worth visiting this shop—on the edge of the Old Town Square—just to see what the free market is bringing to the Wild East. Pimply adolescents come here and sweat in front of gleaming pistols, machetes and shotguns, while furtive survivalists dash in to replenish their stocks of CS gas. Serious self-defence enthusiasts can also buy ski-masks and 40,000-volt cattle prods. AE, MC, V.

Books

Reading is a national pastime. The government, and a fair number of proud Praguers, used to recite sales statistics showing that Czechs read twice as much/quickly as the rest of Europe. The achievement was always a questionable one, given that much officially-available literature was dross, and recent years have shown that given a choice Czechs will happily sink to the lowest common denominator. Science-fiction and westerns are perennial favourites, while translated accounts of out-of-body experiences and the like can set the capital alight. That said, an honourable minority of true bibliophiles remain. They can often be found in the innumerable second-hand bookstores (*antikvariát*) that have sprung up since 1989, which can be useful places to pick up cheap prints, English prewar curiosities and a potboiler for the trip home. The following shops are the most interesting for English-speakers.

Akademické knihkupectví, Národní 9. *Mon 1–6, Tues–Fri 10–6, Sat 9–2, Sun 12–5.* Contains a branch of London's Collets Bookshop, and a selection of dictionaries, reference books and paperback fiction. Prices are slightly more expensive than in the UK.

Antikvariát Galerie Můstek, 28. října 13. *Mon–Fri 10–6, Sat 10–2.* A wide selection of old books and prints, with a particularly impressive map collection.

Antikvariát Karel Křenek, Celetná 31. *Mon–Fri 9–5.* Specializes in history, philosophy and art books and prints.

Antikvariát 'U Karlova Mostu', Karlova 2. *Mon–Fri 10–6, Sat 11–4.* One of the best antiquarian bookstores in the capital, selling old Hebrew texts, a broad range of prints, a regular supply of turn-of-the-century Baedekers and much else besides. As you might expect, you pay through the nose. AE, MC, V.

Knihkupectví Melantrich, Na příkopě 5. *Mon–Fri 8.30–8, Sat–Sun 8.30–6.* Centrally located and a useful source of guidebooks, maps and coffee-table albums.

PNS Noviny-Časopisy, Na příkopě 22. *Mon–Fri 7.30–6, Sat 8–1.* The best newsagent in town. Even if you don't understand a word of Czech, a browse through the scores of titles here gives a glimpse into the obsessions and tastes of Prague's reading public: choose from pulp fiction, grainy magazines of 'erotic humour', publications for dog- and fish-breeders, weird political tracts, and virtually any other periodical published in the country.

Regula Pragensis, Jilská 14. *Mon–Sat 10–6*. Handles a range of philosophical and sociological works, both old and new and often in English. Run by a fraternity of intense but hedonistic anarchists.

Zahraniční literatura, in the Philosophy Faculty at nám. Jana Palacha 2. *Mon–Fri 9–5*. Carries a broad range of English paperbacks at prices equivalent to those in the US and significantly lower than in the UK. Also sells Czech language courses and a number of cultural magazines.

Clothes

Modes Robes, Benediktská 5. *Mon–Fri 10–7, Sat 10–4 (summer) 10–2 (winter)*. A small and trendy women's clothes store, with coffee bar and stained-glass window, that slips into the style continuum somewhere between Portobello and SoHo. Sells clothes designed by its two owners, pitched at the younger woman, and bought by some of the most beautiful people in town.

A + G Flora, Přemyslovská 29. *Mon–Fri 10–7, Sat 9–1*. Run by one of Prague's best-known designers, whose clothes are often described as 'flamboyant' by awestruck citizens; in fact, they are often as well-cut and demure as any diplomat could desire. Linen, silk and Japanese are the coming thing in Prague, apparently, and there is a small menswear collection. About 200 Czech designers supply this store with accessories, jewellery, graphics, glass-work, ceramics, photography and toys. AE, DC, MC, V.

Bat'a, Václavské nám. 6. *Mon–Fri 8.30–7, Sat 9–4*. The Bat'a shoe is now part of the furniture in India and many other parts of the developing world, but it only returned to its homeland when properties confiscated from the millionaire family were handed back after the revolution. This shop reopened in March 1992. When built in 1928, the use of glass (and little else) on its façade made the building one of the most innovative examples of Constructivist architecture in Europe, and if you take in the view from the 6th floor you'll sense why. You could even buy a shoe. AE.

Crystal, Porcelain and Jewellery

Bohemian crystal is said to be among the finest in the world. Praguers capitalize on its reputation by producing huge amounts of cut glass. If you are in any doubt, take the suspect article and drop it. Crystal usually bounces.

Bijoux de Bohème, Michalská 11. *Daily 10–7.* Sells nothing genuine at all, but has an excellent collection of cheap costume jewellery. AE.

Dana, Národní 43. *Mon–Fri 9–7, Sat 9–6, Sun 11–6.* Perhaps the widest selection of crystal and coloured glass in the capital, and a substantial amount of porcelain as well. Come here to find what's available and then buy it for a cheaper price somewhere else. MC, V.

Karlovarský porcelán, Pařížská 2. *Mon–Fri 10–7, Sat 10–5, Sun 10–2.* Specializes in the highly-regarded porcelain produced in Karlovy Vary, and if you're after a figurine or soup tureen, this is the place to come. AE, DC, MC, V.

Luna, Na příkopě 16. *Mon–Fri 9–7, Sat 9–4.* Contains some attractive glass and crystal but is most noteworthy for its chandeliers, some of which are truly monstrous. AE.

Sklo-Svítidla, Kozí 9. *Daily 10–6.* One of the best places in central Prague to buy cheap and unfussy crystal and galss. AE, MC, V.

Department Stores

Prague's department stores are in a state of flux. Western investors—notably K-Mart—have been sniffing around and dumping goods on them, and in many departments it is now near impossible to find Czech products. All stores are jockeying for position in a battle for Prague's hearts and wallets, and consumerism, Czech style, is on full display in each of the following.

Bílá labut', (White Swan) on Na poříčí 23. *Mon–Fri 8–7, Sat 8–4.* Cheap and cheerless. However it's the store that's most likely to sell Czech items, and a useful stop if you need something functional and cheap. It's also a convenient place to hunt down what remains of command-economy kitsch.

Krone, Václavské nám. 21. *Mon–Fri 9 am–10 pm, Sat 9–7, Sun 11–6.* For anyone who believes that German workmanship is the best in the world.

Kotva, nám. Republiky 8. *Mon–Wed, Fri 8–7, Thurs 8–8, Sat 8–6.* Likes to think of itself as the Harrods of Prague, and sells an unnecessarily large amount of imports. AE, MC, V.

Máj, Národní 26. *Mon 9–7, Tues, Wed and Fri 8–7, Thurs 8–8, Sat 8–4.* Owned by K-Mart, and the best mid-range store in the capital. Riding the open-plan escalators and the horseys on the ground floor adds to the fun.

Food

Fruits de France, Jindřišská 9. *Mon–Fri 9.30–6.30, Sat 9.30–1.* A superb collection of imported fruit and veg, with some specimens that will flummox all but the best-travelled connoisseur. If you're cooking to seduce, the cheeses, wild mushrooms, condiments and oils here are prerequisites, and there's an excellent wine selection. As well as imported marks, the shop sells bottles from its own vineyards in Moravia: try the excellent Ryzlink.

J. & J. Mašek Zemanová, Karmelitská 30. *Mon–Fri 7–6, Sat 7–5, Sun 11–5.* Sumptuous delicatessen selling poultry and a magnificent selection of creatures of the deep, including smoked salmon steaks, caviare, glistening crustaceans and cooked fish ranging from sprats to sharkfins. Also carries a range of salads and wines. Another essential stop for a stylish picnic.

Obchod čerstvých uzenin, Václavské nám. 36. *Mon–Fri 7.30–7, Sat 8–6, Sun 10–4.30.* The place to pick up a piece of meat. A huge variety of suspended and shelved salamis, sausages and internal organs.

Fur and Leather

Kožešiny, Karlova 11. *Mon–Fri 10–7, Sat 10–1, 2–6, Sun 10–1, 2–5.* The place to come if you love leather and just don't care. No reluctant concessions to animal liberators here: the shop is a joyful mortuary of stoles, pelts, leather jackets and caps, and in case anyone misses the point, there's a stuffed fox sitting dolefully in the window. Its neighbouring sister shop, the **Kožešnictví**, is more restrained, limiting itself to a collection of leather gloves and an attractive selection of (inorganic) hats. AE, MC, V.

Galleries

Other than the places listed below, there are now countless galleries and studios exhibiting and selling the work of contemporary artists. Two with particularly strong reputations are the **Galerie MXM**, hidden in the Baroque courtyard at Nosticova 6, ℂ 53 15 64 (*Tues–Sun 12–7*), and the **Galerie Behémót** on Elišky Krásnohorské 6, ℂ 231 78 29 (*10–6*).

Antikvariát, Celetná 31. *Mon–Fri 10–12, 2–6, Sat 10–2.* An attractive collection of paintings, drawings and sketches from *c.* 1890–1945. Work by many major Czech artists of the period passes through, including manifestoes and work produced by the Devětsil group (*see* pp. 79–83).

Galerie Pallas, Náprstkova 10. *Mon–Sat 10–6.* A superb gallery, as spacious and well laid out as a small museum, and containing a remarkable selection of paintings by all the major Czech artists of the 20th century. It's rather upsetting to think that almost all will be bought up by rich foreigners, but that can only partially dilute the pleasure that this place gives.

Galerie Peithner-Lichtenfels, Michalská 12, tel/fax 26 14 24. *Daily 10–7.* Not as grand as the Pallas, but contains a large collection of work by the second division of 20th-century Czech artists. Under the Gothic vault of the attractive gallery, you'll also find scores of smaller sketches and pictures, useful for presents (albeit fairly expensive ones), and there are hundreds of unframed works to leaf through. The gallery also contains some notable sculpture, particularly modern glasswork. AE, MC, V.

Jednorožec s harfou (Unicorn with a Harp), Bartolomějská 13/Průchozí 4. *Daily 11 am–12 midnight.* A small gallery displaying drawings, paintings and sculpture by mentally and physically handicapped people. The work ranges from airbrushed junk to sometimes disturbing scratched and paint-spattered etchings. The space is fully accessible to wheelchair users and includes a small and popular café.

Středoevropská galerie a nakladadelství (Central European Gallery and Publishing House), Husova 19. *Daily 10–7.* A wide selection of graphic art. AE, MC, V.

Markets

After 40 years of hibernation, Prague's markets are coming alive again. The most central, and one with a centuries-old tradition, is on Havelská. One of its most attractive features is how unorientated towards tourists it is, and although wandering around is great fun, you're unlikely to be tempted by the toilet paper and toothpaste bargains on offer. However, it's a good place to eat fruit and vegetables and smell herbs and spices. There's another market at Bubenské nábř. (Vltavská metro—line C), an odd collection of liquor stands, flower stalls, DIY halls and Ukrainians with pots of caviare, but Prague's most exciting outdoor sale is held on Saturday and Sunday mornings at the Sparta football stadium on Milady Horákové. It's the best market for battered telephones, trainsets and other cheap junk, but the atmosphere is what makes a visit here most memorable. Poles, Vietnamese and Czechs mingle easily among stalls selling leather, dodgy videos, plasticware, and gas canisters; Prague marketing patter, unheard for four decades, rings out under the stadium stands; and marching through it all are phalanxes of skinheads, looking for trouble to kill time before the match starts.

Motor Vehicles

Okase Auto-Moto-Bazar, Argentinská ul. *Mon–Thurs 8–5, Fri 8–3, Sat 9–3.* One of Europe's more unusual second-hand car markets. Among the Škodas, you'll find decommissioned tanks and armoured personnel carriers, howitzers, fire engines, and a couple of engine-less MiG 50 and 55s from the Korean war. Everything is for sale, but the owner regrets that he's unable to arrange export licences.

Music

Classical records and compact discs are cheap and usually well recorded. You can always try before you buy.

Karel Schuss CD-LP, Kožná 12. *Mon–Fri 10–6.* A wide selection of pop CDs, and several thousand second-hand records. The latter include a particularly cheesy selection of works by Karel Gott, Prague's triumphant answer to Cliff Richard and Engelbert Humperdinck, and hundreds of records from the 1950s and 1960s, with titles like 'Music of the Bullring' and 'Acapulco says— "Let's Tango!".'

Popron, Jungmannova 30. *Mon–Fri 9.30–7.30, Sat 9.30–7, Sun 10–6.* Pop and dance in all forms, in all formats.

Studio Matouš, Goltz-Kinský Palace, Staroměstské nám. 12. *Daily 10.30–6.* The broadest selection of classical CDs in Prague. No records. AE, MC, V.

Supraphon, Jungmannova 20. *Mon–Fri 9–6, Sat 9–1.* A sizeable collection of classical records and CDs.

Photographic Supplies

Fotoantique, Pařížská 12. *Tues–Fri 10–6, Sat 9–2.* Leicas, Zeniths, old bellows and black boxes, as well as photography books and some beautiful postcards.

Foto-Kino-Optika-Video, Lazarská 6. *Mon–Fri 8.30–12, 2–6.* As the name implies, this place sells anything that goes click, or whirr, along with photographic accessories from filters to Ilford.

Toys

Dřevěné Hracky (Wooden Toys), Karlova 26. *Mon–Sat 10–8.30, Sun 10–8 (an hour earlier in winter).* Wooden toys are sold all over Prague, but the baskets and shelves of this shop contain one of the widest selections: horses to rock and ride a cock on, abacuses, telephones, trolleys and snakes, and an aerial collection of dangling birds. AE, MC, V.

Obchod Loutkami, Nerudova 47. *Mon–Fri 10–7, Sat–Sun 9–7.* Hand and finger puppets and a nightmare-inducing range of tufted, grinning and contorted marionettes. Not a place to get locked into after closing time. AE, V.

Sports and Activities

Over the last century, Praguers have shown a rather unhealthy attachment to mass-mobilization in the name of sport. Until 1989 the quinquennial highlight of the sporting calendar was a celebration of beauty and youth organized by the Communists, and known as the *Spartakiáda*. Every five years, 160,000 identical gymnasts would perform feats of co-ordinated kitsch in the capital's Strahov stadium, watched by 220,000 awe-struck spectators. Very few Praguers will admit it now, but being selected as a cog in the machine was regarded by many as a great honour, and the festival was only the successor to the even more popular *Sokol* movement, founded in 1862 and devoted to celebrating the physical glory of the Czech race. However, the capital may have finally lost its fascination with sporting crowds and power. The plug was pulled on the June 1990 *Spartakiáda*, and any lingering traces of beauty and youth evaporated two months later when Mick Jagger and Keith Richards strutted the Strahov stage.

Propaganda rallies apart, Praguers have rather sedate sporting habits. There are no queer games to speak of, and although a Sparta v. Slavia soccer match will arouse the passions of the man on the Žižkov omnibus, the interests of most reasonable-minded folk stretch not much further than ice-hockey, skiing and tennis. However, people keep in trim and the city is dotted with community leisure centres and sporting complexes. The most luxurious is on the 25th floor of the Hotel Forum, where you can spend the afternoon drifting between gym, pool, sauna and beauty parlour, and emerge ready to tackle even the most strenuous social engagement.

If you forget your tools, or are bitten by the bug while in Prague, sports goods can be bought at the Dům sportu on Jungmannova 28 (Mon–Fri 8.30–7, Sat 8.30–1), or Pragoimpo at Václavské nám. 28 (Mon–Fri 10–6). There's a repair service at Temposervis on Rybná 3 in case your skis crack or your strings snap (Mon 12–4.30, Tues and Thurs 9–4.30, Fri 9–3).

Boating

Rowing boats can be hired during the summer from several spots along the river, including Žofín (a.k.a. Slovanský ostrov), the island near the National Theatre. The Vltava's sluices and gurgling rapids lock you into a small section of the river, but floating in the sun is a rather matchless way of whiling away a dog day in Prague. A passport is required as a deposit, although the attendant can sometimes be hoodwinked with a library card. During the summer, boat parties regularly set sail from the quays near Palackého most (Palacký Bridge), and most Svatopluk Čecha (Svatopluk Čech Bridge). Be clear about what you're embarking upon before buying a ticket. Cruises have been known to last up to seven hours, which is usually enough to tame even the wildest party animal.

Bowling

The best place to have a bowl in Prague is the Hotel Forum, but the fun's limited. The alley appeals particularly to roisterous coach parties and gangs of bored businessmen letting their cufflinks down for an evening. It sells ten types of beer, which is over twice the number of lanes.

Football

Prague has four soccer teams—Sparta, Slavia, Bohemians and Dukla—but unless you are an underdog-lover, only the first two are of real interest. The season's Sparta-Slavia match is football as any Englander would recognize it: obscene chants, fireworks lobbed at the goalies, and regular invasions of the stands by riot officers. Sparta fans in particular revel in their reputation as ruffians. Unlike their western counterparts, who occasionally confound expectations by giving up seats to pensioners and the like, Sparta's most loyal troops are unreconstructed neo-fascist hooligans. You can see them in action most weekends at Letná Stadium: even if the team's not playing, gangs usually turn up to the morning market (*see* p. 345) to buy tear gas and discuss the game plan. If you fancy some footer yourself, an ex-pat league is organized at the British Embassy by one Sergeant Spinks.

Gambling

Since the 1989 revolution, Lady Luck has been abroad in Prague. Street vendors sell instant-lose lottery tickets to scratching citizens across the capital, and slot machines are doing their bit to kill the art of drunken conversation in almost every one of the city's *pivnices*. Casinos can be found in all the smarter hotels, and at the Fortuna betting shop in the Lucerna passage (Václavské nám. 38) you can have a flutter on virtually any sporting fixture in Europe. Unfortunately, Prague's most spectacular game of chance—its mass coupon privatization—is inaccessible to foreigners.

Golf

If you've come to Prague to putt, you are probably already booked into the capital's only green, at the Motel Golf (*see* p. 320). An exclusive club with an 18-hole course is soon to open near Karlštejn; further information is available at Na příkopě 20, © 26 40 18.

Healing, Holistic Therapy, Sauna and Massage

Innumerable healing centres have appeared in Prague since the Velvet Revolution, bringing to the city all manner of unorthodox treatments. One of the best-equipped places is the Natur Centrum at Dukelských hrdinů 7, © 37 37 91, which has even imported a man from China experienced in acupuncture, massage and acupressure techniques. Advanced sufferers of New Age syndrome can also dabble with hypnotherapy, laser-guided cosmetic surgery and something called auriculodiagnostics. The Fit Centrum Dlabačov on Bílohorská 24 has a sauna (*women only from 1–2.30 pm, men from 2.30–4 pm and mixing between 4 and 9 pm*), and between 8 am and 9 pm you can also enjoy a massage, sunbed, or even a spot of myostimulation.

Horsey Sports

The city's racecourse is at Velká Chuchle, a 15-minute bus journey from Smíchovské nádraží metro station on line B (Nos. 129, 172, 241, 243 or 245). Steeplechases and hurdle-races hammer the turf on Sunday afternoons from May–Oct, and there are trots all year round on Thursdays. The cruellest steeplechase in the world is held in early October in the town of Pardubice, some 90 km due east of Prague. At just under 7 kilometres in length, it finishes off a fair proportion of its equine contestants each year. As a result, it has begun to attract the attentions of radical vegetarians, who (along with most of Prague's journalists) were beaten up by the local police in 1992. The incident caused a national scandal, and although the animalists have wheeled in a wonder weapon—Brigitte Bardot at the head of a boycott—the race is likely to be the scene of running battles for some years to come. If all that you want is a canter, those who know recommend the riding school at Lišnice (© 0305 92785).

Ice-skating

There are ice-skating rinks at the Exhibition Park (Výstaviště) and Štvanice island, both in Prague 7. Czechs are fierce puckers, having reached the ice-hockey world championships on several occasions, and exciting international matches are often held at the Výstaviště.

Mushroom-picking

Czechs have a fascination with fungi—so much so that five, on average, die each year as a result of eating the wrong ones. If you like to live on the edge, the countryside around Prague is a fine area for mushroom-picking. The wooded hills that stretch from Karlštejn to Křivoklát castles contain scores of edible varieties, and the grasslands around Telč are said to harbour some particularly interesting specimens. Avoid the fate of the five Czechs by taking your 'shrooms to the Československá mykologická stanice (Czechoslovakian [sic] Mycological Station) at Karmelitská 14, © 53 26 93 (*Mon–Tues 8–2, 3–5, Thurs 8–12 noon*). For a small fee (currently two crowns per mushroom), the staff will name your fungus and warn you if eating it would, for example, lead to vivid hallucinations.

Snow Sports

It's fashionable to head out of Prague with your skis in the winter. Slopy pistes can be found at Špindlerův Mlýn, Harrachov and Pec pod Sněžkou, in the Krkonoše mountains east of Liberec near the Polish border. However, you needn't always go so far to have a slide: after a major snowfall, more intrepid Praguers go cross-country skiing through the wider streets, and hundreds of toboggans emerge from the city's cupboards. If you want to join in, equipment is available from both the shops mentioned above.

Squash

Prague's only squash courts are at the Hotel Forum and the Club-Hotel Průhonice (*see* p. 318 and p. 320). An ex-pat league is run by tireless Sergeant Spinks at the British Embassy.

Swimming

There are 25-metre pools in the centre of town at the Hotel Atrium, and at the YMCA on Na poříčí 12, both with attached saunas. At the Exhibition Park (Vystaviště) you can also get a steam bath and a massage (*Tues, Thurs, Fri 3–8, Wed 3–6, Sat and Sun 10–6*). Prague has a 50-metre pool at Podolská 74, but it's a murky affair which has been known to cause gastric rebellions and unusual rashes. Even more suspicious effluents than usual are available at Prague's oldest pool, a neo-classical palace of rickety planks dating from 1840 on the Malá Strana side of the Svatopluk Čech Bridge (*May–Sept*). A section of the foaming Vltava is cordoned off here, and you're invited to float among the cyanides, isotopes and heavy metals. Few of those who come here to sunbathe take up the challenge, but swimming backstroke under the castle and the Charles Bridge certainly *looks* relaxing. Open-air decontamination showers are provided. Good clean fun is to be had at the Šeberák lake in Prague 4, near K Šeberáku, where everyone takes their clothes off. Finally the lake in Šárka park (along Evropská on the way to the airport) is a time-honoured spot for Praguers to go skinny-dipping on steamy summer evenings. Bring wine, blankets, friends and a torch.

Tennis

There are courts peppered across Prague's suburbs, but you'll cause a commotion if you try to get onto one and don't speak Czech. To avoid problems, call 231 12 70 and book one of the tourist courts on Štvanice island in Prague 7. There are also courts on Letná, which you can sometimes reserve (© 37 36 83).

Watersports

Prague is short on coastline, but it's got a very big dam at Slapy, 30 km upstream on the Vltava. Standing over the mammoth concave slope of concrete that separates the two water levels is a thrill in itself, and waterskiing and windsurfing are possible. To get there, catch the signs on the Strakonická highway, which runs south along the river.

If you are looking to abandon your child, you couldn't pick a better city than Prague. Musicians, puppet-shows and jugglers turn the streets into a perpetual playground during the summer; it's still remarkably safe; and should you succumb to remorse, the city's inexplicable way of engineering unexpected meetings would quickly throw you back into each other's arms. Even if you're the responsible type, there are still endless ways to keep the brats from insisting that life was more fun at home.

Maps and (Czech) money are useful ways of drumming up interest before you leave; Good King Wenceslas is another limited way of introducing the country to younger children. There's an easily readable collection of national legends available in English: *Old Czech Legends* by Alois Jirásek, published by Forest Books. Over the years, the country's much-renowned animators have also produced an impressive body of childrens' cartoons (which are sometimes shown at London's National Film Theatre). When packing for a baby, don't go overboard with the nappies; they are now widely available in the city. However, once in the city *do* worry about the water: even the government accepts that it is unsafe for toddlers (although it quibbles about how toddly), and to be on the safe side, all those under 18 months should only drink from cartons of still water (*see* p. 368).

Children's Prague

Sightseeing with children is no problem. The hourly mechanics of the **Astronomical Clock** are a thing of endless fascination to most children, and **tower-climbing** is a game that the city caters for well. You can even have fun on the move. **Trams** can be mightily impressive to someone small who's never seen the beasts before; **horse-drawn buggies** and **rowboats** on the river are less useful as means of transport, but just as good if your child has learnt to walk and had enough already.

All ages will appreciate the **National Technical Museum**, with its clocks and cameras, button-induced noises, and the hundreds of wings and wheels in its transport exhibition. The long tour through the massive coal mine in the basement is a particular adventure, with all the boys sent off on a mysterious Lord-of-the-Flies type mission half-way through the epic journey. (The guide, an ageing team-leader type, lets particularly plucky girls go too.) Significantly less anarchistic is the **Police Museum**, which shows films to teach children how to want to be police officers when they grow up, and has a number of other kiddy-orientated displays. Little Big Brothers will particularly enjoy the bank of closed-circuit TV screens, which enable them to keep tabs on their fellow infants throughout. Best of all is the small electric model car-racing set, intended to help youngsters develop road-safety skills and almost certainly entirely counter-productive.

The funfair and dinky seaside-pier architecture of the Výstaviště (**Exhibition Park**) is filled with a mass of pleasure-inducing marvels including a funfair, planetarium and adventure playground. Up on Letná Park, just outside the National Technical Museum, is a **carousel** (open all year round, weather permitting), and if there's a **circus** in town, it will almost certainly have pitched up on nearby Letná Plain. You or your offspring would have to be beastly to go to Prague's cruel zoo; but there's another set of attractions on Petřín Hill. The **funicular** to the top is a thrill in itself, and at the summit is a **planetarium** and a **mirror maze**.

Several of the city's theatres cater for children, most reliably the **Divadlo Minor** on nám. Maxima Gorkého/Senovážné nám. 28. That puts on marionette shows from Mon–Fri, generally pitched at the 4–5-year-old audience but occasionally serving up early adolescent material. You'll find full listings in *Program* (*see* p. 36), in the theatre section under the heading *pro děti* (for children).

Finally, when you've had enough and want to go on an adult romp through town, you could call the **YMCA** for help. The group is planning to set up a playgroup, and possibly a baby-sitting service in late 1993. Call 287 22 20 or 287 20 91 for further information. Otherwise, the British or US Embassy just may be able to put you in touch with trusty sitters.

Living and Working in Prague

Setting up home in Prague is a prospect that flits through the minds of most visitors. The city inspires dreams, and gives pause to all those who have ever believed that their true destiny is to run a samba-café and write a novella. Amazingly enough, some of the schemes actually come true. Immigration has been boosted further by a barrage of media coverage in the United States portraying Prague as a Paris of the 1920s for the 1990s. Many bright-eyed arrivals, often fresh out of college, come convinced that there is a new Hemingway wandering the city and spend their first months thrusting their hands out to artistic types, or sidling up to strangers in the hope of finally rubbing shoulders with him. Coexisting happily with everyone else are the hard-nosed fellows with suits, who daily draft contracts and liquidate enterprises for the many multinationals that have moved in since 1989. In total, the number of English-speaking resident foreigners now runs into tens of thousands, and an entire ex-pat culture has grown up around them. That can sometimes be just as unpleasant as it sounds, and there are many who have spent a year Prague-side without making a single Czech friend—but that said, life in the Czech capital now has a tremendous vitality and informality that's missing in the staid cities of the west. The city's movers and shakers—Czech and foreign—are a decade or more younger than their western equivalents, and generations more accessible. As a result, the city has become a teeming hothouse of hobos, misfits, yuppies and Bohemians. Strange fruits are already emerging. Even if the new Hemingway is proving elusive, Prague may soon have one of the highest concentrations of piano-playing bankers, busking journalists and nightclub-crawling lawyers in the world.

Getting Ready

The ex-pat community has two gossip sheets—the *Prague Post* and *Prognosis*—which are a useful introduction to the mood of the city. Before leaving home, you could take out a subscription, or better still wangle some free back-issues, at the following addresses:

Prague Post–Politických vězňů 9, 110 00 Praha-1, © 235 94 55, fax 26 51 86.

Prognosis–Africká 17, 160 00 Praha-6, © 316 70 07, fax 36 81 39.

The *Prague Post* is a news-orientated weekly broadsheet and *Prognosis* is a chattier bi-monthly. *Prognosis* usually makes for a more interesting read, although both papers have a similar and rather charming breathlessness about them. Their classified columns are sparse, but it's just possible that they could land you a job or apartment before your arrival.

Form-filling

Ever since the collapse of the totalitarian house of cards in 1989, a largely benign anarchy has been sweeping through the Czech Republic's official institutions; and trying to glean information about the law can be even more perplexing than before. Few can be sure about which directives have been overruled, which amended and which clarified, and you should expect a long haul through the labyrinth before you become legal. The pleasant flipside is that no one really cares what you get up to, and most police stations will regard you with amazement if you turn yourself in at the required times.

In a nutshell the rules are as follows. You change from a normal visitor to a long-stayer after **three months**, and by then you ought to have regularized your position. You may only stay longer if you have a work permit, for which you'll need your employer's help and a form from the Úřad práce at Zborovská 11. You should then cajole the owner of your flat to accompany you to the local State Notary (let him or her find out where it lives) and solemnly swear that you do indeed live where you claim to live. Within **six months**, you should have also obtained a long-stay permit. *That* requires the work permit, the notarized statement, any marriage certificates you might have accumulated, three passport photos, a clean bill of health and a mass of entirely useless information such as the occupations of your children and the employers of your siblings. Take all that to your local police station, let them sit on it for about a month, and you should emerge legally resident in the Czech Republic. If it all sounds too hellish, you could follow the example of many ex-pats and avoid the issue entirely by leaving the country for a few days at three-monthly intervals. Even more people do absolutely nothing and seem none the worse for it. Unfortunately, that is strictly illegal.

More generally, you should beware of the tremendous bureaucracy that still survives throughout the Czech Republic. Triplication is a national hobby, and obfuscation remains to the ex-Warsaw Pact what rhetoric was to ancient Greece. At the same time, liberalization has brought about a tremendous increase in the responsibilities borne by individuals, and it's easy to fall foul of officialdom simply because you had no idea what was expected of you. The tax system is a particular nightmare: often almost incomprehensible and yet enforced by monstrous fines.

Finding a Job

With the country teetering between boom and crash, the jobs of most people in the Czech Republic are unenviably insecure. However Prague is always going to have it better, thanks to its perennial investors and tourists, and somewhat surprisingly, English-speaking foreigners are among those who have it best of all. Thousands of merchant bankers and attorneys now roam the capital, and many others find work in its various foreign-run clubs and cafés. If you are would rather work with the natives you could give English lessons, for which there is an almost inexhaustible demand among young Czechs. Many of the bigger language schools now require a TEFL qualification, but it's easy to freelance. However, people are quick to spot a charlatan, and if you are going to go it alone, brush up on your grammar and bring some interesting materials. A final alternative is to make your money by entertaining people. With millions of tourists each month and a long tradition of street fun, it doesn't take much to fill a hat with cash in Prague. If you are a fire-eating unicyclist you'll make a mint, and even those with fewer skills can eke out a happy summer by using an instrument with imagination.

Enthusiasm and audacity are always essential to a successful job-search, but in Prague the rule is amplified by the fact that few people are yet very sure where the real talent and authority lie. Take advantage of the confusion by contacting people directly and presenting CVs personally. Most embassies can provide a list of companies from their countries that are operating in Prague. If your skill is teaching English, make preliminary enquiries at the larger schools in your home country, and get a list of contacts at colleges in Prague. The noticeboards in the foreign ghettos can also be useful sources of information, particularly that at Laundry Kings (*see* p. 34) Finally, laid-back types could just go to a café and consider their options; Prague is a city where it's actually true for once that something will always turn up.

Finding a Flat

Everyone has accommodation problems in Prague. Years of neglect mean that much of the capital's state-owned housing stock is uninhabitable, and until a much-debated privatization bill gets through parliament, the incentives for tenants to improve their properties remain minimal. A related issue is the conflict between the *restituce* law, under which most confiscated buildings have been returned to their pre-Communist owners, and the powerful legal protection that tenants still enjoy under unrepealed—and rather popular—Communist legislation. As a result, no one really knows what the future holds, and if you want any security of tenure at all, you should be sure to sign a contract.

Turmoil is a good time to make money, and Praguers have been cramming together and urgently subletting their vacant spaces to foreigners since 1989. In the absence of a floating property market, rents fluctuate wildly, conditioned only by greed, gullibility and guile on both sides. A studio apartment can cost foreigners anything from £70 ($105) to £600 ($900) a month, depending on size, location and facilities. It used to be easy to sympathize with Prague's sublessors, who performed an important function for limited reward. Nowadays, with embassies and oil conglomerates prepared to scribble any figure onto the accounts, even the humblest *babička* tosses caution to the wind when asked the rent. Let human emotions wither and die for the duration of your flat hunt. The only rule to remember is that it's dog eat dog out there.

You'll probably start with your sights set on a Baroque loft in **Malá Strana**. So will several others, many of them very rich indeed, and most foreigners eventually find somewhere outside the centre. The areas you might consider are **Vinohrady** (central, green, spacious and elegant), the areas around **Flora** and **Želivského** metro stops (slightly further, but very well connected by transport routes), other parts of **Žižkov**, and **Smíchov** (central, smoky, lively and gipsy), **Letná/Holešovice** (another bustling district, close to the best parks in town) and **Dejvice** (currently being puffed as a centre for new businesses, but still typified by the detached residences of the once-Communist dinner-party circuit, and a clutch of embassies).

Most foreigners arrive in the city with a vision of where they are going to stay. The dream pad usually has high ceilings, prewar furniture, bay windows and parquet floors, with a pastel charm that's not been spoiled by recent improvements to the electrical and drainage system. In fact, you should brace yourself for cramped accommodation, lace, cuckoo clock and crockery decoration, and flushes and pipes that regularly freeze or explode. Then you won't be disappointed.

The best place to begin a flat-hunt is in *Annonce*, the capital's largest classified ads paper. It's published thrice weekly (Monday, Wednesday and Friday) in two editions: what you want is the *Podnájmy-Nabídka* section in edition A. Wake up early and start phoning immediately, as anything worth while is snapped up by about 11 am. Property descriptions follow a certain formula, which you'll need to understand. The two numbers separated by a + sign *(e.g.* 1+1, 2+1) refer to the number of rooms plus the number of kitchens; if the letters *k.k.* or *kuchyňský kout* follow the first number, the flat has a stove and sink tucked away in a corner; and an apartment described as a *garsoniera* is a bedsit. Other terms that are often used in the ads are *byt* (flat), *cena dohodou* (price negotiable), *dlouhodobe* (long-term), *pokoj* (room), *valuta* (hard currency), and *zařizeny* (fully-furnished). If a flat has a telephone (*telefon*), you can assume that that will be stated, and if it does not, don't expect to have one connected: most applications take years to reach the point of decision, let alone success. You could even put your own ad into *Annonce* (under the subheading *Poptávka*) by calling in at its offices on Na poříčí 30.

A week of *Annonce* generally produces results, but many an apartment has been found by the alternative tactic of advertising desires on flyers. The posters should be eye-catching, Czech and pithy, and pasted up across your favourite districts and buildings. Put your name and a number on detachable strips; the contact should be a Czech speaker and ideally one with an answering machine. Another possibility is to check the noticeboards and newspapers mentioned above for any offers. One final method of finding a flat, to be used only if desperate, is to contact an estate agent (*realitní kancelář*), and pay him or her an exorbitant commission to sort out your problems.

Business in Prague

The most distinctive feature of capitalism in Prague is the extent to which old ways live on in the brave new world. Many of the Czechs who have adapted fastest to the free market are the same old Communist officials, often distinguishable by tight brown suits, whose eyes bulge and faces sweat as they clinch lucrative deals over the heads of the workers they once claimed to represent. And while every factory manager has had to take a crash course in how to laisser faire since 1989, ideology can still triumph in the form of stock-takes that match inventories perfectly, and prospectuses that bear no relation to economic reality whatsoever. The command economy of yesteryear has also left behind a rickety infrastructure that needs almost total replacement, but which has to be modernized piecemeal if it isn't to collapse. Only the very rich are allowed to have chequebooks; cash is used by everyone else, and at any given moment millions of crowns are hurtling around the city in guarded vans and bags, without which the economy would seize up.

It all makes doing business in the city very different from what you might be used to. You can get a basic picture of who's laying off whom and the like from the Prague-based and pink *Central European Business Weekly*, published from Malešická 16a, 130 69 Praha-3, © 683 01 95, fax 89 45 04. The Lion's Share Group, the holding company that publishes the *Prague Post*, also produces an annual manual on the legal and economic state of Czech capitalism. An invaluable overview of the city's professional life is provided by *Resources*, a directory published from Lazarská 3, ☏ 20 13 25. The loose-leaf folder, updated every three months, provides contact details for major firms, agencies and every government ministry in both Czech and Slovak Republics. Its appearance has dented, but by no means destroyed, another ubiquitous feature of Prague wheeler-dealing—the business card, or *visitka*. With companies rising and falling like waves in a storm, cards are an essential navigational aid for the city's entrepreneurial community. More are traded in Prague than perhaps any other European capital, and you'll soon assemble a thick wodge. If you want to pass yours around, you could hook up with the Business Club on Karlova 21, ☏ 26 57 01; and when the hard work bears fruit you might even want to apply for membership of the Golem Club on Na perštyně 18, ☏ 231 43 33, open to all *koruna* millionaires (subject to clubbable status). Humbler networkers could also consider the golfing opportunities in Prague listed on p. 350, and might want to touch base with the International Commercial Group, ☏ 36 74 47.

Setting up a company is little problem in free-wheeling Prague. The most demanding requirements are that you have a few thousand smackers and employ an officer who is a Czech resident. Should you need any more details, the American Center for Culture and Commerce (*see* Libraries, below) has a collection of translated company laws and plenty of other commercial materials. There are hundreds of shysters who will happily file, deposit and swear the papers concerned. To make sure that you aren't fleeced more than is absolutely necessary, look up 'Lawyers—Commercial' in the Yellow Pages (*see below*) and spend an afternoon phoning around.

One last obstacle, the bane of a thousand small businesses, is the **telephone network**. Lines lie doggo or pop you into someone else's conversation with frustrating regularity, and several thousand Prague office hours each week are spent coaxing telephones into behaving reasonably. If you have the money and the impatience, you may want to invest in a mobile phone: contact Eurotel at Jindřišská 24, ☏ 628 01 12/3. Unfortunately, they aren't the most streamlined objects, weighing in at several pounds and extending feelers and widgets in several directions. Another mild disadvantage (or perhaps, secret bonus) is that if you yomp through town with one under your arm, Praguers will acknowledge them with the nudges, whispered explanations and double-takes that ended in the west several years ago.

Finally, those who would like to do business in Prague but lack the prerequisites can get help at the Business Club (*see above*) or the Hotel Diplomat. Both pride themselves on their collections of yuppy gizmos, and as well as temporary office space they can rent you anything from a flipchart to a fax machine.

Additional Considerations

Other subjects that you may need to consider while living in Prague are:

Animals

Importing beasts to the Czech Republic is a complex matter. When asked for the regulations, the State Vet replied obscurely that disease lay beyond the law, and that there was a world of difference between a horse and a hen. Less enigmatic sources suggest that as a general rule, a certificate of good health should be obtained before arrival for all creatures, and that dogs should have a rabies vaccination certificate that's less than a year but more than a month old. However for better or for worse, it's the gnomic State Vet who has the final say, and you can consult him at Těšnov 17, © 286 24 84. Once in Prague, your animal is expected to report to Bolzanova 1, © 22 60 32. It should be in tip-top shape: the authorities there apparently have draconian powers of confinement and execution if they spot the pox or a suspect slaver. Ill pets can be dealt with at the 24-hour animal health-care service at Šenova 2136, © 292 88 88, near Chodov metro (line C), and your mutt can be groomed at the Yoco Salon on Bělohorská 49, © 35 08 50 (*open Mon–Fri 6–5*).

If you don't have a creature, but want one, check the *Zvířata* section of *Annonce (B)*, where you can find everything from pythons to the lab rats with which to feed them. The columns are also a good place to contemplate Prague's canine fetish. Dogs as small as voles or as large as ponies are both popular, but the capital's runaway favourite is the *jezevčík* or dachshund. It's particularly adored by the city's *babičky* who often walk around with the tubular dogs in their shopping bags. Until 1989, bagging your pet was necessary to take it onto the metro, and the habit has lived on. The city's attitude to cats is a mysterious one: Praguers claim to love them, but you won't see more than a sackful during your entire stay.

Answering Machines

Contrary to rumour, these *do* work in Prague (although they must always be set to '1 minute' rather than 'Vox'). However, connecting one involves a lot of plug-pulling and wire-jiggling. Experimentation is safe but frustrating, and the best policy is to pop down to your local high-technology store and explain your predicament.

Cars

If you have a right-hand-drive car, think carefully before bringing it to Prague. Even assuming that it survives the rollicking journey on the speed-limit-less German autobahns, it may be put out of action for a long time by Czech bureaucracy. Registration of a right-hand-drive car is near impossible, which means that it's neither entitled to Czech third-party insurance nor a resident parking permit, and enjoys a legal status that's shady at best. But if you love your car too much to leave it behind, get extended third-party cover from an insurer at home and buy the following objects: first-aid kit, warning triangle, a complete set of spare light bulbs, mudflaps and left-hand headlamps. It's then just possible that the police at Olšanská 2 will allow it to be registered. At that point, you'll be entitled to Czech insurance, which you can get at Spálená 14. Most western car manufacturers now have sales and service outlets in Prague, and you can get the relevant addresses before leaving home. A good all-purpose servicing centre (with car wash) is Segar on Václavská 18, near Karlovo nám. (*Mon–Fri 7–6, Sat 8–4*).

Crises

There's a 24-hour Samaritan service at the **RIAPS Crisis Centre** (Krizové Centrum) on Chelčického 39, ✆ 27 54 44, 29 64 02. The staff speak English, and accommodate personal callers, who don't have to explain themselves, for up to seven nights. **Drug problems** are better dealt with at another centre, U Apolináře, on Apolinářská 4, ✆ 20 14 70. **Alcoholics Anonymous** now holds meetings in English on Friday from 12–1.30 pm at the YMCA at Na poříčí 12 and on Sunday from 5.30–6.30 pm in the Church of the Sacred Heart in nam. Jiřího z Poděbrad, ✆ 793 05 02.

AIDS is still rare in the Czech Republic. At the end of September 1992, the country contained 136 people known to be HIV-infected, of whom 27 had AIDS. However, with the massive influx of foreigners, a notorious reluctance among young Czechs to use condoms, and a mattress-hopping tendency prevalent throughout the capital, an explosion is on the way. Anonymous HIV tests are available at the Národní referenční laboratoř pro AIDS (National Reference Laboratory on AIDS) on Šrobárova 48, ✆ 74 94 80. Results are available in a week or, in cases certified as emergencies by a doctor, within 24 hours. The staff speak English, although the level of counselling and support is obviously not as great as it would be at home. *The centre is open from Mon–Fri 7.30 am–1.30 pm.*

Pregnant **women** can receive advice and treatment at the Nemocnice na Homolce (*see* p. 28). Two English-speaking GPs dealing with gynaecological matters there are Dr Berka (✆ 5292 2147) and Dr Čadek (✆ 5292 2150). Czech law permits abortions during the first 12 weeks of a pregnancy; the procedure is safe, but very expensive for foreigners.

Education

Prague's International School teaches a US-style curriculum to over 300 children, aged between 4 and 16. At least six months' notice is required if you're to have any chance of nabbing a place; contact the school at Mylnerovka 2 in Prague 6, ✆ 311 20 44, 311 77 71, fax 311 85 78. Particularly small children can get a good and proper British education, either at the small play group that meets at the embassy (call Mrs Spinks), or at the London International Day School on Belgická 25 in Prague 2, tel/fax 25 00 73. Again, considerable advance notice is recommended. Finally, if you don't mind your child having Czech friends or growing up bilingual, you can enroll him or her in a regular Prague kindergarten or school with little difficulty.

Embassies

The British Embassy will fly your body home if you die alone. It can also help British residents in a number of lesser emergencies and it's worth registering at the embassy if you plan on staying in Prague for some time. Registration means that lost passports are replaced more quickly and cheaply than they otherwise would be, that urgent personal messages can be passed on, and that should war or famine break out, you can be evacuated with all due speed. The embassy also publishes a detailed, regularly updated and extremely useful information booklet for residents. The US Embassy dishes out its own pamphlets and provides the usual range of consular services. It also displays up-to-the-minute State Department telexes, warning US citizens which hotspots they have become unwelcome in most recently, which might come in useful if you are planning to travel elsewhere in Europe, or to Africa, Asia, or Latin America. Embassy addresses are on p. 27.

Environmentalism

Recycling is slowly taking off in Prague. Collection points in the form of plastic domes have sprouted across the capital: the white ones are for clear glass, the greens for green and the blues are for paper. A series of more complex tubs for advanced recyclers is now being introduced as well. If you generate waste on a large scale, a private firm called **BOS** will come to pick up your rubbish. It accepts (and pays for) paper, iron, coloured metals, car batteries, glass and textiles, and can also take plastics after discussion. If it's on the daily round, BOS will even pick up junk from individual wasters. *Call on (0205) 22353 during the following hours: Mon and Wed 7–5, Tues and Thurs 7–4, Fri 7–3, and every first Saturday of the month from 8–12 noon.* More active greenies can do their bit for the world by getting in touch with Greenpeace at U Prášné brány 3, ✆ 232 63 23.

Furniture

There are three halls full of furniture at Libeňský ostrov in Prague. Plywood abounds, but the turnover is rapid and includes anything from walnut bureaux to ancient wirelesses. *The modern warehouses are open from Mon–Wed 8–5, Thurs 9.30–6, and Fri 8–3, and the antique hall from Mon–Wed 8–4 and Thurs 9.30–5.* You could also try the antique and junk shops listed on p. 340.

Homosexuals

A useful source of information on gay initiatives (both male and female) in the capital is **SOHO**, at nám. Maxima Gorkého/Senovážné nám. 2, © 236 36 67. The age of consent is 15, the same as that for heterosexuals. Gay men should be careful of the area around Hlavní nádraží: not only are the prostitutes who frequent it said to be a reservoir of HIV, but the station was also the launchpad for the pick-up murders of two male homosexuals in 1992. *See also* pp. 335–6.

Keys

There's a cutting service on the third floor of the Kotva department store.

Language Courses

An ability to speak Czech is what separates the ex-pat from the foreign resident in Prague. Berlitz now offers regular courses: it has offices at Konviktská 18, © 232 44 73 and Na poříčí 12, © 287 20 74, both in Prague 1. A wide range of classes is offered at the Jazykova škola on Národní 20, and the Philosophy Faculty of the Charles University holds a number of intensive courses each year; write for details to the Fakulta Filosofická Karlova Universita/ nám. Jana Palacha 2/ Praha-1. The Valenová Language Laboratory, © 88 27 19, can also provide cheap and friendly lessons.

Libraries

The British Council on Národní 10 maintains an airy reading room, containing periodicals from the old country, and a booth in which to watch BBC TV World Service (*open Mon–Fri 9–4*). The US Embassy runs the American Center for Culture and Commerce at Hybernská 7A, housed with self-conscious irony in the building in which Lenin sneakily and fatefully took over the Russian Social Democratic Party in 1912. *It's open from Mon–Fri 8–4.30*; its many attractions include up-to-date copies of *Harpers* magazine. The State Library at the Clementinum contains thousands of ancient and modern English tomes, and also has an English-language section; *open Tues and Thurs 1–7.*

Newspapers

Britishers can keep up with the old country through the international editions of the *Guardian* and the *Financial Times*. Both steam off Frankfurt presses and hit

Prague's hotels, street vendors and bookstalls at about noon. US citizens may prefer the *Herald Tribune* or even *USA Today*. At the time of writing, the *European* is still afloat, unlike its founder, the no-longer-bouncing Czech.

Prague's Czech newspapers are likely to be of limited interest to you until the language lessons take hold. However, in order to keep your finger on the pulse, as well as to make snap judgments as to the political and moral calibre of the person opposite on the metro, it's worth having some understanding of Prague's periodical culture. *Lidové noviny* is a former underground weekly and represents the voice of sane, civilized democracy. *Respekt* is its weekly equivalent. *Rudé právo* is the ex-mouthpiece of the Communist Party, and now describes itself simply as 'left-wing'; that's usually a bad idea in gung-ho Prague, but the paper commands a surprising level of respect. *Prostor* and *Telegraf* are right-of-centre dailies. *Mlada Fronta Dnes* provides the news in bite-sized chunks for those who don't have much time. *Expres* is a junky tabloid, favoured by the desultory and the unintelligent, while *Blesk* is a sex-and-scandal sheet that turned a profit within months of opening and is now the most popular paper in the country. Its low point, so far, was a colour photo-spread of the last minutes of a suicidal student as she jumped off the Nusle Bridge in the summer of 1992.

Plants

The shortage of sunlight in many Czech flats has led to a peculiar fondness for bonsai trees and potted cacti. If your bedsit needs brightening, and you feel that stunted vegetation is up to the job, you could head for the Bonsai Centrum at Pod krčským lesem 38, ✆ 471 34 77. Artificial flowers, cloth plants and plastic trees are popular for similar reasons; the ground floor of Kotva has a particularly lifeless selection.

Personal Security

Security agencies have been springing up since 1989 to absorb the talent freed into general circulation by mass purges of the police and army since 1989. Most of the new guards seem to do little but stand outside exchange offices fingering their nightsticks, but should you ever need physical protection—or a sleuth—you could contact Izros at Türkova 1, ✆ 76 57 31. It offers a 24-hour service on 26 40 41.

Radio

The BBC World Service broadcasts non-stop on 101.1 FM. A stream of pop music and occasional snippets of news comes from the Voice of America on 106.2 FM. Over the last couple of years, Prague has been inundated by the same kind of mediocre FM stations that have taken over the rest of the Continent, and if you fiddle with your dial you'll find innumerable stations blasting out the sounds of yesteryear or the tunes of today.

Romance

Only the most socially-challenged swinger would find it hard to make short-term friends in Prague. However, if it's love you're after, and you're a man, professional help is now available in the form of Czechmate. The England-based agency (© +44 58 225960, fax 488339) offers introductions to over a thousand Czech and Slovak ladies who are seeking 'genuine marriage-minded gentlemen'. Alternatively, you'll find several pages of **lonely hearts** under 'Seznámení' in *Annonce (B)*. Both sexes and all preferences advertise. The subsection marked 'Hezké chvíle...' ('Sweet moments') is for people who prefer to skip the preliminaries. The suggestions make for interesting reading, and often the friend who translates them for you doesn't have to be left out of the fun. To clinch, consolidate or repair your relationship, **flower deliveries** can be ordered at Fleurop-Pragoflowers, Vinohradská 14, © 236 08 10 (*Mon–Fri 8–6, Sat 9–12 noon*). Choose your blooms over the phone, pop in to pay, and delivery is then as immediate as practicable. If flowers don't say enough, you can now express your feelings with a **tattoo**; several studios have opened up across the city, including one above a club at Legerova 44 (*open Mon–Sat 1–9*). Given Praguers' notorious penchant for sexual intrigue and infidelity, things may go horribly wrong, in which case you could call the Pavel Lûis Expatriate Commiseration and Therapy Centre on 22 80 61. Alternatively, take the offensive and hire a snoop, or a bodyguard, from Izros (*see above*).

Students

If you're studying at a Czech college or university, you can pick up an ISIC card from the International Union of Students at Pařížská 25. You'll need a photo, some evidence of your status and a handful of crowns. The office is open from Mon–Fri 9–3. Students enjoy discounts in most of Prague's museums, and certain travel bargains are also available (*see* p. 35).

Telephone Numbers

International services are detailed on p. 23. Prague finally has a Yellow Pages (actually *Zlaté stránky* or Golden Pages), with an English index, which you can buy at Na Florenci 29. Information gathering has never been easy in Prague and many of the directory's numbers have been wrong for at least 10 years, but it can be a godsend if you're living in the city. If you have your own phone, there are a number of other services open to you, depending on how much Czech you speak. Directory enquiries are answered on 120 (Prague) and 121 (for numbers elsewhere in the country). Calls within the Czech Republic can be made through an operator on 0102; services offered include fixed-time calls, reverse-charge calls and calls with notification of charges. Telegrams are on 127, alarm calls on 125, the time on 112, and messages will be taken for you in your absence if you ask on 124. To report a fault, call the first two or three digits of your number followed by 2222: that's a rough-and-ready formula which works in about 80 per cent of cases. If yours isn't one of them, you'll find the correct number in the front section of the *Zlaté stránky*.

Television

Three standard channels are now available in Prague—ČT 1, ČT 2 and ČT 3. The last runs a number of foreign-language programmes including several hours of CNN each day.

Translations

Very rarely, you may have to submit a form in Czech in order to receive some benefit or avoid another burden. The best thing to do is to ask a friend for help, since Praguers are generally well versed in the hermetic language of their country's bureaucracy and can usually come up with the phrases, oaths and denials required. If the matter is more serious, contact Babel Service at the Palace of Culture, 5. května 65, © 692 67 41–3, 692 67 58–9, fax 692 67 74.

Water

Toxins have been trickling down to Prague's water table for decades, and if you're in town for a few months you may want to limit the damage with mineral water. Multinational brands are widely available, but far cheaper and just as refreshing is the lightly-carbonated Mattoni, from Karlovy Vary. Blue and white cartons of still table water (marked *Stolní pitní voda*) are also available from many shops. Most supermarkets stock several other Bohemian spa waters, but some have unwanted side-effects. To identify the gentler ones, compare the mineral contents (the fewer, the better), and assess the likely infirmities of other purchasers. However, experimention is only advisable if you have constipation or are following medical advice.

Day Trips from Prague

When you feel the urge to explore beyond Prague, the heart of Europe is your oyster. Some of the day trips below exemplify an aspect of Bohemia's history that throws the capital into its European perspective; others are simply destinations for lazy summer days. Two focus on the centuries of German influence in the country—from the tranquillity of the spa at Carlsbad to the very different silence of the Theresienstadt ghetto—while Kutná Hora contains some of the most superb Gothic architecture from the golden age of Bohemian independence. The Hussite stronghold of Tábor dates from the same era, but its 16th-century town square and tunnels are a picturesque souvenir of a more insane strand of Czech nationalism. The Moravian town of Telč is among the most charming in all the Czech Republic, a minuscule jewel of Gothic and Renaissance architecture, and the perfect destination for a drive and a picnic. Two Gothic castles—Karlštejn and Křivoklát—are covered in another trip. Both are set in rolling hills and forests, and are the best choice if the cobbles and fumes of Prague have become too much, and you need to go wild in the country. České Budějovice (Budweis), where they have been brewing their own for some seven centuries, is an attractive spot for a beer-drinking pilgrimage. As for Český Krumlov, words can hardly do justice to its smoky and decrepit charm. Untouched for at least two centuries, locked into two river bends, and dominated by a fantastic rocky citadel, it's a town you never forget.

Orientation

All these destinations are within 1½–2½ hours of the capital, except Český Krumlov and České Budějovice which are at least a 3-hour journey away. Karlštejn is the closest, and can be seen in an afternoon if you're pressed for time. They are all accessible by road and rail, but details of only the most convenient means of transport are provided. The railway and coach stations from which you set off are covered on p. 13–14. Car-hire details are on p. 12. *If you aren't driving, be sure to establish how you will return to Prague as soon as you arrive; the last return time is often considerably earlier than you would expect.*

Carlsbad was for centuries one of the most elegant watering holes of central Europe. Goethe and Schiller drank deep of its draughts; its casino and promenades were the playground of Russian aristocrats and Europe's monarchs; and it's hard to name a Romantic composer who didn't take the cure.

The frolics ended in the troubled 20th century: as part of the Sudetenland it was stolen by the Nazis in 1938 (Hitler paid a visit), and after the war the remaining toffs were dispossessed by the confiscatory Communists. A dreary parade of postwar potentates, from Haile Selassie to Kurt Waldheim, came to dip their toes in the waters, and the spa doors were thrown open to the public. But although the *beau monde* now frivols elsewhere and has been replaced by an annual reinvasion of German tourists, lovers of bygone charm will find few better spots in Bohemia. Le Corbusier once called Karlovy Vary a 'cream cake'; that's not much of a compliment from a man whose ideas of beauty involved glass skyscrapers and curved concrete, but less doctrinaire types will revel in the architectural confectionery. The town, built along the bubbling Teplá river, climbs wooded hillsides in pastel blocks; and although most of the buildings are less than 150 years old, the tall autumnal façades, genteel lawns and summertime outdoor concerts make for a nostalgic amble back into an age when even gout could be romantic.

The town's fame sprang from its springs, the salty cocktails are forced up from subterranean hot rocks two km below, and reach the surface at temperatures ranging from 30–72°C. They first exploded into life during a geological shift about 500 million years ago, but little Wary was an unknown village of clean and healthy folk until Charles IV stumbled upon it in 1358. He immediately built a bathtower near by, and Wary received its prefix and a royal charter in 1370. Most of the houses still have private supplies of the water on tap; it feeds into the river at innumerable points (hence the name Teplá, which means 'warm'); and 12 of the 60 springs now have established medicinal benefits.

Getting Around

The town is 130 km due west of Prague on the E48 road, which you can join on Milady Horákové, running north of Letná Park. Coaches leave Florenc regularly; and a private company, Čebus, also has a service, leaving at 7.30 am and 10 am and returning at 3.15 pm and 6 pm (its sales booth is near by, just before Križíkova street). The trip takes just over two hours. Trains leave from Hlavní nádraží, but are often considerably slower.

Within Karlovy Vary itself, the local bus service isn't of much use, given that the historic centre is only some 1½ miles long; but if you fancy a wander through the surrounding hillsides, there are two useful funicular railways. The information given below progresses and digresses on a fairly logical route along the Teplá from the Thermal Hotel, a modern landmark of grey and glass which is difficult to miss. While sauntering and sipping, beware of the hypochondriacal regulations that apply along the promenades—no dogs, smoking, or loud noises—and in the colonnades, where the prohibitions also cover prams and whatever is meant by the mystifying term 'long objects'. Hygiene police enforce the rules with on-the-spot fines, but insane though the bye-laws are, they're still less dire than they could be: you can retreat to a café or hilltop to smoke and scream, and Hassidic Jews are no longer regarded as a health hazard, as they apparently were for two centuries.

Treatments/Activities

The town contains clinics that handle a variety of conditions from indigestion to quadriplegia. Courses and accommodation can be booked at overseas Čedok offices, or at Balnea in Prague (*see* p. 16). In the town itself, the *Kur-Info* office next to the Vřídlo fountain (*see below*) can tell you whether Karlovy Vary can do anything for your particular ailment. As well as booking treatments, it can reserve accommodation and entertainments, and provide guides (✆ 017 24097, fax 24667). Of the municipal baths, only Bath I is open to foreigners, and the relaxation possibilities that it has to offer are described on p. 376. If all you want is a dip, there's an outdoor pool on the hillside behind the Thermal Hotel, filled with water from one of the (cooler) springs. Sparklingly clean and commanding a breathtaking view over the town below, there are few more satisfying swims to be had in Bohemia (*open 8–8 pm*).

The town has a few dietary specialities that you may want to try. Look out for *oplatky*, sweet wafers that seem designed to mitigate the disgusting taste of the waters themselves; and the ubiquitous *Becherovka*, a herbal tipple developed by town chemist Dr Becher in the 19th century. Despite rumours to the contrary, it contains no spring waters, but it's still proudly known as Karlovy Vary's 13th and most popular spring. Along with *Becherovka* and porcelain from its highly-regarded factories, the town's most popular souvenirs are its Moser snifters. Those are colossal glasses, blown up to the size of a small balloon which, insofar as they have any practical purpose whatsoever, are meant to make superior cognac taste even more superior.

The route through the town is lined with restaurants and cafés. The elegant **Elefant** at Stará louka 30 is a perennial favourite among the locals and a place to sit and watch the promenaders pass. Its cappuccino is luscious and fruit salads, sundaes and cakes add to the pleasure, but it isn't a place for a solid lunch. On the other hand they don't get much more solid than at the **Chebský dvůr** or the **Hotel Puškin**, next to each other just above the Market Colonnade. Both serve Czech staples, the latter in an oom-pah-pah ambience designed to appeal to Germans, and look down over a jigsaw view of plague column, glass pyramid, Baroque spires and wooden colonnade. If you want to dine in the style that Karlovy Vary deserves, make a reservation at the dark and discreet **Embassy** on Nova louka 21 and gorge yourself on luxuries from smoked eel to asparagus tips, © 017 23049).

To begin a trip through the town, find the Thermal Hotel, and continue walking down the Teplá. On your right is the Dvořákovy sady (Dvořák Park), with lily pond and the last of the garden's wrought-iron colonnades, the lone survivor of a Habsburg hunt for cannon metal during the 1914–18 war. Further downriver is the neo-classical splendour of the **Mill Colonnade** (Mlýnská kolonáda). Five springs hiss and gurgle to the surface here, and it's the favourite ambulatory of the town's hydrophiles, who stroll from fount to fount between the Corinthian columns, drinking through the spouts of their teapot-like *pohárky*. The locals all seem to have their favourite brew, but discrimination needs to be acquired, and you should exercise caution. In the unintentionally honest words of one of the town's tourist brochures, 'even small doses have a striking effect on the alimentary tract', and it's no coincidence that there are well-marked toilets at the end of the colonnade.

The road veering right from the colonnade (Lázeňská) used to be named after Karl Marx, who visited three times. The delighted Communists thus had an excuse—as if one were necessary—to honour him with a statue, toppled long ago, and the museum to your left. That has now reopened under its former name, **The Golden Key** (U zlatého klíče), and proletarian kitsch has been replaced by bourgeois kitsch—notably some sweetly terrible paintings capturing gay scenes of flirtation, dancing and gossiping in 19th-century Karlovy Vary (*open Wed–Sun 9–12, 1–5.*) The street winds into a little junction that was the heart of the medieval town. In the centre is the inevitable plague column from Bohemia's epidemic of 1715; every town in the country built one, although this one seems doubly superfluous if it's true, as the town claims, that the power of the waters has kept the buboes at bay throughout its history. On your right is the wooden **Market Colonnade**, a replacement of a bronze victim of the Habsburg meltdown.

On your left is the fountain that was responsible for Karlovy Vary's rise to stardom. It's the **Vřídlo** ('Spring'), now housed in a glass temple built by the Communists and named until 1989 after another key man in their history of the spa, Soviet cosmonaut Yuri Gagarin, who took the waters twice. Yuri's statue never looked very convinced that it should have been here; and the romper-suited spaceman has now been relocated to the town airport, where few people will ever see him again. The fountain fizzes from rocks more than two kilometres underground, and ends its journey in splutters and spurts of up to 12 metres, at a temperature of 72°C. The various legends agree that Charles IV was on a hunt when he discovered the spring and brought the town its fame and prosperity, but the details are fuzzy: the most widespread story is that he was somehow led to Vřídlo by a deer; others claim that it was the yelp of a boiled dog that tipped him off; while the most intriguing tale insists that villagers carried him here after he had been grieviously wounded in hand-to-hand combat with a boar. The emperor was advised by his physician that, although the water was clearly holy, it was suitable only for bathing. The opinion is understandable when you taste the foul potion; but in 1522, the advantages of taking it orally were publicized by a certain Václav Payer, who steadily increased his recommended dosage until he was suggesting a daily intake of 60 cups and 12-hour baths. Even that was a chaser compared to the prescriptions of some later spa maniacs, but armed with a *pohárek*, you can work out your own optimum shot at the smaller outlets in the hall near the fountain.

If you return to the little junction with the plague column, a detour along the street running up the hill (Zamecký vrch) takes you to the spot where Charles is said to have ended his deer hunt. It leads past the circular colonnade of the **Castle Spring**, under the tower built by Charles and remodelled in the early 17th century (its viewing gallery is occasionally open). Follow the hill until you see a set of steps on your left (next to a house marked 'Marius'), then turn left again and take the second path on the right. The cobbles turn into a root-strewn path, which clambers up to **Stag Leap** (Jelení skok), the tall rock where Charles's quarry is said to have jumped/been wounded/been sighted. The legend was confused further by dotty Count Lützow in the 19th-century, who felt that only a goat could have stood on the crag, and an intrepid little chamois now gazes over the valley. Incidentally, Lützow also commissioned the construction of an iron cat on a pillar, for no known reason, at the other end of town.

Salvation of the soul has always taken second place to the perpetration and repair of sins of the flesh in Karlovy Vary, and churches are thin on the ground. Although Russian aristocrats built themselves an Orthodox church in the late 19th century (on Tř. krále Jiřího, near the junction with Petra Velikého), the town got only one Counter-Reformation masterpiece, the oval **Church of St Mary Magdalene** (Kostel sv. Marie Magdalena), built by Kilian Dienzenhofer in 1736. It's on the hill overlooking Vřídlo from the other side of the river, and one enjoyable, if roundabout, way of approaching it to take the funicular railway (*lanovka*) up the hill and walking down past the bulbous spires. The trains leave every 15 mins from Divadelní nám. 3; you'll find the so-called square in a crescent on your left if you resume your interrupted journey through the town centre. In the same square is the **Vítězslav Nezval Theatre** (Divadlo V. Nezvala), the construction of which was financed by what has always been a lucrative cottage industry in Karlovy Vary, the collection of toilet admission fees. Its stage curtain was painted in 1885 by three Viennese painter/decorators, who included a young **Gustav Klimt**. It dates from about a decade before he began his move towards the stylized beauties for which he's best known, and was one of scores of works that he and his decorative firm painted across Austria and nearby provinces. The curtain is a grandiose tribute to Theatre, filled with the nine Muses (Tragedy hogs the stage; she may well be an early Klimtian *femme fatale*); on the right is a band of troubadours, among whom is rakish Gustav himself, tootling on a flute. *The box office is open from Tues–Sat 1.30–6; if you want to see the curtain, ask to speak to the friendly theatre manager, who knows it intimately.*

The journey through the town continues on the same side of the river with the **Karlovy Vary Museum** (Karlovarské muzeum) at Nová louka 11 (*open Wed–Sun 9–12, 1–5*). The strange set of municipal treasures includes an inordinate number of stuffed sparrows and voles, a hollowed-out tree trunk from the 17th century that formed part of Karlovy Vary's ancient drainage system, and a collection of *pohárky* used by the great and the good. On the other side of the river, the embankment is called Stará louka (Old Meadow), and is lined with some of the oldest houses in town, including the Krásná Královna (Beautiful Queen) café, home of Queen Maria Theresa during her visits to the spa. There's another funicular at the top of Mariánská, on the right at the end of Stará louka, climbing 200 metres up the opposite hillside (*9 am–4 pm daily*). It takes you to an observation tower, a café, and a view that is so good that it's disillusioning, revealing the spa to be a tiny oasis of fertility and colour set within the greyness of a 20th-century town. Back at ground level, Stará louka and the Teplá swerve to the left, diverted by the 500-bed **Grand Hotel Pupp**, the core of which is almost 300 years old but with suburban wings dating back only some 50 years.

The hotel marks the end of the town centre. A few hundred metres down Goetheova stezka is a bust of a very supercilious Goethe, who paid Carlsbad 13 visits, and broke his heart here for one of the last times when, in 1823, he spotted 17-year-old Ulrika von Lewetzöw sipping the waters. She spurned the 74-year-old poet; according to legend he was consumed by a profound, if temporary grief, and penned his *Elegies* as he stormed out of town in his carriage. There's a gallery slightly further along the path with a small collection of 20th-century Czech art (*open Tues–Sun 9.30–12, 1–5*). If you feel like a climb, there's an observation tower on the hill next to the Pupp; and a final way of ending the walk is in the twilight splendour of the neo-Renaissance **Bath 1** (Lazně 1), next to the green opposite the hotel (*open Mon–Fri 7–3.30, Sat 7–12 noon*). A guided tour around the building reveals two pompous paintings, depicting convocations of important Karlovy Vary visitors, and the considerably more exciting imperial bathroom that Emperor Franz Josef had built for himself in 1895. For a fee, your guide will turn on the tap water and retire discreetly, and after you have soaked to your satisfaction, he or she will return to serve mineral water and biscuits while you recline on the imperial couch. Polaroid photos (optional) will record the luxurious experience. According to the proud guide, Barbara Streisand once took a bath here between shoots for *Yentl.* If even that can't tempt you to take the plunge, there are a number of other watery services available, ranging from massages to low-voltage electrocution; and if you have money to burn, and an evening in hand, the casino on the first floor opens at 6 pm.

Telč

The minuscule town of Telč is one of the most stunning in the Czech Republic. It still has the feel of a medieval microcosm, a world within walls, but its fortifications and lakes now enclose the splendid luxury of a Renaissance chateau, and the pastel façades of a square that, on a sunny summer day, can make Prague's Old Town Square look hamfisted.

Getting Around

Although the whole town is lovely, Telč's highlight is its chateau, and you should make sure that it will be open before setting off on this day trip. The opening times are given below, but broadly speaking, don't choose a Monday, Saturday or any month from November to March (inclusive). More generally, Telč isn't a town to visit out of season; for better or for worse, the town depends on the annual influx of tourists from nearby Austria, and it sinks into depressive melancholia as winter approaches.

Telč is about 120 km southeast of Prague, and the only practical way to reach it and return in a day is by road. If you're driving, pick up the Brno motorway from the south of Prague. The two largest feeder roads that loop into it are 5. května and Chodovská. Turn off at the E59 for Jihlava and then follow local signs. There's a regular coach service from Florenc station; the journey takes about 2½ hours.

The centre of Telč itself is so small that a bus would have nowhere to go. Once you've found your way to the centre of town, the sites are a stroll away from each other.

Lunch

There are cafés scattered throughout the town square, but in the summer you'll often be grateful to eat anywhere that has space. You could try the **Restaurace Na Kopečku** on Jihlavská 5, up the hill running from the northern gate of the town. A popular lunchtime haunt of blue-overalled workers, it serves beer and dumplings, meat and potatoes, and a range of filling soups. Alternatively, the town's lakes and chateau gardens are ideal for picnics.

Telč seems to have originated in the early 13th century, but it emerges from obscurity only about a hundred years later, when prodigal John of Luxemburg pawned the town, along with several others in southern Bohemia, to keep the money flowing for his chivalrous jaunts overseas. His son Charles IV redeemed it, but after a spot of complex wheeling and dealing, it fell into the hands of the Hradec family, which constructed the town's fishponds, fortifications and chateau before extinguishing itself through various drinking and drowning mishaps in the early 17th century. The town passed through innumerable noble hands until 1945, but it has hardly changed since the Hradec family left.

There are still only three gates through the town fortifications. From the bus station, you'll enter through the southern entrance, past the lonely Romanesque steeple of the first church in Telč, built in the early 1200s but now otherwise long gone. The cobbled lane emerges into the funnel-shaped town square, nám. Zachariáše z hradce. The 300-metre-long set of cinnamon, lemon and gingerbread façades are preposterously picturesque—so much so that you half expect one to tip over in the wind and a man to scream 'CUT!'. The Telč house is so distinctive that it's a byword for fairytale prettiness within the Czech Republic itself—no mean feat in a country where every tenth town can lay claim to enchanted status. Each of the short buildings has a fiercely quirky independence—some combining *sgraffito* with crenellated rooftops, others surmounted with incongruous gables, which double the height of the house concerned—but all have certain characteristic features. A Gothic arcade runs under the houses along the length of both sides of the square, and, pottering from gallery to café, you'll also notice how unusually deep they are in relation to their narrow jostling exteriors. They originated after a fire in 1530 and combine Gothic structures with Renaissance façades, with plenty of curlie-wurlie Baroque flourishes tossed in for good measure.

As you approach the narrower end of the square, you'll see on your left the towers and domes of the Jesuit church of St James, next to the Order's former college, and on your right the entrance to the Renaissance **chateau** (*zámek*). The home of Telč's lords for centuries, it dates back to Gothic times, but was reconstructed in its present form during the second half of the 16th century. As well as having a sumptuous interior, it contains a museum of the town's history and an art gallery.

The small museum and the interior of the chateau are both open from Tues–Sun 9–4 (April, Sept, Oct), 8–5 (May–Aug), with a lunch break from 12–1. The former would hardly merit a visit, were it not for an awe-inspiring electrical model of the Nativity, painstakingly constructed out of cardboard and papier-mâché by Telčian luminaries Mr and Mrs Vostrý. Ask the curator to switch it on. His face will light up; and few visitors fail to be impressed as angels, cradle and sheep swoop, rock and graze with high-voltage fury in a landscape that's somehow redolent of both Heidi and the Arabian Nights. After taking in the other pinnacles of Telč's cultural history, you can buy a ticket for the guided tour through the chateau from the same ticket office. It leads through rooms that often combine Gothic cross- and net-vaulting with rich Renaissance stucco work and decoration; others with illusionistic painting; some gorgeous furniture and cassetted ceilings; and towards the end, impressive arrays of armour, and hundreds of hunting trophies. The latter collection includes tiger skins, zebra heads and what is claimed by many to be the largest elephant ear in central Europe, one metre in diameter.

The chateau also houses a gallery of the painting of Jan Zrzavý (1890–1977), at the end of the arcade in the gardens. Zrzavý's art is some of the most distinctive and uncategorizable to have been produced by a Czech this century. The paintings on display span his entire career, during which his colourful and simple work teetered back and forth across the range from whimsy to profound humaneness; much of his finest art was produced between 1910 and 1930, under the (very indirect) influence of Cubism and then a form of social realism suffused with a powerful spirituality. *The Gallery's complex opening hours are: Tues–Sun 9–4 (April, Sept, Oct), 8–5 (May–Aug); Tues–Fri 9–4, Sat 9–1, Sun 9–4 (Nov–March). It closes from 12–1 wherever applicable.*

This trip is a none-too-lighthearted excursion through the final chapter of the German presence in Bohemia. Terezín is better known to the outside world as Theresienstadt, a 200-year-old fortress town that was transformed by the Nazis into a concentration camp for deported Jews from across Europe. It lay within the German-speaking Sudetenland, and you can combine the visit with a trip to the nearby town of Litoměřice—formerly Leitmeritz, and a thriving centre of the minority population until its violent expulsion after the war.

Getting Around

Terezín is about 60 km to the north of Prague on the route to Teplice which you can pick up from Argentinská street in Holešovice. The journey by coach takes under 1½ hours; buses leave from Florenc station at 7.45 am, 10 am, 11 am and 11.30 am. Organized tours to the town leave Prague's Old Town Hall every Sunday morning; you can get the times and details from the Jewish Town Hall (*see* p. 168). Trains go to Litoměřice, but the journey is long and involves changing at Lysá na Labem.

The bus to Terezín stops in the main square. The ghetto was in the town itself, and the nearby fortress was a prison, a distinction that isn't always appreciated by visitors. You should make sure to see both; they're separated by a walk of a few minutes. There is a regular bus service to Litoměřice, leaving either from the same stop in the square at which you arrive, or the one just around the next corner. The journey takes about 10 minutes.

Lunch

The best (and almost the only) restaurant in Terezín is the **Restaurant Terezian**, on the opposite side of the main square from the bus stop (*Mon–Fri 10–5*). The pleasant staff will even consider requests for custom-made brunch or lunch. Alternatively, you could try downing a snack in the former SS canteen just inside the gates of the prison camp, although after a visit the prospect is often too nauseating. In Litoměřice, there are a number of tolerable lunchstops around Michalská street, to the west of the town square; the best is **Restaurace Zlata 2** on Pekařská 17 (*Mon–Sat 11–10*). A final possibility is to unpack a picnic in front of St Stephen's church at the end of your visit.

Terezín was established by imperial fiat in 1780. Emperor Joseph II named it after his mother, but sentimentality ended there. Along with the nearby fortress, the chess-board town was designed simply to defend Bohemia's northwest frontier. However, its eminently functional layout made it suitable for any project that required order, and when the Nazis began their *Aktionen* against Bohemian and Moravian Jews in 1941, they had little difficulty in turning it into a concentration camp. Transports were soon arriving from across Europe, to be accommodated temporarily as the finishing touches were put to the Nazis' final solution of the Jewish problem. The first arrivals were put up in the barracks; but in June 1942, all of Terezín's existing inhabitants were expelled, and the entire town was taken over. The Nazis intended it to be the acceptable face of ghettoization; and International Red Cross representatives were shown around here, as and when the organization took an interest in what was happening to Europe's Jews. The relatively lax regime meant that the camp became a bizarre centre of wartime Jewish culture, with clandestine newspapers, plays and concerts, and even a jazz band ('The Ghetto Swingers'), despite a Nazi decree outlawing such Judeo-Negroid deviancy. However, the laxness was very relative indeed; only some 20,000 of around 140,000 deportees survived the war.

Terezín's former (Czech) inhabitants returned after 1945, but the town has a stillness that feels very different from the lazy calm that you might expect of a provincial town. The stark but almost elegant neo-classical grid is permeated with the atmosphere of a terrible museum: after you have left, it's hard to remember seeing a child or hearing birdsong in the town; and little seems to drive on the broad and dusty roads save the occasional truck from its still-functioning garrison. If you leave the square along B. Němcové, and then turn left at Dlouhá, many of the street corners still show the overpainted German markings of the ghetto's blocks. On the right at the far end of Dlouhá is a disused railway terminal, and just beyond it a 100-metre stretch of track. Trains carried 87,000 people to Auschwitz-Birkenau from here, of whom 3000 survived the war. The road parallel to the track (Bohušovická brána) crosses the vast ditch that rings the town and which could be filled by the river in moments of need. On the right, in arches set into the heavy fortifications, are funeral halls built towards the end of the war to impress the last Red Cross delegation. In one of the chambers, Christian services were held for those unlucky enough to be defined as Jews by Nazi race laws. Slightly further along the road, a path to the left leads to a Jewish cemetery and Terezín's **crematorium**. Its four trolley-loaded ovens burned for the last three years of the war, and disposed of 30,000 bodies. *The former inferno is now a silent museum, open from March–Nov 10–5 (closed on Saturdays).* A memorial service is held in the cemetery every year on 20 September.

Although the rest of the town is dotted with plaques and memorials, they were all put up soon after the war, and over the years there seemed to have developed a complicit understanding between residents and municipality that the secrets of Terezín should be allowed to lapse. Many locals have tended to view visitors as unwelcome reminders of a history that has somehow finished; and although it's easy to sympathise with people who only want obscurity, one has to be grateful that a private museum has now opened to tell the story of Terezín. You'll find the **Ghetto Museum** (Muzeum ghetta) on Komenského street, to your left as you face the suitably desolate neo-classical church on the town square. The museum is opposite a small green that represents one of the ghetto's aforementioned secrets: a playground was built here in 1944, just before the International Red Cross came to town, and a group of Terezín children were filmed screaming and playing on the grass shortly before they were transported to Auschwitz.

The museum (*open 9–6*) is extremely well laid out, with most exhibits explained fully in English. One of the most thought-provoking sections is devoted to the efforts made by the Nazis to deceive the Red Cross—which extended to opening a café and establishing an entirely fake cash economy—and the ease with which the international organization was deceived. (The Swiss ICRC delegation head sent his souvenir snaps to the Reich Foreign Ministry, which made good use of them.) At the end of your visit, you can watch a number of films, including a documentary of survivors' testimony and the almost more harrowing *Gift of a Town*, produced by Nazi propagandists to show the German public what the Führer was doing for his Jews.

From the museum, make your way to the **Small Fort** (Malá pevnost), *open daily 8–6.30 (summer) and 8–3.30 (winter)*. It is a 15-minute walk along Pražská (on your left as you leave the museum), which runs over the eastern fortification gullies, filled with straggling allotments, and then crosses the Ohře river. The fort was built by the Habsburgs, but again exploited most effectively by the Nazis. The Gestapo took over in June 1940 and 32,000 inmates passed through, either prisoners-of-war or pinko troublemakers. Their crime wasn't Judaism, and the treatment was correspondingly less harsh. As a result only 2500 died here, and another 5000 in death camps.

On your right as you approach to the main entrance is the **National Cemetery**, containing the graves of some 2400 people, and the ashes of some 25,000 others. A huge crucifix now stands over the rows of simple tablets; it's a recent addition and a questionable one, given that the cemetery contains the remains of innumerable Communists and Jews. The dates on the stones show how many were victims of the typhus that raged through the town in the weeks after its liberation by Soviet forces on 8 May 1945. The epidemic eventually left 3500 dead.

After paying, turn left into the first courtyard, where prisoners registered and were given uniforms and numbers. 'Arbeit Macht Frei' still greets you as you walk into the camp proper. In front of you are collective cells; and if you turn left and left again, you enter a street of solitary chambers for condemned prisoners and those under interrogation. The Nazis weren't the first to use them—and in the first cell on the right, the Habsburgs imprisoned **Gavrilo Princip**. Perhaps the most successful of the many trigger-happy anarchists of the turn of the century, Princip was the man who killed Archduke Francis Ferdinand, heir to the Habsburg throne, at Sarajevo in 1914. The assassination set Europe's war machines into motion, but Princip himself saw none of the action. He was manacled to the cell wall until tuberculosis crept in in 1916, and died in Terezín's military hospital in April 1918. The small exhibition contains mug-shots of Princip and five other members of the bungling Black Hand organization to which he belonged. Their slapstick efforts were consummated only when the Archduke's car stalled next to Princip, half an hour after another conspirator had lobbed a ball of dynamite which missed. The ludicrous Serbs became heroes of Tito's Yugoslavia, and this memorial was unveiled by the ambassador in the 1950s.

The next set of buildings contain showers, and the enamel basins and individual mirrors of a pristine shaving-room, constructed by the Nazis shortly before the 1944 Red Cross visit. Walk through the little passage near by, and on the right is a gate (marked '17') which leads into one of the eeriest parts of the fortress, a dim tunnel stretching for hundreds of metres through its walls (closed in winter). That has nothing to do with the Nazis; but you emerge in front of a gallows and grassy bank where they shot and hanged some 250 inmates. Through the gate to the right is the overgrown site of a mass grave of 601 people, who were exhumed and reburied in 1945. Condemned prisoners arrived through the Gate of Death on the left. As you walk out of it, you'll pass the swimming pool and cinema used by the guards (unless the Red Cross were in town, in which case inmates were ordered to amuse themselves). The cinema now shows documentaries, although you'll need to amass a small group before the staff will show one. Just past the cinema on the left is a small memorial with earth from all the extermination camps fed by Terezín, and beyond that a courtyard and watchtower (the minute rooms to the right housed up to 12 people in the last months of the war). As you retrace your footsteps, there's a museum in the former SS barracks to the left; and the guards' canteen is just before the exit.

As you cross the Labe river on the short journey to **Litoměřice**, you'll see on your left Radobýl Hill, inside which is a now closed factory which operates as part of the Flossenbürg concentration camp. 15,000 involuntary troglodytes worked in the mountain during the war, and a third of them died there.

The centre of the town is in the direction from which the bus arrives. Cross the road and walk down Dlouhá towards the main square. A living town comes as a relief after the barracks and cells of Terezín, but unfortunately Litoměřice is an unkempt mess. There are some sights worth seeing, but you probably won't want to stay long after having had lunch. The town used to be one of the largest in Bohemia, but was almost completely wiped out by Swedes during the Thirty Years War (1618–48). Its recent history has been no happier, as you can begin to appreciate in the **Town Museum**, housed in the town hall, under the arcade on your right as you enter the square (*open Tues–Sun 10–12, 12.30–5*). Scattered among the archaeological junk and medieval paraphernalia (including torture instruments and the tree-like stocks of the old town) are objects that tell the story of the Sudetenland in microcosm, from swastika-laden soup bowls to photographs of the jubilant reception given the Nazis in 1938. What's missing is any mention of what happened to the town's Germans after the war. They were expelled, as they were throughout the Sudetenland—an understandable decision after you've been to Terezín, but one that led to the deaths of thousands, including Jews and relatives of concentration-camp victims. For a decade, the area was filled with ghostly villages; and although Litoměřice itself was repopulated soon after the war, some of its façades are (very) muted echoes of Terezín, with faded German shop signs reappearing from under the crumbling paintwork. The Sudeten Question is by no means closed. Since the 1989 revolution, a few Czechs have reopened the once-taboo subject, and Václav Havel went so far as to apologize to the German government in early 1990. Soul-searching can be politically disastrous in the modern Czech Republic, and Havel's conciliatory efforts have been hugely unpopular. At best they are viewed as naïve; at worst, they are seen as the actions of a dupe, or a traitor. Before leaving the museum, take a look at the *Litoměřice Prayer Book* (pre-1517), which marks an important stage in the development of Czech printing. The titanic tome is usually open at a vibrant technicolour scene of an alarmed Jan Hus preparing to meet his maker, and vice versa.

If you cross the square from the museum, and take Michalská on the left, you'll find the **North Bohemian Gallery** at No. 7 (*open Tues–Sun 9–5*). The small collection runs from Romanesque sculpture to sorry 19th-century efforts, but it also contains the notable work of the Master of the Litoměřice Altarpiece. Technically accomplished and showing a close affinity to the work of Lucas Cranach the Elder, it marks the point in the early 16th century when Czech Gothic art joined the mainstream of the northern Renaissance. A good place to end your day is at the Jesuit **Cathedral of St Stephen** in Dómské nám., which you'll reach if you walk to the end of Michalská and then head left for a couple of hundred metres. It contains a large number of saintly relics and an organ of 3944 pipes. Even if you can't get in, the green in front of the church—lined with the quarters of ageing nuns who have returned from years of Communist-enforced exile—is a tranquil spot in which to unwind after Terezín.

Tábor

Tábor is a town built on fanaticism. Named with fundamentalist fervour after the mountain on which Jesus was transfigured, it was founded in 1420 by radical Hussites fleeing the Catholic rule of Emperor Sigismund in Prague. Tábor was initially intended to be a new form of society, in which all property would be held in common, but the experiment quickly hit the deep doo-doo that all communisms seem to run into. The Táborites' conviction that private property was a mortal sin was optimistically linked to a belief that the godly did not have to work, and the town soon found that it had no property at all, communal or otherwise. Tábor overcame the shortfall by launching righteous raids on surrounding peasant communities, but economic teething troubles were soon the least of its problems. Its religious radicalism soon set it at war with most of Europe: an unenviable challenge, but one to which it arose with zest. For over a decade its armies held out against popes and kings thanks to novel tactics of warfare developed by the brilliant Jan Žižka, whose one-eyed countenance you'll find bearing down on you throughout your day trip. The Táborites were eventually crushed in 1434 (*see* p. 47) and the town's brief moment at the centre of the Continent's religious hatred ended for ever, but around—and under—the pretty Renaissance and Baroque buildings of its historical core, the spirit of Hussite lunacy whispers on.

Getting Around

Tábor lies just under 100 km to the south of Prague. To drive, pick up the E59 towards Brno (running out of town across the Nusle Bridge from behind the National Museum), and take the E55 when you see signs for České Budějovice, about 20 km outside Prague. The drive takes about an hour and 40 minutes.

Lunch

The town contains many nondescript bistros and cafés where you can fill up on chips and fried cheese, but nowhere that you'll want to return to in a hurry. The best it can offer are two restaurants on Žižkovo nám., the main square: the **Restaurant Beseda**, serving Czech staples in the shabby interior of a Renaissance house, and the nearby **Restaurant Zlatý drak** (Golden Dragon Restaurant), owned by a Chinese family and offering tasty Cantonese fare.

When you arrive, find your way to Žižkovo nám., the sloping square at the heart of old Tábor. At its northern end stands the first of the many statues of Žižka you'll see today, and near the centre is a Renaissance fountain presided over by squat and solemn Hromádka, who founded the town along with Žižka. He stands over four toothy pike, who honour the fishy traditions of lacustrine southern Bohemia. (The region contains some 300 artificial lakes, linked during the 16th century into a chain which begins about 30 km south of Tábor.) In the north-western corner of the square is the Gothic **Church of the Transfiguration of Our Lord on Mount Tabor** (*Kostel Proměnění Páně na hoře Tábor*), built on top of an old Hussite church between 1440 and 1512. Its most notable feature is the odd vaulting of the chancel, with ribs formed out of co-ordinating planes and angular faces and looking more like a modernist nod to Gothic motifs than the genuine 16th-century vault that it is.

On your left as you face the church is the **Old Town Hall**, surmounted by three crenellated gables, and a curious one-handed 24-hour clock (apparently, the townsfolk originally ordered a sundial and then decided to use it as a clock instead). The town hall interiors include a stark and impressive Gothic hall, where you can see a small version of Bohumil Kafka's *Žižka*—the largest equestrian statue in the world, which now stands on Prague's Žížkov Hill (*see* pp. 273–4). The town hall also houses the **Hussite Museum** (*open Tues–Sun June–Sept 9–4.30, Oct–May 9–5.30*). As well as several more studies of Žižka and Horse, the collections include what is reputed to be the top of the great man's skull. Eagle-eyed sculpture-watchers may already have noticed that there is no consensus as to where Žižka wore his patch, a question further complicated by the fact that he was totally blinded when his good eye caught an arrow in 1421. It's one of history's less significant mysteries, but one that deserves a moment of silent contemplation while you stare at the fracture lines of his cracked headcase. The museum also contains copies of weapons used by Žižka's forces. Tábor's theoreticians knew that to defeat their well-equipped and numerous enemies they needed cost-effective arms of maximal violence, and over the years the peasant inventors came up with some wily weapons. Scythes and pitchforks metamorphosed into cudgels, spiked bludgeons and flails, while Táborite ordnance included battering rams, catapults and 15th-century superguns. Žižka may also have been the first to use ironclad wagons in defensive laagers, Voortrekker-style. The museum also contains standards and pennants marked with the Hussite symbols of chalice and goose: the former represented the rebels' belief that everyone should drink Christ's blood, while the latter comes from a Czech pun (*husa* = goose).

At the museum box-office you can also buy your ticket for Tábor's strangest attraction, the **tunnel system** that burrows at a level of 7–12 metres under the main square. It is open from a vague point in April to an equally uncertain day in November; however, if you are sufficiently large in number, or sweet enough, you might find a guide outside those dates. About 800 metres are open to the public, although there are over 12 kilometres of passageway in total, built between the years 1430 and 1530. The purpose of the subterranean system is unclear. The constant temperature of about 7° celsius made the tunnels ideal for storing beer and sitting out the blazes that regularly wiped out the town above, and the guides insist that is *all* they were ever used for. Others point out that few, if any, fire escapes or beer cellars are 12 kilometres long, and that the date of construction makes it almost certain that the tunnels originally had a military purpose. It's another of Tábor's historical riddles. But as you roam through the sombre passages, there are definite hints of long-term hide-out strategies and survivalist paranoias: routes wander into the gloom and then suddenly double back, just to throw you off-guard; whiffling flues keep the air fresh; and staircases connect most of the town square's houses to the underground network, just in case flight (or perhaps beer) should become necessary. The tour also takes you past dungeons and pits which were used to hold nagging wives in years past. Interestingly enough, husbands were not allowed alcohol while their scold was held, which presumably limited take-up of the municipal facility quite dramatically.

You'll emerge from the tunnel dazed, disorientated, and at the far (eastern) end of the square from the town hall. From here you could continue eastwards towards the Jordan lake, formed from a river named by the original Táborite settlers and a dam built in 1492, the oldest in Bohemia. In the other direction, along Klokotská at the far southwestern corner of the town, is the 15th-century Bechyně Gate, part of the town's original fortifications. It contains a few pinafores and pots from Tábor's dull pre-Hussite past, but more impressive is the view from the tower over the Lužnice river and the crammed roofs of the old town.

Finally, be sure to stroll through the narrow cobbled alleys to the bell-shaped nám. Mikuláše z Huse. Nothing happens here, but it's a charmer, and just beyond its three lime trees, fountain and geranium-infested cottage is a hillside park where you can contemplate the mysteries of religious mania in peace.

Český Krumlov and České Budějovice

Český Krumlov can have a powerful effect on its visitors. UNESCO has declared its historical and architectural value to be second only to Venice, a ranking that, even if almost meaningless, shows at least how its beauty can flabbergast even a team of men with briefcases. The nearby town of České Budějovice can't match its neighbour, but its ancient network of arcaded streets and the vast town square have their own charm, and as the home of Budweiser lager it attracts several hundred thousand visitors every year. Between them the towns make a memorable weekend trip; a number of boarding houses in Český Krumlov are listed below.

Getting Around

České Budějovice is about 180 km due south of Prague, and Český Krumlov a further 25 km southwest. The drive takes about 3 hours. Follow the route to Tábor (*see above*) and continue, following signs, along the E55. There is a regular coach service to both towns from Prague's Florenc station, which takes just over four hours to reach Český Krumlov.

Reservations

Should you wish to make a hotel or restaurant reservation in Český Krumlov, the telephone code for the town is 0337.

Eating Out

Lunch in **České Budějovice** is a simple matter if your main reason for being there is to drink the beer; almost every restaurant in town has it on tap. One of the best places to sample copious quantities is the **Restaurace Masne krámy** (Meat Market Restaurant), a very long structure on Krajinská 13 about 50 metres from the northwestern corner of the square. The town's butchers used to assemble here, having been ordered by Emperor Charles IV in 1364 to cease and desist from hanging carcasses on the square, but the present building dates from 1554. As well as doing all the honour to butchery that you would expect of a Czech beer hall, it sells tasty potato pancakes (*bramborák*) and pungent beer cheese (*pivní*). A shop on the other side of the street can equip you with Budweiser keyrings, caps, umbrellas, recordings of Czech drinking songs, and even non-alcoholic *Budvar*, should you want a souvenir.

Český Krumlov has a more varied selection of eateries. There is no shortage of cosy places along Latrán street and in the town square; during the summer, there are also a number of picturesque terrace restaurants along the river embankment and near the castle. Some of the more notable spots are listed below.

U šatlavy (The Dungeon), Šatlavská, © 67176. *4 pm–1 am*. Only the chalice hanging above the small door hints at what lies within Český Krumlov's medieval dungeon. The arched ground floor room becomes a nightly feast, with endless supplies of wine and beer flowing while steaks, toasted cheese and sausages spit, pop or smoke on the indoor griddle. Huge fun.

Restaurace Eggenberg, Latrán 27. *11–10*. Broad range of Czech dishes, including fishy, fowl and veggie offerings, in the airy interior of a building that was once the town ruler's armoury and is now the local brewery. A noisier and smokier beer hall is attached.

Rybářská bašta Jakuba Krčína, Kájovská 54, © 67183. *11–10*. Cosy, lively and informal fish restaurant, serving the Freshwater Four of south Bohemia's lakes—trout, pike, perch and eel—in ever-changing spices, herbs and oils. Extremely popular; during high season, reservations should be made at least a week in advance. The restaurant also serves local game dishes, according to season and baggability.

Where to Stay

Český Krumlov has just what Prague so sorely lacks: a thriving bed-and-breakfast culture in the historical centre. Any walk through its alleys will take you past innumerable lodgings, ranging from almost-adapted settee lounges to rug-and-fireplace hideaways of trysting fantasy. The following is a selection of what's on offer; all should be reserved at least a week in advance, and if you don't speak Czech, you should at least be prepared to bark a few salient German phrases (English is a definite third language in Krumlov). *The standard price for B&B is about £30 ($45) for a double room, although you can expect to pay almost three times that at the Hotel Růže.*

Hospoda Na louži (Inn on the Puddle), Kájovská 66, © 5495. A tomato-coloured charmer of crumbling plaster and splintered shutters, in a triangular junction of snoozing Baroque and Renaissance townhouses. At the time of writing the guesthouse is preparing to open for the first time, and it can only be hoped that the rooms match up to the promise of the exterior. Downstairs is a raucous beer room, serving a small selection of cutlets and sausages.

Hotel Růže (Rose Hotel), Horní 153, © 2245 or 5481–3. (AE, MC, V.) A 16th-century Jesuit seminary that has been turned into a plush and hushed hotel, with less rustic charm and more creature comforts than the other spots on this list. The restaurant is rather formal but its dishes can be delicious.

Na Ostrově (On the Island), Široká 171, © 2905. Stay here not for the rooms, clean and comfortable though they are, but for the incredible location—between two arms of the Vltava and under the mountainous face of the upper castle, which rises with epic force from the far side of the river. Considerably less awe-inspiring, but perhaps noteworthy to music-lovers and early sleepers, is the fact that country musicians twang banjos and sing songs on the outdoor terrace, on Thursday and Sunday evenings.

Ve věži (In the Tower), Latrán 28, © 5287. Although perched on the once fortified edge of town, the four rooms of this 16th-century tower offer perhaps the most atmospheric dreaming space in town. Under its wizard's hat of a roof, each slice of room contains little but rough table and chairs, wooden floors, functional bed and Rapunzel window. Showers and loos are shared between two. During high season, you should reserve at least two weeks in advance here.

České Budějovice

České Budějovice was founded back in 1265, when Přemysl Otakar II ordered his engineer to design a town in the south for the German settlers he was inviting into Bohemia (*see* pp. 40–1). To make colonization even sweeter, he included in the town charter the much-prized right to brew beer. Despite passing through all the vicissitudes of Bohemian history, notably wholesale destruction during the Thirty Years War, it has been doing so ever since. Fish-farming, salt-storage and, since 1847, pencil production have also been staple town industries; but for many, it was the introduction in 1894 of bottom fermentation—and thus Budvar lager—that was the most significant event in the town since 1265.

Any wander through the town can only begin (and, it must be said, pretty much end) in the main square, nám. Přemysla Otakara II. Rather larger than two soccer pitches, most of the buildings that frame it date from the 18th and 19th centuries but they stand over long arcades that—in terms of the space between the bricks rather than the bricks themselves—date back to the 13th century. That Gothic hangover, a feature typical of Bohemian architecture, can also be seen in a number of other streets that crisscross the area around the square—their regularity another reminder of the original town plan. The façades, a pastel feast of salmons and avocados, honeys and peaches, are nicely set off by the rough sandstone of the early 18th-century **Samson fountain** at the centre of the square. It shows three pained atlantes supporting the hairy hero on a basin, while he performs an unspeakable act of violence on a very small lion.

There's little of note beyond the square. However, if you exit from the corner opposite the striking town hall (recognizable by its Baroque clock tower and flanking turrets) you'll find St Nicholas's Church and the neighbouring **Black Tower** (Černa věž). The 16th-century tower (*open Tues–Sun: March–June 10–6, July–Aug 10–7, and Sept–Nov 9–5*) commands a splendid view. Assuming you successfully negotiate the mountainous sets of wooden steps (no mean feat, unless you have been sticking to non-alcoholic *Budvar*), the panorama takes in the square below and modern České Budějovice beyond. Sites to note have been thoughtfully marked out: for the most part they are of questionable interest, including several shopping centres and a Škoda factory, but on the far horizon you might just be able to make out the doomsday chimneys of the controversial **Temelín atomic energy reactor**. Due to come on stream in the later 1990s and based on an old Soviet design, its opponents call it ČRnobyl, while supporters hail it as the end of global warming. Even if you wouldn't want it in your back-yard, it's sometimes hard not to feel a twinge of support for the nuclear boys while standing here, on days when Bohemia's coal-fired smog is so thick that not just Temelín but the local Škoda plant are shrouded to the point of invisibility.

Český Krumlov

Český Krumlov dates back to at least the 13th century, but the clock stopped running a couple of hundred years ago. The industrial revolution did little more to its appearance than to add two cast iron sculptures to the main footbridge. Its sand- and wood-coloured houses jostle each other within a 2-shaped bend of the Vltava river, over alleys that flow between them in cobbled waves and under long-extinguished dormers and smoking chimneys. And over it all broods an enormous castle that is more a symbol than a structure, literally built out of a rock and possessing a power that calls up images of fortified universes from Mervyn Peake's *Gormenghast* to Kafka's *The Castle*.

A tour through the town is most conveniently begun at the **Budějovice Gate** *(Budějovická brána)*. (It lies across the small bridge opposite the main coach station, as well as the first car park that you come to on the right if driving from České Budějovice.) The painted tower dates from the late 16th century and is the largest remaining section of the town's medieval defences. Its arch leads into Latrán street, which bends and twists all the way down to the river. The name derives from the Latin *latere* or 'on the flank'; the entire district grew up higgledy-piggledy like limpets clinging on to the castle rock. After some 250 metres, you'll come to the Red Gate (*Červená brána*) on your right which leads into the outer bailey of the castle itself, enclosed by the pharmacy, stable, granary and salt house of the first 14th-century fortress on this site. Looming up ahead of you on the left is a strange 72-metre cylindrical tower—half Renaissance, half pagoda—complete with a circular arcade, and a copper high hat of turrets, prongs and pennants. In its present form it dates from the 16th century, but it sits on top of a squat remnant of its 13th-century preincarnation. The short bridge before the gate ahead of you leads over the **Bear Moat** (*Medvědí příkop*), where you can see the latest members of an ursine family that has been lolling and procreating here since the later 16th century. Through the gate is the second courtyard, which is as old as the first, but remodelled in the late 1500s when the castle assumed its definitive form.

That form begins to reveal itself through the vaulted passage ahead of you that snakes up to the third courtyard. Originally this was a gorge, crossed by a bridge that linked the defensive baileys that you have just walked through with the Upper Castle ahead, but in the 1570s and 1580s the entire complex was remodelled and extended. However, as you only properly appreciate when you see the castle from below, there's an unfathomable quality to the castle's architecture that is an integral part of its mystery. Hidden rooms drive down deep into the cliff on which you're now standing; covered passages and walkways span rocky crevices and somehow link ground floors to rooftops; and the whole complex is characterized by an asymmetry and irregularity that even the two **guided tours of the interior** can't sort out.

Open Tues–Sun: April and Oct 9–12, 1–4, May–Aug 8–12, 1–5, Sept 9–12, 1–5 (last tours an hour earlier). The first Renaissance interiors honour the brotherly duo of **Vilém and Peter Vok of Rožmberk**, who began the reconstruction of the castle and whose emblem of a cinquefoil rose is ubiquitous both here and throughout the town below. The family line died out with the death of Peter in 1611, and between them the two men—the first a Catholic, the second a Protestant—personified the tolerant and humanistic traditions of the Rudolfine era that ended in the same year. Vilém was the Burgrave (very vaguely, Viceroy) to Rudolf II, and his court at Krumlov became one of the most vital in central Europe; when he died in 1592, his brother maintained it until debts forced him to sell up to Rudolf II in 1602. Over the next three centuries, the estate passed through first the Eggenberg and then the Schwarzenberg families, and both also left their sumptuous mark on the interiors. The high point of the tour is the **Masked Ball Room** *(Maškarní sál)*, dating from 1748 and decorated by a Rococo riot of illusionistic frescoes, with scores of masked and costumed revellers stepping in and out of balustrades and boxes. Harlequins, damsels and dragoons make merry while one character casts a *trompe l'œil* reflection in a real mirror, and the artist himself watches the fun over a cup of coffee.

From the Upper Castle, the **Pláštový (Cloak) Bridge** crosses a ravine to the neighbouring hill. The view from here over the tent-like roofs of the old town is exceptional: within the bend of the rushing Vltava, they rise with a sagging, bulging pressure towards the sharp steeple of St Vitus's Church. You can also now see the curiously random pattern of windows and openings that puncture the castle wall, looking like the desperate creations of claustrophobic castle guests.

Perhaps the most amazing sight, however, is the 18th-century bridge itself—but again, that's something you can only appreciate from below. It forms a V-shape between the two hills, and you are standing on the third level of rough stone piers and arches; above you are a further three storeys of covered passageway.

After crossing the bridge, on your right is the **Baroque Theatre** (1766–7), which remains intact down to the props and backdrops. Beyond that lies the **castle gardens**, linked to the castle (and the roof of the theatre) by a spindly extension of the top layer of covered bridge, extending out precariously over bulging pier supports. You can enter the gardens up the lane on your right, and inside you'll find an elegant set of clipped hedges, a Baroque fountain of Neptune and various watery friends, and further on a Rococo summer house and a strange modern revolving theatre.

From the gardens, retrace the long route back through the castle to the first court-yard and on your right you'll find the **Castle Steps** *(Zámecké schody)*, which wind uncertainly back down to the lower reaches of Latrán and the nearby Church of St Jost and infirmary *(Kostel sv. Jošta a špitál)*. Across the Lazebnický Bridge lies the pear-shaped old town proper: bounded by the Vltava loop, its orig-inal name of Chrumbenowe ('curved meadow' in old Czech) is probably the origin of the word Krumlov. The bridge turns into Radniční street, which runs up to the main town square, nám. Svornosti. Its plague column (1712–16) was a belated thank-you to the saints from the survivors of the 1682 epidemic; they clearly thought its construction politic, given that the bacteria were doing the rounds again. From here, wander along nearby Horní street to have a look at the pretty curved stone staircase approach to St Vitus's Church *(Kostel sv. Víta)* and the early 14th-century vaulting of its interior.

From here, your options are numerous. At the end of Horní is a town museum, containing some accomplished late-Gothic statuary. Otherwise there are innumer-able more picturesque streets to meander through. Rybářská, below the southern Vltava bend, has several old fishing cottages, while Parkán, at the north of the old town, is lined with the quaint dwellings of Krumlov's medieval riffraff. Some of the most exceptional houses can be found around Soukenická (once the homes of cobblers, maltsters, gingerbread makers and the like) and Široká street where, at No. 78, you'll find the crumbling house of Anton Michael of Ebersbach, cabalist, alchemist and magician to the court of Vilém of Rožmberk. (Vilém was second only to Rudolf II as a patron of the scientific arts in Bohemia, and among his some-time workers were John Dee and Edward Kelley, whose Bohemian adventures are dealt with in the Visionary Prague section of this book.) Finally, you could wander along to the island at the end of Široká, for its dramatic view up to the six-tiered bridge and sheer walls of the castle that you have just walked through.

Bohemia is full of Gothic castles. Many are mouldering ruins, caught unaware by the discovery of artillery and given up for dead by their fleeing owners, but these two, rising in majestic isolation from the rolling hills and forests to the west of Prague, are among the best preserved in the country. It's possible to visit both in a day, although you'd be pressed for time; the best idea is to plump for one and then spend some hours hiking through the surrounding countryside. Karlštejn is the closer, and probably the most popular tourist excursion of all from Prague, but beware—no matter what anyone else tells you, its most exceptional feature, the Chapel of the Holy Cross, is firmly closed for restoration until some time in the late 1990s.

Getting Around

Both castles are always closed on Monday, and have convoluted opening hours (given below) that you should check before setting off. You can drive to Karlštejn by picking up the signs on Strakonická (southbound), the western embankment of the Vltava; and to get to Křivoklát, you have to then drive on to Beroun and follow local roads towards Rakovník. Most trains to Karlštejn leave from Smíchovské nádraží (the service is generally hourly). If you want to continue to Křivoklát, catch a local train to Rakovník from Beroun, but be especially careful when working out your route back to Prague; if you miss a connection, you can easily find that over an hour has been added to your return journey. Karlštejn is 28 km southwest of Prague, and Křivoklát some 46 km almost due west of the capital; the rail journies take about 35 mins and 1½ hours respectively.

Both castles are a short walk from their respective railway stations, and you can only wander through them in the company of a guide. Walking routes through the surrounding hills are marked on tree trunks, cairns and the like.

Lunch

The road up the hill to Karlštejn is lined with small cafés, none more notable than any other and all eager to sap the pockets of day-trippers. The best advice in high season is to eat before leaving Prague; otherwise, just take potluck with whichever place has a free table. The castle road at Křivoklát isn't as jam-packed with either tourists or traps. There is a small restaurant at the foot of the hill in the **Hotel Sýkora** (Titmouse), and in the other direction you'll find a cheap and moderately cheerful café, **U černých**, a couple of hundred metres further up the road beyond the castle.

Karlštejn

Open Tues–Sun: Mar 9–3, April–May 9–4, June–Aug 8–5, Sept–Oct 9–4, Nov–Dec 9–3. Closed 12–12.30.

Karlštejn is almost too perfect to be believable when you spot its slate roofs and towers from the train, perched on their limestone peak. By the 1700s, it had fallen into complete disrepair, the stalking ground of local peasants taking their pigs for a walk; and in the late 19th century it was restored according to the obsessively purist neo-Gothic theories of Josef Mocker (*see* p. 75). Much of its interior suffered as a result, but it still contains enough to make the short journey from Prague worth while.

Most medieval castles were built as places to hide when the going got rough; but Charles IV had safe houses aplenty, and his ideas for Karlštejn were very different. It was begun in 1348, and by the time its interior had been decorated in 1367, it had been turned into a vast symbol of the strange universe that the emperor inhabited. Its three almost separated components made no sense in defensive terms, but were designed instead to mark a mystical ascent from the mundane level of temporal power, represented by the emperor's quarters, up 260 metres to the pinnacle of the castle, the Chapel of the Holy Cross. As a result of botched 19th-century restoration, the vagaries of guided tours, the closing of the chapel, and—perhaps most importantly—the lost mentality of an age, it's hard to re-create the pilgrim's way that Charles would have followed; but as you advance, there are a few highlights that you should notice in particular.

The first stage takes you through the lowest level of the building, including the richly panelled Audience Hall, past an altarpiece by the north Italian Tommasso da Modena (1325–79)—a leading artist of his day, and one of those most often commissioned by the emperor—into the **Luxemburg Hall**. In the centre of the room is a minuscule model of how the original room looked (until destructive humidity led to the reconstruction of the room in the 16th century). Emperor Charles was less insecure about his position than many other monarchs, but he nevertheless swathed his dynasty in myth to be on the safe side; and the doll's-house room shows the characters whom Charles proudly claimed as his forebears—a lineage that somehow runs from Noah through Troy's King Priam to Charles's father, madcap John of Luxemburg.

The tour then leads up to the **Church of the Virgin**, in which the emperor is still honoured with a requiem on 29 November. It's here that spiritual concerns begin to take over. On the wall opposite the altar are the lively *Relic Scenes*, which are among the earliest known portraits of European art (*c.* 1357). They show Charles receiving a comprehensive set of oddments of the Passion, from Charles V of France (on the left) and an unknown king, and then depositing them in his specially-designed Reliquary Cross. That priceless trinket—which may be back on public display in Prague castle by the time you read this (*see* pp. 134–5)—contained niches for nails and splinters of the True Cross, thorns, and even a shred of the vinegar-soaked sponge. The other three walls are covered with scenes of the Apocalypse; they're sadly fading into undecipherability, but if you peer closely, you can still make out some of the most memorable hallucinations suffered by John on Patmos, including a city collapsing into topsy-turvy destruction, and the fiery seven-headed and ten-horned Beast itself. Next to the church is **St Catherine's chapel**, consecrated to one of Charles's innumerable patron saints, adopted by the emperor after she had saved his life on an Italian battlefield. The oratory is studded with the jaspers, amethysts and chalcedonies that so fascinated the emperor, set in gilt stucco; lining the side of the chapel are paintings of the seven Bohemian patron saints, and on the altar is a votive scene of the emperor kneeling under the Virgin. If you have already seen the Chapel of St Wenceslas in St Vitus's Cathedral (pp. 124–6), the decorative scheme of this chapel will be familiar—but it's in the third and last stage of Karlštejn that the fervent chiliasm of the emperor and his age reaches an unparalleled climax.

The **Chapel of the Holy Cross (Rood)**, accessible only via a corkscrew staircase and fortified with walls that are up to 5½ metres thick, was designed by Charles to house his new crown jewels and Reliquary Cross; but to explain it in functional terms is to mislead. It ended the emperor's questing trek through the castle and represented the promised Heavenly City (an idea that recurs in the Chapel of St Wenceslas), in which he could contemplate the blissful relief of salvation after the tribulation of Revelation in the church below. Under its gilt vaults, studded with hundreds of glass stars, a moon and a sun, he would pray in the light of 1300 candles burning from iron spikes; and the emperor's painter, Master Theodoric painted over 120 saints, prophets and angels to guard Charles and his jewels. The chapel is an extraordinary sight, but a combination of humidity and utter stupidity meant that it had to be closed for long-term restoration in 1981. The ante-chamber shows the condition of the paintings immediately before the work began: not only were the annual exhalations of 300,000 breathless visitors threatening to unglue the chapel, but—almost incredibly—several of the irreplaceable masterpieces by Master Theodoric had been all but destroyed by tourists' graffiti.

Křivoklát

Open Tues–Sun: Feb–April 9–3, May–Aug 9–5, Sept 9–4, Oct–Dec 9–3.

Unlike the *via sacra* of Karlštejn, Křivoklát has never had pretensions to being anything other than a fortified country seat. Its towers, turrets and battlements rise with compact force from deep forest, once filled with the bears and boars so beloved of royal hunters everywhere; and its interior contains all the features that an owner would need, from chapel to torture chamber. Rudolf II was the last Bohemian monarch to spend time in the castle—killing animals was one of his relatively healthy obsessions while young—and Křivoklát declined to merely noble status during the 17th century. However, minor royalty continued to invite itself along for a chase, most notably Archduke Francis Ferdinand, Habsburg huntsman *extraordinaire* until he found himself at the wrong end of a pot-shot at Sarajevo in 1914.

The castle originated in the early years of the 12th century, but its present appearance dates largely from its reconstruction in the late 15th century, during the reign of Vladislav II of Jagellon. As a result, the castle's architecture is typified by the flamboyant Vladislav Style of Bohemian Gothic architecture (*see* p. 68), and among the rich figurative and organic encrustations, the castle is replete with net-vaults and spiralling pillars similar, if on a smaller scale, to those of Prague's Vladislav Hall. The guided tour leads through the castle hall and chapel, filled with panel painting, sculptures and exhibits from the castle's history. As you walk through the King's Hall, take a look at the children's drawings on the walls, which were doodled during a rainy day in 14th-century Bohemia, hidden for an age, and rediscovered only a few years ago. The tour ends in the Queen's Palace, which contains the 53,000-volume library of the Fürstenburg family, thrown in as part of the job lot when the nobles sold their castle to the state in 1937.

The collections of the castle are being reorganized at the time of writing, but a hunting display with exhibits that include ivory-inlaid crossbows, ornate shotguns and gormless trophies should have opened by the time you read this. With luck, the iron maidens and Spanish boots of the castle's torture-instrument collection should also be on show next to the round tower. While looking around that, you could ask after the six skeletons of starved debtors which were found here during the 18th century. Finally, go and look at the Huderka tower, at the other end of the castle. It contains a small exhibition of debris collected after each of the four fires that the castle has experienced, and is one of the many towers scattered across Bohemia from which earless alchemist Edward Kelley is said to have jumped to his death (*see* p. 104).

Kutná Hora means 'mining mountain'. The town grew out of nothing in the late 13th century, when it was discovered that there was silver and copper in that there hill. The Přemysl kings muscled in on the operation, and the city boomed as it began to yield up thousands of tons of precious ores annually. It was granted a royal charter (1308), grew into one of the largest towns in Europe, and became the second home of King Wenceslas IV in 1400—and then in the mid-16th century, its silvery life-blood was finally exhausted. The panhandlers drifted away, the shanty-town suburbs evaporated, and apart from the standard Jesuit-inspired Counter-Reformation encampments, nothing of note was ever built again. But although its glory years were over, its crumbling Baroque and Rococo townhouses are peppered with some of the finest Gothic architecture in Bohemia, all monuments to a silver Klondike of the Middle Ages.

Getting Around

To go by car, pick up route 333 on Vinohradská and drive for about 70 km. Buses leave Prague regularly, from either Želivského or Florenc (pay on board) and take about 1½ hours to arrive. The train journey from Masarykova or Hlavní nádraží is often slightly longer, and sometimes requires a change at Kolín. Kutná Hora's tourist information office is in the main square, Palackého nám. You'll be walking for most of the time, and the town's filled with signposts which are only mildly confusing. If you want to get a bus to Sedlec (*see below*), buy a ticket from any tobacconist.

Lunch

The town contains a bubbling collection of cafés, often in one-time living rooms. Two cosy ones are on Barborská street: at No. 24 is the **Hotel U Hrnčíře**, serving a range of fishy, fowly and steaky Czech dishes, and at 33 is the **Café U hrádku** with a small menu, a large selection of drinks and a charming level of service. Beer, fried cheese and pale lumps of meat in gravy are available at the long-established **U havířů** on Šultysova.

The highlights of the town are packed to the south of the main square. Walk down the narrow Jakubska and you'll be greeted by the **Church of St James** (sv. Jakub), its 82-metre tower rising with incongruous magnificence from a curving lane of pastel cottages. The citizens started to build it in 1330, but splendid as it is, it was just a trial run for their later effort, which you'll see soon. To the east of the church is the **Italian Court** (Vlašský dvůr), *open 9–5 April–Oct and 10–4 Nov–March*. The court was set up as a mint in 1300 by Wenceslas II after

Florentine financial experts, summoned to advise him on monetary reform, suggested that he produce coins. Obvious really, and it worked; the *groschen* became an ECU of its time, used by merchants across Europe in preference to their flabby currencies. There are examples in the building's museum, along with the later *taler*, a name that originated in another Bohemian silver mine at Joachimstal (Jáchymov) and which eventually migrated across the Atlantic to become the dollar. Wenceslas IV moved his royal residence here in 1400, and the building contains his Session Chamber, used by the king whenever his troublesome nobles wanted to have a word. Diets assembled here into the 16th century, and in the far corner is a bench from 1511, which was specially designed—as your guide will gleefully demonstrate—to reverse direction with a flick of the wrist, to enable petulant councillors to turn their backs to their kings more easily. The paintings show the hall at moments of moment: one is of the election of Vladislav II of Jagellon, and the other depicts the issue of the Decrees of Kutná Hora, by which feeble Wenceslas IV agreed to gerrymander the electoral system at Prague's university. The same king built the neighbouring chapel, now smothered by garish neo-Gothic painting from 1904, but the sculptures are original. The hollow Man of Sorrows (*c.* 1520), once used as a safe, has the burly build of a Kutná Hora miner, and shows how closely linked the town's art was to its working traditions.

From the mint, it's a short walk to the **Hrádek Mining Museum** on Barborská 28, where you can explore more deeply into the town's history (*open April–Oct Tues–Sun 8–12, 1–5*). It contains a hoisting—original, but from another town—around which six horses would eke out their sorry lives lifting leather bags of silver and floodwater to the surface. The museum is built over a rediscovered mine shaft which burrows through the surrounding hill and which is the perfect spot to contemplate the drowning, burning and asphyxiation that were the most common forms of premature death in medieval Kutná Hora.

If you can find your way back to where you went into the museum, walk further along Barborská, which goes over the hill through which you've just been crawling—to your right is the former Jesuit College, built in the mid-17th century and their largest outside Prague; to your left is an avenue of the Baroque sculpture of which the Society of Jesus was so fond in Bohemia; and directly ahead of you is the **Church of St Barbara** (Kostel sv. Barbora), built from 1388–1558 and ranking among the most splendid Gothic churches in Europe. Its three steeples and web of gargoyle-bedecked flying buttresses can be seen from across the town; and the church is even more fantastic when you consider that it was no king but ordinary miners who financed it, in honour of their industry's patron saint (shared by anyone who faces sudden death). *The church is open Tues–Sun 8–12, 1–5 April–Sept, 9–12, 2–4 Oct–March.* Enter through the northern door; if it's closed, you can pick up a key at the Jesuit college opposite, through the door just under the tower.

Generations of Bohemia's finest architects worked on the church for over 150 years. Peter Parler or one of his students began the eight eastern chapels, and the most striking feature of the church, the wondrous flowers and stars of the nave's vaulting, was the work of Benedict Ried, who had just completed the equally ingenious Vladislav Hall in Prague (see pp. 131–4). The Jesuits moved in their Baroque baggage when they arrived—the long chapels at the western end have altars dedicated to their founders, SS Ignatius and Francis Xavier—but what remains of the original Gothic decoration is superb. Three of the chapels are covered with frescoes from the late 15th century: the Crucifixion and the Queen of Sheba; a colossal figure of St Christopher fording a fish-filled stream (he was traditionally a giant, but more importantly for Kutná Hora's churchgoers, he is another saint who'll have nothing to do with sudden death); and under one of the windows, pictures of miners at work. Again local traditions have influenced the art of the period, with striking effect when set in the church's architectural grandeur. The feature reappears at the southwest end, where an entire wall is covered with simple images of coiners and angels, neither group more glorified than the other.

There are a few other sites worth seeing as you walk through the streets of the town, notably a late 15th-century **stone fountain** in Rejskovo nám., and a **plague column** of 1715 at the junction of Husova and Šultysova, with detailed Latin inscriptions extolling the powers of various saints against the armpit-virus. There's also the ornate Gothic façade of the **Stone House** (Kammený dům) on Radnická. However, make sure to keep enough time to go to the incredible **ossuary** (kostnice) at Sedlec. Open April–Sept Tues–Sun 8–12, 1–5 (daily between July and August); Oct–March Tues–Sun 9–12, 2–4. It's a couple of kilometres out of town; take any local bus from the stop at the beginning of Masarykova, and get off when you see a church on the right.

The church dates from around 1320, when the Cistercians in their abbey next door (now a tobacco factory) decided to build their very own French cathedral. It still has its original scale (the nave is three times higher than it's broad), but the vault is an 18th-century creation by Giovanni Santini. If the church is open, compare Santini's ribbing with Benedict Ried's in St Barbara's; the joyful abstraction of both is an excellent example of the continuity that linked Bohemia's Baroque and Gothic architectural traditions.

When they built the church, the Sedlec Cistercians weren't just joining the Kutná Hora construction boom. Their cemetery had been pulling crowds of pilgrims ever since Abbot Henry had returned from the Holy Land in 1278 and sprinkled a jar of earth from Golgotha over it. Within decades, it had become one of the most popular resting places in central Europe. Moribund believers converged on the area in droves, and corpses were trundled in from hundreds of miles away. Plague epidemics boosted business, and by 1318 the cemetery contained some 30,000 bodies—roughly the same as the population of London at the time—a state of affairs that gave rise to the creation of the ossuary. It's one of the most macabre sights that you're ever likely to see. You'll find it in the crypt of the All Saints' Chapel (1400), which is at the end of the small lane opposite the church, still surrounded by a functioning graveyard. As you approach, take a look at its tower, which has been an indirect victim of rapacious mining: the vagaries of distant subsidence have left it skew-whiff by 44 cm, and it tilts a few more nanometres every year. *If the crypt is closed at a time when it shouldn't be, you can pick up the keys from House 127, next to the shop just back up the lane.*

The ossuary dates from 1511, when a half-blind monk began gathering together all the bones from abolished graves and putting them in the crypt. It sounds an unenviable task, but it had a practical purpose and was the product of strange times; what's harder to understand is why as late as 1870, a woodcarver was hired to arrange the 40,000 sets of bones into pleasing patterns. Skulls and femurs have been turned into four monstrous bells, over three metres high; the Schwarzenberg family has been honoured with a skeletal coat-of-arms; and cheerful cherubs sit on top of obelisks of skulls, cradling grinning braincases in their laps. Woodcarver František Rint clearly wasn't superstitious—the writing on the wall is his own, a proud and bony signature. His *pièce de résistance* is the eight-branched chandelier that hangs over the crypt, composed of all the bones of the human body, several times over. On All Saints' Day (1 November) and All Souls' Day (2 November), it's traditionally lit with candles and an intoning priest leads a requiem in the fiery charnel-house. There have been recent suggestions that the Masses are macabre, and their continued celebration is in doubt; but if you happen to be in town, you could always turn up (5 pm) on the off chance.

	Rulers	Events
c. 870	Bořivoj	
c. 894	Spytihněv I	
c. 905	Vratislav I	
c. 921	Wenceslas I (Václav)	
c. 935	Boleslav I (The Cruel)	Good King Wenceslas murdered
c. 967	Boleslav II (The Pious)	
c. 999	Boleslav III	
c. 1002	Vladivoj of Poland	
c. 1003–		Dynastic struggle between
c. 1034		Jaromír, Boleslav III
		Boleslav the Brave and Oldřich
c. 1034	Břetislav I	
c. 1055	Spytihněv II	
c. 1061	Vratislav II	
c. 1092	Břetislav II	
c. 1100	Bořivoj II	
c. 1107	Svatopluk	
c. 1109	Vladislav I	
c. 1117	Bořivoj II (second time)	Cosmas of Prague begins making up
		Bohemia's history
c. 1120	Vladislav I (second time)	
c. 1125	Soběslav I	
c. 1140	Vladislav II	
c. 1172	Bedřich	
c. 1173	Soběslav II	
c. 1179	Bedřich (second time)	
c. 1182	Konrád Ota	
	Bedřich	
c. 1189	Konrád Ota	
c. 1191	Wenceslas II	
c. 1192	Přemysl Otakar I	
c. 1193	Břetislav Jindřich	
c. 1197	Vladislav III Jindřich	
	Přemysl Otakar I	
c. 1212	(**Kings**)	Bohemia made a kingdom
c. 1230	Wenceslas I	
c. 1235		Old Town receives royal charter; Jewish
		ghetto set up
c. 1253	Přemysl Otakar II	
c. 1257		Jews relocated; Malá Strana founded
1278	Wenceslas II	
1305	Wenceslas III	

Chronology

1306	Jindřich of Carinthia	
	Rudolf of Habsburg	
1310	John of Luxemburg	
1346	Charles IV	Battle of Crécy; Black Prince steals three feathers from John of Luxemburg's helmet and puts them into Prince of Wales' crest
1348		Charles IV founds New Town; Europe ravaged by Black Death; most of Bohemia escapes
1378	Wenceslas IV	
1380		Bohemia ravaged by plague; most of Europe escapes
1389		3000 Jews killed in pogrom; survivors fined
1415		Jan Hus burnt at stake
1419		Prague's first defenestration
1420	Sigismund	Hussite Wars begin
1438	Albert of Habsburg	
1440	Ladislav the Posthumous	
1458	George of Poděbrady	
1471	Vladislav II of Jagellon	
1516	Ludvik of Jagellon	
1526	Ferdinand I of Habsburg	
1541		Fire on left bank
1556		Jesuits come to town
1564	Maximilian II	
1576	Rudolf II	
1598		Hradčany becomes royal town
1611	Matthias	
1618		Prague's grandest defenestration begins Thirty Years War
1619	Frederick of the Palatinate	
1620		Battle of the White Mountain (bílá hora)
	Ferdinand II of Habsburg	
1621		27 nationalists executed
1635		Treaty of Prague ends Thirty Years War; French start it again
1637	Ferdinand III	
1646	Ferdinand IV	
1648		Thirty Years War ends on Prague's bridge
1657	Leopold I	
1680		Plague returns
1705	Joseph I	
1711	Charles VI	
1715		Plague returns
1740	Queen Maria Theresa	
1743		French besiege Prague
1757		Prussians bombard Prague
1780	Joseph II	

1781		Edict of Toleration abolishes all religious orders that neither nurse nor teach
1784		Prague's four towns united into one municipality
1787		Mozart conducts *Don Giovanni*
1790	Leopold II	
1792	Francis I	
1835	Ferdinand V	
1848	Francis Joseph I	Year of Revolutions
1866		Prussians invade Prague and sign a peace treaty
1875		Horse-drawn trams appear
1891		Electric trams take over
1893		Demolition of Jewish ghetto begun
1916	Charles I	
	(Presidents)	
1918	Tomáš Garrigue Masaryk	Czechoslovakian independence
1935	Edvard Beneš	
1938	Emil Hácha (stooge)	Britain and France sell Czechoslovakia down the river at Munich
1939		Nazis invade; Protectorate of Bohemia and Moravia established
1942		Reinhard Heydrich assassinated
1945	Edvard Beneš	Prague Uprising; city liberated by Soviet forces
1948	Klement Gottwald	
1952		Slánský show trials
1953	Antonín Zápotecký	
1957	Antonín Novotný	
1968	Ludvík Svoboda	Alexander Dubček elected First Secretary; Prague Spring; Warsaw Pact invasion
1969		Jan Palach burns himself to death; Gustáv Husák replaces Dubček as First Secretary
1975	Gustáv Husák	
1977		Charter 77 movement born
1987		Miloš Jakeš elected First Secretary
1988		Soviet foreign ministry spokesman Gennady Gerasimov asked what the difference is between perestroika and Prague Spring; replies '20 years'
1989	Václav Havel	Communist regime collapses; Alexander Dubček becomes speaker of Federal Assembly
1990		First post-revolutionary elections held
1991		Václav Klaus becomes prime minister
1992		Václav Havel resigns; presidency vacant Alexander Dubček dies after car crash
1993	Václav Havel	Czechoslovakia splits into the Czech Republic and the Slovak Republic.

Since the 1989 revolution there has been a steady growth of interest in Czech literature among both publishers and readers, and the number of authors and works available in translation has increased considerably. The best shop in London for books from eastern and central Europe in general is **Orbis Books** at 66 Kenway Rd, London SW5 0RD, ℂ (071) 370 2210. You could also try the library of the **Czechoslovak National House**, 74 West End Lane, London NW6 2LX, ℂ (071) 328 0131. It contains a restaurant, and plenty of émigrés with whom to discuss your forthcoming holiday.

Anděl, Jaroslav and others, *Czech Modernism 1900–45* (Museum of Fine Arts, Houston, 1989). Comprehensive survey of early 20th-century Czech art. The essays ramble, but there are lots of pretty pictures.

Bloch, Chajim, *The Golem: Legends of the Prague Ghetto*. The definitive versions.

Brook, Stephen, *The Double Eagle* (Picador 1988). An expedition through the postwar darkness of the former Habsburg empire, from the land of Kurt Waldheim to the dead zone of 1980s Prague. Marred by a tone that can becomes pompous when it wants to be scathing.

Chatwin, Bruce, *Utz* (Picador 1988). A gentle tale of claustrophobia, escapism and porcelain-collecting in postwar Prague.

Deacon, Richard, *John Dee* (Frederick Muller 1968). Still the best biography of the English alchemist and his scrying sidekick, Edward Kelley.

Evans, R.J.W., *Rudolf II and His World* (OUP 1973). A mad emperor, gathering war clouds and the turning of an intellectual age make for a fascinating read, but Evans plays the potty scholar by hiding the best quotes in untranslated footnotes. Untrained linguists can expect a stuttering read.

Farova, Anna, *Josef Sudek* (John Murray 1990). A short biography of Prague's best photographer, with black-and-white shots that would do any coffee-table proud.

Fermor, Patrick Leigh, *A Time of Gifts* (Penguin 1977). Very English reminiscences of Fermor's trip through a late-1930s central Europe of crunchy snow and jackboots.

Further Reading

Garton-Ash, Timothy, *We the People: The Revolutions of 1989* (Granta 1990). Blow-by-blow account of central Europe's *annus mirabilis* by Garton-Ash, whose huge contribution to keeping the area in the news during the 1980s makes the self-glorifying flourishes of this book almost understandable.

Hašek, Jaroslav, *The Good Soldier Švejk* (Penguin 1990). Hašek was paid by the word for several of the Švejk stories, so pithy they ain't; the humour comes from somewhere between the bar and the toilet; but there are still chuckles aplenty.

Havel, Václav, *Open Letters* (Faber 1991). A series of essays that date back as far as the mid-1960s but show a vitality, consistency and continuing power to illuminate contemporary political issues ranging from ecology to materialism. All are grounded in the day-to-day dirt of Communism, but paradoxically it's the possibility of human integrity that shines out in this remarkable book. Faber also publish *Living in Truth*, which contains several of the same works, alongside tributes to Havel from admirers who include Arthur Miller and Samuel Beckett.

Havel, Václav et al., *The Power of the Powerless* (Hutchinson 1985). Two collections of political essays by writers from across the spectrum of the post-1968 opposition: Catholics, humanists, liberals and Marxists.

Holub, Miroslav, *Poems Before and After* (Bloodaxe Books 1990). A superb collection of works by a noted immunologist and internationally renowned poet. The poems cover a period of 30 years and range in form from terse blank verse to tiny absurdist dramas, but they are all unified by Holub's beautiful economy of expression, the awareness of social context that led him to become one of the original signatories of Charter 77, and the related concern of the humane scientist to retain sight of the big picture while working on the small task. Bloodaxe Books also publishes several other collections of translated Czech poetry.

Hrabal, Bohumil, *I Served the King of England* (Abacus 1989). An effortless flight of history and fantasy by the most popular living Czech author, recounting a waiter's coming-of-age against the backdrop of modern Czech history, taking in touching bordello scenes, Nazi convalescent homes, and a millionaires' prison. Look out for any of Hrabal's other work too, including *The Death of Mr Baltisberger* (Abacus 1990) and *Closely Watched Trains* (Abacus 1990).

Kafka, Franz, *The Complete Novels* (Minerva 1992). Includes *The Trial*, *America* and *The Castle*. Three of the most significant and prophetic novels of the century.

Klíma, Ivan, *My Merry Mornings: Stories from Prague* (Readers International 1985). The daily creation and destruction of dreams in Communist Prague. Many other of Klíma's works have been translated; one of the best is *Judge on Trial* (Vintage 1992) in which Klíma examines the corruption of late totalitarianism with masterful balance, through the moral soul-searching of a Communist judge.

Kovaly, Heda Margolius, *Prague Farewell* (Victor Gollancz 1988). Moving autobiography by the widow of a defendant executed in the 1950s show trials, beginning with her escape from a Nazi death-march and ending with Soviet tanks on Prague's streets.

Kundera, Milan, *The Joke* (Penguin 1984). The dangers of having a humour-less girlfriend in postwar Czechoslovakia.

Lustig, Arnošt, *Darkness Casts No Shadow*, (Quartet, 1989), *Diamonds of the Night* (Quartet 1989), *Night and Hope* (Quartet 1989) and *A Prayer for Katerina Horovitzova* (Quartet 1990). Reports from the death camps by Czechoslovakia's pre-eminent chronicler of the Holocaust.

Lützow, (Count) Francis, *The Story of Prague* (J. M. Dent 1907). A read-able introduction to the city's history, tinged with genteel nationalism.

Mlynář, Zdeněk, *Night Frost in Prague*, (Hurst & Co. 1980). The story of the Prague Spring told by one of Dubček's closest associates, and one of those bundled off to Moscow for comradely intimidation after the invasion. Times change: in 1989, Mlynář was the man that the KGB hoped to install into power.

Pawel, Ernst, *Nightmare of Reason* (Collins Harvill 1988). An excellent biography of Franz Kafka, elegantly written and placing the author squarely within the Prague of his time.

Perutz, Leo, *By Night Under the Stone Bridge* (Collins Harvill 1990). Thickly atmospheric fictional re-creation of Rudolfine Prague by a Prague-born author.

Škvorecký, Josef, *Talkin' Moscow Blues* (Faber 1988). A collection of impressionistic essays on jazz, literature, film and political madness, told with the caustic wit of Škvorecký at his best. Another marvellous read is *The Miracle Game* (Faber 1991), a fictional sweep through modern Czechoslova-kian history up to the 1968 invasion, written with equal measures of humour, anger and confidence during the first years of the author's exile in Canada.

Shawcross, William, *Dubček* (Hogarth 1990). Biography of an *aparátník* who grew to fit extraordinary times. Hastily updated after 1989. The joins are often apparent, but the comments of the reformed Dubček of 1990 are a fasci-nating insight into how Communism destroyed its own dreams in Czechoslovakia.

Vaculík, Ludvík, *A Cup of Coffee with my Interrogator* (Readers International 1987). Powerful collection of essays on the meanness and mediocrity of Czechoslovakia's post-1968 thought police, written contempora-neously and circulated underground.

Weil, Jiří, *Life with a Star* (Fontana 1990). An unforgettably powerful fictional record of the tightening of the noose in Nazi-occupied Prague. Weil, a Czech Jew, writes from the unique perspective of a man who success-fully faked suicide to escape death. He is also the author of *Mendelssohn is on the Roof* (Flamingo 1992), the bizarre story behind which is mentioned on pp. 161–2.

It's sometimes difficult to imagine how Czech could be more alien to English-speakers—although if you want to try, remember that St Cyril provided the Czechs with the script named after him when he arrived. The language seems to have given English nothing other than the words 'pistol', 'robot' and 'Semtex'; and, a few Germanic oddities like 'bratr' (brother) notwithstanding, the only English-tinged Czech words are the same 20th-century neologisms that the rest of the world has also borrowed. The language is Slavonic, with Latin influences, and in its modern form it dates from the 19th century. After 200 years of Germanization in Bohemia, it was painstakingly re-established by a few scholars, with the help of mumbling peasants, a few old texts, and Polish, Serbo-Croat, Bulgarian and Russian dictionaries.

If you try to speak a few words of Czech it's appreciated by most people, although Prague's surly waiters and shop assistants are more likely to treat you as an imbecile than to break into a kindly smile. Since the revolution, English and German have been jockeying for position as second language in the country and it has recently begun to look as though English is pulling ahead. Most older Praguers speak some German—although lingering memories sometimes make the words unutterable—but many of the economic reasons once given by students for learning the language of the Deutschmark have been turned on their head now that the US has become the largest foreign investor in the country. Even more importantly, the English-speaking resident community of yuppies, bums and jokers have the back-up of a postwar pop culture that Germany cannot match. The crucial battle is being fought in the country's schools and the coming generation, encouraged by video nasties and the need to understand pop lyrics, are increasingly turning towards English. As a result, you'll almost certainly be cornered by someone eager to perfect his or her conjugations and learn a few more obscenities. French is limited to a few sophisticates. Two entire generations were forced to learn Russian; it's widely understood, but almost universally reviled, and even if you're fluent in the language, use it only as a last resort.

Czech is a phonetic language (pronounced consistently according to its spelling) with none of the shenanigans of silent letters and the

Language

like. That's simple enough—the problem is learning how to pronounce the letters. If the language of the English southern middle class is used as a benchmark, the main differences are that *c* is spoken as 'ts', *j* is a vowel sound like the English 'y', and *r* is rolled at the front of the mouth. *Ch* is a consonant in itself—it's pronounced as in the Scottish 'loch', and you'll find it after 'h' in the dictionary. A *haček* (ˇ) above a consonant softens it: thus *č* is pronounced 'ch' as in 'chill', *š* is 'sh', and *ž* is the 'zh' sound in 'pleasure'. With *ř*, you venture into territory uncharted by the English language, and every other known language in the world. Even Czech children have to be taught how to pronounce the sound properly; the closest you're likely to get to it is by rolling an 'r' behind your teeth and then expelling a rapid 'zh'. You'll amuse a lot of people by trying to say '*strč prst skrz krk*'—it's a Czech tongue-twister that means 'put your fingers down your throat'.

Vowels are less complicated—*a* is the 'u' in 'up', *e* is as in 'met', *i* and *y* are both as in 'sip', *o* as in 'hot', and *u* as in 'pull'. The sounds are lengthened if the vowel is topped with an accent (´) (or in the case of *u*, also the symbol °)—they're pronounced like the vowels in, respectively, 'bar', 'bear', 'feed', 'poor', and 'oooooh!'. The letter *ě* is pronounced as though it were 'ye' as in 'yet' and softens the consonant that comes before it. Accents affect only the sound of a vowel; and when pronouncing a word, it's *always* the first syllable that's stressed.

You don't use a subject (I, you, etc.) with a verb, since the ending in itself makes clear who's doing the deed. The English pronoun 'you' has two forms, as in many European languages: *vy* is polite and is used in most everyday situations (and always where more than one person is being addressed); *ty* is widespread among young people, and can be used to address anyone whom you could call your friend (you can also use it to be contemptuous to someone you've never met before). Beware also of the bewildering number of endings any ordinary word can have, depending on which of the seven cases, three-and-a-half genders and two categories it belongs to; if you're looking something up in a dictionary, plump for whatever looks closest. Finally, be alert to the fact that Czechs generally say *no* or *ano*, when they're agreeing to something that's in doubt. Those who still feel eager to learn more can find details of language courses in the section on Living and Working in Prague.

Useful Words and Phrases

yes/no	*ano/ne*	pen	*pero*
I don't understand	*nerozumím*	stamp	*známka*
I don't know	*nevím*	envelope	*obálka*
Do you speak English?	*mluvíte anglicky?*	express mail	*expres*
I am English	*jsem angličan(ka)*	telegram	*telegram*
Please	*prosím*	telephone	*telefon*
Please speak slowly	*mluvte prosím pomalu*	fax	*telefax*
Thank you (very much)	*děkuji (moc)*	I'd like to make a call to ...	*rád bych zavolal do ...*
You're welcome	*prosím*	I'd like to reverse the charges ...	*na učet volaného*
Not at all	*není zač*		
I'm sorry	*promiňte*	The number is ...	*číslo je ...*
Call a doctor	*zavolejte lékaře*	I need the number of ...	*potřebuji číslo ...*
Let me through,	*pusťte mě,*		
I'm a doctor	*já jsem lékař*	telephone directory	*telefonní seznam*
Who?	*kdo?*	soap	*mýdlo*
What?	*co?*	toothpaste	*zubní pasta*
Where (is)?	*kde (je)?*	sun-protection cream	*krém na opalování*
Where (are you going)?	*kam (jdete)?*	medicine for/against	*lék na/proti*
From where?	*odkud?*	headache	*bolest hlavy*
When?	*kdy?*	cough	*kašel*
Why?	*proč?*	sore throat	*angina*
How/what kind of?	*jak?*	thermometer	*teploměr*
How much/many?	*kolik?*	plaster	*náplast*
Do you have ... ?	*máte ... ?*	bandage	*obvaz*
post office	*pošta*		

Conversation

Good morning	*dobré ráno*	Do you have a telephone?	*máte telefon?*
Good day	*dobrý den*		
Good evening	*dobrý večer*	May I have the number?	*dáte mi číslo?*
Goodbye	*na shledanou*		
Allow me to introduce myself	*dovolte, abych se představil*	Would you like to come in for a quick coffee?	*nechceš zajít na kávu?*
Let me introduce you to ...	*dovolte, abych vám představil*	What did you say?	*co řikáte?*
My name is ...	*jmenuji se ...*	What did you say? (rude)	*co kecáš?*
I'm pleased to meet you	*těší mě, že vás poznávám*	What are you looking at?	*na co se díváte?*
How are you?	*jak se máte?*		
Do you come here often?	*chodíte sem často?*	What are you looking at? (very rude)	*co čumíš?*

Hotel and Shopping

Do you have a free single/double room?	*máte volný pokoj pro jednu osobu/pro dva?*	pharmacy	*lékárna*
		supermarket	*samoobsluha*
		tobacconist	*tabák*
I'd like the room for ... night(s)	*potřebuji pokoj na ... noc(i)*	antique	*starožitnost*
		book	*kniha*
May I pay by credit card?	*mohu platit credit card?*	cigarettes	*cigarety*
		crystal	*krystal*
How much does it cost?	*kolik to stojí?*	food	*jídlo*
		glass	*sklo*
greengrocer	*zelinář*	newspaper	*noviny*
hairdresser	*kadeřnictví*	porcelain	*porcelán*
laundry	*prádlo*		

Sightseeing

I'd like to go to a (concert)	*chtěl bych navštívit (koncert)*	chapel	*kaple*
		monastery/convent	*klášter*
Two tickets for ... please	*prosím, dva lístky na ...*	castle	*hrad*
		cinema	*kino*
Do you have a map of the town?	*máte plán města?*	theatre	*divadlo*
		gallery	*galerie*
What building is that?	*co je to za budovu?*	museum	*muzeum*
How old is it?	*jak je to staré?*		
When are you open?	*jak máte otevřeno?*		
May I take photographs here?	*mohu zde fotografovat?*		
church	*chrám/kostel*		

Numbers

zero	*nula*	sixteen	*šestnáct*
one	*jedna*	seventeen	*sedmnáct*
two	*dva*	eighteen	*osmnáct*
three	*tři*	nineteen	*devatenáct*
four	*čtyři*	twenty	*dvacet*
five	*pět*	twenty-one	*dvacet-jedna*
six	*šest*	twenty-two	*dvacet-dva*
seven	*sedm*	thirty	*třicet*
eight	*osm*	thirty-one	*třicet-jedna*
nine	*devět*	forty	*čtyřicet*
ten	*deset*	fifty	*padesát*
eleven	*jedenáct*	sixty	*šedesát*
twelve	*dvanáct*	seventy	*sedmdesát*
thirteen	*třináct*	eighty	*osmdesát*
fourteen	*čtrnáct*	ninety	*devadesát*
fifteen	*patnáct*	one hundred	*sto*

one hundred and one	sto-jedna	six hundred	šest set
two hundred	dvě stě	seven hundred	sedm set
three hundred	tři sta	one thousand	tisíc
four hundred	čtyři sta	two thousand	dva tisíce
five hundred	pět set	million	milión

Colours

black	černý	blue	modrý
white	bílý	pink	růžový
yellow	žlutý	violet	fialový
red	červený	golden	zlatý
orange	oranžový	brown	hnědý
green	zelený	grey	šedý

Days

Monday	pondělí	Friday	pátek
Tuesday	úterý	Saturday	sobota
Wednesday	středa	Sunday	neděle
Thursday	čtvrtek		

Months

January	leden	July	červenec
February	únor	August	srpen
March	březen	September	září
April	duben	October	říjen
May	květen	November	listopad
June	červen	December	prosinec

Time

What time is it?	kolik je hodin?	century	století
morning	ráno, dopoledne	tomorrow	zítra
afternoon	odpoledne	yesterday	včera
evening	večer	the day before yesterday	předevčírem
night	noc		
minute	minuta	the day after tomorrow	pozítří
hour	hodina		
(to)day	dnes	now	teď
week	týden	later	potom
month	měsíc	before	před
year	rok	after	po
this year	letos	during	během
next year	příští rok		

Travel

How can I get to … ?	jak se dostanu na ?	bus	autobus
I would like to go to …	rád bych do …	tram	tramvaj
		train	vlak
Where is … ?	kde je … ?	taxi	taxi
How far is it to … ?	jak je to daleko do … ?	car	auto
		small boat	lodička
How long does the journey take?	jak dlouho trvá cesta?	pleasure steamer	parník
		ticket	lístek
How much does it cost?	kolik to stojí?	seat reservation	místenka
		on the left	na levo
May I have a ticket to … ?	prosím jízdenku do … ?	on the right	na pravo
		straight ahead	rovně
Can I buy a ticket on the bus?	mohu si koupit lístek v autobusu?	nearby	blizko
		far away	daleko
Do I have to change?	musím přestupovat?	north	sever
		south	jih
When does the … leave?	kdy odjíždí … ?	east	východ
		west	západ
Do I need a reservation?	potřebuju reservaci?	crossroads	křižovatka
		street	ulice
May I have a couchette?	mohu dostat lehátko lůžko?	square	náměstí
		bridge	most
What's the name of this station?	jak se jmenuje tato stanice?		
Let me out	pusťte mě ven		
airport	letiště		
bus- or tram-stop	zastávka		
metro station	stanice		
(railway) station	nádraží		
taxi-rank	stanoviště taxi		
aeroplane	letadlo		

Mealtimes

Do you have a table for (one/two)?	máte volný stůl pro jednoho/dva?	vegetarian dishes?	jídlo?
Is this seat free?	je toto místo volné?	Excuse me, I'm ready to order	promiňte, mohu si objednat
Could I make a reservation for (one/two)?	mohu reservovat jednou místo/dvě místa?	That was delicious/ disgusting	bylo to výborné/hnusný
May I see the menu?	mohu vidět jídelny lístek?	Bon appétit!	Dobrou chuť'!
		breakfast	snídaně
What would you recommend?	co doporučujete?	lunch	oběd
		dinner	večeře
Do you have	máte bezmasé	tea	čaj
		coffee	káva

with lemon	*s citrónem*	mineral water	*minerálka*
with milk	*s mlékem*	beer	*pivo*
without milk	*bez mléka*	soda water	*sodovka*
milk	*mléko*	wine (white, red)	*víno (bílé, červené)*
lemonade	*limonáda*		
cola	*cola*		
juice	*džus*		

The Menu

dušené	braised	*předkrm*	appetizer
na rožni	grilled	*obloha*	bits and pieces of onion and cabbage served as a side dish
pečené	roast		
smažené	fried		
vařené	boiled	*ovčy sýr*	sheep cheese
hranolky	french fries	*salát*	salad
polévka	soup	*sýr*	cheese

Meat, Fish and Poultry

bažant	pheasant	*roštěná*	stewed meat (usually beef)
biftek	steak		
candát	perch	*sardelka*	anchovy
divočák	wild pig (can also be used to describe sexually potent man)	*sardinka*	sardine
		sekaná	mincemeat
		špíz	kebab
		srnčí	venison
drůbež	poultry	*štika*	pike
hovězí	beef	*šunka*	ham
humr	lobster	*svíčková*	sirloin
husa	goose	*telecí*	veal
játra	liver	*těstoviny*	pasta
jelení	stag	*tuňák*	tuna
kachna	duck	*uhoř*	eel
kapr	carp	*uzeniny*	sausage
klobás(a)	sausage	*velryba*	whale
krab	crab	*vepřové*	pork
králík	rabbit	*žralok*	shark
krocan	turkey		
kuře	chicken		
ledvinka	kidneys		
maso	meat		
platýz	plaice		
pstruh	trout		
pštros	ostrich		

Fruit and Vegetables

ananas	pineapple	*meruňka*	apricot
banán	banana	*mrkev*	carrots
brambory	potatoes	*okurka*	cucumber
broskev	peach	*ořechy*	nuts
česnek	garlic	*pomeranč*	orange
chřest	asparagus	*rajčata*	tomato
cibule	onion	*rýži*	rice
houby	mushrooms	*třešně*	cherries
hruška	pear	*tuřín*	swede
jablka	apple	*žampion*	mushroom
jahoda	strawberry	*zeli*	cabbage

Dessert

koláč	cake	*šlehačka*	whipped cream
kompot	compote	*smetana*	cream
palačinka	pancake	*zmrzlina*	ice-cream
pohár	ice-cream sundae		

Numbers in *italics* indicate maps. Numbers in **bold** indicate main references. Chapels are grouped under entry 'Chapels', and churches and basilicas under 'Churches'.

Index